WJEC EDUQAS GCSE (9–1)

Design and Technology

Ian Fawcett

Andy Knight

Jacqui Howells

Dan Hughes

Chris Walker

Jennifer Tilley

Although every effort has been made to ensure that website addresses are correct at time of going to press, Hodder Education cannot be held responsible for the content of any website mentioned in this book. It is sometimes possible to find a relocated web page by typing in the address of the home page for a website in the URL window of your browser.

Hachette UK's policy is to use papers that are natural, renewable and recyclable products and made from wood grown in well-managed forests and other controlled sources. The logging and manufacturing processes are expected to conform to the environmental regulations of the country of origin.

Orders: please contact Hachette UK Distribution, Hely Hutchinson Centre, Milton Road, Didcot, Oxfordshire, OX11 7HH. Telephone: +44 (0)1235 827827. Email education@hachette.co.uk Lines are open from 9 a.m. to 5 p.m., Monday to Friday. You can also order through our website: www.hoddereducation.co.uk

ISBN: 978 1 5104 5134 6

© Ian Fawcett, Jacqui Howells, Dan Hughes, Andy Knight, Chris Walker and Jennifer Tilley 2019

First published in 2019 by

Hodder Education,

An Hachette UK Company

Carmelite House

50 Victoria Embankment

London EC4Y 0DZ

www.hoddereducation.co.uk

Impression number 10 9 8 7 6 5 4

Year 2023 2022

Cover photo © pavlofox – stock.adobe.com

Illustrations by DC Graphic Design Limited.

Typeset in India.

Printed in India.

A catalogue record for this title is available from the British Library.

Contents

Introduction to WJEC Eduqas GCSE (9-1) Design and Technology   iv

Acknowledgements   vi

Section 1   **Technical principles: core knowledge and understanding**   **1**

Chapter 1   Design and technology and our world   2

Chapter 2   Smart materials, composites and technical textiles   23

Chapter 3   Electronic systems and programmable components   30

Chapter 4   Mechanical components and devices   39

Chapter 5   Materials   48

Practice questions   63

Section 2   **In-depth knowledge and understanding**   **65**

Chapter 6   Electronic systems, programmable components and mechanical devices   66

Chapter 7   Paper and boards   111

Chapter 8   Natural and manufactured timber   140

Chapter 9   Ferrous and non-ferrous metals   173

Chapter 10   Thermosetting and thermoforming polymers   200

Chapter 11   Natural, synthetic, blended and mixed fibres, and woven, non-woven and knitted textiles   226

Practice questions   267

Section 3   **Core designing and making principles**   **269**

Chapter 12   Develop and apply core knowledge, understanding and skills   270

Practice questions   306

Section 4   **Preparing for assessment**   **307**

Chapter 13   Component 1: Design and Technology in the 21st Century   308

Chapter 14   Component 2: Design and make task   312

Glossary   327

Index   333

Introduction to WJEC Eduqas GCSE (9–1) Design and Technology

This book has been written to help you to master the skills, knowledge and understanding you need for WJEC Eduqas GCSE (9–1) Design and Technology. Throughout the course you will develop your ability to identify and solve real problems by applying a broad knowledge of materials, components, technologies and practical skills to design and make high-quality, imaginative prototypes. You will learn about the wider influences on design and technology, including historical, social/cultural, environmental and economic factors; and you will learn how to communicate your design ideas effectively and to critique and refine them to ensure design solutions meet the needs, wants and values of users.

The book is structured to reflect the subject content in the WJEC Eduqas GCSE (9–1) Design and Technology specification. It is divided into six sections:

1 Technical principles: core knowledge and understanding

This section includes five chapters (Chapters 1–5), which are designed to develop your knowledge and understanding of how design and technology has an impact on people's lives. You will need to study all five chapters to make sure you develop an understanding of emerging technologies, and how to make effective choices when selecting materials, components and systems.

2 In-depth knowledge and understanding

This section includes six chapters (Chapters 6–11). You will need to study **at least one** of these chapters to ensure you have in-depth knowledge and understanding of at least one specific material area and/or components and systems. Each of these chapters also covers the in-depth knowledge, understanding and skills of designing and making principles you will need when designing and making prototypes as part of your non-exam assessment (NEA), and when applying knowledge and understanding of designing and making in the written exam.

3 Core designing and making principles

This section includes one chapter (Chapter 12), which will help you to develop and apply core knowledge, understanding and skills when designing and making prototypes as part of your non-exam assessment (NEA). You will also be assessed on these designing and making principles within the Design and Technology in the 21st Century written examination.

4 Preparing for assessment

Section 4 of the book takes a closer look at the two assessment components of your GCSE course. Chapters in this section (Chapters 13 and 14) include useful advice on preparing to complete the designing and making activity within the non-exam assessment (NEA), and on how to revise and prepare for the written examination.

Summary of assessment

The table below summarises how you will be assessed for WJEC Eduqas GCSE (9–1) Design and Technology.

Component	Assessment type	Time	Marks available	% of qualification
Component 1: Design and Technology in the 21st Century	Written examination	2 hours	100 marks	50%
Component 2: Design and make task	Non-exam assessment	Approx. 35 hours	100 marks	50%

Features in this book

Throughout each chapter you will find a range of features to support your learning.

Learning objectives

By the end of this chapter you should have developed a knowledge and understanding of:
- how new and emerging technologies have had an impact on industry and enterprise

Clear learning objectives for each chapter explain what you need to know and understand.

Activity

In pairs, make a list of five advantages and five disadvantages of the global production of products on culture and people.

Short activities are included to help you to understand what you have read. Your teacher may ask you to complete these.

Know it

1 Give one example of a product created because of market pull and one product created due to technology push.

These short questions test your knowledge and understanding of the topics covered.

KEY WORDS

Market pull: a new product is produced in response to demand from the market.

All of the important terms are defined.

KEY POINTS

- New products are usually developed because of a want or need (market pull).

Summaries of key points appear at the end of each chapter to help you remember the most important aspects of a topic, and to help you with revision.

Practice questions

These questions appear at the end of each section and are designed to help you prepare for the written exam.

Acknowledgements

The authors and publishers would like to thank the following schools, and their teachers and students, for the examples of student work:

- Abingdon School, Oxford
- Mrs Stacey Jenkins, Ysgol Stanwell School, Penarth, Cardiff
- Mr Jason Cates, St. John the Baptist Church in Wales High School, Aberdare
- Mr Gethin Williams and Mr Siôn Jones, Ysgol Dinas Brân, Llangollen.

Thanks also to Mr Phillip Robinson, Technician at Thrybergh Academy, Rotherham, for his assistance with photographs.

Picture credits

The Publishers would like to thank the following for permission to reproduce copyright material.

P.1 © Tomasz Zajda/stock.adobe.com; p.2 top © Soonthorn/stock.adobe.com; Fig.1.1 © Maroš Markovič/stock.adobe.com; Fig.1.2 © Tsiumpa/stock.adobe.com; Fig.1.4 © Antonioguillem/stock.adobe.com; Fig.1.5 © Tomhanisch/stock.adobe.com; Fig.1.6 © Goodluz/stock.adobe.com; Fig.1.7 Dan Hughes; Fig.1.8 © Ekaterina Kupeeva/123RF; Fig.1.9 Dan Hughes; Fig.1.10 © xiaoliangge/stock.adobe.com; Fig.1.11 © European Union; Fig.1.12 © Simon Belcher/Alamy Stock Photo; Fig.1.13 © Petovarga/123RF; Fig.1.15 Fairtrade; Fig.1.16 © Svet110/stock.adobe.com; Fig.1.17 © Soonthorn/stock.adobe.com; Fig.1.18 © Grigory_bruev/123RF; Fig.1.19 © Tim W/stock.adobe.com; p.23 top © Prakasitlalao/stock.adobe.com; Fig.2.1 Dan Hughes; Fig.2.4 © Will Thomass/Shutterstock.com; Fig.2.5 © dpa picture alliance/Alamy Stock Photo; Fig.2.6 © Prakasitlalao/stock.adobe.com; Fig.2.7 © Richard Heyes/Alamy Stock Photo; Fig.2.8 © diter – Fotolia; Fig.2.9 © RichLegg/E+/Getty Images; Fig.2.10 © kalpis/stock.adobe.com; p.30 top Chris Walker; Fig.3.2 © Tiago Zegur/Alamy Stock Photo; Figs 3.3, 3.16 Chris Walker; p.39 © Nikkytok/stock.adobe.com; Fig.4.1 © Westend61/Getty Images; Fig.4.2 © Anton Samsonov/123RF; Fig.4.3 © Marek/stock.adobe.com; Fig.4.4 © Spinetta/stock.adobe.com; Figs 4.8, 4.9 Chris Walker; Fig.4.12 © Sergey Lavrentev/stock.adobe.com; Fig.4.13 © Nikkytok/stock.adobe.com; Fig.4.14 © Vladimir/stock.adobe.com; Fig.4.15 © John Hopkins/Alamy Stock Photo; p.48 © Digital Genetics/Shutterstock.com; Fig.5.4 © Francesco Gustincich/123RF; Fig.5.5 © Wichien Tepsuttinun/Shutterstock.com; Fig.5.8 © YOR/stock.adobe.com; Fig.5.9 © Cherv/stock.adobe.com; Fig.5.12 © Robert Doran/Alamy Stock Photo; Fig.5.13 © Digital Genetics/Shutterstock.com; Fig.5.14 © Unkas Photo/Shutterstock.com; Fig.5.15 © Coprid/Shutterstock.com; Fig.5.16 © jcsmilly/123RF; Fig.5.17 © Horizon International Images Limited/Alamy Stock Photo; Fig.5.18 © Standard Studio/Shutterstock.com; Fig.5.19 © Mahirart/stock.adobe.com; Fig.5.20 © Dianagrytsku/stock.adobe.com; Fig.5.22 © Ruzanna Arutyunyan/stock.adobe.com; p.65 © Liptakrobi/stock.adobe.com; p.66 © Marcus Harrison – technology/Alamy Stock Photo; Figs 6.5, 6.7, 6.21, 6.27 Chris Walker; Fig.6.29 © lapis2380/stock.adobe.com; Fig.6.31 Chris Walker; Fig.6.37 © Powered by Light/Alan Spencer/Alamy Stock Photo; Fig.6.38 © DBURKE/Alamy Stock Photo; Fig.6.39 © Raymond McLean/123RF; Fig.6.40 © Marcus Harrison – technology/Alamy Stock Photo; Fig.6.41 Ethical Trading Initiative; Figs 6.44, 6.47, 6.48, 6.49, 6.52, 6.53 Chris Walker; Fig.6.56 Dan Hughes; Fig.6.63 © Alfred Hofer/123RF; Fig.6.64 © StockphotoVideo/Shutterstock.com; Fig.6.65 Andy Knight; Fig.6.66 © Kbwills/E+/Getty Images; Fig.6.67 © Danielle Nichol/Alamy Stock Photo; Fig.6.68 © Randall Schwanke/Shutterstock.com; p.111, Fig.7.3 © Paketesama/stock.adobe.com; Fig.7.4 © Yuri Tuchkov/123RF; Fig.7.6 © Kitch Bain/Shuttetstock.com; Fig.7.7 © Paul Smith/123RF; Fig.7.11 © Peter Gudella/Shutterstock.com; Fig.7.12 © Adisak Rungjaruchai/Shutterstock.com; Fig.7.16 © Carolyn Jenkins/Alamy Stock Photo; Fig.7.24 © Jame Pakpoom/Shutterstock.com; Fig.7.25 © le Moal Olivier/Alamy Stock Photo; Fig.7.27 © Zoonar GmbH/Alamy Stock Photo; Fig.7.28 © Quang Ho/Shutterstock.com; Fig.7.29 © Robert Ashton/Massive Pixels/Alamy Stock Photo; Fig.7.30 © B Christopher/Alamy Stock Photo; Fig.7.31 Andy Knight; p.140 top © Ftfoxfoto/stock.adobe.com; Fig.8.1 © Kletr – Fotolia; Fig.8.4 based on an illustration in E.J. Wynter, *Woodwork*, Longman (1970); Fig.8.5 © Avalon/Construction Photography/Alamy Stock Photo; Fig.8.6 Dan Hughes; Fig.8.7 © Zoonar GmbH/Alamy Stock Photo; Fig.8.8 © nito500/123RF; Fig.8.9 © Forest Stewardship Council® – FSC® – www.fsc.org; Fig.8.10 © Peter Lopeman/Alamy Stock Photo; Fig.8.12 © Tetra Images, LLC/Alamy Stock Photo; Fig.8.13 © Oleksiy Maksymenko Photography/Alamy Stock Photo; Figs 8.14, 8.15 © Donatas1205/stock.adobe.com; Fig.8.16 © Ftfoxfoto/stock.

adobe.com; Fig.8.17 © Justin Kase z12z/Alamy Stock Photo; Fig.8.20 © Dreamsquare/Shutterstock.com; Fig.8.22 Dan Hughes; Figs 8.24, 8.29–34, 8.36, 8.40, 8.41 Ian Fawcett; Fig.8.54 © Olekcii Mach/Alamy Stock Photo; Fig.8.60 © Mark Vorobev/123 RF; Fig.8.62 © Audrius Merfeldas/123RF; Figs 8.63–65 Ian Fawcett; Fig.8.66 © Jodie Johnson/stock.adobe.com; Fig.8.67 © Rocky Reston/123 RF; Fig.8.68 © Alex Hinds/Alamy Stock Photo; Fig.8.69 fotoknips/123 RF; Figs 8.70–72 Dan Hughes; Fig.8.73 © Steven Heap/123RF; Fig.8.74 © Arch White/Alamy Stock Photo; p.173 © Paul Broadbent/Alamy Stock Photo; Fig.9.3 © samum/123 RF; Fig.9.6 © STA17/Shutterstock.com; Fig.9.8 © Flegere/Shutterstock.com; Figs 9.10, 9.11, 9.19, 9.20, 9.22, 9.23, 9.26, 9.27 Ian Fawcett; Fig.9.44 © oYOo/Shutterstock.com; Fig.9.45 © Showcake/stock.adobe.com; Fig.9.46 © Dinga/Shutterstock.com; Fig.9.47 © Walter Nurnberg/SSPL/Getty Images; Fig.9.48 © Paul Broadbent/Alamy Stock Photo; Fig.9.49 Dan Hughes; Fig.9.50 © Brilliant Eye/stock.adobe.com; Fig.9.51 © David J. Green/Alamy Stock Photo; p.200 © Unkas Photo/Shutterstock.com; Fig.10.3 © Yevgeny Vershinin/stock.adobe.com; Fig.10.4 © Kanok Sulaiman/123 RF; Fig.10.5 © Standard Studio/Shutterstock.com; Fig.10.7 © Esbeauda/stock.adobe.com; Fig.10.8 © Severija/stock.adobe.com; Fig.10.9 © Colin Christopher Rowlands/123RF; Fig.10.10 © Dario Lo Presti/123RF; Fig.10.11 Dan Hughes; Fig.10.12 © Trifonenko Ivan/stock.adobe.com; Fig.10.13 © Maxisport/stock.adobe.com; Fig.10.14 © EpicStockMedia/stock.adobe.com; Fig.10.15 © Unkas Photo/Shutterstock.com; Fig.10.16 © Coprid/Shutterstock.com; Fig.10.17 © KRIANGKRAI APKARAT/123RF; Fig.10.18 © Achim Prill/123 RF; Fig.10.19 © Elena Abduramanova/Shutterstock.com; Figs 10.20, 10.21 Dan Hughes; Fig.10.22 © Konstantin Yuganov/stock.adobe.com; Figs 10.23, 10.26 Ian Fawcett; Fig.10.27 © C R Clarke & Co (UK) Limited; Fig.10.29 © Severe/stock.adobe.com; Fig.10.30 © Zoonar/Alexander Strela/Alamy Stock Photo; Fig.10.31 © Damirkhabibullin/stock.adobe.com; Fig.10.32 © Guy J. Sagi/Shutterstock.com; Figs 10.36, 10.37 Images provided by TechSoft UK Ltd; Fig.10.39 © C R Clarke & Co (UK) Limited; Fig.10.40 © Mohamed Osama/123RF; Fig.10.43 © John Howard/Science Photo Library; Fig.10.44 © Giro Sport Design; Figs 10.45, 10.46 Dan Hughes; Fig.10.47 © Alvey & Towers Picture Library/Alamy Stock Photo; Fig.10.48 © Akulamatiau/stock.adobe.com; p.226 © Liptakrobi/stock.adobe.com; Fig.11.1 © Keith Morris/Alamy Stock Photo; Fig.11.5 © v_sot/stock.adobe.com; Fig.11.6 © Fotofabrika/stock.adobe.com; Fig.11.7 © Chamillew/stock.adobe.com; Fig.11.11 © Seramoje/stock.adobe.com; Fig.11.12 © Andreja Donko/stock.adobe.com; Fig.11.15 © Studiomode/Alamy Stock Photo; Fig.11.16 © Eightstock/stock.adobe.com; Fig.11.17 ©Joan Wakelin/Art Directors & TRIP/Alamy Stock Photo; Fig.11.18 © Mamunur Rashid/Alamy Stock Photo; Fig.11.19 © China Photos/Getty Images News/Getty Images; Fig.11.20 www.trashtocouture.com; Fig.11.22 © Givaga/stock.adobe.com; Fig.11.23 © Maarigard/Dorling Kindersley/Getty Images; Fig.11.24 © Alexei Gridenko/123RF; Fig.11.25 © Toeytoey/Shutterstock.com; Fig.11.26 © Witthaya/stock.adobe.com; Fig.11.27 © Anton Oparin/123RF; Fig.11.28 © Jesiya/stock.adobe.com; Fig.11.29 © Mahmut Akkaya/Shutterstock.com; Fig.11.31 © Cherryandbees/stock.adobe.com; Fig.11.32 © Fotoinfot/stock.adobe.com; Fig.11.33 © Sabdiz/stock.adobe.com; Fig.11.34 © Apugach/123RF; Fig.11.35 © Dee Cercone/Everett Collection/Alamy Stock Photo; Fig.11.39 © Vvoe/stock.adobe.com; Fig.11.40 Jacqui Howells; Fig.11.41 © Pincasso/stock.adobe.com; Fig.11.42 © Olganik/stock.adobe.com; Figs 11.46, 11.47 Jacqui Howells; Fig.11.48 © tapui/stock.adobe.com; Fig.11.49 Jacqui Howells; Fig.11.50 © ksena32/stock.adobe.com; Fig.11.52 Yin USA Inc; Fig.11.53 © Amnarj Tanongrattana/123RF; Fig.11.54 © Roger Grayson/Alamy Stock Photo; Fig.11.57 © dpa picture alliance/dpa/Alamy Stock Photo; Fig.11.58 © KHURSAINI BIN A FATAH/123RF; Fig.11.59 © vvoe/stock.adobe.com; Fig.11.60 © Claudette/Stockimo/Alamy Stock Photo; Fig.11.61 © Michael White/Alamy Stock Photo; Fig.11.62 © dreamtimestudio/Getty Images; p.267 bottom right © Nys/stock.adobe.com; p.269 © Windsor/stock.adobe.com; p.270 top © Illustrart/123RF; Fig.12.1 © SergValen/stock.adobe.com; Fig.12.3 © Mushy/stock.adobe.com; Fig.12.5 © Steve Mann/123RF; Fig.12.6 © Santiago Rodriguez Fontoba/123RF; Figs 12.7, 12.8 © Dyson; Fig.12.9 © Duncan Snow/Alamy Stock Photo; Fig.12.10 © Af8images/stock.adobe.com; Fig.12.11 © Stefan Rousseau/PA Archive/PA Images; Fig.12.13 Tefal cordless kettle designed by Seymourpowell – Photo by Seymourpowell; Fig.12.14 Dan Hughes; Fig.12.15 © Suricoma/123RF; Figs 12.17, 12.18 Dan Hughes; Fig.12.19 © Illustrart/123RF; Figs 12.20–22 Dan Hughes; Fig.12.23 © BENOIT TESSIER/Reuters/Alamy Stock Photo; Fig.12.24 © Radub85/123RF; Figs 12.25–27 Dan Hughes; Fig.12.28 Jennifer Tilley; Fig.12.29 Chris Walker; Figs 12.30, 12.36 Dan Hughes; pp.307, 308, 312 © shotsstudio/stock.adobe.com; Fig.14.8 (right) Copyright and Photography by Sass Tetzlaff.

Every effort has been made to trace all copyright holders, but if any have been inadvertently overlooked, the Publishers will be pleased to make the necessary arrangements at the first opportunity.

Section 1

W0198355

Technical principles: core knowledge and understanding

Chapter 1 Design and technology and our world..2

Chapter 2 Smart materials, composites and technical textiles................................23

Chapter 3 Electronic systems and programmable components.............................30

Chapter 4 Mechanical components and devices..39

Chapter 5 Materials...48

Practice questions...63

Chapter 1
Design and technology and our world

Learning objectives

By the end of this chapter you should have developed a knowledge and understanding of:
- how new and emerging technologies have had an impact on industry and enterprise
- the impacts that new products can have on the environment, and how products can be designed and manufactured in a sustainable way
- the effects that global production has on culture and people
- legislation that affects products
- consumer rights and protection for consumers when purchasing and using products

- moral and ethical factors related to the manufacturing, sale and use of products
- the advantages and disadvantages of computer-aided design (CAD) and computer-aided manufacture (CAM)
- how computer-aided manufacture (CAM) equipment can be used in a variety of applications
- how the critical evaluation of new and emerging technologies informs design decisions
- how energy is generated and stored in order to choose and use appropriate sources to make products and to power systems.

KEY WORDS

Mass production: when hundreds or thousands of the same product are produced (usually on a production line).

Assembly line: a line of workers and equipment in a factory. A product is gradually assembled as it moves through each stage of the line until it is completely assembled.

Automated production: the use of automatically (computer) controlled equipment or machinery to manufacture products.

1.1 The impact of new and emerging technologies

New technologies that change the way in which we live our lives are constantly being developed. As designers it is important to be aware of new and emerging technologies and both the positive and negative impacts they can have on society and the environment. This helps us to make effective decisions about the materials, components and systems we use when designing and making new products.

The impact of new and emerging technologies on industry and enterprise

Throughout history developments in technology have had an impact on our industry and business activities. Think about the Industrial Revolution in the late 1700s and early 1800s: the use of steam to provide power led to huge innovations in machinery and manufacturing equipment which meant that products could be produced more quickly and economically by machines rather than by hand. The ability to generate electricity allowed factories to house larger machines for the **mass production** of products on **assembly lines**.

Developments in computer technology and electronics mean that modern factories increasingly make use of **automated production**. Thousands of identical products of consistent high quality can be produced quickly and cheaply. Robots are used to carry out some of the repetitive and monotonous tasks that were previously performed by humans.

Figure 1.1 The car industry often uses robot arms to carry out tasks on assembly lines.

Activity

Create a mind map or list examples of ways in which technology has changed the way we work (think about how we communicate in the workplace and how we manufacture products). Compare your examples with two or three other students.

Market pull and technology push

Market pull describes the development of new products in response to demands from users. Through market research a designer identifies a need or discovers a problem that requires a solution. Designers then produce new or revitalised products driven by the needs and wants of the users. The mobile phone is an example of a product developed because of market pull – people wanted a way to be able to contact each other when they were away from the home or office.

Technology push is when developments in materials, components, or manufacturing methods lead to new or improved products being developed. Tablets and smartphones are examples of products created because of technology push – developments in electronics mean that small, powerful components can be put into these devices, which allow them to perform a range of functions.

The development of new materials is also an example of technology push. For example, the development of graphene is likely to lead to a host of new products that make use of the strength, light weight, flexibility, transparency, and the ability of this new material to conduct heat and electricity. Graphene is likely to have applications in a wide range of industries, including transport, medicine, electronics and energy.

Consumer choice

Development of new products is led by consumer choice. Designers and manufacturers aim to ensure that people want or need the product they design. New technologies can influence the products a consumer wants to buy, as people often want to own the latest technologies and products. When a mobile phone company releases a new model, many people will want to replace their existing phone with one that includes the latest technology and design.

Product Life Cycle Analysis (LCA)

The product **life cycle** is an important concept in marketing. It describes the four stages a product goes through from its initial introduction to the market until it is replaced or withdrawn because it is not selling well enough. The four main stages of the cycle are introduction, growth, maturity and decline (see Figure 1.3).

Figure 1.2 Technology push: developments in electronics allowed smartphones and tablets to be produced.

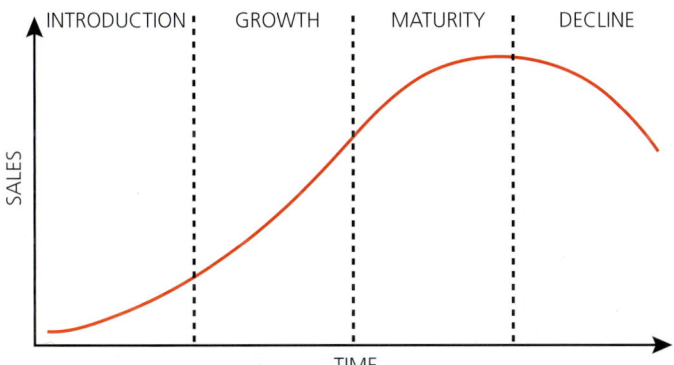

Figure 1.3 The product life cycle

- **Introduction:** this is when new products are launched and are heavily publicised so that consumers know that they are available. This might be a new product or a new version of an existing product, for example a new model of a smartphone with a larger memory or longer battery life.
- **Growth:** once the product is available, sales will grow as more people become aware of the product and buy it to replace previous products or older models.
- **Maturity:** sales of the product reach their peak. Companies will want this stage to last for as long as possible so that they get the maximum number of sales.
- **Decline:** at this stage, most interested consumers have already bought the product or a newer model will be available, at which points sales will begin to fall.

Activity

Look at these different types of product life cycle and identify a product that each of the curves might apply to.

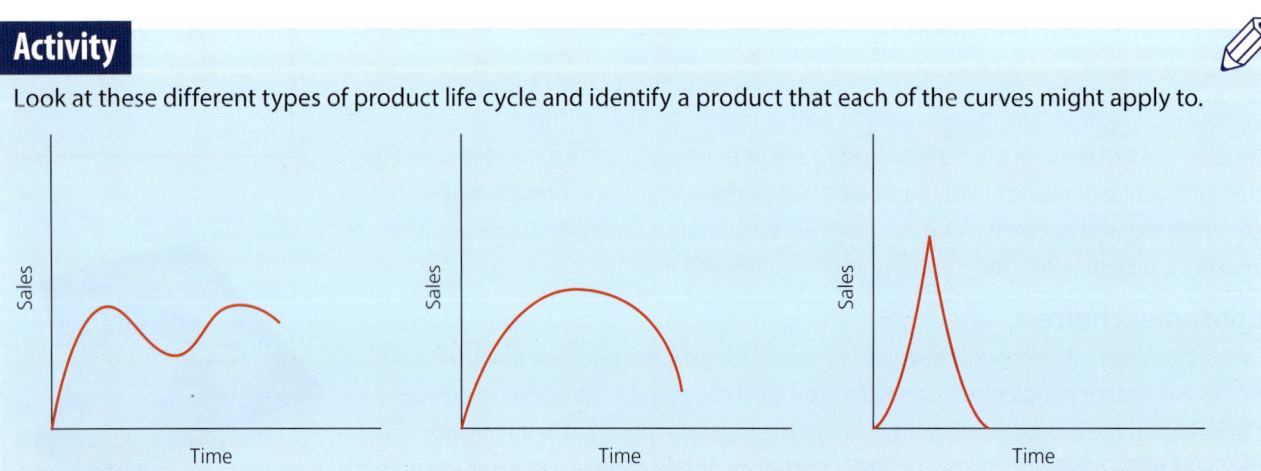

Activity

Carry out some research into a new technology that is likely to reduce the impact that products have on the environment. Write a short summary of what the technology is, its benefits and drawbacks.

The product life cycle will depend on the product being sold. A product which is popular for a short time will have a short life cycle with a steep growth period and an equally steep decline. Some products may decline and then start growing again, for example an item of clothing that comes in and out of fashion.

People, culture and society

Technology can also have an impact on our lifestyle, values and beliefs. When designing and manufacturing products we need to consider how they will affect our society and their moral and ethical implications. Designers also need to ensure they abide by legislation and protection that has been put in place to protect consumers.

Global production and its effects on culture and people

We live in an increasingly global society. Developments in transport mean that products are now shipped all over the world. Components and parts for some products may be produced in several different countries and transported between countries during the manufacturing process. Increasing automated production in factories has speeded up production processes, helping to reduce manufacturing costs.

Similarly, developments in communications technology and the internet mean that we can work with, sell to and buy products from people almost anywhere in the world. This means there is greater competition between companies to market and sell their products, which keeps prices low and helps us to get the best deal. Mobile technology and the internet means we can now communicate with people all over the world at any time and in any place through email and social media. These developments make us better connected and can increase our awareness of other cultures and societies.

However, there are downsides to these new technologies and global production. Importing cheaper products from other countries instead of buying products produced locally can lead to job losses in our own society. It may have been possible to produce those products more cheaply in another country, but this may be because workers in that country are paid low wages and work in poor conditions; this can be detrimental to their lives and health. We need to question the ethical and moral implications of making these choices.

Increasing automated production may have freed up our time, reduced manual labour and stopped us from having to carry out menial tasks, but has caused job losses in some industries as fewer people are needed to perform these roles.

While mobile technology may have increased the frequency of our interactions with other people, it may lead to us having fewer face-to-face interactions, which causes us to feel isolated. Being constantly connected is not always seen as a positive; many people feel it has blurred the boundaries between their work and leisure time and has a negative impact on their sleep and mental well-being.

As designers, we also need to question the cultural implications of global production. We need to be sensitive to the ideas, values, beliefs and customs of different cultures when we are designing products – what may be acceptable in one culture or society may be misunderstood or seen as offensive in another culture. Colours, patterns and symbols, for example, can have different meanings for different people and we need to bear this in mind when making choices for our products to ensure we do not offend. Global production can threaten the traditional industries, skills and techniques of some cultures; we need to consider carefully the impact new products may have on these traditions.

Figure 1.4 Mobile technology and social media means we are better connected than ever before, but it may make us feel isolated.

Activity

In pairs, make a list of five advantages and five disadvantages of the global production of products on culture and people.

KEY POINTS
- New products are usually developed because of a want or need (market pull), or because of developments in technology (technology push).
- Developments in technology have changed our industry and enterprise: automated production and robotics mean we can now produce products quickly and cheaply with a smaller workforce.
- Producing new products uses materials and energy; designers have a responsibility to consider the impact a product will have on the environment at every stage of its life cycle and to produce products with sustainability in mind.
- In our global economy products are sold to people in different societies and with different cultures; we need to consider the positive and negative implications of this and think about how the products we design will affect people, their communities and cultures.

Legislation and consumer rights

The Consumer Rights Act 2015

When you buy products or services, the Consumer Rights Act 2015 protects you when things go wrong, such as buying a defective product or not receiving the expected level of service. The law covers you for faulty goods, **counterfeit** goods, poor services and problems with builders, including rogue traders and contracts. The law states that goods must be of satisfactory quality, as described or seen when purchased, and fit for purpose. The Act also covers digital products and buying online.

You can claim a refund, repair or replacement when something you purchase does not meet the following standards:

- The product should function as intended and you should be able to use it as explained to you by the seller at the time it was purchased. This includes advertising content as well as a verbal exchange, and applies to an actual product and digital downloads. For example, a Bluetooth portable speaker should play music on instruction or a downloaded film should play without interference. The product should always be fit for purpose.

- The product should be of satisfactory quality. It should not be damaged or be defective in any way when you receive it. The law does not protect you if you bought faulty goods knowingly, as sometimes happens with sale items. If you buy goods over the internet it is best to check the quality immediately on receipt.

- The product should be as it was described at the time of purchase. This is particularly important when buying online. Clothing, for example, should be in the colour and size you ordered or if a sports shoe is described as leather it should not be made of cheaper synthetic imitation leather.

The law also protects consumers when a service that has been agreed fails to meet expectations. The provider is still legally bound to offer some form of **compensation** even if it is not practical to bring it in line with what the customer originally purchased (for example if the service and catering at a restaurant for a party was not as agreed). The seller should at least offer a partial refund.

If a product develops a fault or is defective in some way, you have up to 30 days from the day you received the product to get a full refund. You can ask for a repair or replacement if that is your choice. Outside 30 days, the seller should offer a repair service if it is feasible and reasonable to do so. If the repair is unsuccessful then you can ask for your money back or a reduction in price. The same rules apply for digital content; in addition, you might be entitled to additional compensation if a device has been damaged as a result of the faulty downloaded digital content.

The Consumer Rights Act also covers contracts like those for mobile phones. Terms and conditions should be clearly displayed with no additional charges or unfair terms hidden in the small print.

Activity

Discuss the following scenarios.

1   Thomas has downloaded a game for his computer. Initially all was fine – the game was great until his computer seemed to get a virus. Thomas cannot access any of his computer files and the game no longer plays either. What are his rights?

2   Jasmine organised a pool party for her 5-year-old niece's birthday. On arrival at the leisure centre along with 20 invited guests, they were told the pool was closed for repairs so the leisure centre would organise a few games in the hall instead. What are her rights?

3   Alex's new designer sunglasses that were purchased online are great. They even came with a certificate of authenticity. They seem a bit more like plastic than they appeared on the website but they still look really cool. Ten days after receiving them one lens falls out and one of the arms is loose. What are the issues here?

Moral and ethical factors related to manufacturing products and the sale and use of products

A global free market allows unrestricted trade. People who want to make a profit by growing their business leads to healthy competition, which in turn should help workers improve their lives by having an income through regular employment. There is, however, no obligation for companies to support workers in their employ in this way. Businesses are constantly making decisions but not all are considered ethical or morally acceptable. In many areas of global trade not everyone is treated equally and fairly.

Businesses have a moral duty to supply goods and services that are fit for purpose, safe to use and as advertised. Sadly, some businesses put profit above everything else. This could mean poor working conditions and pay for workers and inferior products for unsuspecting consumers.

Some manufacturing companies follow a more ethical approach to trade. These companies focus on how their goods and services directly benefit consumers but also support socially responsible and environmental causes. They also aim to provide advertising that is honest and trustworthy. Ethical traders share a breakdown of costs for products – this transparency is important to them. For other manufacturing companies, costs are not revealed for a number of reasons – for instance, if profit margins and cost breakdowns were disclosed for a specific product, it could reveal poor wages and working conditions for some workers. This is particularly true of the garment manufacturing industry. Organisations like Fairtrade, discussed later in the chapter, seek to redress the balance in trade.

Sustainability

Designers, manufacturers and consumers have become increasingly aware of the negative impact that new technologies and the development and disposal of products can have on the environment, and many now look for ways in which they can reduce their environmental impact.

Sustainability is about meeting today's needs without compromising the needs of future generations. When developing new products, designers and manufacturers have a responsibility to do so with sustainability in mind. See Section 1.2 for examples of how sustainability can affect design.

KEY WORD

Sustainability: producing goods and services without impacting on the needs of future populations.

Figure 1.5 Hybrid technology is helping to reduce CO_2 emissions associated with traditional petrol and diesel car engines.

KEY WORD

Fossil fuels: finite resources that cannot be replaced.

There are many examples of ways in which new and emerging technologies can be utilised to help us to use, manufacture and dispose of products in a more sustainable way. For example:

- **Hybrid technology and electric cars** – the development of hybrid cars, which use both petrol or diesel and an electric motor, reduces fuel consumption and means the car emits less carbon dioxide. Fully electric cars have similar advantages, and as technology develops they are likely to become more popular.
- **Developments in renewable energy** – technology that will help us to make better use of alternative sources of energy and reduce our reliance on **fossil fuels**. Wind, solar, tidal and hydroelectric power technologies are becoming increasingly efficient and helping us to maximise the use of these renewable sources of energy. See page 18 for more on renewable and non-renewable energy sources.
- **Recycling technology** – we recycle only small amounts of the plastic we consume, and products such as Styrofoam cups and plastic bags are difficult to recycle. Recycling companies are focusing on developing technologies that can break down these plastics more effectively and safely.

KEY POINTS
- Know that the Consumer Rights Act 2015 protects consumers when they purchase products, including digital downloads and online purchases. All goods should be as advertised or described, be fit for purpose and of satisfactory quality.
- Know that if we continue to live as we currently do we will cause irreparable damage to the environment. Simple adjustments like buying sustainable products is a good start.
- Think before throwing something away – has it got another use? Reduce land mass currently being used for landfill.

Production techniques and systems

Computer-aided design (CAD)

Figure 1.6 CAD designer

Computer-aided design (CAD) has become one of the most valuable tools available to designers and manufacturers. Once a highly specialised and expensive tool, CAD packages are becoming easier to use, more powerful and their cost is dropping dramatically. It has improved the quality of design work at all stages in the design process, from generating and communicating initial ideas, through to producing 3D models and subsequently extracting working drawings.

Making drawings by hand was extremely time consuming, required a huge level of skill, and errors or adjustments often resulted in the drawing being restarted. Now CAD is accessible to all, from people planning the basic layout of their new kitchen, to engineers developing CAD drawings that can be used to manufacture working prototypes.

CAD models can also be used by manufacturers to simulate how potential products will perform in a particular environment. Simulations of the aerodynamic performance of a car or how a given product may perform under a particular force can all be undertaken using a 3D CAD model. This saves money, time and resources.

Cloud-based technology is an emerging technology which has made collaborative work easier. Designers can share projects in the cloud, allowing for different components to be developed simultaneously by designers who could be working on the other side of the planet. This improvement in communication has improved efficiency and reduced the amount of travelling between designers and manufacturers.

CAD software is accessible to all, but if a complex design or component is needed, the level of skill and knowledge of the CAD designer must be comprehensive. Generative design is a new development that makes use of mathematical algorithms to design components based on a set of parameters or design requirements. This often generates unique and highly efficient designs that would have not been possible to create using traditional skills.

The advantages of CAD:
- The quality of presentation is generally higher than hand-drawn ideas.
- 2D and 3D CAD models can be created, amended and edited easily.
- Textures and colours can be applied to make models photorealistic.
- The design can be securely stored, shared and worked on collaboratively.
- The 3D model can be exported to CAM machines which can produce a working prototype.
- Ideas, concepts and models can be exposed to the clients/users and opinions sought to further develop products.
- CAD can speed up the designing process and reduce lead-in time to get the product to market quicker.

The disadvantages of CAD:
- Powerful computers are necessary for 3D modelling and rendering.
- Designers and other users will need training to use the software to its full potential.
- It requires a high level of expertise to use efficiently.
- It can be slower to generate initial ideas than with pen and paper.
- Software is continually being updated and can be expensive to keep up to date.
- Hardware such as 3D printers can be expensive and quite slow to manufacture large objects.

Computer-aided manufacture (CAM)

CAM machinery is used to produce products and components directly from CAD drawings. A CAD drawing is converted into a code that can be interpreted by a CAM machine. Most CAM machines operate on the principle of a head that moves along an X, Y and Z axis. The code is a series of numerical commands that tell the machine where to move and at what speed, in order to cut out, print or machine the CAD design. As a result of this code they are also often referred to as Computer Numerically Controlled (CNC) machines.

CAM machines are frequently found in industry, where the need to manufacture large volumes of identical and consistent quality products occurs. The initial costs of these machines can be expensive and workers need extensive training to programme and operate them effectively. They have the benefit of being able to run for long periods without breaks, and as such they are much more efficient than the human workforce that they replace. They do however need ongoing servicing and maintenance which can be expensive and impact on the output of a production line.

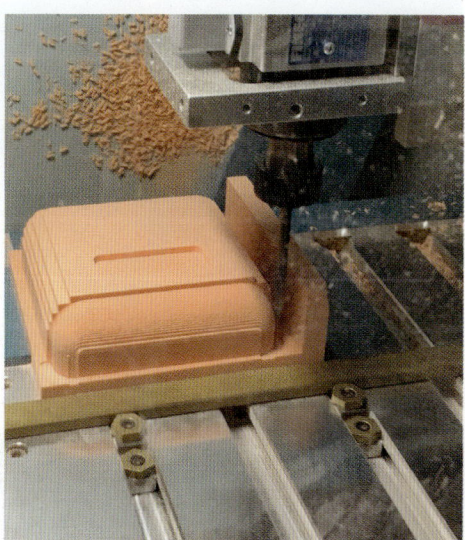

Figure 1.7 CNC router machining a prototype from polyurethane modelling foam

KEY WORDS

CAD: Computer-Aided Design.

CAM: Computer-Aided Manufacture.

CNC: Computer Numerically Controlled.

CAM machines are also found in some schools: vinyl cutters, laser cutters and more recently 3D printers. They are usually smaller than their commercial equivalents but are perfect for cutting and shaping thin materials such as self-adhesive vinyl, card, plywood and acrylic.

The advantages of CAM:

- CAM processes are generally faster than traditional manufacture.
- A high degree of manufacturing accuracy is achievable.
- Consistent and repeatable processes are achievable.
- Less waste is produced than in traditional manufacturing processes.
- It allows for flexible manufacturing systems to be implemented in industry.

The disadvantages of CAM:

- CAM machinery can be expensive.
- CAM machinery can need regular maintenance and servicing.
- Traditional skills and workforces can be displaced.
- Costs generally inhibit CAM use in small-scale manufacture.

Using CAM equipment

CNC embroidery

CAD designs can be sewn or embroidered into a range of textiles and fabrics. CNC embroidery lends itself well to flexible manufacture by being able to personalise garments with dates or names. Designs can be saved or shared to allow for short or long production runs. Uses include the manufacture of school uniforms or applications where branding or logos need to be applied.

Figure 1.8 A CNC embroidery machine producing a multi-coloured logo

Vinyl cutting

Using a roll of self-adhesive vinyl, a simple pattern is cut out from a CAD drawing using a sharp cutting blade. The colour of the design in determined by the vinyl loaded. This process is used to produce lettering or shapes for sign writing or for applying branding to vehicles. Vinyl cutters are probably the most affordable CAM machines, which makes them commonplace in schools.

CNC routing

A rotating router cutter is used to cut around a path or shape determined by the CAD drawing. The profile of the cut can be changed by fitting alternative cutting tools and the depths of the cut are usually determined by different colours being used on the CAD drawing.

More comprehensive 3D shapes can be produced on CNC routers that have attachments that rotate the workpiece while being machined.

Laser cutting

Laser cutters use a directed laser beam to cut through or vaporise material, leaving a high-quality accurate cut. They can be used to cut or engrave a wide range of materials, with some of the more powerful machines cutting through metal. One of the advantages of a laser cutter is that the workpiece can be easily held as there is no force from a rotating cutter or blade. This means that intricate patterns can be cut out, for example jigsaws and decorative designs in greetings cards.

3D printing

3D printing is becoming ever more popular as the price of the printers is decreasing, and the popularity and flexibility that the process offers designers increases. 3D printing, also known as **additive manufacture**, uses a thermoforming polymer roll or spool of filament that is heated and extruded through a head that moves on an x and y axis, much like a laser cutter and CNC router. Following the printing of the first layer, the bed of the printer moves down and the next layer of polymer is extruded. The strength of the product printed can be determined by the type of material used and also the inner design of the print.

Using 3D printing, a working prototype can be quickly produced. Designers can test products and bring them to market without the need for the expensive tooling previously needed to manufacture plastic products. It also means that small-scale manufacture is possible.

Case study: Underarmour ArchiTech footwear

One company that has been looking at how CAD and CAM can allow them to further develop their products is Underarmour. They used generative design to develop a sole for their 'ArchiTech' shoe, which has a lattice structure that has excellent cushioning properties. The complexity of the design is such that it can only be produced by 3D printing. Although the time taken to produce each sole has limited the scale of production, it gives an indicator of how CAD and CAM are going to be integral to many more products that we take for granted.

> **KEY WORD** 🔑
> **Additive manufacture**: the process of building up a physical shape layer by layer.

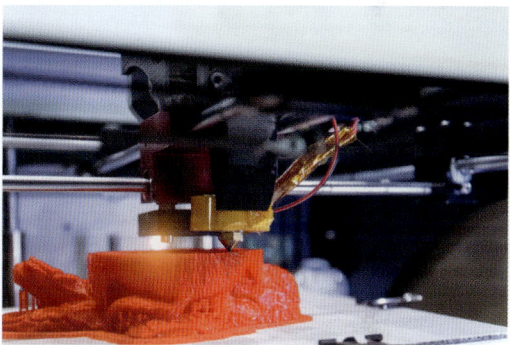

Figure 1.9 3D printer

Figure 1.10 3D printing layer by layer

Activity

Find out more about how generative CAD design and advancements in 3D printing are shaping skateboard design and manufacture by researching 'Project T.O.S.T'.

KEY POINTS 🎯
- Additive manufacture is the process of building up a physical shape layer by layer.
- Rendering is the process of applying a colour or textures to a drawing.
- CAD is an effective method of drawing, editing and presenting design work digitally.
- CAM is the process of using machinery to produce products. CAM machines run from instructions produced from CAD drawings.

1.2 How the critical evaluation of new and emerging technologies informs design decisions

New technologies are always emerging. Some of these are disruptive and can cause significant changes to our lifestyle. Others create a brief fashion which soon disappears.

The internet has massively changed the way we shop, communicate and entertain ourselves. In some ways, the internet has reduced the amount that we need to travel, but in other ways it has increased our 'road miles' because we expect online goods to be delivered to our door. In this section, we look at how important it is for future designers to make decisions based on consideration for the environment.

The importance of sustainability issues and environmental issues when designing and making

Designers, manufacturers and consumers all have a role to play in promoting a sustainable design strategy. Sustainable design involves:

- Materials – choosing materials for manufacturing that have a low impact on the environment (materials which are recycled, such as paper and card, non-toxic and do not need as much energy to process).
- Manufacturing methods – designing products which are manufactured using efficient, low-energy methods.
- Build quality – products with a higher build quality are likely to work more effectively, for longer and break down less.
- Packaging – reducing unnecessary product packaging and making all packaging recyclable, e.g. cardboard.
- Transportation – reducing the energy needs for transporting the raw materials and the finished product, for example by local manufacturers using locally sourced materials where possible.
- Energy needs – designing energy-efficient products, for example using LED lights instead of filament lamps.
- Product life expectancy – designing products to last, avoiding early obsolescence and designing products to be serviced and repaired.
- End of product life – consideration of what happens to the product when it is no longer needed. Ease of product recyclability.
- Fair trade – designing products which provide a fair income for workers at all stages in the supply and production chain.

KEY WORD

Environmental directive: a type of law to provide protection for the environment.

There is a great deal of international pressure on governments in all countries to reduce energy consumption, reduce pollution and eliminate the disposal of hazardous substances into the environment, and to increase recycling. There are many **environmental directives** (types of laws) which stem from the European Union and from bodies such as the World Energy Council which specify targets to achieve these aims. There are also international agreements on climate change, air pollution and the protection of wildlife.

Manufacturers can apply to have their product awarded the European Ecolabel. To qualify, products have to meet a tough set of environmental criteria which take into account the whole product life cycle. The EU Ecolabel is intended to simplify consumer choice in seeking out products which are good for the environment.

Figure 1.11 The EU Ecolabel

Products displaying the EU Ecolabel tell the consumer that they have achieved environmental excellence, which manufacturers hope will promote sales of the product.

Social, cultural, economic and environmental responsibilities

In addition to environmental directives, designers and manufacturers face pressure from consumers who are becoming more conscious about buying products which are better for the environment.

Many new domestic appliances carry an energy rating label which helps consumers choose energy-efficient products. The label rates the product on a scale from A+++ (most efficient) to G (least efficient). The EU claims that the introduction of the energy rating label, together with consumer education, will reduce energy consumption by an amount equivalent to the annual energy consumption of Italy, saving consumers hundreds of pounds on their annual energy bills.

Linear and circular economy

In a **linear economy**, products are made as cheaply as possible. Resources are extracted and taken from the earth, made into products and then sold. Once the product is broken or no longer wanted it is simply disposed of.

The use of certain materials and processes when manufacturing products can have an extremely detrimental effect on wildlife, the environment and our climate. As a result, there has been a shift in people's perceptions and attitudes. Many people choose not to purchase products that are not environmentally friendly.

Figure 1.12 Energy rating label on a washing machine

A sustainable strategy ensures that, when a product reaches the end of its life, the useful materials in the product are recovered for reuse. Manufacturers have had to change the way they source, process and package products or they risk losing sales. The Government has also forced manufacturers to meet more stringent laws relating to the amount of pollution they produce and how they dispose of waste products.

This 'make–use–recycle' strategy is called the **circular economy**. The circular economy uses as few resources as possible and extracts the maximum from them, using them for as long as possible. Products are manufactured in such a way that they can be repaired or so that as many parts as possible can be reused or recycled once they are broken or no longer required.

Circular economy links with **cradle-to-cradle** production (compared with cradle-to-grave) where a manufacturer considers the stages of a product's life, from its birth, through its use and death, then recycling and ultimate rebirth into a new product.

The six Rs of sustainability

Table 1.1 shows the six Rs of sustainability, which are intended to help consumers ask questions about their lifestyle, how they choose and use products, and how it impacts on the environment.

KEY WORDS

Circular economy: considering how to recover the assets from a product at the end of its life and invest them in a new product.

Cradle-to-cradle: considering a product's complete life cycle, including its rebirth into a new product.

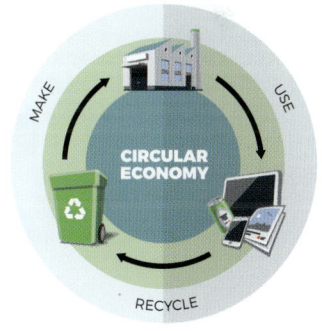

Figure 1.13 Circular versus linear economy

A designer can apply the six Rs during product development, so that excellent environmental qualities are designed into the very heart of the product.

	Questions a designer might ask
Rethink	Does the product do its job well? Is there a better way to solve the problem which is less damaging to the environment?
Reduce	Can we reduce the amount of materials used in the product or its packaging? Are there parts which are not needed? Many products are over-packaged – can this be reduced?
Recycle	At the end of the product's life, can the materials be easily separated and then recycled in order to make new components for new products?
Reuse	Can the product (or parts of it) be used for some other purpose once it has reached the end of its primary life? Can packaging be reused rather than being discarded?
Refuse	Is it necessary to use the product at all? Is it an unethical product? Where is it made, and what are the conditions for the workers who make it? Do they get a fair wage? Is the product Fairtrade? By refusing to buy unethical products, consumers can put a great deal of pressure on manufacturers.
Repair	Can the product be repaired if it breaks down? Can it be better designed so that regular servicing extends its life?

Table 1.1 The six Rs of sustainability

Life-cycle analysis

A life-cycle analysis is carried out to assess the environmental impact of a product during its entire life cycle, from cradle-to-cradle. It looks at the use of materials, the use of energy, and the impact of transporting the materials, parts and the product itself at various points in its life. Table 1.2 lists a series of questions that can be useful when carrying out a life-cycle analysis.

Figure 1.14 Life-cycle analysis

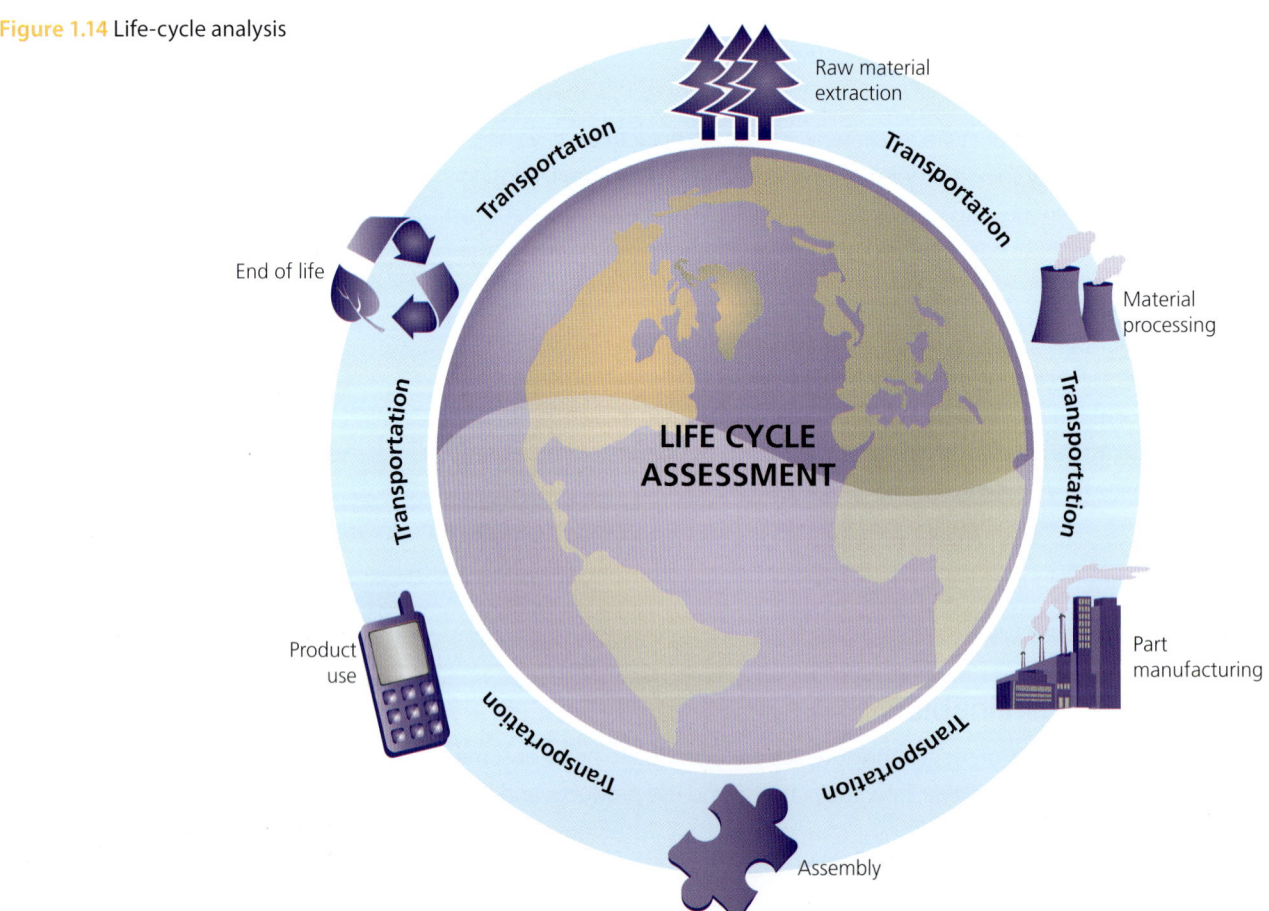

Stage	Questions to ask
Acquiring raw materials	• What is the environmental impact of extracting or harvesting the raw materials (e.g. drilling for crude oil)? • How much energy is used in the extraction? • Could recycled materials be used instead?
Material processing	• How much processing is required to convert the raw material into a usable material (e.g. converting crude oil into polymer)? • How much energy is required? • Does the processing use renewable energy sources? • Does the processing use harmful chemicals, or produce pollution or waste products?
Manufacturing	• What manufacturing method(s) is used? Is there an alternative? • How much energy is required (e.g. for machines, factory lighting/heating, etc.)? • Does the manufacturer use renewable energy sources? • Does the manufacturing use harmful chemicals, or produce pollution or waste products (e.g. bleach used during textile dyeing)?
Use	• How much energy does the product use, if any? • Does the product consume energy when not being used (e.g. when on standby)? • Where does the energy come from? Is it a renewable source? • Does the product create pollution or waste products (e.g. a car exhaust)? • Can it be made more energy efficient?
End of life	• Can the product easily be dismantled into component parts? • Are the parts recyclable? • Do the parts contain hazardous chemicals (e.g. mobile phone batteries)? • How much energy is needed to process the product for recycling or disposal?
Transportation	• How far are parts, product and waste transported? • What fuels are used for transportation? • What is the carbon footprint? • Could local materials be sourced? • Could the product be manufactured close to where it is used?

Table 1.2 The stages of a product life-cycle analysis

Activity

Carry out a life-cycle assessment on an electric kettle. Construct a grid with the six stages shown in Table 1.2. In your grid, answer some of the questions asked in the table.

Fairtrade

A key ethical issue for a designer is the working conditions for the people who make the products. Many raw materials are mined or harvested from all over the world, and designers have a responsibility to ensure that materials are ethically sourced. Not all farmers, workers and miners who are involved in the production of products are treated equally and fairly. Many do not share in any of the benefits and profits associated with trade.

Fairtrade sets up partnership schemes between producers, businesses and consumers that offer a different approach. Social, economic and environmental standards are set for all companies, producers and workers involved in the supply

Figure 1.15 FAIRTRADE Mark

Exploit: unfairly take advantage of.

Global warming: a rise in temperature of the Earth's atmosphere caused by pollution and gases.

Fairtrade products and ingredients	
Bananas	Herbs
Cereals	Ice cream
Chocolate	Nuts
Cocoa	Olive oil
Coffee	Rice
Cosmetics	Soft drinks
Cotton	Spices
Flowers	Sugar
Footballs	Tea
Gold	Wine

Table 1.3 Some Fairtrade products

chain. One of the aims of Fairtrade is to connect disadvantaged producers and consumers by setting up fairer trading conditions. If disadvantaged producers get a better share of profits and fairer wages for the work they do, it will help improve their lives and combat poverty. Producers who work under the Fairtrade agreement have an equal say in more aspects of the trade chain. Working conditions have to be of a satisfactory standard, to tackle **exploitation** and protect workers' rights.

Products made under the Fairtrade agreement that meet all the standards can carry the Fairtrade mark. This helps shoppers to make decisions about whether a product they are thinking of buying is ethical, or manufactured from materials or ingredients that have been ethically sourced.

Carbon footprint

A carbon footprint is a measure of the amount of greenhouse gases released as a result of our activities. The figure is expressed as kilograms or tonnes of carbon dioxide (CO_2). Carbon dioxide is a greenhouse gas, which means that it traps the Sun's heat at the surface of the Earth. Greenhouse gases cause **global warming**. The more CO_2 an individual generates the bigger the impact on the environment.

Using energy from fossil fuels adds to our carbon footprint. Heating our homes with gas, oil or coal emits CO_2 and makes our carbon footprint bigger. Even if using electricity does not directly give off CO_2 the power station that generated it does! The waste we generate also produces CO_2 and another gas called methane when it goes to landfill. Table 1.4 lists some activities which each have a carbon footprint of 1 kg of CO_2.

Activities which each release 1kg of CO_2
• Driving 4 miles in a car.
• Travelling 7 miles on a bus or train.
• Flying 1.4 miles in a plane.
• Leaving your computer switched on for a day.
• Manufacturing two plastic bottles.
• Producing 100 g of beef (cows produce large amounts of methane gas in their guts).

Table 1.4 Carbon footprint examples

Activity

Use an online carbon footprint calculator to work out your own carbon footprint for your lifestyle. There are many online calculators, such as the one at http://footprint.wwf.org.uk which compares your carbon footprint to the UK annual average.

Across the world, the average annual carbon footprint per person is 4 tonnes. In the UK, the average annual carbon footprint is 10 tonnes per person.

Some carbon-based fuels are carbon neutral. This means that they do not contribute to the amount of CO_2 in the atmosphere. Wood is an example of a carbon neutral fuel. When the wood grew, the tree absorbed CO_2 from the atmosphere and locked the carbon into the wood. When the wood is burned, the same amount of CO_2 is released, resulting in no overall CO_2 change in the atmosphere. All biofuels (Section 1.3) are close to being carbon neutral, although fossil fuels may still be used in their production (for example, to power farm machinery). Energy sourced from renewable sources (Section 1.3) creates no carbon at all.

Activity

Think of one product or gadget you own. Consider its carbon footprint and how that indirectly affects your carbon footprint. Think about:

- Where was it made?
- Were the materials and components made there too?
- Where did you get it from?
- Has it travelled far from its early concept stage to be in your possession?
- Does it need power to use it? Think about that carefully!
- What do you intend to do with it when you no longer want it?
- Has it added much to your carbon footprint? Could you change any actions as a result of this analysis? If so, how or in what way?

(HINT: Denim jeans/clothing are good for this exercise.)

Ecological footprint

A person's **ecological footprint** is the area of the Earth that they need to produce the resources, and absorb the waste, to sustain their lifestyle. It gives us a measure of the impact human activity has on the environment. Our ecological footprint weighs up how quickly we consume resources and generate waste against how quickly nature can absorb our waste and generate new resources.

Resources include food (plants, livestock, fish and drinking water), building materials (timber, mined materials), fuels (fossil fuels, renewable energy farms), other consumables (clothes, paper, etc.). Waste is mainly carbon emissions.

Table 1.5 illustrates what the land is mainly used for that makes up our ecological footprint.

KEY WORDS

Ecological footprint: a measure of the impact that human activity has on the environment.

Ecological deficit: a measure to indicate that more natural resources are being used than nature can replace.

Use	What land is used for
Infrastructure	land needed for buildings – houses and industrial; transportation – roads and railways; reservoirs for hydropower and energy plants
Forestry	land needed to supply timber for products, furniture and construction, wood fuel, pulp, paper; also needed to absorb CO_2 from fossil fuels
Water	fishing grounds for the food commodities from oceans and rivers; water is vital to sustain all life; needed in industry and agriculture
Cropland	land required to grow the food we eat – fruit, grain and vegetables; fibre for textiles such as cotton and linen; animal feed, bio fuel
Grazing land	needed to raise livestock for meat and dairy, wool and leather products
Disposal	land needed to dispose of all the waste we generate
Fossil fuels	production, transportation, heating and cooling

Table 1.5 Ecological footprint

In the UK, the average ecological footprint of each person is 5.6 hectares. One hectare is about the size of a rugby pitch, so each person requiring 5.6 hectares is simply not sustainable. The global sustainable level is 1.8 hectares per person.

Worldwide, humanity's ecological footprint is currently the equivalent of 1.7 Earths. Put another way, it takes Earth 18 months to regenerate what we use in 12 months. If we continue to use up the world's natural resources quicker than nature can replace them, we will create an **ecological deficit**.

Activity

Use an online footprint calculator to work out your (and your family's) ecological footprint.

- Investigate how you could lower your ecological footprint by making small changes to the way you currently live your life.
- Discuss how your school could lower its ecological footprint.
- Describe what product designers could do to help consumers lessen their ecological impact.

KEY POINTS

- Sustainable design involves choosing the correct materials, manufacturing methods, packaging, transportation, energy needs and end-of-product-life considerations.
- Environmental directives are laws which aim to protect the environment by controlling use of hazardous materials, energy use and pollution.
- Know the six Rs of sustainability, and how they can be applied to reduce a product's environmental impact.
- A life-cycle analysis is carried out to assess the environmental impact of a product during its entire life cycle, from cradle-to-cradle.
- Products that carry the Fairtrade logo have been certified to meet Fairtrade standards. This helps shoppers to make decisions about whether a product they are thinking of buying is ethical, or manufactured from materials or ingredients that have been ethically sourced.
- Fairtrade lobbies governments for fairer trade deals for disadvantaged producers, and campaigns to make the public aware of the unfair issues associated with trade. The Fairtrade Foundation works closely with and supports farmers in developing countries.
- Carbon footprint is a way of measuring the contribution an activity makes towards global warming.
- Your carbon footprint is the total CO_2 you generate; the more you generate the bigger impact you have on the environment.
- Ecological footprint is a measure of the area of land required to support an activity.

1.3 How energy is generated and stored in order to choose and use appropriate sources to make products and to power systems

As a Design and Technology student, you will need to consider ways that energy is used to:

- manufacture products
- power products and systems.

Energy is always needed to cause something to move, to heat something up, to create light or sound, or even to perform calculations in a computer chip. Energy is also needed to process a material (for example to extract, refine, mould, bend, cut or drill it). Basically, the manufacture and use of products and systems requires energy, and an assessment of this was discussed under life-cycle analysis in Section 1.2.

Types of renewable and non-renewable energy sources

You will have learned in science that energy cannot be created or destroyed, it can only change from one type of energy into another type. When we 'generate' energy, such as electricity, we are transforming another source of energy into electricity. We constantly need sources of energy to supply the demands of industry and consumers.

The energy sources available to us on earth can be classified into **non-renewable** and **renewable** sources. Non-renewable sources are fuels that are extracted from the earth. Once used, they cannot be replenished; they are **finite** sources and they will eventually run out. Renewable energy sources will not run out.

Source	Explanation
Coal (fossil fuel)	Mined from the ground. Burning coal releases heat energy which is used in power stations to generate electricity, which is then distributed around the country through a national grid.
Oil (fossil fuel)	Crude oil is extracted from the earth by drilling deep into the ground. It is then refined to produce a variety of liquid fuels, such as petrol, diesel and aviation fuel. These hydrocarbon fuels can be used in motor vehicle engines, or aircraft jet engines to produce movement. They can also be burned in central heating systems for buildings, or for generating electricity in power stations.
Gas (fossil fuel)	Natural gas is largely methane, a combustible hydrocarbon. It is used as a fuel in some vehicles. Gas is extracted by drilling, and then it is piped through a national grid pipeline into houses and factories where it is used as a fuel for heating and cooking. Some power stations use gas-powered turbines (similar to a jet engine) to generate electricity.
Nuclear	Uranium ore is mined from the earth. It undergoes a purification and enrichment process to be transformed into nuclear fuel which is then used in a nuclear reactor to generate heat which is converted to electricity in a nuclear power station. Nuclear fuel is not burned. The heat energy is released when the large, unstable uranium atomic nuclei split into two smaller nuclei. This is called nuclear fission.

Table 1.6 Non-renewable energy sources

Figure 1.16 Coal is a fossil fuel.

Source	Explanation
Wind	A wind turbine is designed to extract energy from the wind. The rotating blades are connected to a generator which produces electricity. The hub of the turbine can turn so that the blades always face into the wind.
Solar	Photovoltaic (PV) panels produce electricity when exposed to sunlight. In the northern hemisphere, they normally face south and are angled so that they receive the maximum possible sunlight throughout the day. They produce a low voltage, direct current (DC). This can be used to charge batteries, or it can be converted to high voltage AC and fed into the mains electricity grid. Solar water heating panels can be used to directly heat water for domestic and industrial use.
Geothermal	Cold water is pumped underground where it is heated by the Earth's natural heat. The hot water (or steam) that returns can heat homes, or it can be used in a power station to generate electricity.
Hydroelectric	A dam is built to trap a natural river, forming a lake. The water is released, under control, and the pressure of the escaping water turns turbines which generates electricity. Some small hydroelectric generators do not need a dam, relying instead on the energy of a fast-flowing river.
Wood/biomass	When a tree is harvested, the wood which is not of interest to the timber industry is chipped (or pelleted) and used as fuel in place of burning coal. This can provide heating for houses, or it can be used to generate electricity. In other biomass schemes, plants are grown to produce materials which can be processed into biofuels. Sugar cane is fermented to produce bioethanol, and soy beans can be processed into biodiesel; both these liquid fuels are useful in transportation. A digester unit will process waste food into a burnable biomass fuel, such as converting used cooking oil from restaurants to biodiesel.
Wave	A mechanism is used to convert energy from waves on the sea into electricity. Wave power is not widely used. Tidal power is a more promising aspect for future energy needs. This is a type of hydroelectric scheme which extracts energy from the rising and falling tides.

Table 1.7 Renewable energy sources.

Issues surrounding the use of fossil fuels

Fossil fuels (coal, oil and gas) currently provide around 80 per cent of the world's energy needs. They are a store of chemical energy, which they release as heat energy when burned. Using fossil fuels has a significant environmental cost. They produce waste products which are emitted into the atmosphere, mainly carbon dioxide gas, but also pollutants such as sulphur dioxide (which raises the acidity of rain) and fine particulates which can cause breathing problems for people. Carbon dioxide is a **greenhouse gas** which means that it traps the Sun's heat at the surface of the Earth. Most scientists agree that carbon dioxide emissions from burning fossil fuels is actively contributing to global warming.

Figure 1.17 Solar PV panels and wind turbines

KEY WORD

Greenhouse gas: atmospheric pollution which traps heat at the Earth's surface.

Fossil fuels cannot be replaced. Estimates vary about when they will run out, but we are currently using oil at a much faster rate than coal or gas.

Fossil fuels have a very high energy density, which means they hold a lot of chemical energy per kilogram of fuel. This makes them ideal for use in transportation (cars, ships, aircraft, etc.) because they contain a lot of energy for not much weight. They are also quick to refuel – it only takes a couple of minutes to fill a car with petrol. The alternative fuel sources, such as batteries in electric cars, are heavy, offer limited range and take hours to recharge. Battery technology will improve, but fossil fuels are, currently, more convenient.

There is a great deal of international pressure on governments to reduce the pollution from fossil fuels. This pressure is passed on to vehicle manufacturers to make cleaner cars, and it is passed on to consumers in the form of fuel tax and vehicle tax. Eventually, fossil fuel-powered vehicles will be made too expensive to run and drivers will be forced to switch to vehicles powered by cleaner, renewable sources of energy.

The advantages and disadvantages of renewable energy sources

Except for biomass fuels, renewable sources of energy produce no atmospheric emissions and are, therefore, non-polluting.

When biomass (such as wood) is burned it releases carbon dioxide, but new trees are planted which absorb carbon dioxide as they grow, so the process is classed as **carbon neutral**. Biomass fuel availability can be seasonal, and there is a need for the fuel to be transported to where it is needed.

The equipment needed to extract renewable energy can be expensive, so there is often a high initial outlay. However, once installed, it produces free energy.

Wind and solar energy are not always available, so they cannot be relied on as our only energy source. The energy output is also quite small, so several wind turbines are often clustered together in a wind farm. Some people say that wind farms and fields full of black solar panels are unsightly and spoil the natural environment.

There are also environmental considerations for hydroelectric power, as it often involves building large dam structures in rural areas, which flood the countryside and might upset the habitat for wildlife.

Geothermal energy units are very expensive to install and are only profitable in some areas where the underground rocks are particularly hot near the surface.

Increasing numbers of manufacturers are investing in renewable energy schemes to power their manufacturing systems. Solar panels and wind turbines can both generate energy which the manufacturer uses to power their factory. Many factories will also install equipment to recover 'waste' energy, such as the heat energy wasted from moulding thermoforming polymers, and use the recovered energy to heat their offices. This will reduce their energy bills and demonstrates a responsible and ethical attitude towards the environment, which can improve the company image.

Figure 1.18 This solar-powered garden lamp recharges during the day.

Renewable energy sources for products

There are opportunities to use compact, renewable energy sources with some products. Small solar PV panels will produce a small current during daylight hours which will recharge a battery. Small wind generators can recharge a battery providing there is enough wind. The power output from either method is quite small, so only relatively low-power products are suitable. A renewable energy source is sometimes the only option for products when mains power is not accessible. Some electronic roadside signs are powered by a solar PV panel mounted on top of the signpost.

Figure 1.19 A wind-up torch that needs no batteries

A clockwork wind-up mechanism can also provide a temporary source of power for electronic and mechanical products. The user winds up a spring which stores potential energy. This is released slowly to generate electricity when the product is used. Some wind-up products do not use a spring; instead, the user generates electricity as they wind and this is stored in a capacitor and released when the product is used. Wind-up radios, torches and phone chargers all operate on free energy, without the need for batteries.

Energy generation and storage in a range of contexts

Motor vehicles

Most cars use chemical energy stored in petrol or diesel (fossil fuels) as their energy source. As mentioned above, their convenience and high energy density makes them challenging to replace. Electric cars use batteries as their energy source which are recharged by plugging them in to a mains electricity source. The car produces no emissions, although the source of mains electricity may still come from a fossil fuel power station. Electric vehicles are efficient because they can recover some of their kinetic energy when the driver brakes and store this energy in the battery. The battery can take hours to fully recharge, and the car's range is limited. Nonetheless, sales of electric cars are increasing as they are cheap to run and they avoid the ban (or tax) that some cities are now imposing on fossil fuel-powered vehicles.

Activity

Find and photograph five products which are powered by their own renewable energy source. Try to find products around your home and school, or use images from the internet if you have to.

A rechargeable hybrid car uses a combination of electric motors for city driving, and a petrol engine for long distances. The petrol engine can also recharge the battery. They can be quickly refuelled with petrol or plugged in for an overnight charge. Therefore, rechargeable hybrid cars combine lower emissions with a good driving range.

Mains-powered products

Products which do not need to be portable can be plugged in to the mains electricity supply, which provides an 'unlimited' supply of energy and avoids the need for recharging. However, the number of mains products which are left 'on standby' is causing concern as these products are continuously using energy when they are not being used.

Activity

Go through every room in your house and itemise the products which are plugged in (or permanently wired in) and 'on standby'. Examples include TVs, microwave ovens, intruder alarms, phone chargers, etc.

Battery-powered products

Mobile phones, cordless vacuum cleaners, smart watches, etc. are powered from the energy stored in their rechargeable battery. Many torches, TV remotes, toys, etc. use non-rechargeable batteries, which are used once then replaced. Used batteries should be disposed of responsibly through proper recycling facilities. These batteries store chemical energy which is released as electrical energy when the product is used.

Some outdoor products use a solar PV panel to recharge a battery within the product. The energy is stored within the battery and released as electricity when the product is used. Solar garden lights and some burglar alarms and security cameras use solar panels as a renewable energy source.

KEY POINTS
- Energy sources are either non-renewable or renewable.
- Using fossil fuels has a significant environmental impact.
- Renewable energy sources are 'clean' but not always available, and they can be expensive.

Know it

1 Give one example of a product created because of market pull and one product created due to technology push.
2 Discuss the advantages and disadvantages that automated production has had on industry, people and society.
3 If a company is producing 1000 units of an item, why would they choose to use CNC manufacture where possible?
4 List the six Rs of sustainability and give examples to explain how each one could be put into practice.
5 Explain what is meant by a circular economy.
6 Explain the terms 'carbon footprint' and 'ecological footprint'.
7 Describe how renewable energy sources can be useful in products.
8 Explain how Fairtrade supports disadvantaged producers and workers.
9 Explain how the Consumer Rights Act protects consumers when purchasing digital products.

Chapter 2
Smart materials, composites and technical textiles

Learning objectives

By the end of this chapter you should have developed a knowledge and understanding of:
- the range of smart materials and the condition that triggers a change in their property
- how smart materials can be used to enhance the function of a product
- different types of composites and how they can be used to enhance a product
- different types of technical textiles and how they can be used to enhance a product.

2.1 Smart materials

Smart materials are those whose physical or mechanical properties react to a change in their environment. This reaction, which can include a change in colour, shape or resistance, can be in response to a change in temperature, light, moisture, pressure or an electrical input.

The change is temporary and reversible. The material should return to its previous state when the environmental factor that initialised the change is removed.

Electroluminescent material

Electroluminescent materials provide a visible light when exposed to an electrical current. They are most easily identifiable by their blue glowing light, but other colours are also produced.

Electroluminescent wire, often referred to as EL wire, is made from a thin copper wire core that is coated in a phosphor powder that, when subjected to an alternating electrical current, provides a bright glowing light. The colour emitted can be determined by the pigment being added to the phosphor used. EL wire is used in applications where the wire's flexibility is most beneficial, such as decorative lighting, signage and as a decorative element in clothing.

Electroluminescent technology can also be found in the form of flexible films or thin panels. Here, the light-emitting phosphor is sandwiched between a pair of conductive electrodes and emits light when subjected to an AC current. The brightness of the panel or film will increase in line with the voltage applied. EL films are replacing traditional LCD displays in some applications as they can be flexible, they do not generate heat, and have increased reliability and durability. EL film is also used in applications such as mobile phones, car dashboard displays, watch illumination and signage.

Quantum tunnelling composite (QTC)

Quantum tunnelling composites are flexible polymers that contain conductive nickel particles. They are categorised as smart materials as they can be either a conductor of electricity or an insulator. When a force is applied to the material the conductive particles come into contact with each other and the conductivity increases. The more force with which they are compressed the more conductive and less resistant they become. When the force is removed, the material returns to its original state and becomes an electrical insulator.

KEY WORDS

Smart material: a material whose properties change in response to an external change in environment.

Electroluminescent: a material that provides a visible light when exposed to a current.

Quantum tunnelling composites: materials that change from insulators to conductors when under pressure.

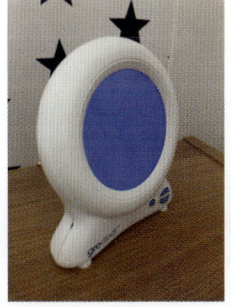 

Figure 2.1 The Groclock uses electroluminescent technology.

Door bolt

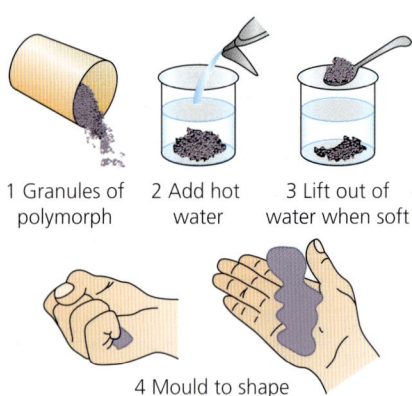

Compression spring keeps SMA wire stretched and bolt in 'locked' position

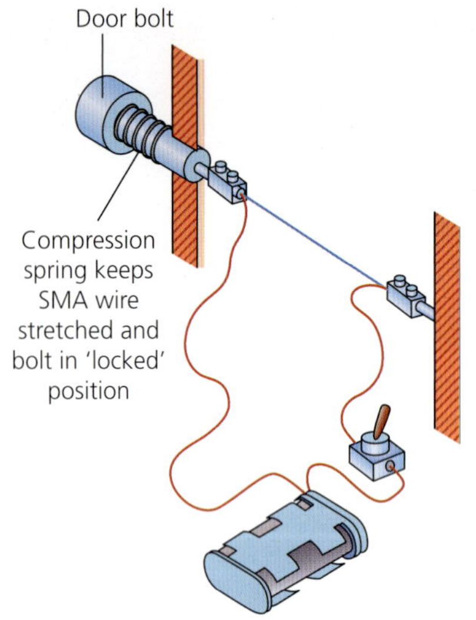

Figure 2.2 In some systems, the heat needed to make the SMA return to its predetermined state can be achieved by passing an electric current through the material in a thin wire form.

1 Granules of polymorph

2 Add hot water

3 Lift out of water when soft

4 Mould to shape

Figure 2.3 The four stages of polymorph

Figure 2.4 Thermochromic pigment in children's spoons. The spoons on the right have been heated.

KEY WORD

Micro-encapsulation: the process of applying microscopic capsules to fibres or fabrics.

They are found in applications such as variable speed controllers, membrane switches, mobile phones and pressure sensors.

Shape memory alloys (SMAs)

Most metals can be shaped into different forms, but few have a 'memory' that will allow them to return to their original shape if heated. Nitinol is an alloy of titanium and nickel and is one of the more commonly known shape memory alloys. A product manufactured from nitinol can be shaped and deformed, but when heated the metal will return to its original state.

It is found in many medical applications, such as medical fastenings used in bone fractures, and dental implants such as braces. In both of these applications the SMA reacts to the natural heat of the body, keeping the wire of the braces under tension and preventing the medical fixings from becoming loose.

Polymorph

Polymorph is a thermoforming polymer that is usually supplied in a granular form, often categorised as a smart material due to it becoming soft and pliable at a low temperature. When heated in water to 62°C, polymorph becomes soft, the granules merge together and create a volume of material that can be easily moulded by hand, solidifying when cool.

It is a versatile modelling material that can be machined and shaped with hand tools when solid, and will become soft and pliable if reheated in water. It is often used in schools when modelling ergonomic features on a product.

Photochromic pigment

Photochromic pigment changes colour in response to light intensity. It can be found in applications such as sunglasses where the lens will become darker or lighter in response to the UV radiation.

Thermochromic pigment

Thermochromic pigments change colour in response a change in heat. They can be engineered to respond to a specific temperature or temperature range and are often used in applications where a visual indicator is needed when a specific temperature has been reached, such as the temperature of a baby's bath or to indicate when their food is cool enough to eat. Drinks companies have used thermochromic ink in their labels, to show when the ideal chilled temperature has been reached.

Micro-encapsulation

Micro-encapsulation is a process of applying microscopic capsules to fibres or fabrics. The capsules can contain vitamins, therapeutic oils, moisturisers, antiseptics and anti-bacterial chemicals, to name a few. These substances are released through friction when in contact with the skin. Micro-encapsulated fabrics have many potential uses, for example:

● Medical textiles: antiseptics embedded on dressings delivered directly to the wound, aiding the healing process and with a potential reduction in infection. Dressings may need to be changed less often.

- Sportswear: micro-encapsulated with chemicals to repel odour and prevent fungal infections.
- Children's wear or clothes for people with sensitive skin: encapsulated with moisturisers and oils to soothe and heal.
- Household textiles: lavender and camomile are known for their soothing properties. They can now be encapsulated into bedlinen to aid relaxation.

Biomimetics

Biomimicry is when the inspiration for new fabrics comes from the natural world. These smart technical fabrics mimic different situations found in nature. Fastskin, developed by Speedo for performance enhancing swimwear, mimics the shark's natural sandpaper-like skin by reducing drag in the water. Such was its success that it was banned from competitive swimming in 2009 for giving swimmers an unfair advantage!

2.2 Composites

Composites are produced by combining two or more materials together to make use of their individual properties in the creation of a new enhanced material. Most composites are made from just two materials. One is known as the matrix, the other the fibre or reinforcement. The two materials combined usually have significantly different properties and maintain these properties in the new composite.

Carbon fibre reinforced polymer (CFRP)

Carbon fibre reinforced polymer (CFRP) is a composite of carbon fibre strands woven together and encased in a polymer resin. The resin, which is lightweight and rigid, encases the carbon fibre strands, which have a high tensile strength to create a high-performance engineering material. CFRP is instantly recognisable due to its woven appearance.

CFRP is found in the manufacture of both racing bikes and mountain bikes due to its strength-to-weight ratio and stiffness along with the ability to produce streamlined shapes. Other common uses of CFRP include Formula 1 components, high-performance sports equipment and in the aerospace industry.

Glass reinforced plastic (GRP)

Glass reinforced plastic (GRP) is a composite of glass fibres and polyester resin. It is a more common composite polymer than CFRP due to its lower cost and more accessible manufacturing methods. The polyester resin makes GRP tough and lightweight with the glass fibres providing rigidity.

GRP has a less attractive surface finish than CRFP and is usually seen with a pigmented finish. Common uses of GRP include boats, canoes, hockey sticks and car body work.

Due to the nature of a composite, when the matrix has set or cured it is impossible to reverse the process. Due to this, most composite materials are very difficult to recycle.

Kevlar

Kevlar® is a tradename for a fibre that is manufactured by DuPont. It is a lightweight, flexible and extremely durable fibre that has excellent resistance to heat and damage from chemicals. It is often used in protective clothing such as police body armour, where the fibre is woven

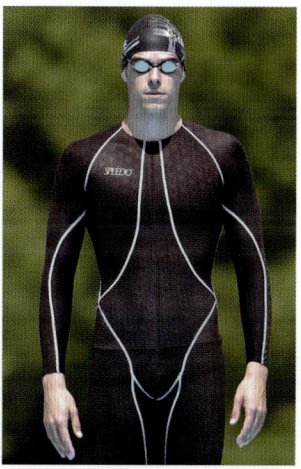

Figure 2.5 The all-in-one Fastskin swimsuit streamlines the body when in water.

Figure 2.6 CFRP matting

Figure 2.7 CFRP has been used to provide an aerodynamic frame that is lightweight and stiff for this track bike.

Figure 2.8 Kevlar stabproof vest

in a lattice that provides protection against knife attack. It is also used as a fibre thread in sportswear, such as motorbike clothing and protective padding worn by mountain bikers and skateboarders.

It is not a composite in its own right, but is often used as the fibre component of other resin-based composites due to its high tensile strength and durability.

Activity

Using the internet, research some sports accessories that are manufactured from CFRP. What properties of CFRP have made it a suitable choice for the product? As an extension, try to research the material that it has replaced. Why has that development taken place?

2.3 Technical textiles

Technical textiles are engineered with specific performance characteristics that suit a particular purpose or function. Recent advances in technology have seen a rapid growth in demand for more technically advanced performance-related fabrics.

Interactive textiles

Interactive textiles, or integrated textiles, are when electronic devices and circuits are integrated or embedded into textile fabric and clothing to interact and communicate with us. Conductive fibres and threads developed from carbon, steel and silver can be woven into textile fabrics and made into clothing, or conductive threads can be sewn into a product to connect a circuit. Common uses include heart-rate monitors, performance monitors for athletes, GPS tracking systems, heating and flexible solar panels, as well as communications devices such as mobile phones. There are many practical applications for this technology, but one example is a heart-rate/performance monitor embedded into the shirt of a professional rugby or football player. Coaches are able to monitor specific aspects of a player's performance and fitness levels and make informed decisions on whether to substitute them or allow them to continue playing.

The rapid growth in this area of textiles is due to the increased availability of the technology. Further advances in technology will increase the possibilities within this field as market pull demands.

Microfibres

Microfibres are extremely fine synthetic fibres, usually made from polyester or nylon very much finer than a human hair. They are lightweight and versatile and have a number of useful properties including excellent strength-to-weight ratio, water-resistance and breathability. Microfibres are very versatile and used in a number of applications including clothing, cleaning cloths and insulation. When used for cleaning, the fibres attract dirt and dust, making them more efficient than regular cleaning cloths. When used in printing fabrics, the size of the fibre does not distort images, giving good definition. Examples of microfibres include Tactel® and Tencel™ (Lyocell).

Figure 2.9 The latest technology allows the development of new products such as the solar-powered bag. It includes photovoltaic cells ready to supply eco-friendly energy for mobile phones or laptops.

Phase-changing materials

Materials that change from one state to another are called **phase-changing materials** (PCMs). PCMs have the ability to absorb, store and release heat over a small temperature range. In this heat storage system, PCMs change from liquid state to solid and vice versa. PCMs absorb energy during the heating process (returning to liquid) and release energy to the environment during cooling (returning to solid). PCMs can be micro-encapsulated into textiles or applied as a coating to make thermo-regulating smart textile fabrics. In cold weather clothing, PCMs encapsulated into the fabrics allow body heat to be stored within the fabric and then released when needed. Outlast® fabrics use phase-changing materials and were originally developed for use in space.

Breathable fabrics

Breathable, waterproof and windproof fabrics function by allowing the flow of air in and out. The most commonly known breathable fabric is Gore-Tex. This laminated fabric consists of three or more fabrics laminated together with a breathable membrane making up one of the middle layers. This structure works on the principle that warm air and tiny droplets of moisture, from perspiration, are allowed to permeate out though the breathable membrane, but moisture from larger rain droplets and wind cannot enter. This, when used on high-performance clothing and footwear, offers the wearer the means of regulating the body temperature by maintaining a constant temperature.

Rhovyl

Rhovyl® is a synthetic fibre, known as a chlorofibre, made from forms of polyvinyl chloride (PVC), a derivative from the petrochemical industry. For more on the properties of PVC, see Chapter 10. Rhovyl is a leading manufacturer of PVC-based fibres. Rhovyl is non-flammable, crease resistant, has good thermal and acoustic properties, is anti-bacterial, waterproof and dries quickly. When spun and woven into fabric these fibres are soft and comfortable to wear, which is why they are particularly used in the manufacture of clothing. The construction of the fibre gives fabrics the ability to wick away moisture, such as perspiration, through the fabric. As it is non-absorbent and dries quickly it is easy to care for, and as it does not retain odours it is commonly used on socks! Other uses include casual wear and underwear, and technical clothing such as high-performance sportswear.

Sun-protective clothing

One of the best ways to protect yourself from the sun's harmful ultraviolet rays (UVR) is to cover up. However, not all clothing is effective in protecting us. It depends on the type of knit or weave used in the construction of the fabric. While most fibres are capable of naturally absorbing some UV radiation, it is the closeness of the knit or weave that makes the difference. A tightly woven or knitted fabric reduces the spaces between the yarns that are created during the construction of the fabric. In a tight weave the gaps are significantly reduced, preventing harmful UV rays getting through. Elastane fibres reduce the spaces even further, making fabrics containing these even more efficient and protective. Synthetic fibres such as polyester and nylon with a natural lustre reflect the sun's UV rays more than matt fibres such as cotton which tends to absorb them.

KEY WORD

Phase-changing materials: encapsulated droplets on fibres and materials that change between liquid to solid form within a temperature range.

Nomex

Nomex® is an **aramid synthetic fibre** developed by the DuPont chemical company in the 1960s. It is primarily used where resistance to heat and flames is essential, typically in firefighters' uniforms and racing car drivers' clothing, but also in oven gloves and fire-resistant insulation on buildings. It is an extremely strong fabric and can withstand exposure to the most extreme conditions.

Nomex and Kevlar are often combined in a composite, making a lightweight material with a very high strength-to-weight ratio. This composite was used in the construction of the Airbus 380 aeroplane, making a much lighter aircraft, which in turn improves fuel economy.

Geotextiles

Geotextiles are woven or bonded, synthetic or natural, permeable fabrics made originally for use with soil, with the ability to filter, separate, protect and drain. They have many uses and applications in civil engineering, road and building construction and maintenance, for example:

- the control of coastal erosion and drainage, on embankments, roads, railways, airfields and retaining structures
- protection and development of crops in agriculture
- textile 'roofs', such as on the Eden Project in Cornwall and the O2 arena
- linings on canals to prevent water draining away.

Figure 2.10 Geotextiles are used to line embankments and prevent soil erosion.

Activity

Conduct some further research into biomimicry.

- Find out what Velcro® has to do with biomimicry.
- What is spider silk?
- What have blue butterflies got to do with biomimicry?

KEY POINTS

- Smart materials change their properties in response to a change in the environment.
- Any change in a smart material's property is only temporary.
- Composite materials combine the properties of the materials combined to make them.
- Composites are very difficult to recycle.
- Technical textiles are engineered with specific performance properties to meet a particular need. You should be able to apply named technical textiles to specific situations and explain their importance.
- Electronic circuits or devices embedded or integrated into textile fabric interact with the user. Technology drives this area of textiles.
- The potential for interactive and integrated textiles are vast and are only limited by current technology. Be aware of new developments as they come onto the market.

Know it

1 Define the term 'smart material'.
2 Name the material whose colour changes in response to light and illustrate an appropriate use.
3 Name three applications of thermochromic pigment.
4 Define the term 'composite'.
5 Justify the use of a carbon-reinforced polymer in the manufacture of a sporting product of your choice.
6 Explain how biomimetics has benefitted swimmers.
7 Describe the advantages to the user of phase-changing materials when used in cold weather clothing.
8 Describe how an integrated heart monitor in clothing supports the care of a post-operative patient.

Chapter 3
Electronic systems and programmable components

Learning objectives

By the end of this chapter you should have developed a knowledge and understanding of:

■ how electronic systems provide functionality to products and processes

■ principles of a control system: input, process, output and feedback

■ analogue and digital signals and interfacing

■ control systems used in familiar products

■ the use of programmable components to embed functionality into products

■ programming techniques.

3.1 How electronic systems provide functionality to products and processes

Electronics permeate our lives in so many ways. It is hard to imagine going through a day without using an electronic device at some point: a smartphone, tablet, computer, TV or radio. The car we travel in is bursting with electronic systems to control the engine, to ensure our safety and to help with navigation. The heating and ventilation in the buildings where we work and live are monitored by electronics, not to mention security systems, CCTV, and so on.

Electronic control systems

An electronic system can be broken down into smaller parts called **subsystems**, and these in turn can be classified into inputs, processes and outputs. A **system diagram** (sometimes called a block diagram) is drawn to show how the subsystems are interconnected.

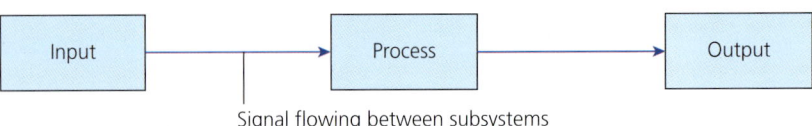

Signal flowing between subsystems

Figure 3.1 A generic electronic system

Inputs consist of **sensors**, which are the 'eyes and ears' of an electronic system. They allow the system to monitor and measure a range of **physical quantities**, such as light level, temperature, weight, etc. A push button is a very commonly used input component that senses when it has been pressed. A sensor produces an electrical **signal**. Some systems have several sensors producing multiple input signals.

The signals from the input sensors are fed into the process subsystem which responds in a specific way to control the output devices. The exact function of the process subsystem will depend on the needs of the product. Process subsystems can be complex electronic circuits containing semi-conductor components such as transistors and **integrated circuits (ICs)**. These systems are described in depth in Chapter 6. In this chapter we will focus on using only a programmable **microcontroller** as the process component, as these powerful and flexible devices offer a designer the chance to significantly enhance the function of a product.

Figure 3.2 Push buttons are frequently used as inputs.

Microcontrollers can perform various tasks, such as:

● counting – such as keeping track of the scores in a sports game, and displaying these on an electronic scoreboard

● switching – such as switching on a streetlamp when the light level falls

● timing – such as in a cooking timer or turning on a security light for a period of time after movement is detected.

A microcontroller is a miniature, programmable computer integrated into an IC or mounted on a small circuit board. In industrial systems, a full-size PC computer is sometimes used to control electronic systems. However, in the kind of products you are likely to design for GCSE, a microcontroller is more useful as these can be programmed and then permanently embedded into the product.

The output components of an electronic system produce a physical output in response to signals from the process subsystem. Outputs can produce light, sound, motion, etc.

Activity

1 Find five electronic products from around your home (for example, kitchen scales, coffee machine, TV remote control, satnav, central heating room thermostat, burglar alarm control panel). Identify the input sensors and the output devices (some of these may not be visible). Make sure you consider sensors and components that may be hidden inside the product.

2 Look carefully at an electronic central heating room thermostat to see if you can find the temperature sensor.

3 Where does the 'beep' sound from a microwave come from?

Input sensors

Sensors can be broadly classified into two types:

● **Digital sensors** are used for detecting a yes/no situation, for example:
  ○ Is the button pressed?
  ○ Is movement detected?
  ○ Has the product fallen over?

● **Analogue sensors** are used when it is necessary to measure 'how big' a quantity is, for example:
  ○ how bright a light is
  ○ what a temperature is.

The different types of sensor need to be **interfaced** to the appropriate analogue input or digital input on the microcontroller.

Light sensor

The light-sensing component in an electronic system is a **light-dependent resistor (LDR).**

When an LDR is connected in an electronic circuit, it produces an analogue signal that rises when the light level increases. When an LDR is used to provide an input signal to a microcontroller, the microcontroller will convert the signal into a number, in a process called analogue-to-digital conversion (ADC); the larger the number, the brighter the light detected. The microcontroller can then process this number or make decisions depending on how bright the light is.

KEY WORDS

Digital sensor: a sensor to detect a yes/no or on/off situation.

Analogue sensor: a sensor to measure 'how big' a physical quantity is.

Interfacing: connecting sensors and output devices to electronic control circuits.

Figure 3.4 is a **circuit diagram** showing how an LDR is interfaced to a microcontroller. Notice that an analogue input (A$_o$) is used on the microcontroller. The LDR and the 10k (10 kilo-ohm) resistor form what is called a potential divider; these are fully explained in Chapter 6.

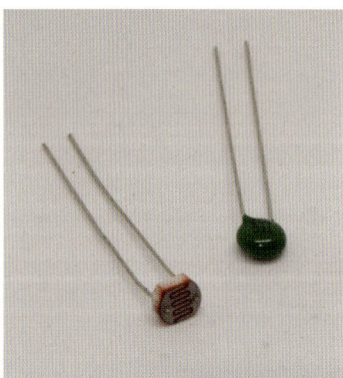

Figure 3.3 An LDR and a thermistor

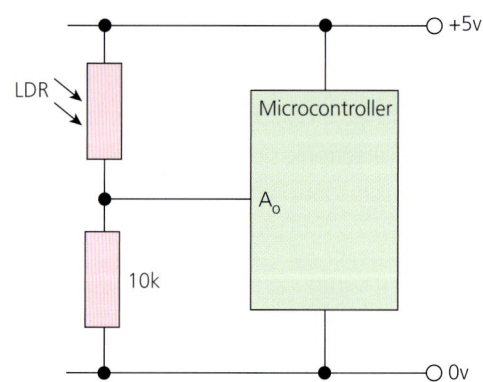

Figure 3.4 An LDR connected to an analogue input of a microcontroller

Temperature sensor

A **thermistor** is a temperature-sensing component. Two types are available, a negative temperature coefficient (ntc) type and a positive temperature coefficient (ptc) type. The ntc thermistor has a high resistance when it is cold and a low resistance when hot. When interfaced to a microcontroller, as shown in the circuit in Figure 3.5, it produces an analogue signal that rises when the temperature rises. The ptc thermistor is less commonly used; its resistance is low when cold, and rises as the temperature increases.

Switch sensor

When a push-button switch is used as a sensor, it produces a digital signal which is on (high) when the switched is pressed, and off (low) when the switch is released. Figure 3.6 shows how to interface a switch to a digital input of a microcontroller.

A circuit diagram shows the electrical interconnections between components in a circuit. It does not show the physical positions of the components. Standard circuit symbols are used to represent the components. A great deal of information is carried in a circuit diagram, including component types and values.

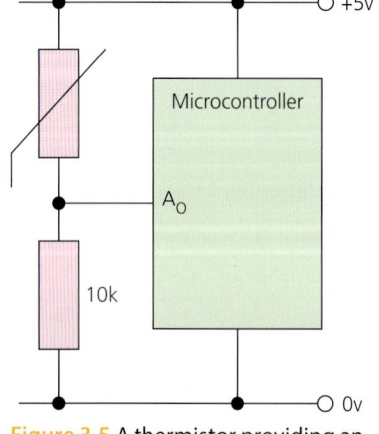

Figure 3.5 A thermistor providing an input signal to a microcontroller

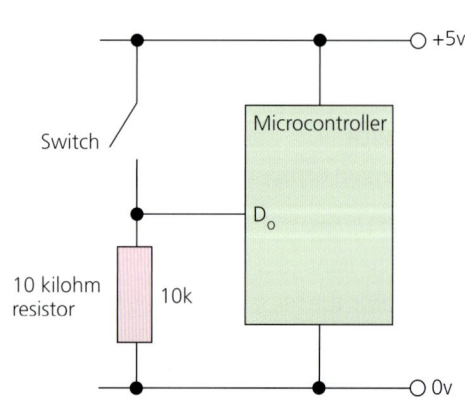

Figure 3.6 Method of using a switch as a sensor

Output devices

Buzzer

A buzzer produces an audible tone when it receives power. A microcontroller could be programmed to turn a buzzer on and off rapidly to produce a beep-beep-beep sound, which is very effective at attracting attention. Figure 3.7 shows how a buzzer is connected to an output pin of a microcontroller.

Light-emitting diode (LED)

LEDs are available in an enormous range of sizes, colours, brightnesses and shapes.

Figure 3.8 shows how an LED is used with a microcontroller. Notice that a 330 ohm resistor must also be used to limit the current flowing, otherwise the LED will burn out.

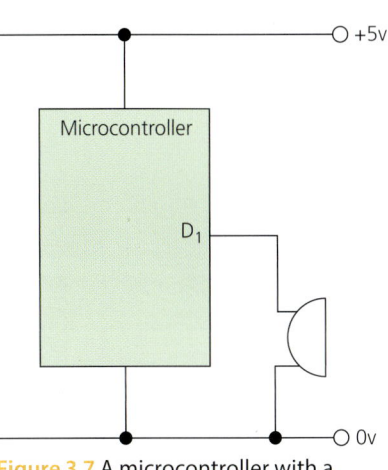

Figure 3.7 A microcontroller with a buzzer output

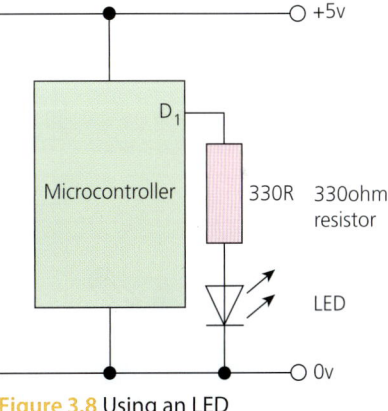

Figure 3.8 Using an LED

Control systems in familiar products

Street light

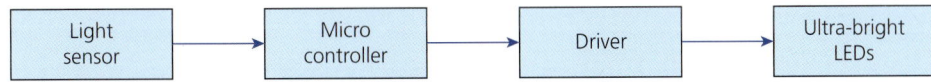

Figure 3.9 System diagram for a street light

The light sensor sends an analogue signal into the microcontroller. When the light level drops below a set value, the microcontroller will turn on the LEDs. The **driver** is a subsystem to boost the output signal.

Electric oven

The microcontroller receives a signal from the temperature sensor and compares it to the temperature-setting control. If the temperature is too low, the heater will be turned on. The temperature sensor monitors the oven temperature and feeds the information back into the microcontroller; this technique is called **feedback** and it is frequently used in systems to achieve precise control.

> **KEY WORDS**
>
> **Driver**: a subsystem to boost a signal.
>
> **Feedback**: achieving precise control by feeding information from an output back into the input of a control system.

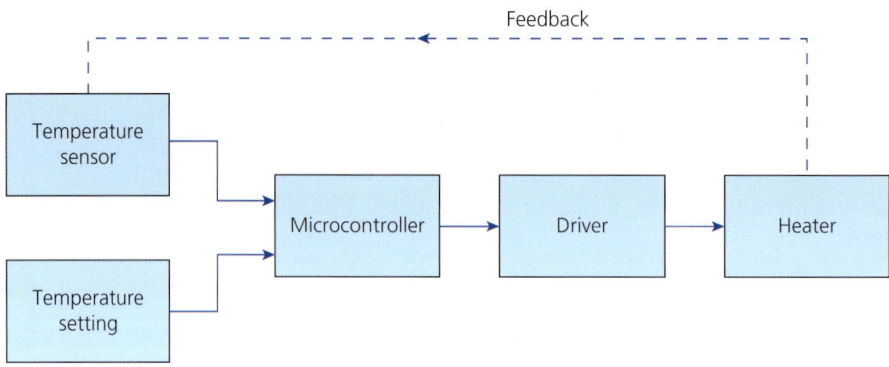

Figure 3.10 System diagram for an oven

Cruise control

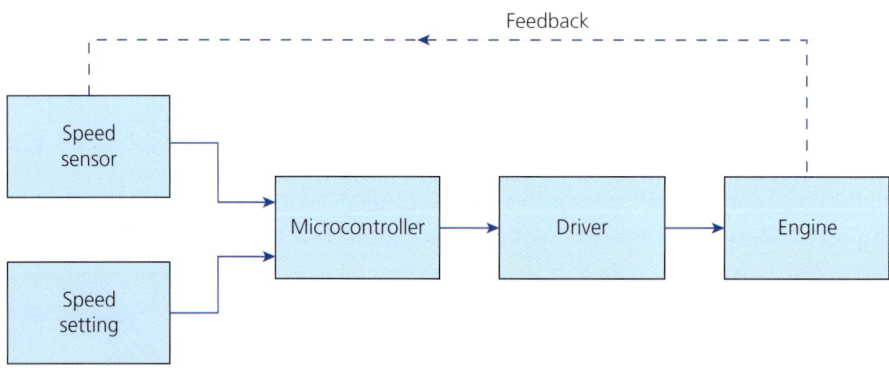

Figure 3.11 System diagram for a car cruise control

Activity

Draw system diagrams for:

- a cooking timer
- a variable speed cordless drill.

A cruise control allows a car driver to program a set speed, which the system will then maintain. A feedback loop is created by the sensor feeding speed information from the output back to the input, where it is compared to the set speed value. The microcontroller then adjusts the engine speed to match the set speed.

3.2 The use of programmable components to embed functionality into products in order to enhance and customise their operation

Programmable microcontrollers are electronic components that can add incredible functionality to a product or a system. Microcontrollers take information from sensors and other inputs and then process this information in order to control a variety of outputs. Microcontrollers all start off blank, but the designer then writes a **program** that is downloaded into the microcontroller's memory. Microcontrollers can be repeatedly reprogrammed, which is essential during the iterative development of the program.

The program is a set of instructions that tells the microcontroller how to carry out a task that is specific to a product. This process of customising a generic microcontroller to a specific application and placing it permanently within the product is called **embedding**.

Microcontrollers are increasingly being used in products, and their small size, versatility and relative ease of use make them an attractive new technology. In many basic products the full potential of the microcontroller is never used. In a kettle, for example, the microcontroller simply needs to switch on the heating element until it senses that the water has reached

KEY WORD

Embedding: permanently installing a microcontroller into a product.

boiling point, then to switch the heater off. Nonetheless, it is usually more cost effective to use a microcontroller for this simple task than to design a bespoke electronic system from scratch. Designers now realise that, once a microcontroller has been selected for a design, there is the potential to add advanced features that can enhance the product. For example, a kettle could have a 'keep warm' feature added, or it could heat the water to different temperatures that the user has programmed or sound an alert when the water is ready.

Microcontrollers are relatively expensive components, and they require the designer to learn a programming language.

Flowchart programs

The system diagram shown in Figure 3.12 is a design for a bicycle safety lamp. There is a single push-button input and three ultra-bright LED outputs. The microcontroller could be programmed to operate the lamp as follows:

- First push of the button turns on all three LEDs.
- Second push of the button flashes all three LEDs.
- Third push turns off all LEDs.
- The cycle then repeats.

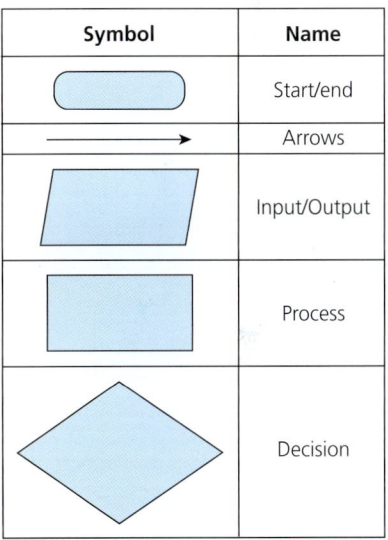

Figure 3.12 A system diagram for a bicycle safety lamp

At this point, the flexibility of the microcontroller becomes clear, in that it would be simple to reprogram it to add enhanced features to the product. For example, a fourth push of the button could make the LEDs flash independently in an eye-catching pattern.

The program should initially be written down as a **flowchart**, which is a simple way of breaking down the microcontroller task by showing the key steps involved. At a later stage in the design development the flowchart may need to be converted into a specific programming language, depending on the microcontroller used.

A microcontroller can perform only one instruction step at a time, in sequence. When the program is run, each instruction is carried out extremely quickly, so the user would not normally notice any delay between the instructions, unless WAIT commands are inserted in the flowchart to deliberately slow things down. Figure 3.13 shows the five symbols used for drawing flowcharts.

Symbol	Name
	Start/end
→	Arrows
	Input/Output
	Process
	Decision

Figure 3.13 System diagram symbols

Study the flowchart in Figure 3.14 and note the following points:

- The program will begin at the 'START' box.
- The instructions will be executed one after another at very high speed. Consequently, 'WAIT' instructions are used to control the speed through particular sections of the program.
- The two 'WAIT 1' instructions are needed to give the user time to release the button after pressing it, before the program reaches the next 'Is the button pressed?' decision.
- There is no END box because, after the third press of the button, the cycle repeats from the start.

Subroutines

As a microcontroller program is developed to add functionality to a product, the program can become very complex. **Subroutines** can be used to give some structure to a complicated program to make it clearer to write and easier to **debug**. A subroutine (sometimes called a macro, procedure or function) is a set of program instructions, packaged as a separate unit, that perform a specific task.

KEY WORDS

Program flowchart: a set of instructions that tells a microcontroller what to do.

Subroutine: a small program within a larger program.

Debug: find and remove errors in a microcontroller program.

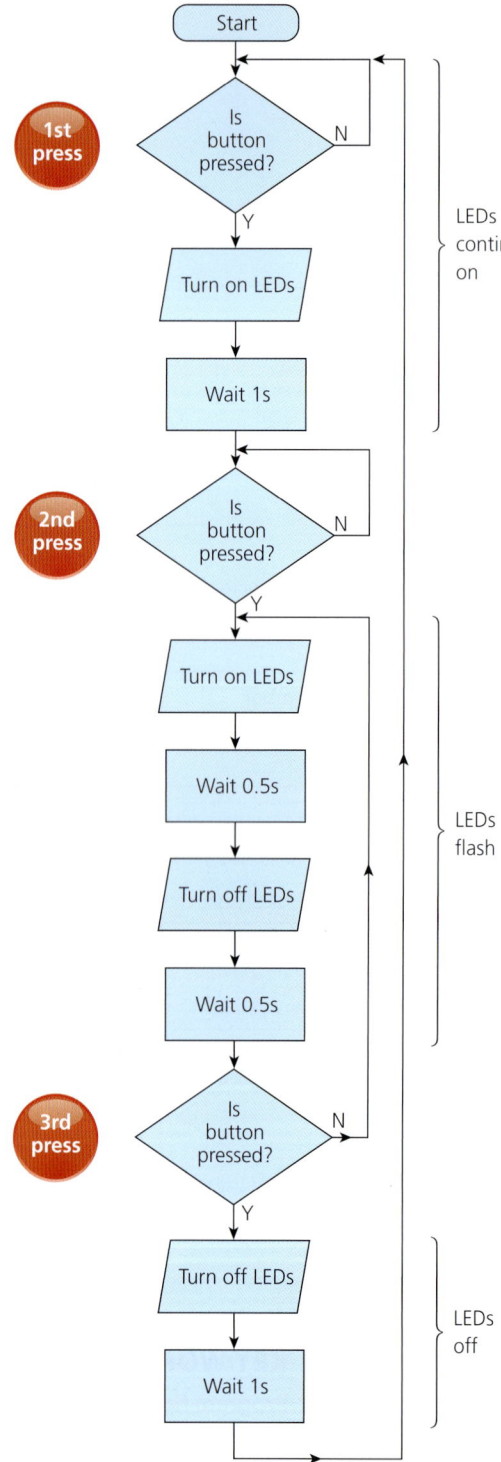

Figure 3.14 Flowchart program for the bicycle safety lamp

The main program can 'CALL' the subroutine any time it needs to carry out that task. The program flow then jumps to the subroutine. A RETURN command at the end of the subroutine returns the flow back to the main program. There can be several subroutines, each assigned to carry out a different task.

The flowchart in Fig 3.15 shows an alternative program for the bicycle safety lamp, using two subroutines named **Flash 1** and **Flash 2**. The main program loop is on the left. Study this flowchart to see that, after the first press of the button, the program will repeatedly call **Flash 1**, causing the LEDs to light up sequentially. If the button is pressed a second time, **Flash 2** is repeatedly called, flashing the LEDs in a different pattern. A third press of the button will switch all LEDs off. Notice the RETURN commands at the end of each subroutine.

Success with microcontrollers

Several different kinds of microcontroller are available, each one offering benefits for different applications.

The choice of microcontroller for a specific application will depend on:

- the technical requirements of the application, such as the number of inputs/outputs needed
- the programming language
- the range of dedicated accessories available, such as sensors or output devices, which make the interfacing much easier.

Some microcontrollers are designed for designers with little previous knowledge. Others will need you to design your own **printed circuit board (PCB)** and solder them in place. Some, for example, are aimed at applications in textile or wearable projects. Some are intended to be connected temporarily with crocodile clip leads, others with conductive thread. As with all projects, start simple and gradually build up the complexity of the system and the program as you iteratively develop your design.

PICAXE is a popular range of microcontrollers for use in school projects. A wide range of PICAXE devices is available, depending on the needs of your project, along with several dedicated sensors and displays. If you do not want electronics to be the focus of your project, but you would like to enhance its function with a PICAXE,

KEY WORD

Printed circuit board (PCB): the support and connections for the electronic components in a product.

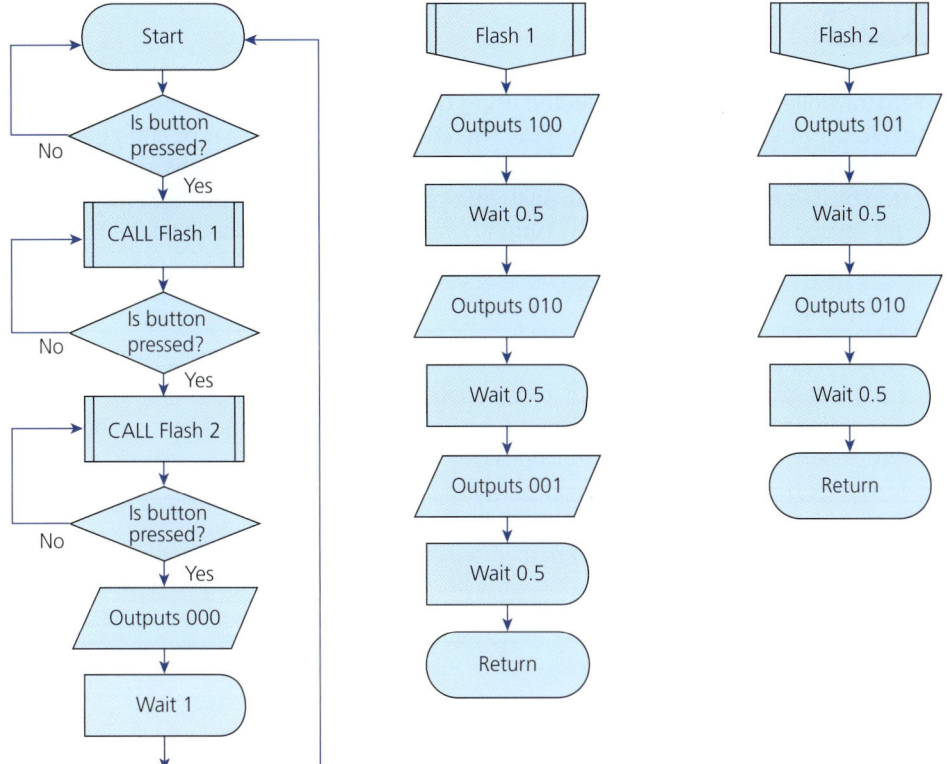

Figure 3.15 An alternative program for the bicycle safety lamp, structured around subroutines

then it is possible to buy a range of pre-built 'project boards' which include various sensors, and drivers for output devices. These boards simplify the electronics somewhat, but you will still need to develop and test a program specific to your design.

The detailed use of PICAXEs goes beyond the scope of this book, but a wealth of information and support, and an active online community, can be found at www.picaxe.com.

Activity

Consider a relatively straightforward product found in the home – for example a tap, a vacuum cleaner or a doorbell. Write down ways in which a microcontroller could enhance the product's functionality so that the user has a better experience interacting with the product.

Figure 3.16 Microcontrollers

Activity

Experiment with a microcontroller. If you have never used one before, choose a microcontroller that can be connected using crocodile clips. Start by programming the microcontroller to flash a single LED. Then flash a few LEDs in a repeating pattern. Program it to play a simple tune or sound effect. Then try detecting when an input button has been pressed. Then use analogue commands to sense the light level from a light sensor input and respond by turning on LEDs or making sounds as the light level gets progressively darker.

KEY POINTS

- Electronic systems consist of input, process and output subsystems.
- A microcontroller is a powerful process subsystem which can be programmed and embedded in a product to add functionality.
- Sensors and output devices are interfaced to a microcontroller.
- Signals in a system can be analogue or digital.
- Feedback is used in a control system to improve the control function of the system.
- A microcontroller program is a set of instructions that tells the microcontroller how to function in a product.

Know it

1 Explain the differences between a system diagram, circuit diagram and flowchart.
2 Name the sensors used to sense temperature and light. Sketch a circuit diagram to show how each one is interfaced to a microcontroller.
3 Explain how a microcontroller processes an analogue signal from an input sensor.
4 Give two advantages of using subroutines in a microcontroller program.
5 List four parameters a designer should consider when selecting an LED for use in a product.

Chapter 4
Mechanical components and devices

Learning objectives

By the end of this chapter you should have developed a knowledge and understanding of:

- the functions of mechanical components and devices to produce different sorts of movement
- mechanical systems which change the magnitude and direction of forces and movement
- the principle of a mechanical system in terms of input, process and output
- simple calculations involving mechanical systems
- how mechanical systems are used in everyday, familiar products.

4.1 The functions of mechanical devices to produce different sorts of movement, changing the magnitude and direction of forces

Movement and **motion** bring products to life. Even a very basic product, such as a pair of scissors, relies on movement for its operation. In some cases, the entire product might move, such as a vehicle. In other cases, just part of the product will move, such as in an electric fan. The motion might be clearly visible (for example a food mixer) or it might take place inside the product and not be immediately visible from the outside, as in a computer printer.

- Motion occurs when an object moves its position over time.
- A **force** is a push, a pull or a twist. Forces are measured in units called newtons (N).
- A **mechanism** is a series of parts that work together to control forces and motion in a desired way.
- A **mechanical system** will take an input force (or motion) and process it to produce an output force (or motion). This may involve increasing or decreasing the size of the force or motion, or transferring it to the place where the force or motion is needed.

Different types of motion

Rotary motion

This is motion that follows the path of a circle. Rotary motion is very common and can easily be seen in the rotation of wheels. The output shaft of an electric motor also moves in rotary motion. Rotary motion can be measured by counting the number of revolutions in a set period of time. Revolutions per minute (rpm) is a common measurement of rotational speed.

$$\text{Rotational speed} = \frac{\text{number of revolutions}}{\text{time taken}}$$

KEY WORDS

Motion: when an object moves its position over time.

Force: a push, pull or twist.

Mechanism: a series of parts that work together to control forces and motion.

Mechanical system: takes an input force (or motion) and processes it to produce an output force (or motion).

Figure 4.1 Items on a conveyor belt move with linear motion.

Linear motion

Linear motion is motion in a straight line. This is commonly seen, for example, when a vehicle is travelling in a straight line or in items travelling on a conveyor belt. The speed at which objects travel in a straight line is measured by dividing the distance they travel by the time taken:

$$\text{Speed} = \frac{\text{distance travelled}}{\text{time taken}}$$

Speed is often measured in units of metres per second (ms^{-1}) or kilometres per hour ($km\ h^{-1}$).

Oscillating motion

Oscillating motion is similar to rotary motion, but the rotation moves back and forth in a circular path. Oscillating motion is quite common but you need to look carefully to spot it; a good example is the oscillating head of an electric toothbrush. The rate of oscillating motion is measured in oscillations per second or per minute.

Reciprocating motion

This is back-and-forth motion in a straight line (for example the needle on a sewing machine). Oscillating and reciprocating motions are similar in that they are both measured in oscillations per second or per minute.

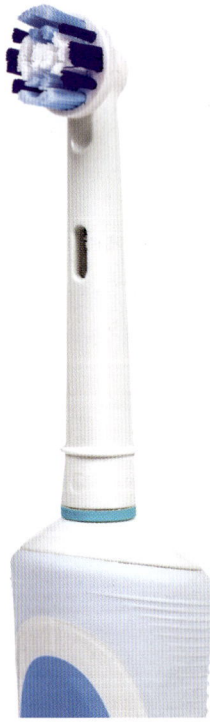

Figure 4.2 An electric toothbrush head uses oscillating motion.

Activity

Find examples of products which exhibit each of the four types of motion. Take a photo of each and annotate the image to identify exactly which part of the product performs the motion.

For clarity, describe the motion involved when the product is used for a complete cycle. For example, you might describe the movement of an automatic sliding door as 'linear motion', but a complete operating cycle involves the door opening and then closing, so 'reciprocating motion' would be a better description.

Mechanical systems

A mechanical system will take an **input** force (or input motion) and **process** it to produce a desired **output** force (or output motion). In most mechanical systems, it is necessary to consider forces and motion at the same time. This is because, if the mechanism is to do any useful work, a force is needed in order to make something move.

Take a pair of scissors as an example. The user provides an input force from their hand on the scissor handles. This is transferred to the blades which then output the force onto the material being cut. At the same time, the user will squeeze the handles together, and this input motion is transferred to the blades which output the motion to the material being cut. The process part of the mechanism is a pair of **levers** which may increase or decrease the force and the movement produced.

In the door-latching mechanism shown in Figure 4.4, the user provides input movement to the door handle in the form of oscillating motion. The latch mechanism inside the door processes this motion and outputs it as reciprocating motion of the door catch.

When a simple mechanism takes input forces and movement and processes them to produce an output, there is a simple but very important principle which you must remember:

● the mechanism can increase the force, but reduce the distance moved, or
● the mechanism can reduce the force, but increase the distance moved.

There is always a trade-off between force and distance moved – one can increase, but only if the other decreases. This means that mechanisms can be used to **amplify** (make bigger) forces so that very heavy objects can be lifted by one person – for example a car jack, but the trade-off is that the person must move the input lever of the jack through a much further distance than the car gets lifted up.

Figure 4.3 Scissors are a simple mechanical system.

Figure 4.4 A mechanical door latch system

KEY WORDS

Lever: a rigid bar that pivots on a fulcrum.

Amplify: to make something larger.

Activity

Take four simple mechanical products from around your home and identify the input motion and the output motion produced when they are being used. Examples you could look at include: key-operated door locks, window blinds (various types) and curtains, stapler, hole punch, can-opener, garlic crusher, kettle flip-up lid button, various hand tools, various toys, etc.

KEY POINTS:
● There are four common types of motion.
● Mechanical systems transfer forces and motion in a controlled way, and they may convert from one type of motion to another type.
● Mechanical systems can change the magnitude and direction of forces and motion.
● A simple mechanism trades-off forces against distances moved. If one increases, the other must decrease.

Mechanical components

In this section we will look at the 'process' parts of mechanisms and the components that can be used to increase or decrease forces and movement.

Levers

The simplest example of a mechanism that controls and changes motion is a lever, which consists of a rigid bar that pivots on a **fulcrum**. The input force is often called the **effort** and the output force is called the **load**.

A car brake pedal is an example of a lever. The input (effort) force applied by the driver's foot creates an output (load) force, which is used to apply the car's brakes. In Figure 4.5 the forces are represented by arrows that show the direction in which the forces act.

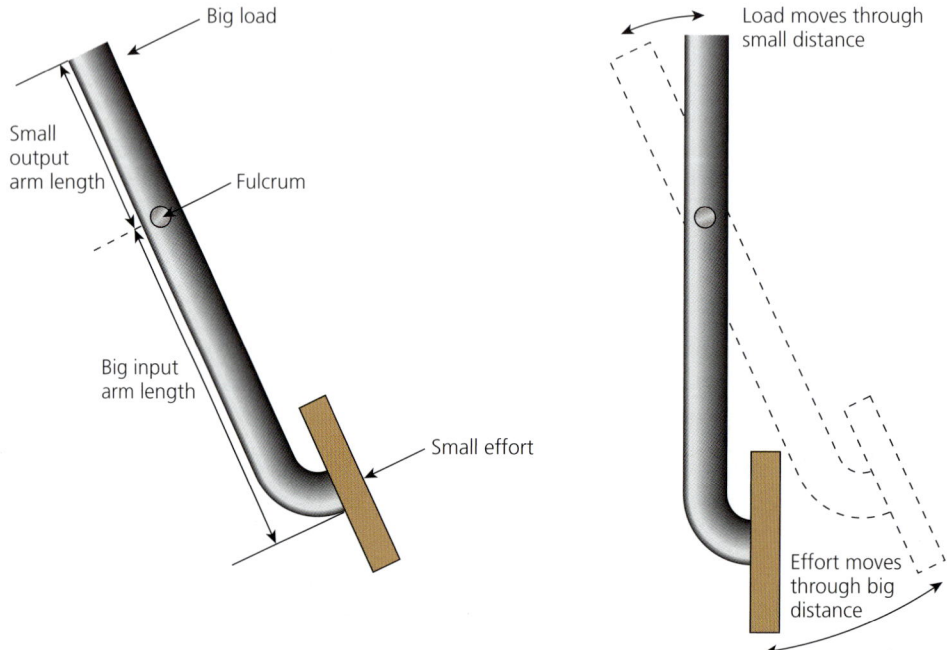

Figure 4.5 A brake pedal is a lever.

The diagram shows that, because of the position of the fulcrum, the effort moves through a larger distance than the load, so this lever has **reduced the distance moved** from input to output. Therefore, according to the trade-off principle described above, the lever must have **increased the force** between input and output. This means that the brake pedal has effectively amplified the force applied by the driver's foot. This leads to the idea of 'leverage'.

The distance between the fulcrum and the force is called the **lever arm length**. The larger the arm length, the larger the distance the force must move.

For a simple lever:

    bigger arm length = bigger distance moved = smaller force

So, for a lever to increase an input force, the input arm length must be greater than output arm length.

The arm length is in inverse proportion to the force. In other words, if the output arm is half as long as the input arm, the output force will be twice as big as the input force. The trade-off is that the output will only move half the distance that the input moves.

Not all levers are used to amplify forces; in some applications, the load will intentionally be less than the effort.

A wheelbarrow is a lever with the fulcrum at one end. The input arm length (the distance from the handles to the fulcrum) is 950 mm. The output arm length (the distance from the load to the fulcrum) is 380 mm. If the user can comfortably apply an effort force of 300 N to the handles, calculate the load force that can be carried in the wheelbarrow.

First, work out the ratio of the input and output arm lengths:

$$\frac{\text{input arm length}}{\text{output arm length}} = \frac{950}{380} = 2.5$$

This means that the lever will increase the input force 2.5 times.

So, if the input force (the effort) is 300 N, then the output force (the load) will be:

output force = input force × 2.5

output force = 300 × 2.5 = 750 N

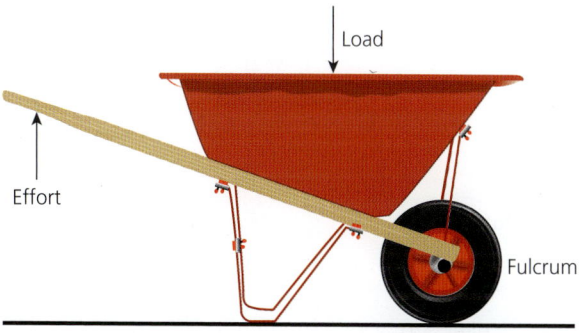

Figure 4.6 A wheelbarrow is a type of lever.

Some levers operate in pairs, such as scissors or pliers. Each half operates as an independent lever; when they are used, the same force is applied to each lever but in opposite directions. There is more information about the different classes of lever in Chapter 6 (pages 85–7).

Activity

Find three examples of levers from around your home. These could be complete products or parts within products. Photograph the products and annotate the images to identify the fulcrum and the points where the effort and load are applied. State whether each lever increases or decreases the input force. Products could include a pair of kitchen tongs, nail clippers, tweezers, can-opener, wheelbarrow, stapler, etc.

You might notice that, in some levers (such as tweezers) the fulcrum is at one end, in other cases the fulcrum will be part way along (such as scissors).

Linkages

A **linkage** is a component used to direct forces and movement to where they are needed. A linkage will often change the direction of motion, and it might also be used to convert between different types of motion.

- A **simple pulley** is used to change the direction of motion of a cord. A cord can only apply a pulling force (it cannot push) and a pulley can help to direct this pulling force to where it is needed.

KEY WORD

Linkage: a component to direct forces and movement to where they are needed.

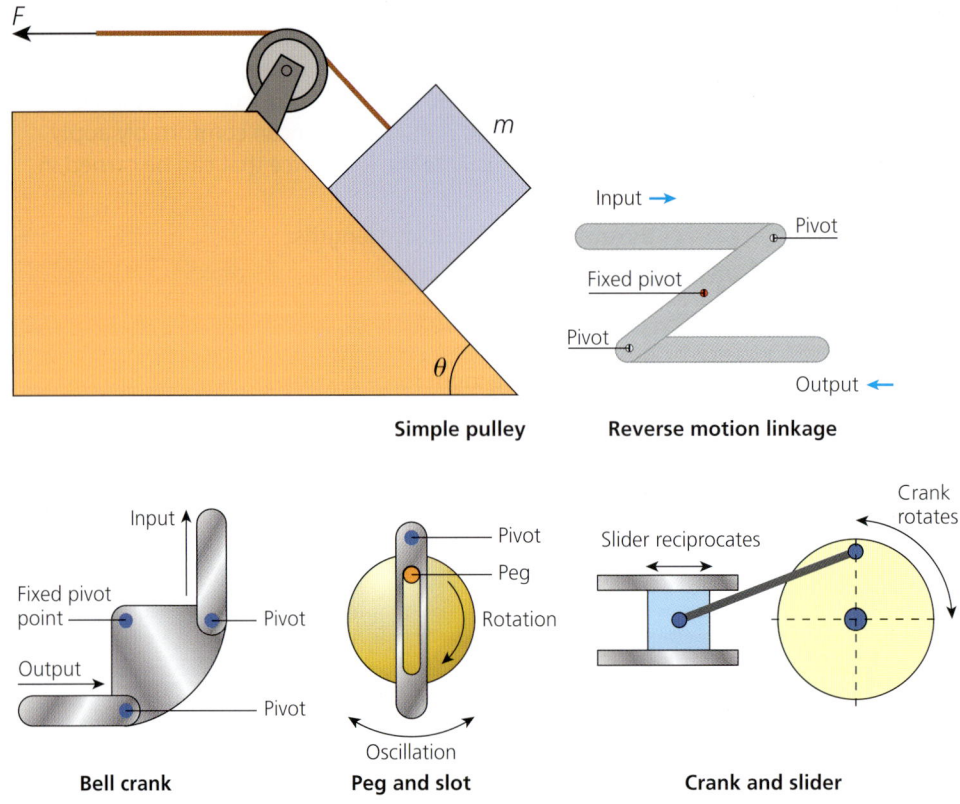

Simple pulley

Reverse motion linkage

Bell crank

Peg and slot

Crank and slider

Figure 4.7 Examples of linkages

- A **reverse motion** linkage will reverse the direction of input motion.
- A **bell crank** will change the direction of motion. It can transfer motion around a corner.
- A **peg and slot** is used to convert rotary motion to oscillating motion.
- A **crank and slider** will convert rotary motion to reciprocating motion.

Many common products contain these linkages, or variations of them.

Figure 4.8 Pulleys change the direction of motion of the pull-cords in a window blind.

Figure 4.9 A bicycle brake lever is a bell crank, changing the direction of pull applied by the rider's fingers by 90°.

Cams

A **cam and follower** is a mechanism to convert rotary motion into reciprocating motion. A cam is a specially shaped wheel and the follower rests on the edge of the cam. As the cam rotates, the follower moves up and down. Cams are used extensively in machinery and engines, and in some toys, to produce a desired motion.

The profile (shape) of the cam determines the motion of the follower throughout one rotation cycle. For the three cams shown in Figure 4.10:

- The snail cam causes the follower to rise steadily, followed by a sudden drop. Can you see why this type of cam is only able to rotate clockwise?
- The pear-shaped cam creates a sudden rise and fall, followed by a long period where the follower does not move.
- The eccentric cam creates a smoother rise and fall motion throughout its rotation.

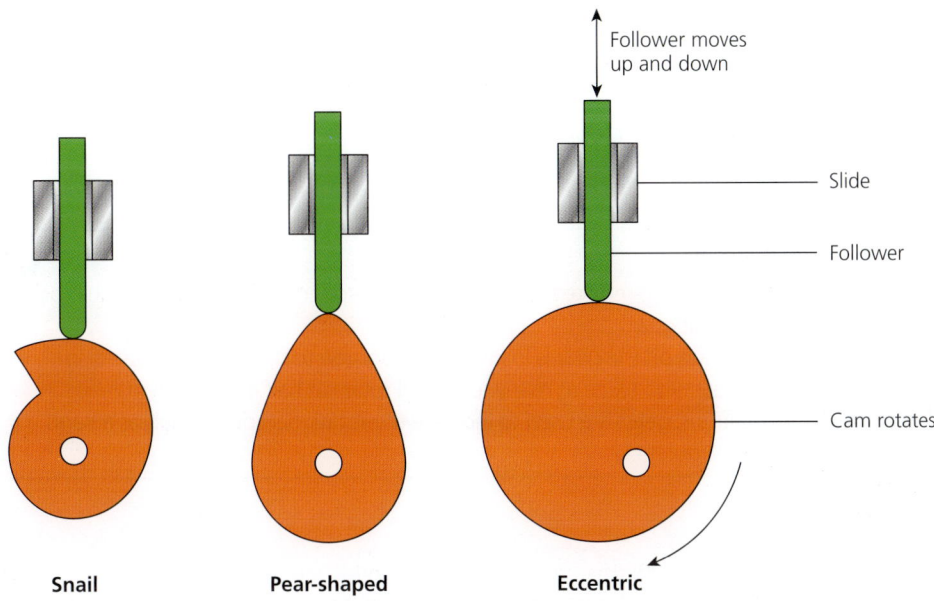

Figure 4.10 Three types of cam

Gears

Gears process rotary motion.

A **spur gear** is a wheel with teeth around its edge. These teeth are designed to mesh with (link into) the teeth on another spur gear, which is usually of a different size – this pair of gears is called a **simple gear train** and consists of an input gear (the driver) and an output gear (the driven). If the input gear is the smaller gear, it is sometimes called a **pinion**. For compound gear trains, see Chapter 6.

Gears are mounted on **shafts**, which carry the rotation to a different part of the mechanism.

> **KEY WORDS**
>
> **Spur gear**: a gear wheel with teeth around its edge.
>
> **Pinion**: a small input gear.
>
> **Shaft**: a rod which carries rotation to different parts of a mechanism.

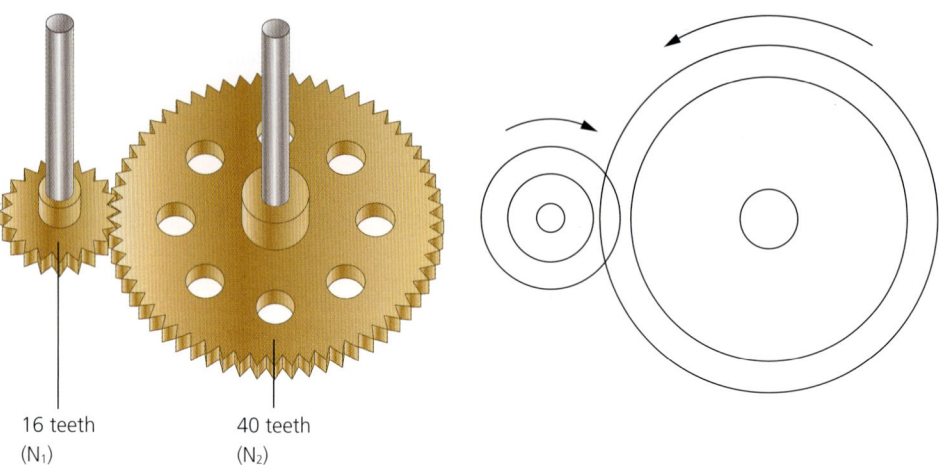

16 teeth
(N_1)

40 teeth
(N_2)

Figure 4.11 A simple gear train

If the two gears are different sizes they will rotate at different speeds. There are two simple rules to remember:

- The smaller gear will rotate faster than the larger gear.
- The two gears will rotate in opposite directions.

Figure 4.12 A hand drill uses a simple gear train.

> **KEY POINTS**
> - For a simple gear train to reduce the input rotational speed, the output gear must be larger than the input gear.
> - The number of teeth on the gear is in inverse proportion to the speed it rotates. In other words, a gear with twice as many teeth will rotate at half the speed.
> - In some applications, gears are used to increase the rotational speed, such as a hand drill, as shown in Figure 4.12.

Calculation

In a hand drill, the user rotates an input gear containing 48 teeth. The output gear (which rotates the drill bit) contains 12 teeth. Calculate the speed increase between the input and the output.

Calculate the ratio of the number of teeth on the output and input gears.

$$\frac{\text{number of teeth on output gear}}{\text{number of teeth on input gear}} = \frac{12}{48} = 0.25$$

This is also the ratio of the speeds of the gears. The input gear is the larger gear, so it will rotate at 0.25 times the speed of the output. In other words, the output will rotate four times faster than the input.

Belt drives

Spur gears provide one method of transferring rotary motion between two shafts. An alternative method is to use a **pulley and belt** drive, which behaves in a similar way to a simple gear train but with the following differences:

- The input shaft and the output shaft can be separated by a greater distance than can be achieved with spur gears.
- The input and output shafts rotate in the same direction.

A pulley and belt drive can provide speed reduction or increase in a similar way to the simple gear train.

Figure 4.13 shows a belt drive being used in a domestic washing machine to transfer rotation from the motor (the small pulley) to the wash drum (the large pulley). This system will result in a very big speed reduction between motor and drum.

Rack and pinion

A **rack and pinion** is a gear system to change between rotary and linear motion. As the pinion rotates, it moves along the rack.

In the stairlift shown in Figure 4.15, the rack is stationary and is attached to the stairs. The pinion inside the stairlift is driven by a motor and the pinion 'climbs' up the rack. In other systems, such as sliding automatic doors, the pinion stays in one position and, as it rotates, it causes the rack to move sideways, which opens the door.

Figure 4.13 A belt drive in a washing machine

Figure 4.14 A rack and pinion

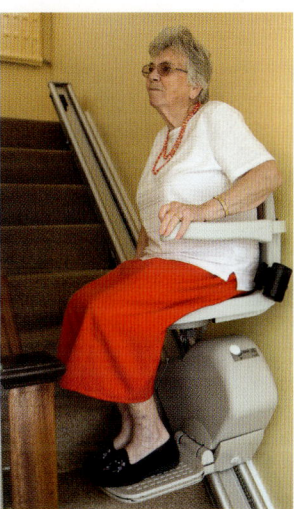
Figure 4.15 A stairlift uses a rack and pinion.

Activity

Investigate a wide range of simple mechanical products and systems to see how they work. Present your findings about one product to your peer group. Use correct technical vocabulary for the mechanical parts and explain how forces and movement are transferred and changed.

This may involve opening or dismantling products. Make sure you have permission to do this and get supervision from someone who fully understands the safety issues. Take care, but the best engineers and inventors are inquisitive and are keen to find out how things work!

KEY POINTS

- Levers and linkages are simple mechanisms which can control forces and motion.
- Cams, gears, belts and pulleys all process rotary motion.

Know it

1 Give an example of each of the four types of motion.
2 Identify the conversion of motion associated with each of the following mechanisms:
   a crank and slider
   b rack and pinion
   c peg and slot
   d cam and follower.
3 A motorcycle brake lever has an input arm length of 100 mm. The output arm length is 25 mm. If the rider applies a force of 80 N, calculate the output force produced.

4 A simple gear train consists of an input gear with 15 teeth and an output gear with 75 teeth. The input rotates clockwise at 1000 rpm. Calculate the speed and direction of rotation of the output.
5 Describe the output motion produced by a snail cam system.
6 Give two reasons why a belt drive system might be used in place of a simple gear train in a mechanical system.

Chapter 5
Materials

Learning objectives

By the end of this chapter you should have developed a knowledge and understanding of the categorisation and properties of:

- papers and boards
- natural and manufactured timbers
- ferrous and non-ferrous metals
- thermosetting and thermoforming polymers

- natural, synthetic, blended and mixed fibres, and woven, non-woven and knitted textiles.

This chapter provides an overview of each of the types of material. For more detail see the In-depth knowledge, understanding and skills section where each of the materials is covered in greater detail.

5.1 Papers and boards

Paper and board are widely used by designers for a range of purposes, from the sketching, drawing and planning of ideas through to the modelling and prototyping of design solutions. They come in a wide range of different thicknesses, sizes and types. They are available in standard sized sheets ranging from A10, which is approximately the size of a postage stamp, through to 4A0, which is larger than a king-size bed sheet. The most common sizes used by designers are between A6 and A0.

Size	A10	A9	A8	A7	A6	A5	A4	A3	A2	A1	A0	2A0	4A0
Length (mm)	37	52	74	105	148	210	297	420	594	841	1189	1682	2378
Width (mm)	26	37	52	74	105	148	210	297	420	594	841	1189	1682

most common sizes used by designers

Figure 5.1 A paper sizes

Each sheet size is twice the size of the one before (for example, A3 is twice the size of A4). In the same way, if you fold a sheet of paper in half it then becomes the next size below – for example, an A1 sheet folded in half becomes A2 size, as shown in Figure 5.3.

For more information on paper and board sizes and types, see Chapter 7.

The thickness of paper is known as its 'weight' and this is measured in **grams per square metre**, often abbreviated as g/m² or **gsm**. This is the weight in grams of a single sheet of paper measuring 1 m × 1 m (1 m²) in size. A weight greater than 170 gsm is classified as a board rather than a paper.

Boards are usually classified by thickness as well as by weight. This is because, depending on the type of board, different sheets may be the same weight but different thicknesses. For example, a sheet of corrugated cardboard and a sheet of mounting board may both be the same thickness but will weigh different amounts. The thickness of board is measured in **microns**; a micron is one-thousandth of a millimetre.

> ### KEY WORDS
>
> **Grams per square metre (gsm)**: the weight of paper and card.
>
> **Micron**: one-thousandth of a millimetre – used to measure the thickness of paper.

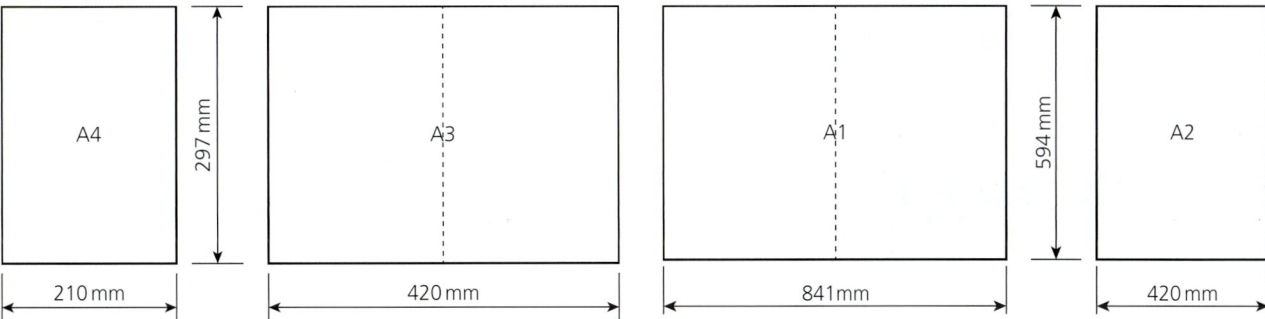

Figure 5.2 The dimensions of A4 and A3

Figure 5.3 The dimensions of A2 and A1

Paper

Common paper types include the following.

Layout paper:
- used for sketching and developing design ideas
- has a smooth surface for both pencil and pen work
- weighs around 50 gsm
- thin enough to trace and copy parts of designs when developing ideas
- cheap to buy.

Tracing paper:
- used for making copies of drawings and fine details
- thin and transparent
- weighs around 40 gsm
- hardwearing and strong despite its lack of thickness
- mistakes in pen can be scratched off using a sharp blade.

Copier paper:
- used extensively for printing, photocopying and general office purposes
- weighs approximately 80 gsm
- smooth surface, making it ideal for most printers and photocopiers.

Cartridge paper:
- available in different weights between 8 –140 gsm
- thicker and more expensive than layout and copier paper
- has a slightly textured surface and is slightly creamier in colour
- used by artists for sketching, drawing and painting
- ideal surface for pencil, crayons, pastels, water colour paints, inks and gouache.

Virgin fibre paper

Paper and card are made from wood fibres called cellulose. Chemicals are used to break down or 'pulp' the fibres by removing the lignin which is the natural 'glue' that holds them together. Further chemicals can be added to bleach or colour the paper and give it a special texture. The pulp is sprayed out in thin layers onto fine mesh, then compressed and dried out by running through heated rollers. Paper made from 'new' wood fibres is called **virgin fibre paper**.

KEY WORD

Virgin fibre paper: paper made entirely from 'new' wood pulp.

Figure 5.4 Paper pulp

Recycled paper

Because of the environmental impact of making virgin fibre paper, it is becoming more expensive. **Recycled paper** is commonly used instead. Recycled paper is made by soaking and mixing waste paper in water to separate the fibres back into pulp. The pulp is then refined to remove any unwanted contaminants, such as staples, plastic, etc. that may have been mixed in with the waste paper, then sprayed and compressed in the same ways as virgin fibre paper.

Each time paper is recycled the fibres get shorter, and as a result, the strength and flexibility of the paper produced is reduced. However, the water absorption properties of the paper are increased. For these reasons, the higher the proportion of recycled pulp that is used, the lower the quality of paper produced.

Most recycled paper is a mixture of virgin pulp and pulp from recycled paper. The higher the proportion of recycled pulp, the lower the quality of paper produced:

> **KEY WORD**
>
> **Recycled paper**: paper made from wood pulp using some re-pulped paper.

Virgin pulp	Pulp from recycled fibres	Products and uses
85% to 100% (approx.)	0% to 15% (approx.)	High-quality printing and graphic paper, publication paper
70% to 85% (approx.)	15% to 30% (approx.)	Household and sanitary applications (e.g. toilet paper, kitchen roll)
50% to 70% (approx.)	30% to 50% (approx.)	Newspaper
20% to 50% (approx.)	50% to 80% (approx.)	Paper and cardboard packaging

Table 5.1 Composition and uses of recycled paper

Card and cardboard

Card

Thin card is slightly thicker than paper, around 180 to 300 gsm in weight. Like paper it is available in a wide range of colours, sizes and finishes, including metallic and holographic shades. Thin card is easy to fold, cut and print on, making it ideal for greetings cards, paperback book covers and so on, as well as for simple modelling applications.

Cardboard

Cardboard is available in many different sizes and surface finishes, with thickness from around 300 microns upwards. Cardboard is widely used for the packaging of many different products – for example cereal boxes, tissue boxes, sandwich packets, etc. – because it is relatively inexpensive and can be cut, folded and printed on to easily. Cardboard can be used to model design ideas and is often used to make templates for parts and pieces of products, which once correct can then be made from metal or other more resistant materials.

For more on how cardboard is produced, see Chapter 7.

Folding boxboard

Folding boxboard is similar in thickness to cardboard, but is more rigid and lightweight. Boxboard has a thick centre made of layers of mechanical pulp sandwiched between two thinner outer layers of chemical pulp. A coating is then usually applied to one side to give it a smoother texture and white colour. Because of its low density and good stiffness, boxboard is often used as packaging, particularly for products such as frozen foods, medicines and beauty products.

Corrugated cardboard

Corrugated cardboard is a strong but lightweight type of card that is made from two layers of card with another, fluted sheet in between. It is available in thicknesses ranging from 3 mm (3000 microns) upwards. The fluted construction makes it very stiff and difficult to bend or fold, especially when folding across the flutes. Because of the spaces between the two layers created by the fluted sheet, corrugated card can absorb knocks and bumps. This makes it ideal for packaging fragile or delicate items that need protection during transportation. It is also widely used as packaging for takeaway foods, such as pizza boxes, as the fluted construction gives it good heat-insulating properties compared to normal cardboard.

Figure 5.5 Corrugated cardboard packaging

Board sheets

Mounting board is a rigid type of card with a thickness of around 1.4 mm (1400 microns) and a smooth surface. It is available in different colours, but white and black are the most commonly available and used colours. Mounting board is often used for picture framing mounts and architectural modelling.

Laminating

Surface coatings applied during the paper-making process are sometimes called laminates. These spray-on coatings can reduce absorbency to give clearer printing and increase strength.

The other form of laminating involves applying a film of clear plastic between 1.2 and 1.8 mm thick to either one or both sides of paper or thin card. It is usually applied to finished documents such as menus, posters, signs, identity badges and other printed documents to:

- improve their strength and resistance to bending, creasing or ripping
- waterproof the document, allowing it be wiped clean and prevent it smudging or going soggy
- improve the appearance, making the document shiny
- increase the lifespan of the printed document.

The three methods of laminating a document are outlined in Chapter 7.

Laminated layers

Laminated layers include various other materials that come in sheet form, like paper and cardboard, and can be used in similar ways. Examples include foam board, Styrofoam and Corriflute. For more details, see Chapter 7.

Activity

1 Do some research into the paper-making process. There are numerous videos to be found online showing the process.
2 Find out what percentage of new paper is made using recycled paper.
3 What are the most common uses for recycled paper?

5.2 Natural and manufactured timber

Timber is a common material that is used for many popular products. It is recyclable, reusable and renewable. Different timbers are easily identified by their weight, colour, grain, texture, durability and ease of working.

Timbers are readily available as planks, boards, strips, dowels, mouldings and square sections.

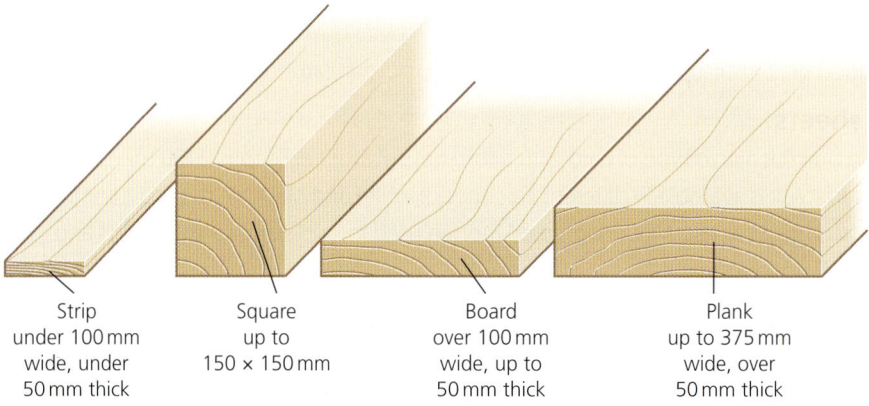

Strip	Square	Board	Plank
under 100 mm wide, under 50 mm thick	up to 150 × 150 mm	over 100 mm wide, up to 50 mm thick	up to 375 mm wide, over 50 mm thick

Figure 5.6 Common timber stock forms

Timber is a natural material; its original source is trees. It can be categorised into two groups: hardwoods and softwoods.

Hardwoods

Hardwoods, such as oak and beech, come from deciduous trees. Deciduous trees are those that generally lose their leaves in autumn, but there are a few exceptions to the rule. Holly is a hardwood but keeps it leaves all year around. Deciduous trees take a long time to mature before being able to be felled and turned into useable timber; as a result, they tend to be more expensive than softwoods. They can be identified by their broad leaves and have branches that are grouped at the top of the tree.

Softwood:
- mostly evergreen
- retain leaves all year round
- needle- or scale-like leaves
- bear cones.

Hardwood:
- mostly deciduous
- shed leaves each autumn
- typically flat leaves.

Figure 5.7 Hardwood versus softwood

Hardwoods are generally harder and stronger than softwoods, although this is not always the case. Balsa is categorised as a hardwood, but you can make an indent into it by pushing hard with your thumb and cut it with a craft knife. Hardwoods generally have a close grain structure that gives them their strength. They can be sanded to a finer, smoother finish and be given a higher-quality finish.

Ash is commonly used for the manufacture of cricket stumps and bails because it is a tough and flexible material, making it durable enough to withstand the impact from a cricket ball travelling at speeds of up to 100 mph.

Softwoods

Softwoods, such as pine and spruce, come from coniferous trees, also known as evergreens. Coniferous trees are quick growing and take around ten years to reach maturity before felling; this makes them an extremely sustainable group of materials as they are renewable. They can be easily identified as they have needles instead of leaves and bear cones instead of fruit. Their branches are located along the whole length of the trunk.

Softwoods are most commonly found in interior products and joinery, as most have poor resistance to decay and require the addition of preservatives before being used outside. Most softwoods have an open grain and are generally less dense and not as strong as hardwoods.

Larch is one of the few types of softwood that can be used outside. It is used in the manufacture of fencing and cladding for sheds, due to its toughness and natural resistance to rot from moisture. It is so durable in a moist environment that the piles and poles on which Venice is held above the water are built almost exclusively from larch.

Finishes for natural timber

Natural timber products usually require a finish to be applied to them before they can be used. A finish has two main functions; it protects the natural timber and enhances its appearance.
- A wood stain will change the colour of the timber but offers little protection.
- A wood preservative allows natural timbers to be used outdoors in products such as fences and sheds. It gives protection against the weather and can also be coloured.
- A varnish finish gives protection against weather when used outdoors and can also be coloured. Varnishes that are used indoors are typically used as a clear protective coating that enhances the natural look of the wood.
- Oil finishes such as 'Danish oil' are used indoors. They give a shine to the surface of the wood but offer low-level protection.
- Painting changes the colour of wood and gives it protection from the weather.

For more information on finishing timber see Chapter 8.

Manufactured boards

Manufactured boards were developed as an alternative to natural timbers. They proved so popular and versatile that in many applications they have almost completely replaced the use of natural timber. Kitchen manufacturing and developments in self-assembly furniture are just two areas where manufactured boards are almost exclusively used.

Manufactured boards fall into two categories. **Laminated boards** are produced by gluing large sheets or veneers together, and **compressed boards** are manufactured by gluing particles, chips or flakes together under pressure.

KEY WORDS

Softwoods: timber that comes from coniferous trees.

Manufactured boards: man-made boards that are available in large flat sheets.

Figure 5.8 Plywood

Figure 5.9 Chipboard

Plywood

Plywood consists of a number of layers (veneers) of wood that are glued together with the grain of each veneer running adjacent to the next. This creates a very strong, flexible board, especially when produced in thin sheets.

Medium-density fibreboard (MDF)

Medium-density fibreboard is a common, cost-effective manufactured board. It is made from fine particles of wood that have been produced from recycled and poor-grade timber. It has a very flat smooth surface but is easily affected by moisture. The glue used to bind it together is abrasive on tools and can also be detrimental to your health if breathed in.

Chipboard

Chipboard is made by compressing 'chips' of wood together with a resin. This cost-effective board is often veneered with natural timbers to improve its appearance.

Hardboard

Hardboard is a low-cost manufactured board that is generally used as a packing material and as a backing for products such as wardrobes and drawers. It has one smooth surface and one meshed surface. It has little strength and is easily affected by moisture.

Finishes for manufactured boards

As with natural timbers, most manufactured boards are given a finish before use. However, because of their porous nature, manufactured boards such as MDF and hardboard must be sealed before a final finish can be applied. Sealing involves coating the board with a sealer such as a thin layer of PVA glue.

Veneered boards

Most manufactured boards will accept a veneered finish. A veneer is a thin sheet of natural timber that is often used as a decorative layer on top of bland manufactured boards such as MDF.

Activity

Have a look around your house and identify five wooden products. Can you determine what timber they are manufactured from? Think about their function, the environment that they are found in and their appearance. Are they made from hardwood or softwood?

KEY POINTS
- Hardwoods come from deciduous trees, softwoods come from coniferous trees.
- Hardwoods take approximately ten times as long to mature as softwoods.
- Manufactured boards come in larger sizes than natural timbers.
- Manufactured boards are more stable than natural timber and will not split or twist.
- Veneers and laminates can be added to manufactured boards to improve their appearance.

5.3 Ferrous and non-ferrous metals

Metals play an integral role in the manufacture of buildings, vehicles and household products.

Metal is a naturally occurring material and is mined from the ground in the form of ore. The raw metal is extracted from the ore through a combination of crushing, smelting or heating with the addition of chemicals and huge amounts of electrical energy. Most metals can be recycled, saving natural resources and limiting the amount of materials imported from abroad.

Metals can be identified by their properties and characteristics, such as colour, hardness, toughness, tensile strength, malleability, elasticity and conductivity.

Metals are readily available in a variety of stock forms, such as sheet, rod, bar, tube and angle. They are categorised into two groups: Ferrous metals and non-ferrous metals.

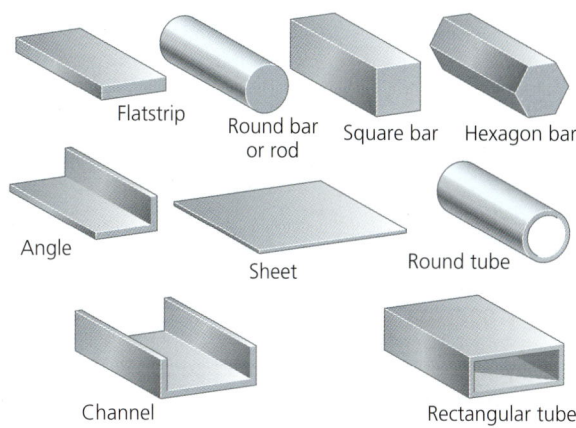

Flatstrip   Round bar or rod   Square bar   Hexagon bar

Angle   Sheet   Round tube

Channel   Rectangular tube

Figure 5.10 Standard metal forms

Ferrous metals

Ferrous metals are those that contain iron. Most are magnetic, which is a useful property when it comes to sorting out metals when recycling. Their carbon content means that most are prone to corrosion, in the form of rust, when exposed to moisture and oxygen.

A good way of remembering that ferrous metals contain iron is to remember the periodic table symbol for iron. **FE** = iron = ferrous.

The properties of ferrous metals, such as hardness and malleability, are directly related to their carbon content. For example, the more carbon that is found in steel, the harder and less malleable the steel becomes.

Mild steel is one of the most widely used of the ferrous metals. It has excellent tensile strength and, when fabricated into an I-beam cross-section, it can be used to produce rolled steel joists (RSJs). These are widely used in the construction of buildings.

Medium-carbon steel contains more carbon than mild steel and is therefore harder. It is typically used in the manufacture of tools such as spades, trowels and gardening equipment.

High-carbon steel, as the name suggests, contains even more carbon and is used for cutting tools such as saw blades and drill bits.

Cast iron is hard, but can be brittle. It is used for intricate castings, such as the metalwork vice you use in the workshop.

Finishes for ferrous metals

Most ferrous metals require a finish to be applied to prevent rusting. Painting, galvanising, plating and polymer coating are typical ways of protecting ferrous metals and are used to enhance their appearance.

Non-ferrous metals

Non-ferrous metals are those that do not contain iron. The absence of iron makes non-ferrous metals desirable for their malleable properties and for their resistance to corrosion. Most non-ferrous metals are not magnetic, which means that they can be used in electronic devices and wiring.

After steel, aluminium is the most widely used metal. Aluminium is produced from alumina, which is extracted from an ore known as bauxite. In addition to heating, several chemicals are used to help the separation process, including caustic soda and lime. The alumina then goes through an electrolysis process from which liquid aluminium is obtained. This processing takes a huge amount of energy, which is why aluminium is so regularly recycled.

Figure 5.11 Iron in the periodic table

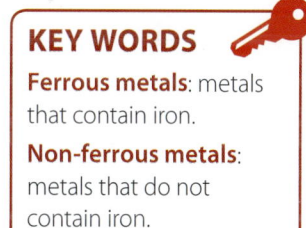

KEY WORDS

Ferrous metals: metals that contain iron.

Non-ferrous metals: metals that do not contain iron.

Figure 5.12 RSJs used in buildings

It takes around 95 per cent less energy to recycle aluminium than to produce the raw material from bauxite.

Copper is a versatile material due to its wide range of desirable properties. It is commonly found in plumbing fixings and heating systems because it is easy to solder and will not corrode when in contact with moisture.

Alloys

KEY WORD

Alloy: a mixture of two or more different metals.

Metals in their pure form can be useful for many purposes, but it is often desirable to adjust their mechanical and physical properties in order to produce a more suitable material for a particular use. An **alloy** is a material that is produced by combining two or more elements together to produce a new material with refined properties. Alloys can be categorised as ferrous alloys or non-ferrous alloys, depending on the main pure metal that they contain.

Brass is a non-ferrous alloy that can be cast into detailed shapes and is used extensively for plumbing fittings such as water taps and pipe connectors. It is an alloy of copper and zinc. The zinc adds hardness to the copper while retaining its resistance to corrosion.

Bronze is also a non-ferrous alloy, which is used widely by metal sculptors to produce large pieces of artwork. Its ability to be cast into intricate shapes and its resistance to corrosion makes it ideal for outdoor projects.

Finishes for non-ferrous metals

Non-ferrous metals have the advantage of not rusting. However, they do oxidise. Oxidation is when the surface of the metal is affected by air and water. The surface of aluminium becomes white, the surface of copper becomes green and other metals will become dull and eventually turn black.

To prevent oxidation occurring, non-ferrous metal should have a finish applied. Processes such as chrome plating and anodising are often used as well as more conventional finishing techniques such as painting.

For more information on finishes, see Chapter 9.

Activity

Complete the table by:
- naming the metal used to make each product
- categorising it (ferrous, non-ferrous, alloy)
- explaining its properties.

Product	Metal	Category	Properties
Greenhouse			
Wedding ring			
Kitchen sink			
Water tap			

KEY POINTS
- Ferrous metals contain iron and are normally magnetic.
- Non-ferrous metals do not contain iron.
- Alloys are combinations of two or more pure metals with other elements.

5.4 Thermoforming and thermosetting polymers

The ability of **polymers** to be coloured, shaped and formed, along with their cost and versatile range of working properties, has allowed designers and manufacturers to improve the performance of products and replace the use of more traditional materials. Polymers can be identified by their weight, hardness, elasticity, conductivity/insulation, toughness, strength and mouldability.

The majority of polymers are known as synthetic polymers and are manufactured from the non-renewable resource crude oil. The use of crude oil is not sustainable and chemical engineers are constantly looking for reliable alternatives. The environmental impact of polymer use has grown and designers must consider this when selecting materials for use.

Natural polymers are known as **biopolymers** and come from renewable sources, such as corn starch. The development of natural polymers is relatively new and there are far fewer examples of this type of polymer. Polylactate acid (PLA) is the most common biopolymer; you may be using it if you have a 3D printer in school.

Polymers are readily available in a number of different stock forms including sheet, film, bar, rod, granules, powder and tube.

KEY WORDS

Polymer: a scientific term for a substance or fibre that has a molecular structure made up of much smaller units which are bonded together; can be natural or manufactured.

Natural polymers (biopolymers): polymers made from natural sources, such as corn starch.

Thermoforming polymers: polymers that can be softened by heating, shaped and set over and over again.

Figure 5.13 Acrylic (PMMA) sheet

Figure 5.14 Polypropylene (PP) tubing

Figure 5.15 Polyvinyl chlorine (PVC) granules

Polymers can be categorised into two groups: thermoforming polymers and thermosetting polymers.

Thermoforming polymers

Thermoforming polymers are the most commonly used and are found in the manufacture of a huge range of products. They can be moulded into almost any shape and have pigment added to them, so therefore can be found in a wide range of colours, and most importantly they can be recycled.

Thermoforming polymers can be softened by heating. Once softened, or plasticised, they can be shaped and formed using a wide variety of processes. Once the desired shape has been achieved, the polymer cools and maintains its new shape. This process can take place over and over again with minimal damage to the properties of the polymer.

Polythene (PE) is a very widely used polymer. Low-density polythene (LDPE) is a tough flexible polymer that is easily moulded into shape. Carrier bags, bin liners and washing up liquid bottles are typically made from LDPE. High-density polythene (HDPE) is a harder, stiffer version of polythene and is used for milk crates and wheelie bins.

Polystyrene (PS) is a food-safe polymer. Disposable plates and cutlery are made from polystyrene. Expanded polystyrene (EPS) is a lightweight polymer used in packaging. The white moulded foam used in packing TVs or monitors is made from EPS.

Polypropylene (PP) is a polymer that is often chosen for applications where there is a hinge moulded into the product. PP has excellent resistance to fatigue, so the hinge can be opened and closed without breaking or work-hardening.

Polyvinyl chloride (PVC) is a very common, cost-effective polymer. It is stiff, hard and durable and is easily moulded and extruded into shape. Rain water pipes and guttering are made from PVC.

Thermosetting polymers

Thermosetting polymers can also be shaped and formed by heat, but in contrast to thermoforming polymers this process can only occur once. Thermosetting polymers cannot be reheated or reformed. This makes them excellent insulators but also means that thermosetting polymers cannot be recycled.

Melamine formaldehyde (MF) is found in the manufacture of picnic crockery. It is hard and so it resists scratching, which enables it to maintain its aesthetics while being used and cleaned. It is also more durable than ceramic or glass alternatives.

Urea formaldehyde (UF) is used extensively in the manufacture of electrical fittings, such as the electrical plug. It is hardwearing, durable, a non-conductor of electricity, and most importantly, it will not change its shape if it should become hot.

Polyester resin (PR) is used to bond together strands of glass fibres to produce tough, waterproof mouldings, such as the hull of a yacht.

Epoxy resins (ER) are commonly found in the school workshop and are used as an adhesive to glue together dissimilar materials.

Figure 5.16 Melamine crockery

Figure 5.17 Urea formaldehyde (UF) plug

Activity

Gather a selection of polymer products from around your home; they could be children's toys, kitchenware, or packaging.

Look for the polymer identifying symbol on the product. It will look like the one in Figure 5.18.

Name the polymer and suggest reasons for its use.

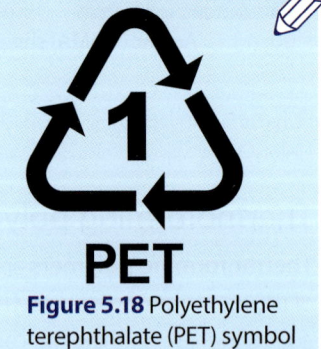

Figure 5.18 Polyethylene terephthalate (PET) symbol

KEY POINTS
- Thermoforming polymers can be repeatedly heated, formed and cooled.
- Thermosetting polymers can only be formed with heat once.
- Thermosetting polymers cannot be recycled.

5.5 Natural, synthetic, blended and mixed fibres, and woven, non-woven and knitted textiles

Fibres are very fine hair-like structures that are spun (or twisted) together to make yarns. These yarns are then woven or knitted together to create textile fabrics. The source of each fibre determines its performance properties or characteristics and affects what it can be used for.

Fibres, also known as polymers, are classified into natural polymers and manufactured (or synthetic) polymers.

Natural polymers

Natural polymers come from plants (**cellulosic fibres**) and animals (**protein fibres**). As they are derived from a natural source they are sustainable and biodegradable. The sources of natural fibres are:

- Plant polymers:
  - cotton, linen (flax), hemp, jute – from the stem or seeds of the plants
  - viscose, rayon – cellulose-based fibres extracted from, for example, wood pulp; chemicals are added in the extraction process (part natural, part artificial). These fibres are also known as regenerated fibres.
- Insect polymer:
  - silk – extracted from the mulberry silkworm cocoon.
- Animal polymer:
  - wool – fibre from the hair or fleece of sheep; other wool fibres include mohair (goat), cashmere (goat), angora (rabbit), alpaca, camel (hair).

Figure 5.19 The cotton boll (green pod shown) contains the plant's seeds; the cotton fibre is found inside the boll protecting the seeds.

Fibre	Properties	Uses
Cotton	Absorbent, strong, cool to wear, hardwearing, creases easily, smooth, easy to care for, flammable, can shrink	Clothing, sewing and knitting threads, soft furnishings, medical dressings, bed sheets, canvas, car tyre cords
Linen	Strong, cool to wear, absorbent, hardwearing, creases very easily, has a natural appearance, handles well, flammable	Lightweight summer clothing, soft furnishings, table linen
Hemp	Absorbent, non-static, anti-bacterial, naturally lustrous, strong	Clothing, carpets and rugs, ropes, mattress filling
Jute	Very absorbent, high tensile strength, anti-static	Bags, sacking, carpets, geo textiles, yarn and twine, upholstery, clothing (but to a lesser extent)
Silk	Absorbent, comfortable to wear, can be cool or warm to wear, strong when dry, has a natural sheen, creases, good feel	Luxury clothing and lingerie, knitwear, soft furnishings
Wool	Warm, absorbent, low flammability, good elasticity, crease resistant, strong, shrinks easily	Warm outer clothing including coats, jackets and suits, knitwear, soft furnishings including carpets and blankets

Table 5.2 Properties and common uses of natural polymers

Manufactured polymers

Manufactured, or **synthetic**, polymers are artificial fibres derived from oil, coal, minerals or petrochemicals. These are known as monomers. The monomers are joined together in a process called polymerisation, and then spun into yarns before being woven or knitted into fabrics. An advantage of synthetic fibres and yarn is that they can be engineered for specific purposes.

Most synthetic polymers are non-biodegradable and from unsustainable sources. The most common synthetic fibres are outlined in Table 5.3.

Fibre	Properties	Uses
Polyester	Strong when wet and dry, flame resistant (but will melt), thermoforming, hardwearing, poor absorbency, crease resistant	A very versatile fabric used throughout textiles
Nylon (polyamide)	Strong and hard wearing, melts as it burns, thermoforming, good elasticity, poor absorbency, resistant to chemicals and perspiration	Clothing, carpets and rugs, seat belts and ropes, tents, rucksacks
Polypropylene	Thermoforming with a low melting point, strong, crease resistant, non-absorbent, resistant to chemicals, hard wearing and durable	Engineered for specific uses to include: carpet backing, sacks, webbing, twine, fishing nets, ropes, some medical and hygiene products, awnings, geotextiles
Acrylic	Strong except when wet, thermoforming, burns slowly then melts, poor absorbency, good insulator	Knitwear and some knitted fabrics, fake fur products (including toys), upholstery
Elastane, Lycra®	Very elastic and stretchy, lightweight, strong and hardwearing	Clothing, but particularly swimwear and sportswear where stretch, comfort and fit is critical
Aramid fibres	Engineered for strength and heat resistance, no melting point, five times stronger than nylon, resistant to abrasion, low shrinkage, ease of care	Flame-resistant clothing, protective clothing, accessories, armour, geotextiles, aeronautical industry, ropes and cables, high-risk sports equipment

Table 5.3 Properties and common uses of synthetic polymers

Figure 5.20 Sports and active clothing often contains Lycra or elastane. This allows the fabric to fit tight to the body – it stretches and recovers easily and makes the clothing comfortable to wear during activity. The fabric used is a knitted construction which supports the fabric's ability to stretch.

Microfibres

Microfibres are extremely fine fibres which are 60–100 times finer than a human hair. Microfibres can be engineered for specific qualities and functions. Fabrics constructed from microfibres are generally lightweight, strong, crease resistant, soft and with good draping qualities. Polyester and polyamide (nylon) are particularly good for producing fine fibres, so recent developments have focussed on these. Products made from microfibres include sportswear, underwear and high-performance garments, but they are increasingly used throughout the clothing industry. Examples of microfibres include:

● Tactel® is a high-tech polyamide (nylon) fibre with a very fine and silky feel. It is hardwearing and easy to care for as it dries quickly. It is often blended with cotton or linen. It is used in clothing, but mostly for underwear and active wear.

● Tencel™ is a sustainable fabric and one of the most environmentally friendly. It is a regenerated fibre made from wood cellulose which makes it biodegradable. It is strong, but is soft, absorbent, resists creasing, and drapes well. It is widely used throughout textiles, particularly for clothing.

Blending and mixing fibres

Fibres are often mixed or blended together to improve the properties of the yarn or fabric. The process combines the best properties from each fibre. Reasons for blending or mixing fibres include:

- to improve the quality, for example to make it stronger or easier to care for
- to improve the appearance, such as the texture, tone or colour
- to improve functionality, for example to improve the handle of the fabric so that it drapes better
- to improve the cost of the yarn or fabric, for example by blending an inexpensive yarn with an expensive yarn to reduce the overall cost.

Mixed fibres

Fibres are mixed by adding yarns of different fibres together during the production of the fabric. This is done by using one yarn for the warp yarns that run along the length of the fabric and a different one for the weft yarns that are combined with the warp yarns across the fabric (see Figure 5.21). Cotton yarns are often mixed with elastane or Lycra to improve the fabric's elasticity.

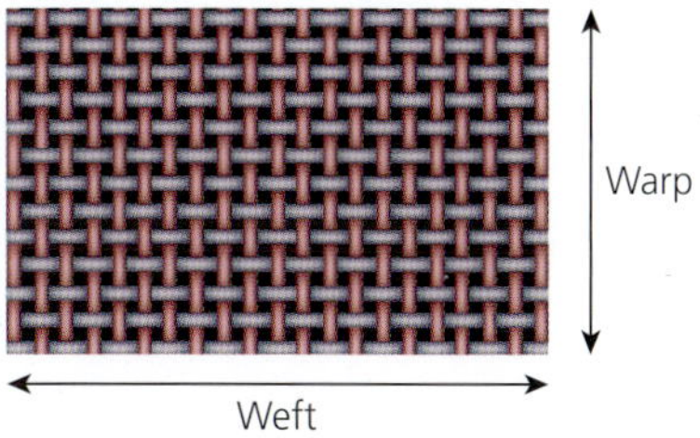

Blended fibres

A fibre blend consists of two or more different fibres being spun together to make a single yarn. The most common blend is polyester cotton. Cotton is absorbent, soft and strong, whereas polyester is hardwearing, quick-drying and elastic. The combined properties create a versatile fabric that is comfortable and cool to wear like cotton, but with the added features of being quick-drying and crease resistant.

Woven, non-woven and knitted textiles

Woven textiles

A woven fabric consists of warp and weft yarns. The warp yarns run vertically along the length of the fabric and the weft yarns are woven horizontally in an under/over configuration – the weft yarn goes over one warp yarn and under the next warp yarn. The most basic weave is a plain weave, which provides an even surface on both sides of the fabric and is generally considered stable and strong. A woven construction might be used for, for example, a polyester/cotton school shirt, cotton bedding or a polyamide (nylon) school/sports bag.

Variations in weaving formations create fabrics with different textures, patterns and strength. Denim jeans, for example, are made from cotton but with a **twill weave** pattern. The weave adds strength to the fabric.

Knitted textiles

Knitted fabrics are made by creating a series of loops in the yarns that interlock together. The main characteristic of knitted fabric is stretch. Knitted fabrics are also considered much warmer to wear as the loops trap air and prevent body heat from escaping. Knitted fabrics are used for many textile products, particularly where some stretch is needed on the product, for example in casual leisurewear and sportswear, underwear, jumpers and accessories such as hats, gloves and scarves. Knitting allows fabrics to stretch and recover which makes clothing in particular more comfortable.

Warp

Weft

Figure 5.21 In a mixed-fibre fabric, the warp yarns indicated in red would be one fibre, such as cotton; the weft yarns indicated in blue would be a different fibre, such as polyester.

Figure 5.22 A selection of plain weave fabrics. Different coloured yarns have been used to create stripes and checks.

> **KEY WORD**
>
> **Twill weave**: recognisable by the characteristic diagonal line pattern created by the weft yarn going over two warp yarns and under one, with a 'step', or offset, between rows to create the diagonal pattern.

Non-woven textiles

Non-woven textiles are constructed from a web of fibres. The web is held together either by adhesive or by stitching. Most non-woven fabrics are not considered strong enough to be made into garments but are often used to reinforce woven and knitted fabrics. Some non-woven fabrics are used to make disposable or single-use products such as surgical gowns and masks, cleaning cloths including wet and dry wipes, and protective suits for crime scene investigators.

Activity

Find three items of clothing and three different products made from textile fabrics.

For each product:

- Identify the method of fabric construction for each product; explain why that method is suitable for each product.
- Examine the label which shows the fibre content for the fabric; state why the properties of each named fibre make it suitable for each product.

KEY POINTS

- Fibres are the raw materials of textiles; each fibre has its own special properties. When the fibre is spun into yarn then made into fabric, the properties determine what the fabric can be used for.
- Natural fibres are all biodegradable, whereas synthetic fibres are not. This should be considered when choosing fabrics for textile products.
- The two main methods of constructing textile fabrics are weaving and knitting. Woven fabrics are more stable and strong while knitted fabrics are useful for their ability to stretch.
- Fibres can be mixed or blended to improve the properties of the yarn and/or fabric.

Know it

1 What is lignin?
2 Why can paper fibres only be recycled so many times?
3 What are board thicknesses measured in?
4 What are the major differences between a hardwood and softwood?
5 Name a hardwood and a softwood and give a use for each.
6 What are the advantages of using manufactured boards?
7 How can ferrous metals be protected from rusting?
8 What is a non-ferrous alloy?
9 What are the environmental issues with using thermosetting polymers?
10 State the two main sources of natural fibres and the main source of manufactured fibres.
11 a Describe the benefits of using cotton or linen for summer clothing.
   b Explain why nylon (polyamide) would be a suitable fabric for a school rucksack-style bag.
   c Give one reason for incorporating elastane into textile fabrics for use in clothing.

Exam practice questions

1 A manufacturer is looking to produce a new handheld games controller.
  a Discuss the benefits that CAD modelling would provide the manufacturer.   [4 marks]
  b Suggest the most appropriate CAM process for producing a physical
      prototype of the controller.   [2 marks]

2 A laser cutter and a CNC router can both be used to manufacture the pieces
of a slot-together product such as a model dinosaur. Evaluate the suitability
of each manufacturing process.   [6 marks]

3 a Describe two environmental problems created by the use of fossil fuels.   [4 marks]
  b Give two reasons why fossil fuels are still the primary fuel source for transportation.   [2 marks]
  c Describe one way in which biomass is used as an energy source.   [3 marks]
  d Use sketches and notes to explain how a garden lamp can be powered using a solar
      PV panel.   [4 marks]

4 Modern developments in technology have led to an increase in smart materials.
  a Define the term smart material.   [1 mark]
  b Explain how micro-encapsulation benefits the medical industry. Include examples
      to help explain your answer.   [4 marks]
  c Explain how nature supports the development of new fabrics.   [4 marks]

5 Technical textiles have been engineered and developed with specific properties to
suit a particular need.
  a Name a fabric that would be suitable for a racing car driver and describe the
      properties that will allow it to protect the driver.   [3 marks]
  b Explain why Rhovyl® would be a suitable fibre for use in sportswear.   [2 marks]

6 a Name and draw the circuit symbol for the electronic component which
      senses a change in light level.   [2 marks]
  b Explain the difference between a digital quantity and an analogue quantity.   [2 marks]
  c A system diagram for an electric kettle is shown.

    Explain how feedback is used in this system to switch off the heater when the water
    reaches 100°C.   [3 marks]

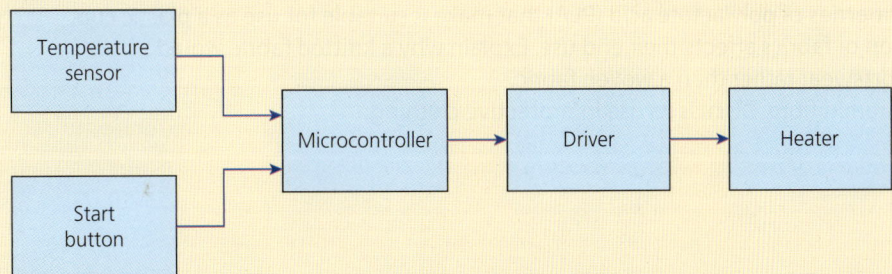

7 An electric toothbrush is being developed, controlled by a microcontroller. The input subsystem is a push button,
and the output is an electric motor. When the user presses the button, the motor turns on at full speed. Pressing
the button again reduces the motor to half speed. A third press turns the motor off, and the cycle then repeats.

  Draw a flowchart program to achieve this function.   [8 marks]

8 a Rotary motion is one type of motion found in mechanisms. Name and give examples
      of two other types of motion.   [4 marks]
  b Sketch a labelled diagram of a crank and slider mechanism and state the conversion of
      motion that takes place in this mechanism.   [4 marks]
  c State two functional differences between transferring rotary motion using a simple
      gear train and a belt drive mechanism.   [2 marks]

9 Pizza boxes are made from corrugated card.

  a State **two** properties of corrugated card that make it suitable for holding pizzas. [2 marks]

  b A pizza restaurant uses menus made from thin card. The menus are A4 size folded into shape as shown below.

  State the overall dimensions of the open menu: ………… mm × ………… mm [2 marks]

  c In use, the menu becomes quickly dog-eared and tatty. Describe **one** method of improving the menu's lifespan. [2 marks]

10 Describe two characteristics of medium-density fibreboard (MDF) that make it suitable for self-assembly furniture. [4 marks]

11 Explain why stainless steel is often used to manufacture kitchen sinks. [4 marks]

12 Discuss the properties of polylactate acid (PLA) that make it suitable for use as a plastic cup. [4 marks]

13 The construction of fabrics affects their end use. Explain why a knitted fabric would be used for sportswear rather than a woven fabric. [6 marks]

14 Nomex® is an aramid fibre. Discuss its use in protective clothing. [6 marks]

Section 2

In-depth knowledge and understanding

Chapter 6   Electronic systems, programmable components and mechanical devices 66

Chapter 7   Paper and boards 111

Chapter 8   Natural and manufactured timber 140

Chapter 9   Ferrous and non-ferrous metals 173

Chapter 10 Thermosetting and thermoforming polymers 200

Chapter 11 Natural, synthetic, blended and mixed fibres, and woven, non-woven and knitted textiles 226

Practice questions 267

Chapter 6
Electronic systems, programmable components and mechanical devices

Learning objectives

By the end of this chapter you should have developed a knowledge and understanding of:

- the working properties of electronic and programmable components and systems:
  - functions of electronic components, circuits and systems
  - input devices
  - process components
  - output devices
- the working properties of mechanical components and systems:
  - simple and compound systems
  - mechanical advantage and velocity ratio

- the sources and origins of components and systems and their ecological and social footprint
- factors which influence the selection of components and materials
- the effect of forces and stresses on components and materials
- stock sizes and values of components and materials
- processes used to manufacture products to different scales of production
- specialist techniques and processes that can be used to shape, fabricate, construct and assemble a high-quality prototype
- surface treatments and finishes for electronic and mechanical devices.

6.1 Sources, origins, physical and working properties of components and systems, and their ecological and social footprint

Functions of electronic and programmable devices/systems

Basic concepts

The **voltage** at a point in a circuit is a measure of the electrical 'pressure' trying to cause a **current** to flow, and current is a measure of the actual electricity flowing. The units of voltage and current are volts (V) and amps (A), respectively, although milliamps (mA) are commonly measured in electronic systems:

1 mA = 0.001 A

In most electronic circuits, the voltage at a point is always measured relative to the **zero volt rail** in the circuit; the zero volt rail is the negative (−) connection on the battery or the power supply unit. In practice, this means that when you use a **multimeter** to measure voltage, the black multimeter probe always connects to the zero volt rail, and the red multimeter probe connects to the point where the voltage is being measured.

Resistors

The relationship between voltage and current is explained by **Ohm's law**, which can be summarised by this formula:

voltage = current × resistance

$V = IR$

Resistance is measured in ohms (Ω), although you will regularly encounter kilohms (kΩ) and also megaohms (MΩ):

$$1 \text{ k}\Omega = 1\,000\ \Omega$$
$$1 \text{ M}\Omega = 1\,000 \text{ k}\Omega = 1\,000\,000\ \Omega$$

Resistors are used to control the current flow through different parts of a circuit. Also, because current, voltage and resistance are related, resistors are also used to produce specific voltages at different points in a circuit.

Resistors are only available in certain values, called **preferred values**. The **E12 series** is the set of 12 resistor values shown below:

| 1.0 | 1.2 | 1.5 | 1.8 | 2.2 | 2.7 | 3.3 | 3.9 | 4.7 | 5.6 | 6.8 | 8.2 |

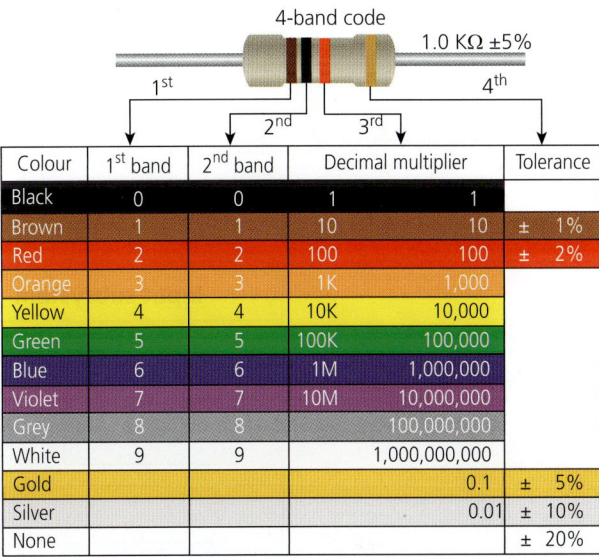

Resistors are available in these values, and their multiples of 10. For example, you can buy a 2.7 Ω resistor, and you can also buy resistors of 27 Ω, 270 Ω, 2.7 kΩ, 27 kΩ, 270 kΩ and 2.7 MΩ. An E24 series is also available which fills in the gaps in the E12 series. When you use Ohm's law to calculate a resistor value, you will rarely obtain a preferred value, so you will generally need to select a resistor with the closest preferred value. For most applications, it does not matter if you use a resistor that is not the exact value you calculated.

Most resistors have their resistance marked on them with four coloured bands. Three of the bands indicate the resistance, and the fourth is a tolerance band which tells how accurate the resistance will be to the indicated value. The resistor colour code is shown in Figure 6.1.

Colour	1st band	2nd band	Decimal multiplier		Tolerance	
Black	0	0	1	1		
Brown	1	1	10	10	±	1%
Red	2	2	100	100	±	2%
Orange	3	3	1K	1,000		
Yellow	4	4	10K	10,000		
Green	5	5	100K	100,000		
Blue	6	6	1M	1,000,000		
Violet	7	7	10M	10,000,000		
Grey	8	8		100,000,000		
White	9	9		1,000,000,000		
Gold				0.1	±	5%
Silver				0.01	±	10%
None					±	20%

Figure 6.1 Resistor colour code

Calculation

Calculate the value of a resistor which will cause a current of 20 mA to flow when it is connected across a 12 V battery.

Use the Ohm's law formula:

$$V = IR$$

Rearrange in terms of resistance, R:

$$R = \frac{V}{I}$$

Remember that the current must be in units of amps. 20 mA = 0.02 A

$$R = \frac{12}{0.02} = 600\ \Omega$$

Select the closest preferred value of resistor and identify its colour code.

The closest preferred value is 560 Ω.

The colours on this resistor will be green (5), blue (6), brown (one zero).

KEY WORD

Preferred value: the range of actual component values (e.g. resistors) that are manufactured.

Electronic system diagrams

In Chapter 3 we learned how the 'systems approach' is a useful way for a circuit designer to approach an electronic design problem. By breaking down a system into input, process and output subsystems, the designer can begin to consider what subsystems are required, how they are interconnected, and the nature of the signals that flow between the subsystems. In Chapter 3, the only process subsystem we considered was the programmable microcontroller, and, while microcontrollers are incredibly useful and powerful devices, they are not the only process subsystems that an electronic designer has at their disposal when developing electronic systems.

Figure 6.2 shows a range of input subsystems, and Figure 6.3 shows the process subsystems that you are required to understand for your GCSE course. The output subsystems are shown in Figure 6.4. An output subsystem contains a **transducer** – a device to convert an electrical signal into a physical output, such as light or motion.

Each subsystem is explained in more detail over the following pages. Notice that some subsystems deal with analogue signals, some deal with digital signals, and some convert analogue to digital.

> **KEY WORD**
>
> **Transducer**: a device to convert an electrical signal into a physical output.

Input subsystem	Description	Output signal
Switch	Several types of switches can be used as inputs (e.g. push, slide, tilt, vibration or reed switches)	Digital
Light sensor	Output signal rises as light level rises	Analogue
Temperature sensor	Output signal rises as temperature increases	Analogue
Moisture sensor	Output signal rises as probes are dipped further into water	Analogue

Figure 6.2 Input subsystems

Process subsystem	Description	Signals processed
Transistor (MOSFET)	A transistor is an amplifier, turning a small signal into a bigger one – usually used to drive a transducer	Digital or analogue
Thyristor	A latching component – once triggered, it stays switched on	Digital
Monostable	When triggered, the output switches on for a period of time	Digital
Astable	Produces an output signal which continually switches on and off	Digital
Voltage comparator	Compares two analogue input voltages and produces a digital output depending on which input signal is the largest	Analogue inputs, digital output
Voltage amplifier	Takes a small input signal and increases it to produce a larger output signal	Analogue
Logic gates	The logic state of the output depends on the combination of the states on the inputs	Digital

Figure 6.3 Process subsystems

Output subsystem	Description	Signal required
Lamp	Emits light – largely replaced by LEDs in modern designs	Digital (on/off) or analogue (to vary brightness)
LED	Available in a wide range of shapes, sizes and colours	Digital (on/off) or analogue (to vary brightness)
Buzzer/ siren	Emits a tone; a siren is a particularly loud or noticeable buzzer	Digital
Loudspeaker	Reproduces music or speech when driven with a sound waveform	Analogue sound waveform
Piezo sounder	Produces audible tones in 2 kHz to 4 kHz range	Digital waveform
Motor	Produces rotary motion	Digital (on/off) or analogue (to vary speed)
Solenoid	Produces a pulling force	Digital
Relay	Placed before some output subsystems to control a higher voltage or current device from a lower voltage or current circuit	Digital

Figure 6.4 Output subsystems

Figure 6.5 Different types of switch

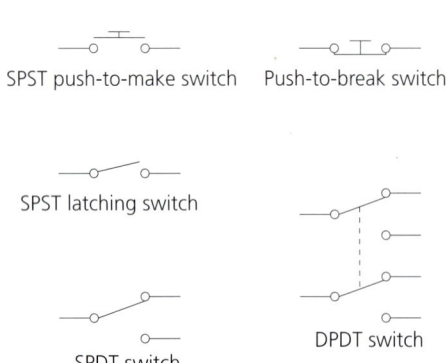

SPST push-to-make switch   Push-to-break switch

SPST latching switch

SPDT switch

DPDT switch

Figure 6.6 Switch circuit symbols

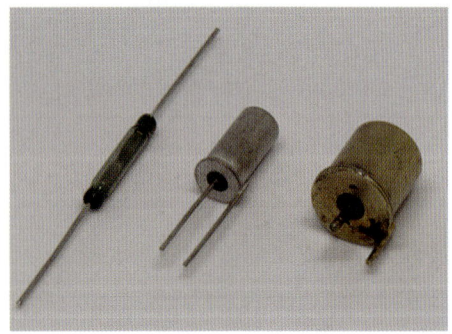

Figure 6.7 Reed, tilt and vibration switches

Input devices

Switches

A switch is a very simple electronic component that can be either off or on. When a switch is acting as an input for an electronic system it will produce a digital signal, either low or high. Most people are familiar with simple push button switches which are on when pressed; these are called **push-to-make** switches. A **momentary-push-button** switch turns off again when the button is released; a **latching** switch stays on until the button is pressed a second time.

Less common is the **push-to-break** switch which is normally on, but which switches off when pressed.

Some switches are operated by a slide or a lever toggle, as seen in Figure 6.5.

A simple push-to-make switch has two terminals. It is known as a single-pole-single-throw (SPST) switch. A single-pole-double-throw (SPDT) switch has three terminals. Look at the circuit symbols in Figure 6.6 and you should see that a SPDT switch can be on in either position. SPDT switches are often used to route a signal to one of two destinations.

A double-pole-double-throw (DPDT) switch consists of two SPDT switches 'ganged' together, so they operate with a single lever. DPDT switches are used for simultaneous control of two circuits.

A **tilt switch** is on when it is upright, and off when the switch is inverted. This switch senses being tilted, which is useful for detecting if a potentially dangerous product, such as a room heater, has fallen over. A slight variation on this is the vibration switch, which produces a brief signal when it is moved; this can be used in a security system to sound an alarm if a valuable object is tampered with.

A **reed switch** is operated by a magnet. When the magnet is next to the reed switch, the switch is on. As the magnet moves away, the switch turns off. Reed switches do not require any physical contact to operate, so they can detect the proximity of a magnet (within about 10 mm). They are widely used to sense doors being opened in burglar alarm systems, and to detect the closing of a laptop lid, or a tablet cover, which generates a signal to make these devices go into standby mode.

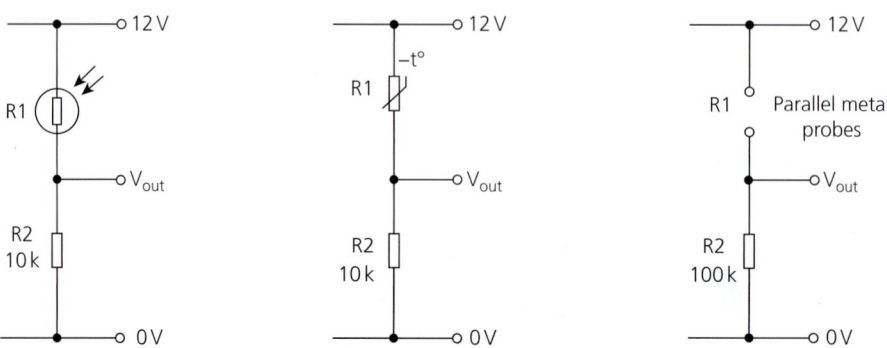

Figure 6.8 Potential dividers to sense light, temperature and moisture

Analogue sensors

Two components for sensing light and temperature were introduced in Chapter 3. The resistance of a light-dependent resistor (LDR) decreases as light level increases. The resistance of a thermistor decreases as temperature increases. These resistive devices are connected in a **potential divider**, as shown in Figure 6.8, to produce an analogue output voltage which *increases* when light level or temperature increases.

It is worth noting that if the potential divider is inverted, so that the LDR or thermistor becomes the bottom resistor, then the output voltage will *decrease* when the light level or temperature increases.

A moisture sensor is useful in Design and Technology projects to sense the presence of water. A moisture sensor can simply be made from two metal probes, held parallel to each other about 10 mm apart. The probes act as a resistor and they are connected in a potential divider. When the probes are out of water, the potential divider output will be 0 V. When they are dipped into water, the output voltage will rise increasingly as the probes are dipped further into the water. This could be used as a way of sensing the level of water in a storage tank.

Process components

Transistor (MOSFET)

A transistor is an amplifying component, which means that it turns a small signal into a bigger one. For your GCSE course, transistors will be used to amplify a signal so that the signal can be used to switch on an output transducer; this is called **driving** a transducer. In its simplest application, the transistor is the sole processing subsystem, connected between the input subsystem and the output transducer, as shown in Figure 6.9. It acts as a sort of switch, to turn on the output transducer when the input signal rises.

The type of transistor used in this circuit is called a **MOSFET**. It has three terminals, labelled drain (d), gate (g) and source (s). The source goes to the zero volt rail and the transducer connects between the positive supply rail and the drain terminal. The gate is the input terminal which is used to control the MOSFET.

The MOSFET behaves like a SPST switch connected between the drain and source terminals. When the input signal on the gate is 0 V the MOSFET switch is off, which means that the transducer is off. When the signal on the gate rises above approximately 2.5 V the MOSFET switch is on, allowing current to flow through the transducer, which causes it to operate. The simple circuit in Figure 6.9 will turn on the lamp when the LDR goes dark.

The limitation of this circuit is that the lamp does not turn on sharply at the switching point but increases gradually in brightness as the light level continues to drop. Better control of the lamp can be achieved using some of the process subsystems described later in this chapter. A MOSFET is usually used as the final output stage in a system, as a transducer driver.

MOSFETs are available with different current ratings. Two common types are shown in Figure 6.10.

KEY WORDS

Potential divider: two resistors, used to produce a known output voltage signal.

MOSFET: a type of transistor, used as a transducer driver.

Calculation

The potential divider formula can be used to calculate the output voltage, V_{out}:

$$V_{out} = V_s \times \left(\frac{R2}{R1+R2} \right)$$

where:
- V_s is the power supply voltage
- R1 is the top resistor in the potential divider
- R2 is the bottom resistor.

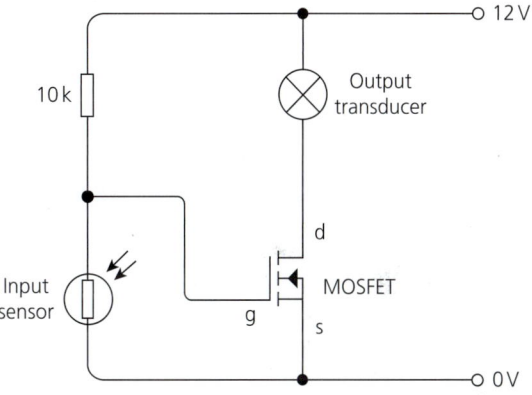

Figure 6.9 A MOSFET used as a switch

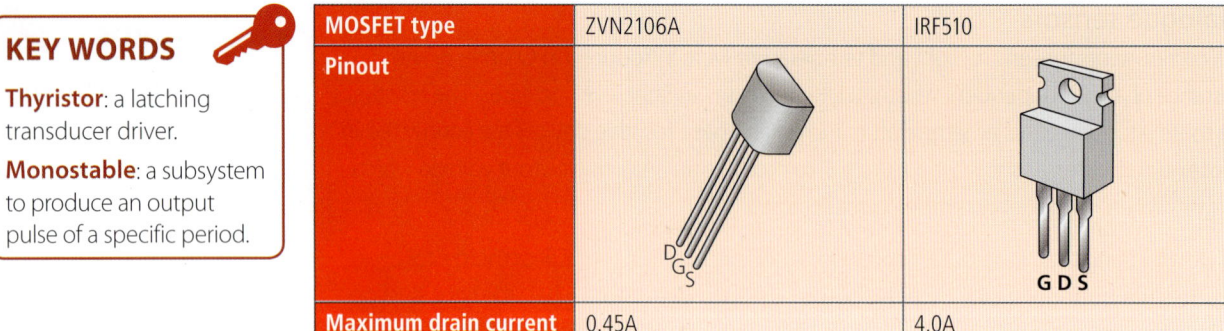
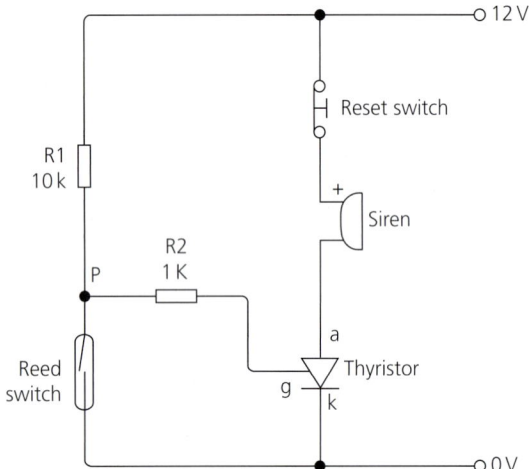

Figure 6.11 A thyristor in use in a latching burglar alarm

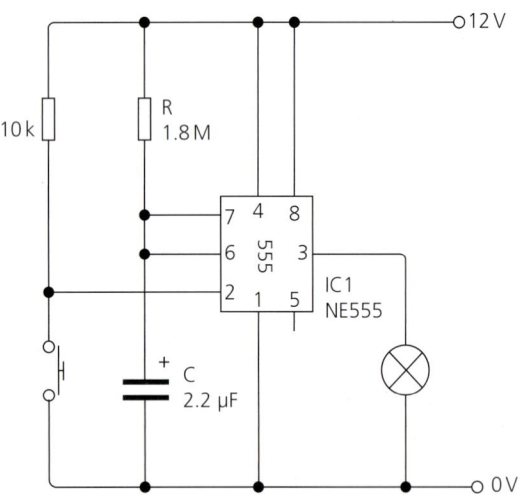

Figure 6.12 A 555 monostable circuit

Thyristor

A **thyristor** is similar to a transistor in that it can drive an output transducer, under the control of an input signal. The circuit in Figure 6.11 shows a thyristor being used in a burglar alarm. When the magnet moves away from the reed switch, the voltage at point P will go high, allowing a small current to flow through resistor R2 into the thyristor's gate (g) terminal. This small current will trigger the thyristor, allowing a bigger current to flow between the anode (a) and cathode (k), causing the buzzer to sound.

However, unlike a transistor, once the thyristor is triggered it **latches** and stays switched on, even if the input signal is removed (even if the magnet is replaced in the burglar alarm). The only way to reset the thyristor is to stop the current flowing through the transducer. In the burglar alarm circuit, this is achieved by pressing the push-to-break switch.

A thyristor is sometimes called a silicon-controlled rectifier (SCR).

Monostable

A **monostable** is a very useful subsystem for Design and Technology projects. It is a timer circuit. When triggered by an input signal, the output of a monostable turns on for a period of time, then it turns off again. The length of time the output stays on is determined by the values of two components in the monostable circuit, a resistor and a capacitor.

Figure 6.12 shows the circuit diagram of a monostable circuit, built around a 555 integrated circuit. In this circuit, the trigger signal is provided by a push-to-make switch, but the signal could come from a different input subsystem. The 555 monostable is triggered by a low logic level on its trigger input (pin 2 on the IC). When the push button is briefly pressed, the lamp will light for a period, then it will turn off.

Capacitors

A capacitor is a component that can temporarily store electric charge. When a capacitor is used along with a resistor, the time taken for the capacitor to charge (fill) to a certain level can be accurately predicted. Therefore, capacitors and resistors are often used in circuits where a repeatable time period is required.

Capacitance is measured in units called farads (symbol F), although microfarads (μF) or nanofarads (nF) are more common:

$1\ \mu F = 1 \times 10^{-6}\ F$

$1\ nF = 1 \times 10^{-3}\ \mu F = 1 \times 10^{-9}\ F$

Capacitors smaller than 1 µF are usually a **ceramic** or **polyester** type. These are non-polarised, meaning that it does not matter which way round they are used in a circuit.

Capacitors 1 µF and above are usually **electrolytic** type. These are **polarised** and their negative lead is usually marked with an arrow or a band on the capacitor's case.

Calculation

The time period for a 555 monostable is given by the formula:

$T = 1.1RC$

- T is in seconds
- R is resistance, in ohms, Ω
- C is capacitance, in farads, F

The monostable circuit in Figure 6.12 has:

$R = 1.8\ M\Omega = 1.8 \times 10^{6}\ \Omega$

$C = 2.2\ \mu F\ (microfarads) = 2.2 \times 10^{-6}\ F$

Therefore, the time period will be:

$T = 1.1 \times 1.8 \times 10^{6} \times 2.2 \times 10^{-6}$

$T = 4.4\ seconds\ (to\ 1\ d.p.)$

Astable

An **astable** subsystem produces an output signal which continually switches on and off. It produces a constant stream of output pulses. The number of pulses produced every second is called the **frequency**. The astable circuit is also built around a 555 integrated circuit. The frequency is determined by the values of two resistors and a capacitor in the circuit.

Figure 6.13 shows a 555 astable circuit which will pulse a buzzer on and off.

Calculation

The frequency of the pulses from a 555 astable is given by the formula:

$f = \dfrac{1.44}{(R_1 + 2R_2)C}$

- f is in hertz, Hz (pulses per second)
- R1 and R2 are resistances, in ohms, Ω
- C is capacitance, in farads, F

The astable circuit in Figure 6.13 has:

$R1 = 1\ k\Omega = 1000\ \Omega$

$R2 = 68\ k\Omega = 68 \times 10^{3}\ \Omega$

$C = 4.7\ \mu F\ (microfarads) = 4.7 \times 10^{-6}\ F$

Therefore, the buzzer will pulse at a frequency of:

$f = \dfrac{1.44}{(1000 + (2 \times 68 \times 10^{3})) \times 4.7 \times 10^{-6}}$

$f = 2.24\ Hz\ (to\ 2\ d.p.)$

To keep the frequency calculations simple, resistor R1 is often chosen to be 1 kΩ.

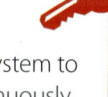

KEY WORD

Astable: a subsystem to produce a continuously pulsing output at a specific frequency.

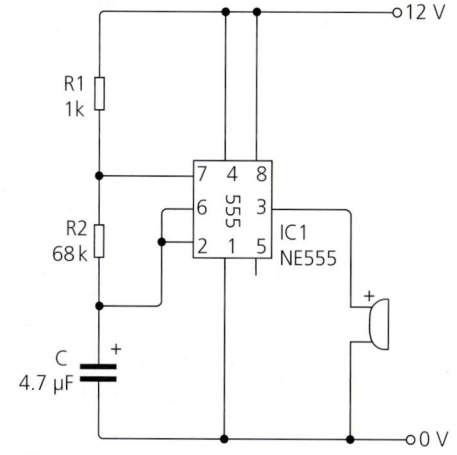

Figure 6.13 A 555 astable circuit

By selecting different values for R2 and for C, the astable circuit can be modified to produce either very slow (low frequency) pulses, or very rapid (high frequency) pulses, depending on the needs of the application.

Typical pulse frequency	Possible application
Less than 1 Hz	Slow flashing of a lamp Intermittent sounding of a siren in an alarm
1 Hz to 5 Hz	'Urgent' flashing of an LED to attract attention 'Urgent' on/off sounding of a buzzer
Above 300 Hz	Higher frequencies fed into a piezo sounder or a loudspeaker will be heard as a 'tone', which could be used: • as part of an electronic musical instrument • to create alarm noises

Table 6.1 Pulse frequencies and their applications

Voltage comparator

This subsystem compares two analogue input voltage signals and produces a digital output which will be either high or low, depending on which input signal is the largest. A voltage comparator is an analogue-to-digital converter.

Figure 6.14 shows a system diagram which will switch on a fan when the temperature rises above a set level.

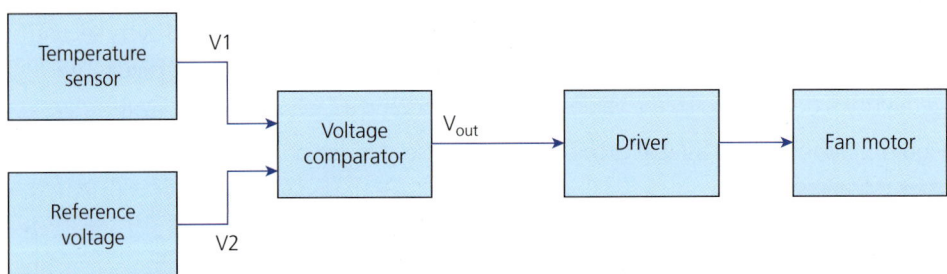

Figure 6.14 A voltage comparator system

The voltage signal from the temperature sensor (V_1) will increase as the temperature increases. The reference voltage (V_2) is fixed and does not change. The voltage comparator behaviour can be explained with the statements below:

If $V_1 > V_2$ then V_{out} is logic 1

If $V_2 > V_1$ then V_{out} is logic 0

Therefore, at low temperatures $V_2 > V_1$, so the comparator output is low, and the fan motor is off. As the temperature increases V_1 will rise, and when $V_1 > V_2$ then the comparator output will go high. This high signal will cause the transducer driver to turn on the fan motor.

The circuit diagram of the **voltage comparator** is shown in Figure 6.15.

The voltage comparator component IC1 is called an **operational amplifier (op-amp)**. These are often packaged in an 8-pin dual-in-line (DIL) package as shown in Figure 6.16.

KEY WORD

Voltage comparator: a subsystem to compare two analogue input voltages, and produce a digital output.

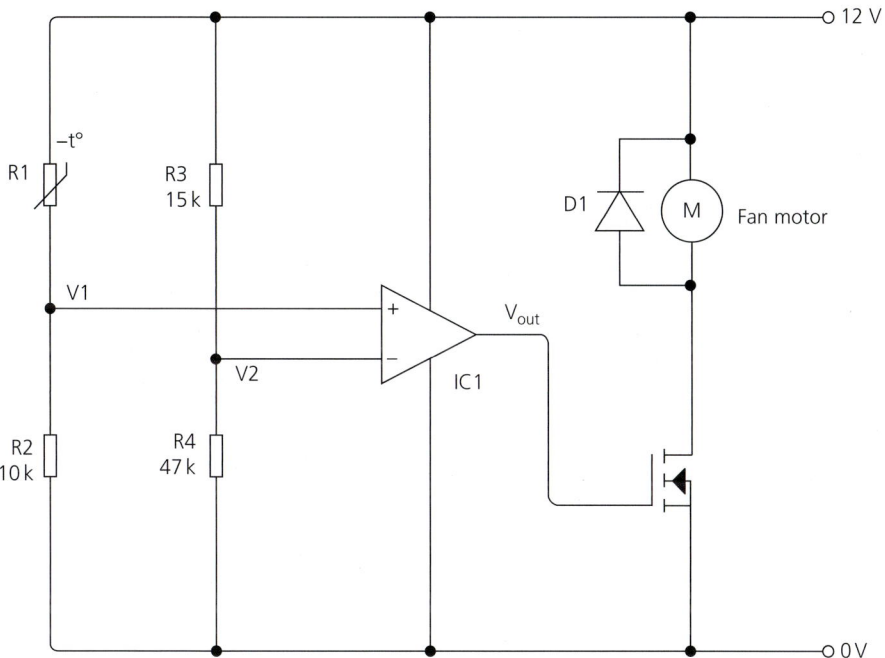

Figure 6.15 A voltage comparator circuit based around an op-amp

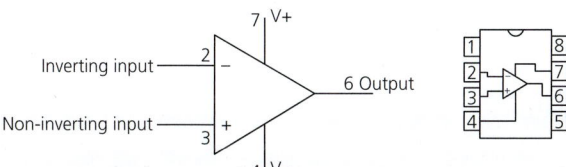

Figure 6.16 Op-amp IC pinout

In Figure 6.15, the switching point of the voltage comparator will occur when the output voltages from each of the two potential dividers are both equal ($V_1 = V_2$). This will happen when the ratio of the resistors in each potential divider are the same:

$$\frac{R_1}{R_2} = \frac{R_3}{R_4} \quad \text{(R_1 is the resistance of the thermistor)}$$

Notice the MOSFET in this circuit, which is being used as a transducer driver for the fan motor. The diode D_1 is used to remove **back emf**, which is explained later in this chapter.

Operational amplifiers and gain

Voltage amplifier

An **amplifier** subsystem receives a small analogue input voltage signal (V_{in}) and increases its magnitude to produce a larger analogue signal (V_{out}). Sound systems rely on amplifiers to increase the weak signals generated by a microphone up to a level where they can be heard from a loudspeaker.

The amplification factor is called the voltage **gain**.

$$\text{Voltage gain} = \frac{V_{out}}{V_{in}}$$

> **KEY WORDS**
>
> **Amplifier**: a subsystem to increase the magnitude of an analogue voltage.
>
> **Gain**: the amplification factor of an amplifier.

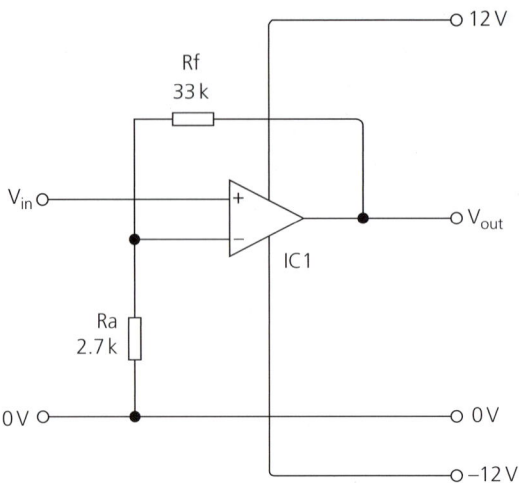

Figure 6.17 Voltage amplifier using an op-amp IC

The circuit in Figure 6.17 shows how an op-amp can be used, along with two resistors, to produce a voltage amplifier.

Calculation

The voltage gain of an amplifier is controlled by the values of the two resistors:

$$\text{Voltage gain of amplifier} = 1 + \frac{R_f}{R_a}$$

The amplifier circuit in Figure 6.17 has:

$R_f = 33\,k$

$R_a = 2.7\,k$

The voltage gain of this amplifier will be:

$$\text{Voltage gain} = 1 + \frac{R_f}{R_a} = 1 + \frac{33}{2.7} = 13.2$$

If a 0.2 V signal is fed in to this amplifier, the output voltage will be:

$$\text{Voltage gain} = \frac{V_{out}}{V_{in}}$$

$$V_{out} = V_{in} \times \text{voltage gain} = 0.2 \times 13.2 = 2.64\,V$$

KEY WORD

Logic gate: a digital integrated circuit component whose output logic state depends on the combination of states on its inputs.

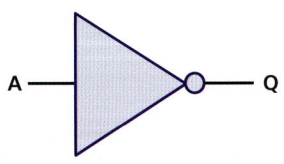

A	Q
0	1
1	0

Figure 6.18 A NOT gate and truth table

Logic gates

Logic gates are digital electronic components where the logic state of their output depends on the combination of the states on their inputs. There are six types of gates: NOT, AND, OR, NAND, NOR and EOR. Each gate has a **truth table** which shows how the gate behaves. It is important to remember that logic gates process digital signals: logic 0 (low) and logic 1 (high).

A NOT gate is the simplest gate. It has a single input. The output is always the opposite logic state to its input. It is sometimes called an **inverter** because it changes logic 0 to logic 1, and vice-versa.

Figure 6.19 shows the 2-input logic gates and their truth tables.

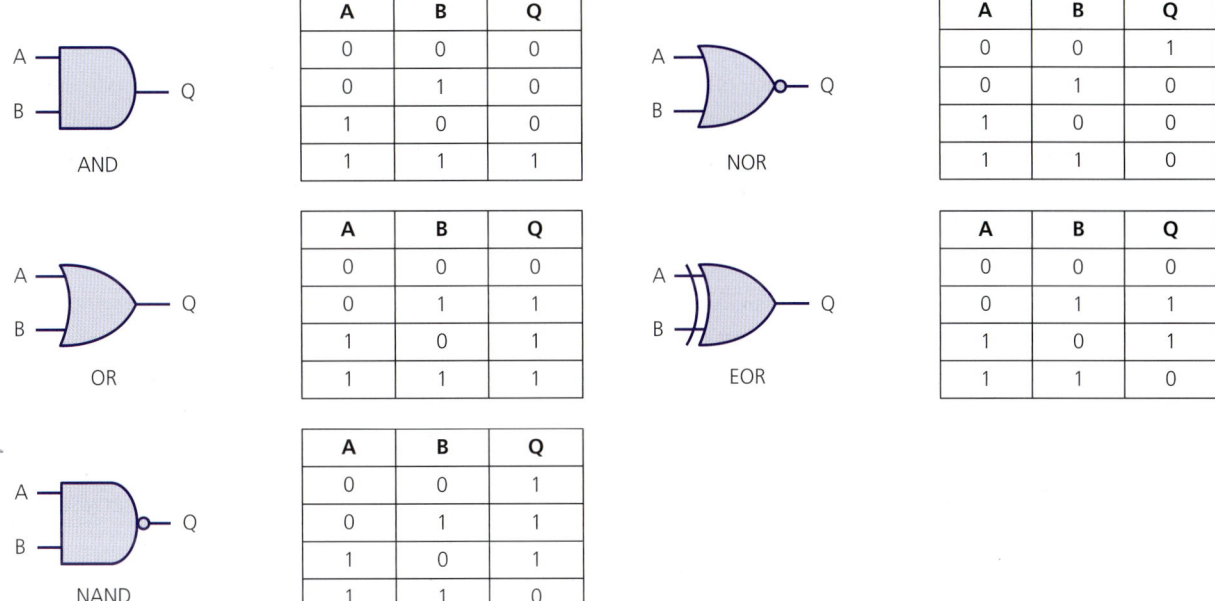

A	B	Q
0	0	0
0	1	0
1	0	0
1	1	1

AND

A	B	Q
0	0	1
0	1	0
1	0	0
1	1	0

NOR

A	B	Q
0	0	0
0	1	1
1	0	1
1	1	1

OR

A	B	Q
0	0	0
0	1	1
1	0	1
1	1	0

EOR

A	B	Q
0	0	1
0	1	1
1	0	1
1	1	0

NAND

Figure 6.19 Logic gates and truth tables

Logic gates are particularly powerful when used in combination. Look at the logic circuit in Figure 6.20, and its truth table. Three push switches (A, B and C) provide digital input signals for this circuit. To work out the function of the circuit, the connections between the logic gates have been labelled X and Y and these columns are also in the truth table. X is the output of a NOT gate, so X = 1 when A = 0. Y is the output of an AND gate, so Y = 1 when B AND C are both 1. The final output Q can be deduced by considering that Q = 1 only when X AND Y are both 1.

The three 10k resistors below each switch are called **pull-down resistors**. They are used with switches in digital circuits to ensure that a logic 0 input signal is produced when the switch is not pressed.

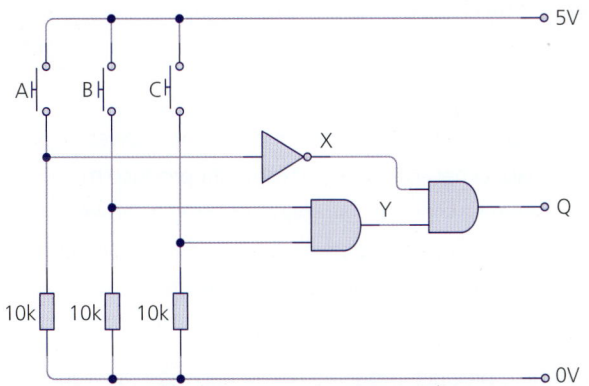

A	B	C	X	Y	Q
0	0	0	1	0	0
0	0	1	1	0	0
0	1	0	1	0	0
0	1	1	1	1	1
1	0	0	0	0	0
1	0	1	0	0	0
1	1	0	0	0	0
1	1	1	0	1	0

Figure 6.20 Combining logic gates

Output components

Light output

Lamps have largely been replaced by light-emitting diodes (LEDs) in many modern products. LEDs are more energy efficient than lamps, do not get as hot, have a longer working life, and are available in a wide range of sizes, shapes and colours. Lamps still have their uses, but for most new designs, LEDs are usually the preferred choice.

The 'standard' size LED is 5 mm in diameter. These are available in every visible colour as well as colours that are not visible, such as infrared and ultraviolet.

A standard brightness LED is suitable for use as an indicator on a control panel (for example, to show that something is switched on). High brightness types are best for illumination applications or for attracting attention, such as warning indicators. Some very high brightness LEDs can light up an entire room, and care needs to be taken not to look directly at these as they can damage the eyes.

An LED needs a resistor to be placed in series with it to limit the current flowing, otherwise the LED will burn out.

Calculation

The series resistor for an LED can be calculated using Ohm's law:

$$R = \frac{V_s - V_{LED}}{I}$$

where V_s is the power supply voltage, V_{LED} is the voltage drop across the LED, and I is the current the LED needs to light up. The values for V_{LED} and I can be looked up for the LED you intend to use.

For a 5 V power supply, and a red LED for which V_{LED} = 2.0 V and I = 10 mA:

$$R = \frac{5 - 2}{0.01} = 300 \ \Omega$$

When selecting a resistor for an LED, it is wise to protect the LED by always choosing a preferred resistor value greater than the calculated value so that the actual current flowing is slightly less.

In this example, a 330 Ω resistor would be chosen from the E12 range.

Sound output

A buzzer is different from a loudspeaker. A buzzer will produce a tone when it receives power, but that is all it can do; it cannot make other sounds and it cannot reproduce music or speech. Similarly, a loudspeaker will not emit a tone if it is simply connected to power; it can only reproduce the electrical sound waveform that it receives. So, if a designer wishes a loudspeaker to produce a tone then they will need to design a circuit to create a waveform at an appropriate frequency.

Buzzers are used when it is only necessary to produce the same sound, such as in an alarm system. Some buzzers are extremely loud, and these are usually known as sirens.

Figure 6.21 Loudspeaker, buzzer and siren

A piezo sounder is a miniature loudspeaker component which is particularly good at producing audible tones in the 2 kHz to 4 kHz range. They can be connected directly to the output pin of a microcontroller without the need for a transducer driver, as shown in Figure 6.22. The microcontroller can then be programmed to produce tones or even tunes from the piezo sounder.

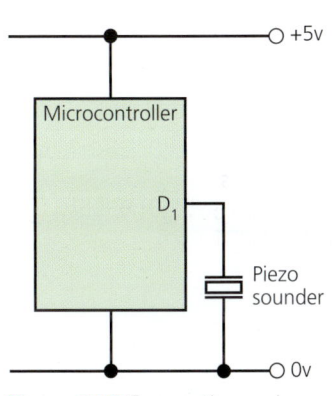

Figure 6.22 Connecting a piezo sounder to a microcontroller output pin

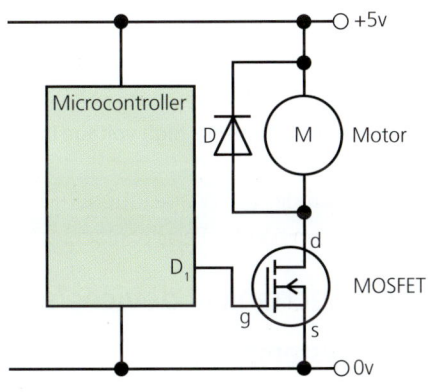

Figure 6.23 Using a MOSFET to drive a motor

Movement output

Electric motors are used to generate rotary motion in products. A MOSFET transducer driver is always necessary to provide sufficient current to operate a motor. Figure 6.23 shows how a motor can be controlled by a microcontroller.

The **diode** (D) is included in this circuit as a protection device for the MOSFET. The diode is needed because electric motors generate **back emf**, which is a type of electrical noise. This unwanted back emf would damage the MOSFET if it were not removed by the diode. Other output devices which require the use of a back emf diode are a solenoid and a relay coil.

A solenoid is an electromagnet which can produce a pulling force (or a pushing force) when current is switched on. They do not produce continuous movement, just a short linear **stroke** of a few mm. Solenoids are used in electronic door locks, and in valves which control the flow of water or air.

KEY WORD

Stroke: the linear distance moved in a reciprocating system.

Relay

A **relay** is a type of driver, consisting of a switch (called the contacts) which is operated by an electromagnet (called the coil). When current passes through the coil, the contacts are activated. Relays are useful because they allow control of a higher voltage or current device from a lower voltage or current circuit.

Figure 6.24 shows how a MOSFET and relay allow a 24 V lamp to be controlled from a 5 V microcontroller circuit.

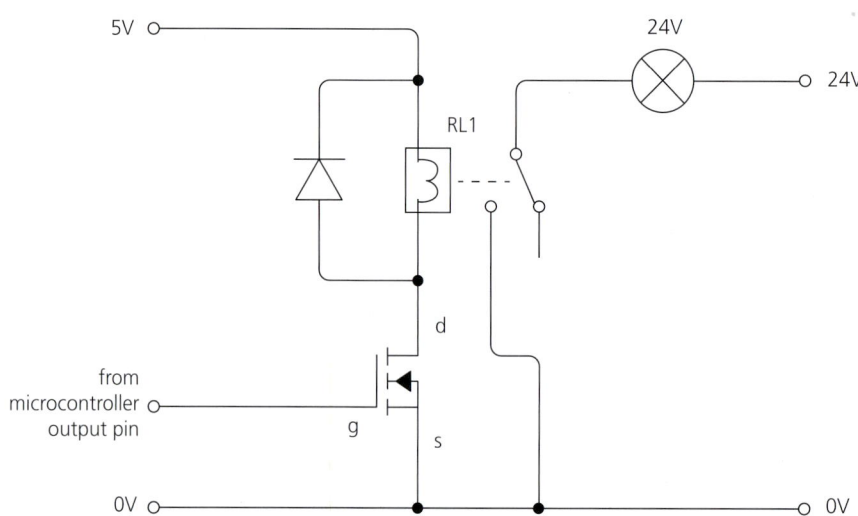

Figure 6.24 Using a relay to control a high voltage lamp

Relays are specified by their coil voltage (often 5 V, 6 V or 12 V), and the maximum voltage/current their contacts can handle. Relay contacts are usually SPDT or DPDT.

Functions of mechanical devices/systems

Rotary motion systems

Rotating mechanical systems are very common. Most engines and electric motors produce a rotary output, which usually needs to be altered in speed or direction or to be transferred to a different place.

Comparisons between rotary systems and linear systems

In Chapter 4 we discovered the 'trade-off' principle that all simple mechanisms obey:

If the mechanism increases the force, then the distance moved must decrease.

Force is a push or a pull in linear systems. The equivalent turning force in a rotary system is called **torque**. Distance moved in a linear system becomes **rotational velocity** (or rotational speed) in a rotary system. Therefore, for a simple rotary mechanism the trade-off principle is written:

If the mechanism increases the torque, then the rotational velocity must decrease.

So, rotary mechanisms can either:

- increase the torque, but reduce the rotational velocity, or
- reduce the torque but increase rotational velocity.

Simple gear train

The simple gear train, consisting of two spur gears, was introduced in Chapter 4. Figure 6.25 shows a simple gear train consisting of a driver gear with N_1 teeth and a driven gear with N_2 teeth.

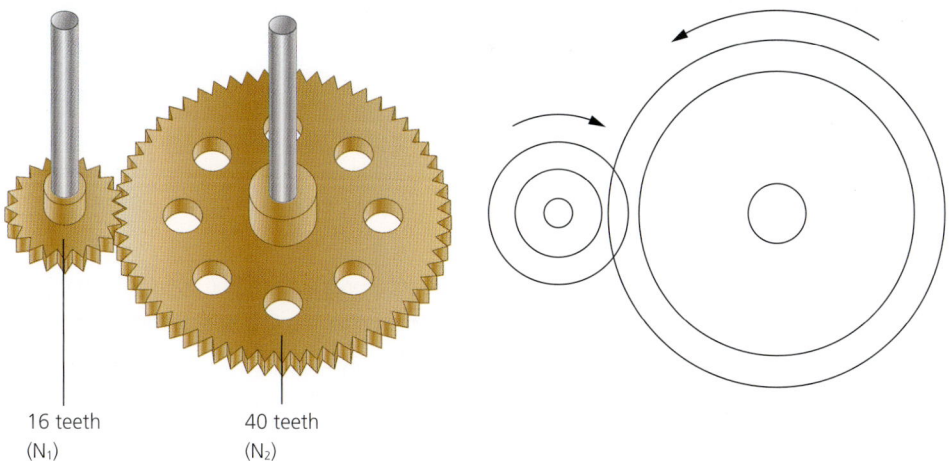

16 teeth
(N_1)

40 teeth
(N_2)

Figure 6.25 A simple gear train

Remember that the two gears will rotate in opposite directions, and the rotational velocity of each gear is inversely proportional to its diameter – the smaller gear rotates faster than the larger gear.

Velocity ratio

A key term used in mechanical systems is **velocity ratio**, which is the factor by which the system **reduces** the rotational velocity:

$$\text{Velocity ratio} = \frac{\text{rotational velocity of input}}{\text{rotational velocity of output}}$$

For a simple gear train:

$$\text{Velocity ratio} = \frac{\text{number of teeth on output (driven) gear}}{\text{number of teeth on input (driver) gear}}$$

Since the above two equations express the same thing, they are equal to each other, so:

$$\frac{\text{rotational velocity of input}}{\text{rotational velocity of output}} = \frac{\text{number of teeth on output (driven) gear}}{\text{number of teeth on input (driver) gear}}$$

This equation is sometimes rearranged and written as shown below:

(RV of input) × (number of teeth on input) = (RV of output) × (number of teeth on output)

(where RV stands for rotational velocity)

In a simple gear train, the velocity ratio is sometimes called the **gear ratio**. Gear ratio is the same thing as velocity ratio.

In a perfect mechanism (where there is no friction), by the trade-off principle, the velocity ratio is also the factor by which the system **increases the torque**.

>
> **KEY WORD**
>
> **Velocity ratio**: the factor by which a mechanical system reduces the rotational velocity.

Calculation

For the simple gear train in Figure 6.25, calculate the rotational velocity of the 16-tooth input gear if the 40-tooth output gear needs to rotate at 10 rpm.

(RV of input) × (number of teeth on input) = (RV of output) × (number of teeth on output)

(RV of input) × 16 = 10 × 40

$$RV \text{ of input} = \frac{400}{16}$$

RV of input = 25 rpm

Compound gear train

A compound gear train consists of several pairs of gears working together, usually so that there is a very large overall velocity ratio. A compound gear train is just two or more simple gear trains placed one after the other. The overall velocity ratio is:

Overall velocity ratio = (velocity ratio of stage 1) × (velocity ratio of stage 2)

Driver gear A 16 teeth   Gear B 32 teeth   Driven gear D 42 teeth

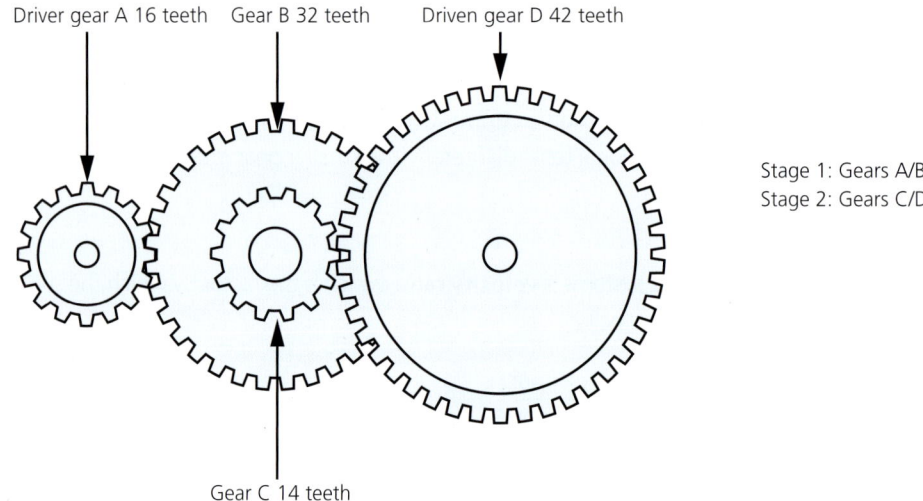

Stage 1: Gears A/B
Stage 2: Gears C/D

Gear C 14 teeth

Gears B and C are locked together

Figure 6.26 A compound gear train

Look at the compound gear train in Figure 6.26. Gear A is the input pinion and gear D is the final output spur gear. Gears B and C are part of a single compound gear, which means that they are two gears locked together so that they rotate as one.

The first stage consists of gears A and B. The velocity ratio is:

$$\text{Velocity ratio of first stage} = \frac{\text{number of teeth on driven gear (B)}}{\text{number of teeth on driver gear (A)}}$$

$$\text{Velocity ratio of first stage} = \frac{32}{16} = 2$$

The output of the first stage becomes the input of the second stage, consisting of gears C and D:

$$\text{Velocity ratio of second stage} = \frac{\text{number of teeth on driven gear (D)}}{\text{number of teeth on driver gear (C)}}$$

$$\text{Velocity ratio of second stage} = \frac{42}{14} = 3$$

The overall velocity ratio of the compound gear train is:

Overall velocity ratio = (gear ratio of first stage) × (gear ratio of second stage)

Overall velocity ratio = 2 × 3 = 6

Remember that each gear rotates in the opposite direction to the previous gear. So, in Figure 6.26, if gear A rotates clockwise, compound gear B/C will rotate anticlockwise, and gear D clockwise.

Compound gear trains are used extensively in mechanical systems, such as the gearbox on the DC motor shown in Figure 6.27.

Figure 6.27 This motor/gearbox features a compound gear train

Calculation

For the compound gear train in Figure 6.26, gear A is replaced by a pinion with 10 teeth.

To calculate the new overall velocity ratio of the system:

overall velocity ratio = (gear ratio of first stage) × (gear ratio of second stage)

$$\text{overall velocity ratio} = \frac{32}{10} \times \frac{42}{14}$$

overall velocity ratio = 3.2 × 3 = 9.6

To calculate the RV of the output if the input is driven by a motor at 3000 rpm:

$$\text{velocity ratio} = \frac{\text{RV of input}}{\text{RV of output}}$$

$$9.6 = \frac{3000}{\text{RV of output}}$$

$$\text{RV of output} = \frac{3000}{9.6} = 312.5 \text{ rpm}$$

Pulley and belt drive

A simple pulley and belt drive system, introduced in Chapter 4, can transfer rotary motion between two shafts which can be separated by some distance. The input and output pulleys rotate in the same direction and there can be an increase or decrease of rotational velocity.

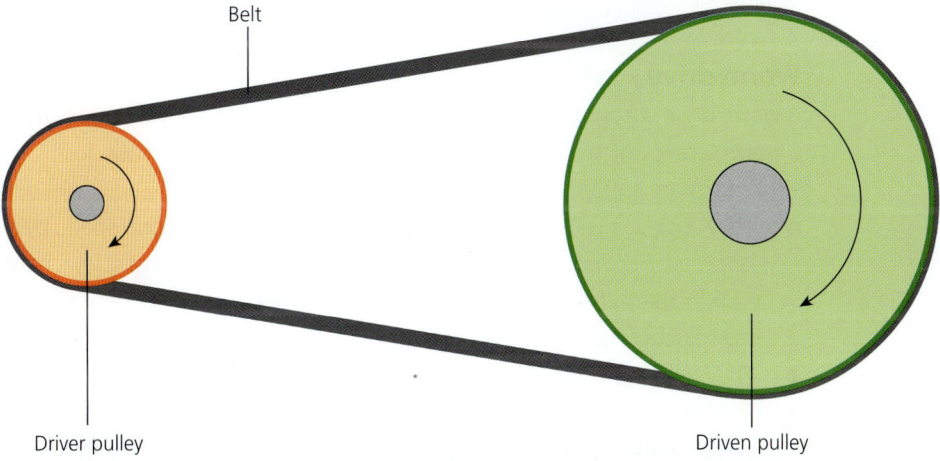

Belt

Driver pulley

Driven pulley

Figure 6.28 Transferring rotary motion with pulleys and a belt

For the purposes of calculations, **pulley and belt drive systems behave in exactly the same way as simple gear trains**, except that we replace the number of teeth on each gear with the **diameter** of each pulley. Therefore, the key equation is written:

(RV of input) × (diameter of input pulley) = (RV of output) × (diameter of output pulley)

In the same principle as a simple gear train, the rotational velocity of each pulley in a belt drive is inversely proportional to its diameter – the smaller pulley rotates faster than the larger pulley.

A pulley and belt drive will be very quiet in operation compared to gears, which tend to 'whine' or rumble.

Calculation

The pulley and belt drive shown in Figure 6.28 is being used to reduce the speed of a drive shaft. The input pulley is 60 mm in diameter and a velocity ratio of 3 is required. To calculate the diameter of the output pulley that is needed:

$$\text{Velocity ratio} = \frac{\text{diameter of output (driven) pulley}}{\text{diameter of input (driver) pulley}}$$

$$3 = \frac{\text{diameter of output (driven) pulley}}{60}$$

diameter of output pulley = 3 × 60 = 180 mm

Figure 6.29 Multiple belts and pulleys used to transfer rotary motion in an engine

Compound pulley system

A compound belt and pulley system consists of two or more simple pulley stages one after the other, just like a compound gear train, usually so that there is a very large overall velocity ratio:

Overall velocity ratio = (velocity ratio of stage 1) × (velocity ratio of stage 2)

Activity

With supervision from your teacher or a technician, look for examples of belt and pulley drive systems on machinery in your Design and Technology workshop. There is usually one on the bench drill, for example.

Worm drive

A **worm drive** is a unique type of gear system. The driver is a screw thread called a **worm screw**, which meshes with a **worm wheel** (which is like a spur gear). There are three important things to note about worm drives:

● They achieve a very high gear ratio, so they can reduce rotational speed by a large factor or increase torque by the same amount. Most worm screws have a single thread from end to end (known as a 'single start'). In these systems, the velocity ratio is simply the number of teeth on the worm wheel.

● They transfer the direction of rotation through 90°.

● They are self-locking, which means that the input shaft (the worm screw) can drive the output, but the output cannot drive the input. This feature can be useful in some applications, for example when it is important that the output does not slip if the input drive is turned off, such as in a winch or a lift mechanism.

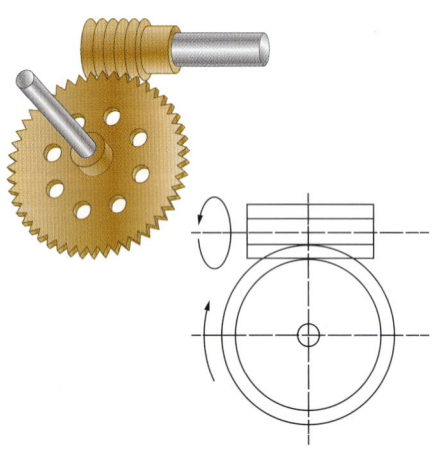

Figure 6.30 A worm drive

Figure 6.31 shows a worm drive mechanism inside an electric whisk. Note that the worm screw (which is rotated by the electric motor) drives two worm wheels which are attached to the two whisks. Can you work out why each worm wheel will rotate in opposite directions?

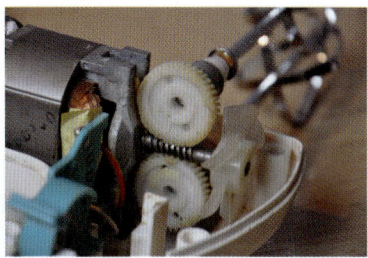

Figure 6.31 A worm drive inside an electric whisk

Calculation

An electric whisk uses a single start worm, and worm wheels each with 30 teeth.

To calculate the output speed of the whisks if the motor rotates at 12 000 rpm:

The velocity ratio of this system is simply equal to the number of teeth on the worm wheel.

velocity ratio = 30

$$\text{velocity ratio} = \frac{\text{RV of input}}{\text{RV of output}}$$

$$30 = \frac{12\,000}{\text{RV of output}}$$

$$\text{RV of output} = \frac{12\,000}{30} = 400 \text{ rpm}$$

Bevel gears

Bevel gears have their teeth cut at an angle and they are used when it is necessary to transfer the direction of the drive shaft by 90°. The velocity ratio is calculated in exactly the same way as for a simple gear train.

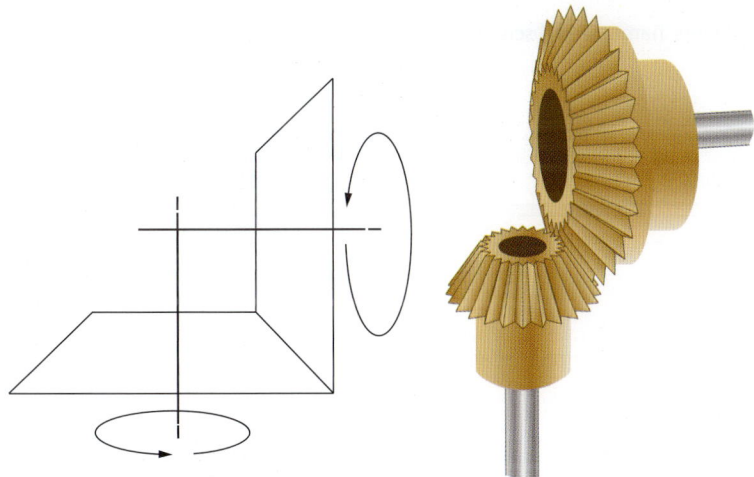

Figure 6.32 Bevel gears

Levers

Levers were introduced in Chapter 4, as a simple mechanism that can change forces and motion.

Depending on where the fulcrum is positioned relative to the effort and load, a lever can amplify force or can amplify distance moved, but it cannot do both at the same time – remember, there must be a trade-off. The position of the fulcrum can also result in effort and load moving in the same direction, or in opposite directions. There are three variations, or 'classes', of lever:

● In a first-class lever, the fulcrum is between the load and the effort. Examples include scissors, and a claw hammer extracting a nail.
● In a second-class lever, the load is between the effort and the fulcrum. Examples include a bottle opener and a nutcracker.
● In a third-class lever, the effort is between the load and the fulcrum. Examples include tweezers and a staple extractor.

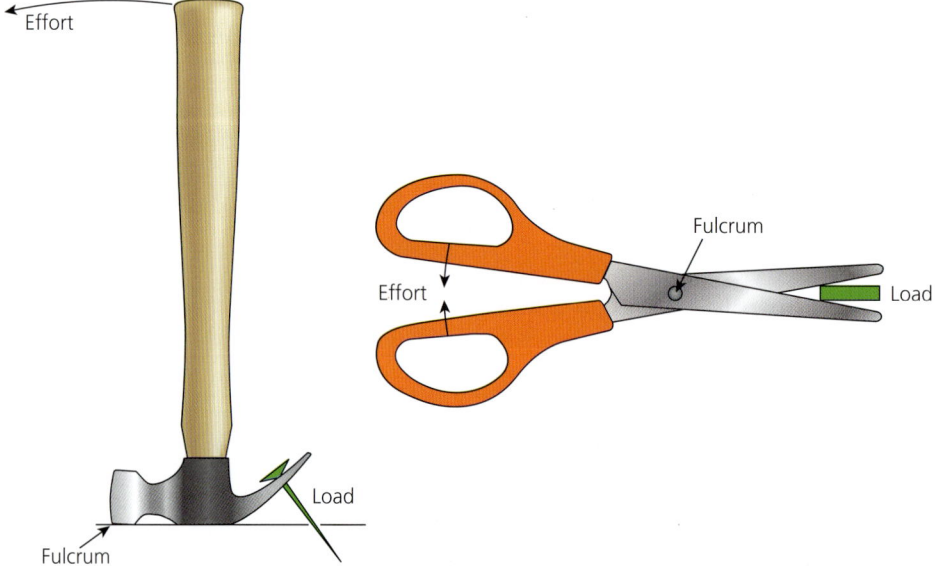

Figure 6.33 First-class levers: hammer and scissors

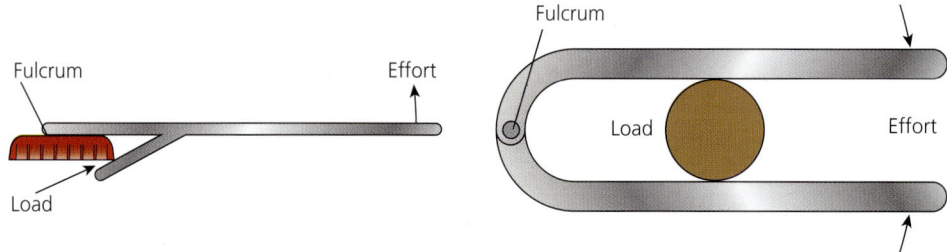

Figure 6.34 Second-class levers: bottle opener and nut cracker

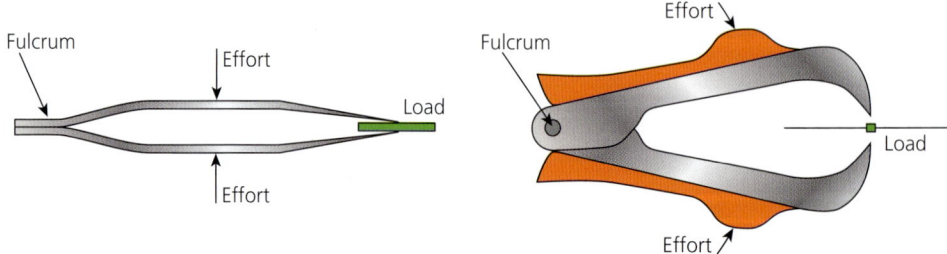

Figure 6.35 Third-class levers: tweezers and staple remover

Mechanical advantage (MA)

Another key term used in mechanical systems is **mechanical advantage**, which is the factor by which the system **increases** the force:

$$\text{Mechanical advantage} = \frac{\text{output force (load)}}{\text{input force (effort)}}$$

For a simple lever, the mechanical advantage is equal to the ratio of the input and output arm lengths:

$$\text{Mechanical advantage} = \frac{\text{input arm length}}{\text{output arm length}}$$

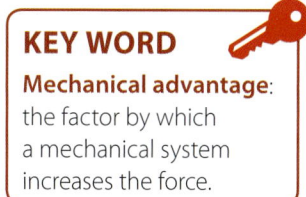

	Effect on an input force	Mechanical advantage	Effect on the input distance moved	Effect on the input direction moved
First class	Depends on input/output arm lengths	Depends on input/output arm lengths	Depends on input/output arm lengths	Reverses the direction
Second class	Amplifies	Greater than 1	Reduces the distance moved	Output moves in same direction
Third class	Reduces	Less than 1	Increases the distance moved	Output moves in same direction

Table 6.2 Classes of lever

Principle of moments

The forces acting on a lever can be calculated by using the principle of moments.

In a mechanical system:

moment = force × perpendicular distance to fulcrum

When the forces on a lever cause it to balance, the moment created by the effort is equal to the moment created by the load:

effort moment = load moment

Therefore:

(effort force) × (input arm length) = (load force) × (output arm length)

Other mechanical devices/systems

Rack and pinion

A **rack and pinion** was introduced in Chapter 4, as a system to change between rotary and linear motion.

Ratchet and pawl

A ratchet and pawl allows rotation in one direction only. The pawl prevents the ratchet from turning in the opposite direction. This mechanism is widely used in ratchet spanners, in turnstile systems, and in lifting mechanisms where the load must not fall after the lifting handle has been released.

The pawl can be moved away from the ratchet to allow free rotation if desired.

Crank and slider

A **crank and slider** was introduced in Chapter 4, as a system to convert between rotary and reciprocating motion. It is widely used in engines and machinery.

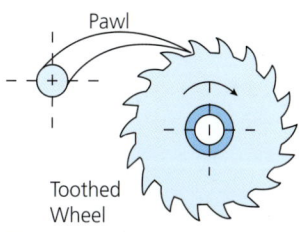

Figure 6.36 A ratchet and pawl

Cams

Cams were introduced in Chapter 4 as a mechanism for converting rotary to reciprocating motion. They are frequently used in engines, sewing machines and other products. The cam profile is designed so that it produces the required kind of reciprocating motion.

Activity

Find examples of all the mechanisms in this chapter. The best way is to photograph examples as you see them in use in products around you. Failing that, get images from the internet. Present your findings to your peer group. Use technical vocabulary and, where possible, calculate velocity ratios and mechanical advantages.

Ecological and social footprint

Changing society's view on waste

In Chapter 1, we learned how pressure from governments and consumers is forcing designers to produce products which have the minimum possible impact on the Earth's resources and ecosystems. Television and the internet have raised people's awareness of the problems created by our throwaway society, and consumers are becoming more conscious and concerned about what happens to products after they dispose of them.

Figure 6.37 Waste printed circuit boards ready to be recycled

Living in a greener world

Electronic and mechanical products may contain hundreds of different components and a wide range of raw materials, many of which will be toxic. Some of the hazardous materials used in electronic components include lead, cadmium, mercury, sulphuric acid and radioactive substances. If products are disposed of in normal waste they will go straight to landfill, where they will decompose and the hazardous materials will leak into the environment. This means they will get into the water system and potentially cause serious health problems for humans.

The average UK citizen will dispose of over 3 tonnes of electrical and electronic products in their lifetime. The **Waste Electrical and Electronic Equipment (WEEE) directive** now requires all manufacturers and producers to take responsibility for what happens to their products at the end of their lives. In practical terms, this means that retailers of electronic products must now provide a free take-back service for customers to hand in the unwanted product they are replacing. The retailer must then dispose of the products at an approved treatment facility. You may have spotted in your local supermarket the collection bin for old batteries – all battery retailers must now provide this take-back facility.

Local councils are also required to offer recycling facilities for electronic products. Some councils will collect old electronic devices when they empty the household refuse bins. There is significant value in some of the materials that can be recovered from electronic products, such as copper and gold, and entrepreneurial recyclers have been quick to spot this and develop ways to extract the valuable materials.

Recycling is only financially realistic if the product can be easily separated into its component materials. Redesigning existing products to make this possible inevitably raises the production costs which makes the products more expensive to buy. However, as more manufacturers move over to producing easily-recycled products, the costs are likely to fall again due to market competition between manufacturers. In the meantime, paying a little more for a greener product is something that environmentally-conscious consumers seem prepared to do.

The WEEE Man is a thought-provoking sculpture based at the Eden Project in Cornwall, constructed from the typical quantity of electronic products an average person will throw away in their lifetime.

Life cycle analysis of a product

The concept of a life cycle analysis was explained in Chapter 1.

Figure 6.38 The WEEE Man

> ### Activity
>
> Carry out a life cycle analysis on an electronic and/or mechanical product. Choose something simple, such as a torch, calculator or portable fan; these products generally have a limited lifetime. Ideally, you will be able to open the product to see what is inside.
>
> Carry out a life cycle analysis of the product as explained in Chapter 1.

Sustainable design

Electronic products quickly become obsolete. Some products become obsolete very quickly, such as mobile phones. Perhaps the software has become slow, or the battery does not last for long, or there is a new model now on sale. A product can also become obsolete if the manufacturer stops supporting it (for example, by no longer selling spare parts).

The point at which it is better for the environment to buy a new product rather than keep using an old one is called the breakeven point. The typical breakeven point for a mobile phone is 7 years, but the average user will exchange their phone for a new model after just 11 months.

In a **sustainable design** strategy, a designer will consider how to minimise the environmental impact caused by the continuous manufacture of rapidly updated products, such as mobile phones, so that the manufacturer can sustain the supply. Earth only has a finite supply of raw materials. A sustainable strategy ensures that new materials are always available and ensures that the useful materials in the discarded products are recovered for reuse, which also lowers the material costs. This **circular economy** is morally and financially the correct strategy, and it boosts the product image with environmentally-conscious consumers. Trade-in deals and upgrades also form part of a good business model to help encourage brand loyalty and help drive the sales of the latest products.

Fashion is a huge driver in product obsolescence. As long as there is a massive consumer demand for the newest model, the businesses will strive for their market share, which is why a sustainable design strategy is so important.

> ### KEY WORDS
>
> **Sustainable design**: product design which minimises the environmental impact of manufacturing and using the product.
>
> **Circular economy**: the idea of recovering the valuable resources from an obsolete product for use in a new product.

- Voltage, resistance and current in a circuit are related by Ohm's law.
- System diagrams are used to explain electronic systems in terms of input, process and output subsystems.
- The different input subsystems can create digital or analogue signals.
- A wide range of process subsystems are available to the electronic designer.
- Different process subsystems deal with digital or analogue signals, and some convert analogue to digital.
- Output subsystems contain a transducer which converts an electrical signal into a physical output.
- Rotary mechanisms trade-off torque against rotational velocity.
- Velocity ratios can be calculated for simple and compound rotational systems.
- A wide range of rotational gear and drive systems are available to the mechanical designer.
- Levers can be categorised into three classes.
- Mechanical advantage relates the output force to the input force in a mechanical system.
- In a lever, moment = force × perpendicular distance from fulcrum.
- Designers have a responsibility to help protect the environment through good design.
- Designers can help to change society's view on waste and encourage recycling.
- Sustainable design involves minimising environmental impact so that manufacturers can sustain the supply of rapidly updated products.

6.2 The way in which the selection of materials or components is influenced by a range of factors

A designer will be faced with multiple factors when selecting components and materials, all of which should be considered before a final choice is made.

- Function – the first thing is to identify what the component needs to do in the system, such as choosing a resistor in an electronic circuit or a spur gear in a rotational mechanism. Following this, the designer may use calculations to select a specific component value (for example, a 680 Ω resistor, or a 40-tooth spur gear). For some components there will be further functional considerations, such as choosing the material the spur gear is made from, or the method by which it will be locked to a drive shaft. These decisions will be influenced by the needs of the application, and the need for compatibility with other components in the system.
- Aesthetic – if the material is on show, then its appearance may be of importance, such as using a brushed aluminium control panel in preference to a plastic panel to create an expensive, high-quality appearance.

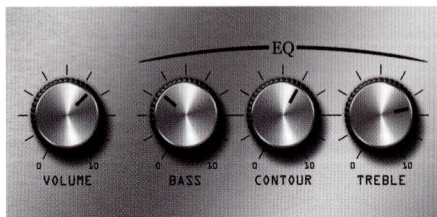

Figure 6.39 A brushed aluminium control panel

- Environmental – some designs will be exposed to a wide range of environmental factors, such as dirt, water or extremes of temperature. The outside environment is very harsh and the product will be exposed to rain, ice, temperature extremes and long periods of sunlight. The materials and any internal components need to be able to operate in these conditions.
- Availability – sometimes a supplier is out of stock of a particular component, or they only have limited stocks, which means that a manufacturer may not be able to manufacture a batch of products in the desired quantity.
- Cost – a designer needs to be constantly aware of the ongoing costs of a design as it develops.
- Social, cultural and ethical issues – this is covered in the section below.

Some factors will be more important than others in a given design and, in many cases, it will be necessary to compromise and use the component or material that best fits the above factors.

Components and their functional benefits or limitations

Electronic components are extremely reliable as long as they are operated within their limits. The **rating** of a component is the maximum value of a specified quantity the component can handle. If this value is exceeded, the component will be damaged, perhaps instantly, or the component may continue to work but its life expectancy will be drastically reduced. Sometimes, the manufacturer will state that it is permissible to exceed the rating briefly.

Some electronic components have a limited lifespan. Rechargeable batteries are one example; after several hundred charge–discharge cycles the battery's capacity reduces to the point where it may not be able to hold enough charge to usefully power the product for a long period. You may have noticed such problems with your mobile phone or laptop battery.

Mechanical components generally have shorter lifespans because moving parts always involve some degree of friction, which causes wear. Higher-quality mechanical components will use harder-wearing materials that last longer, and provision may be made for servicing mechanical parts, such as renewing lubrication or changing individual parts that are known to wear quickly. Mechanical components that are operated within their design ratings should have a long and predictable life cycle.

Miniaturisation

The manufacturing methods used to produce an electronic prototype in a school workshop are different to those used at larger scales of production.

The printed circuit boards (PCBs) produced industrially for modern products differ from school made PCBs in that they are usually double-sided and have copper tracks on both the top and bottom of the board. This allows more complex designs to be achieved without the problem of tracks crossing each other. In fact, many modern PCBs are multi-layered, and these can be thought of as several thin single-sided boards laminated together. Multi-layered boards allow highly complex circuits to be constructed in a very compact space. They are used in products such as mobile phones.

Electronic prototypes made in a school workshop will generally use through-hole components which sit on one side of the PCB and their wires pass through the board to be soldered on the reverse side. Industrially produced electronic products use **surface mount technology (SMT)**, where the components do not have wires and are placed directly on and soldered to the surface of the PCB.

Some of the resistors and capacitors used in SMT are less than a millimetre in size and they are placed on to the PCB by a pick-and-place machine. The components are temporarily held in place by a sticky solder paste. These machines operate at astonishing speed, typically placing five or more components per second. The PCB is then passed through a reflow solder oven, in which the board is raised to a temperature high enough to melt the solder paste.

Surface mount technology permits highly complex circuits to be miniaturised, which is essential for portable products such as mobile

KEY WORDS

Rating: the maximum value of a specified quantity that a component can handle.

Surface mount technology (SMT): the industrial method of using robotic assembly to manufacture miniaturised electronic circuit boards.

Figure 6.40 A SMT PCB showing an IC, resistors and capacitors

The only way to keep a rectangular framework rigid is to make the corner joints very strong, for example by using large screws, strong adhesive or welds. This is the only practical method in some designs, but a better approach is to design the frame using **triangulation**, which is where the frame is composed of triangles rather than rectangles.

A triangular frame cannot change its shape – it is naturally rigid and does not rely on the stiffness of the joints to keep its shape. Adding a diagonal **cross-member** across a rectangular frame creates two triangles and this makes it become a naturally stable framework.

If a design prevents a full cross-member being used, then **gusset plates** can be used to achieve a partial approach to triangulation and, therefore, increase the rigidity of the framework.

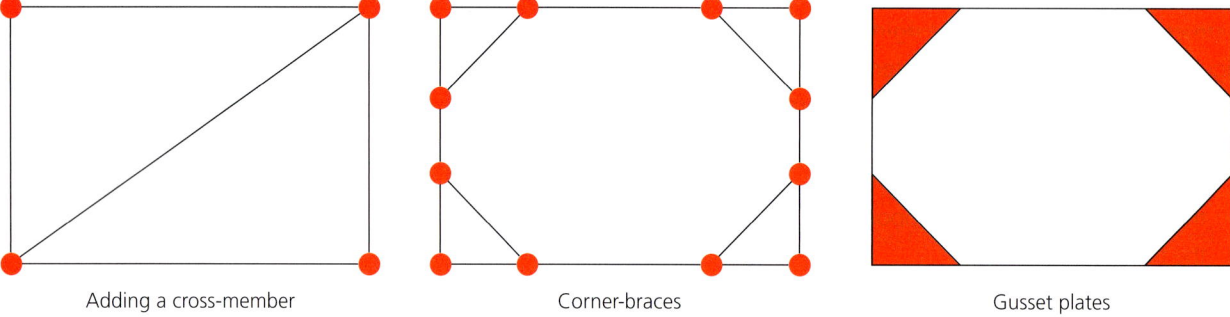

Adding a cross-member   Corner-braces   Gusset plates

Figure 6.46 Methods of triangulating a framework to increase its rigidity

Casing and protecting electronic components

Electronic systems are usually housed in a case of some kind, often because the circuit board, batteries and other components need to be hidden for aesthetic reasons. However, a casing may also be used for functional reasons, to provide structural support for the product and/or to protect the components inside from the environment.

Water ingress can be extremely damaging to electronic and mechanical products, and it is very difficult to make a product fully waterproof. However, by careful design, it may be possible to make the product 'splashproof' and more durable at withstanding accidental

Figure 6.47 Splashproof covers on a control panel

Figure 6.48 Waterproof seal on a sports camera case

splashes, such as may occur in a kitchen, for example. Figure 6.47 shows the control panel of PCB chemical tanks. Notice the flexible plastic covers over the rocker switches and the clear plastic splash-screen over the entire control panel.

It may be tempting to try to completely seal the casing of a product using adhesive so that water cannot enter, but this needs balancing with the need to open the case to service the device and change batteries, etc. A better solution would be to use a rubber seal at the point where the case parts join. A suitable seal in a GCSE project would be the self-adhesive rubber strip used to seal against draughts around doors.

For very demanding, fully waterproof solutions it will probably be necessary to purchase a waterproof 'project case' and place the system inside this. Remember, however, that whenever a hole is drilled in the case for cables, switches, etc., then the waterproofness may be compromised.

Activity

1   Find five examples of products that use hollow or angled cross-section pieces to achieve rigidity. Photograph the examples and annotate the photos to explain your findings. You may need to look carefully to find examples; remember that, in many products, hollow tubes or box sections will have plastic end caps to finish the product nicely – these end caps are a clue that the material is hollow!

2   Find and photograph five examples of products that feature indents or ribs to achieve rigidity. You may need to look inside or underneath the products, as ribs are often hidden because they spoil the aesthetics of a smooth, flat surface.

3   Find five examples where cross-members have been used to achieve triangulation in a framework. Photograph and annotate your findings. Look for large-scale frameworks in towers and buildings, but also for smaller examples around your house or school.

KEY POINTS
- A structure is a collection of members which provide support against forces.
- The rigidity of a member depends on various factors.
- Sheet materials can be made more rigid by adding folds, indents or ribs.
- Frameworks can be made more rigid by triangulation.
- Electronic and mechanical systems need protection from harsh environments.

6.4 Stock forms, types and sizes in order to calculate and determine the quantity of materials or components required

Standard stock electronic component sizes

Many electronic components that are used in schools have pins which are designed to fit on a 2.54 mm (0.1 inch) grid. This standardised pin spacing means that designers can confidently design printed circuit boards knowing that the component pins will fit through the holes drilled in the PCB. If you use a prototyping board (breadboard) for building electronic circuits, you will be very familiar with the 2.54 mm (0.1 inch) grid spacing for the holes.

In addition to the standard physical dimensions of components, resistors, capacitors and some other components are manufactured in certain specific values, called preferred values. This is covered in section 6.1.

Dual-in-line standard for electronic ICs

Integrated circuits (ICs) that are used for prototyping have pinouts which match the 2.54 mm (0.1 inch) grid. The standard IC package is known as dual-in-line (DIL), referring to the two parallel rows of pins. Figure 6.49 shows 8-pin and 18-pin DIL ICs.

One end of the DIL package has a notch, and pin number 1 is to the left of this notch. Pin 1 is also sometimes indicated by a small dot on the case. It is vital that you correctly identify pin 1 by looking for the case markings – applying power to an IC the wrong way round is very likely to destroy it! In Figure 6.50 notice how all the other pins are numbered anticlockwise from pin 1.

Figure 6.49 DIL ICs

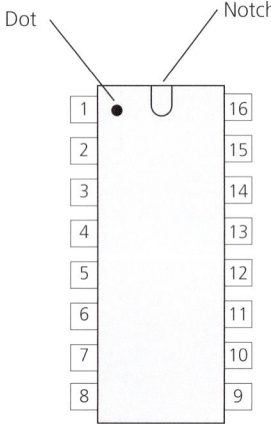

Figure 6.50 DIL pin numbering

When building a prototype PCB, it is good practice to solder in DIL sockets for each IC. Once the PCB assembly is complete, the ICs are then plugged into their sockets. Using IC sockets has the following advantages:

- It avoids soldering the IC pins, which can overheat and damage the IC.
- ICs can easily be removed for testing, or if they have failed, or if they have accidentally been inserted the wrong way round.
- Some ICs are sensitive to static electricity, so they can be left in their protective package until just before they need to be inserted.

The disadvantages of using DIL sockets are that they increase costs slightly and take up a little more space on the PCB.

Not all IC packages are DIL. Many modern ICs are designed for SMT robotic manufacturing methods (see Section 6.2) and there are a large range of package sizes and pin spacings. The IC in Figure 6.40 has pins on all four sides with a spacing of 0.8 mm. Some of these ICs are available on **breakout boards** which convert the SMT package to a DIL package. This is more convenient for prototyping, although it increases the effective size of the package.

Stock materials for the manufacture of products

In addition to using a range of electronic and mechanical components, you will also need to use conventional materials to manufacture casings, chassis, linkages, and other special parts when producing your GCSE projects.

It is necessary to know the **stock forms** that are available for you to use. Knowing the sizes and shapes of materials that are available means that you will design your project around the materials, which is much more efficient than trying to find and modify non-standard materials to fit your design.

> **KEY WORD**
>
> **Stock form**: the standard shapes and sizes of materials that are commonly available.

Woods

Wood materials are available as lengths of natural timber or as sheets of manufactured boards. For use as a structural material, a low-cost softwood such as Scots pine will usually suffice. Timber is available in standard sections which are strips, squares, boards and planks; see Chapter 5 Figure 5.6. For further information on types of timber, see Chapter 8.

For electronic and mechanical products, you will probably want to use timber that has been planed all round (PAR) as this has a smoother surface which is usually more useful in an engineered product and has a better aesthetic. It is worth noting that the specified dimensions of PAR timber are usually the measurements of the rough sawn timber before it is planed smooth. Consequently, the actual sizes of PAR will be about 3 mm less on every surface, so a quoted cross-section of 75 mm × 25 mm will actually measure about 69 mm × 19 mm.

It is important to remember that timber is a natural material, so its properties will vary between batches and it may twist or warp as the weather changes.

Manufactured board is very useful for chassis in engineered products as it provides a large, rigid base on which to mount other components. Engineered boards are much more stable than timber. Plywood and MDF (medium-density fibreboard) are both available in a range of standard thicknesses from about 2 mm up to 25 mm. A full sheet measures 2440 mm × 1220 mm, although these are often cut down to make them more manageable in schools.

Dowel is a solid round rod of wood, available in a variety of diameters up to about 25 mm. Apart from its use in wood joints, dowel is useful in mechanical projects for axles, linkages, pivots, etc.

Metals

The metal materials most useful for manufacturing parts in an engineered project are mild steel, aluminium and brass. Other metals, such as copper or stainless steel, are also used, but for more specialist applications.

Steel is a ferrous metal, therefore it is magnetic and prone to rusting. Aluminium and brass are non-ferrous, they are not magnetic and will not rust so they will be safe to use in a wet, outdoor environment without any special finishing treatment. Aluminium is relatively lightweight for its strength and brass has a good aesthetic finish.

All these metals are available as sheets. The thickness of a metal sheet is sometimes called its gauge, and a variety of standard thicknesses (gauges) are available, for example, 0.7 mm, 1.6 mm, 2.0 mm.

Commonly used metals are available as long bars of various profiles, as shown in Figure 6.51. Section 6.3 explains why different cross-section profiles might be used to achieve structural rigidity.

For more details of types of metals, see Chapter 9.

Polymers

There is a wide range of polymers for use in schools. Most are thermoforming polymers, which means they soften when heated and can be formed into shape. Various stock forms are available:

- Sheets – these come in a range of standard thicknesses. They are useful for vacuum forming, laser cutting and line bending amongst other uses.
- Foamed – these can be sheets (such as Plastazote) which are very lightweight and rigid, or blocks (such as Styrofoam) which are popular for sculpting 3D models.
- Extruded sections – these include rods, tubes and a variety of other shapes that have a continuous profile.
- Reels – lengths of polymer 'wire' are popular for feeding 3D printers.
- Powders – powdered polymers can be used to coat metals with a plastic finish.
- Granules – not used much in schools, but in industrial manufacturing they are used in various moulding processes.

For more on different forms of polymers, see Chapter 10.

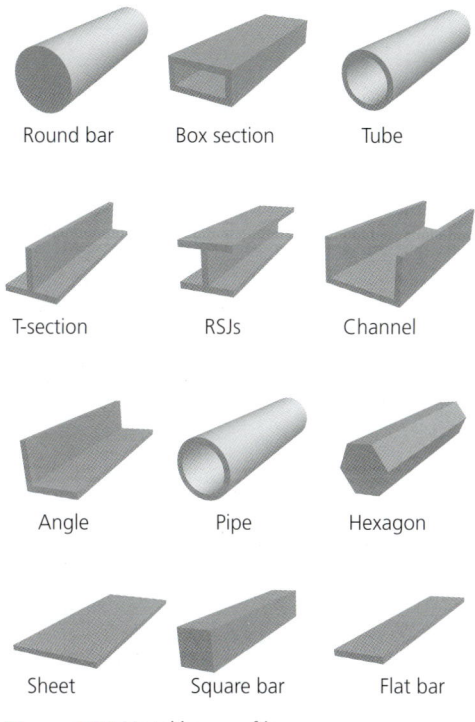

Round bar   Box section   Tube

T-section   RSJs   Channel

Angle   Pipe   Hexagon

Sheet   Square bar   Flat bar

Figure 6.51 Metal bar profiles

Activity

Produce a chart of the stock forms that are kept in stock in your school's Design and Technology store. Narrow down your task to either wood, metal or polymer. Photograph the different stock forms and measure them. Present your findings on one side of A4.

Calculate cost of materials and components for products

The following stages are carried out to calculate the cost of materials that you use in a project:

i   Find the cost of a full length (or a full sheet).
ii Calculate the cost per unit length (or unit area).
iii Measure the length (or calculate the area) you have used.
iv Calculate the cost.

Calculation

A 2.4 m length of PSE timber costs £8.40. To calculate the cost of using 600 mm of this timber:

i   Cost of a 2.4 m length is £8.40.

ii Cost per m is $\frac{8.40}{2.4}$ = £3.50.

iii Length used is 600 mm, which is 0.6 m.

iv Cost of timber = 3.50 × 0.6 = £2.10.

A sheet of plywood measures 2440 mm × 1220 mm. The cost of the sheet is £27.40. A piece measuring 200 mm × 150 mm is cut from the sheet. To calculate the cost of this piece:

i   Cost of sheet is £27.40.

ii Surface area of sheet (in m²) is 2.44 × 1.22 = 2.9768 m².

Cost per m² is $\frac{27.40}{2.9768}$ = £9.20

iii Surface area of piece used (in m²) is 0.2 × 0.15 = 0.03m².

iv Cost of piece = 9.20 × 0.03 = £0.276 = 28p (to the nearest penny).

KEY POINTS
- Many electronic components have pins on a standard 2.54 mm (0.1 inch) grid.
- Many ICs feature a dual-in-line (DIL) package design.
- Woods, metals and polymers are available in stock forms for use in projects.
- It is necessary to calculate the cost of materials used, given the price per length or per sheet.

6.5 Alternative processes that can be used to manufacture products to different scales of production

A project's design brief and initial market research will determine how many products need to be manufactured. The method of manufacture will be directly influenced by the scale and speed of production required.

One-off production

One-off prototypes are quite common in electronic and mechanical design, for example a **bespoke** control system for part of a manufacturing process. A one-off design is usually expensive because the designer needs to receive payment for their time spent developing the prototype as there will not be any future product sales to bring in a long-term income. The designer may spend significant time on the iterative development of the product until it functions to the client's satisfaction.

One-off production usually involves a high degree of manufacturing skill, much of which may be carried out manually. In some cases, manufacturing may be contracted out to specialists, adding to the costs. Rapid prototyping may be useful for manufacturing bespoke parts, and software for a microcontroller will need to be written and developed.

Batch production

For a scale of production that is beyond a few items, a manufacturer will organise the production in a more efficient way. The exact manufacturing process will depend on the product and the manufacturing facilities. Generally, the manufacturer will focus on producing an entire batch of products in one go. Once the batch is complete, the manufacturer may then switch production to an entirely different product.

The production will be organised to make the most efficient use of the machinery available and the skills of the workers. In the case of manufacturing a small batch of a simple mechanical product, this might be:

- Day 1: The entire factory manufactures chassis parts.
- Day 2: The chassis are assembled.
- Day 3: The final components are added.
- Day 4: Product testing.
- Day 5: Packaging and dispatch.

This approach requires every member of staff to be skilled in carrying out all the processes, because every worker must be kept busy every day. This might be the case in a smaller factory, but in a larger manufacturing plant staff tend to have skills in certain areas so the manufacturing would be organised differently.

Batch production describes the way the manufacturer organises the production and the fact that a target quantity is agreed before manufacturing starts. There is no limit on batch size. A larger, more complex product may be manufactured in a batch of ten, while a simpler product may be produced in a batch of 10 000.

Mass production

Mass production involves the manufacture of very large numbers of products. Such manufacture is typical for commonly used components such as screws, connectors, batteries, etc. Mass producers are usually specialist manufacturers that have invested large sums in machinery capable of producing large volumes of parts, with repeatability and reliability being important. Once the production is underway it is often most cost-effective to leave machinery running continuously, with staff working shifts to monitor the process. This is called **continuous flow production**, where production continues 24 hours per day, 7 days a week. The sheer scale of production and economies of scale mean that mass production is the cheapest method of manufacture.

Just-in-time manufacturing

A manufacturer that is producing a product batch will need to order materials and components that are specific to that product. Consequently, for production to start on day one, the manufacturer relies on receiving delivery of the materials just before manufacturing starts. They will not want to take delivery of materials too early because this causes problems storing them. The materials are ordered to arrive just in time for manufacturing to commence.

Activity

Reorganise the five-day manufacture of the mechanical product described above for a factory in which some workers are skilled only at manufacturing, some are skilled only at assembling, and others are skilled only at testing and packaging.

Just-in-time (JIT) manufacturing depends on reliable suppliers that will deliver on time, because a missed delivery will hold up the entire production. In practice, the process works surprisingly well, as every part of the supply chain realises that their reputation depends on meeting production promises.

Manufacturers are usually keen to ship out the products as soon as they are completed, as this clears the factory ready for the next production run to commence. The whole JIT process is aimed at producing efficient 'flow' through the factory.

The use of CAD/CAM in production

Electronic and mechanical designers make use of digital technologies that can link to various CAM machines to aid the manufacture of systems. 2D CAD software can output cutting information to a laser cutter, allowing sheet materials to be repeatedly cut to accurate dimensions and intricate shapes.

Other industrial sheet material cutting machines include plasma cutters, CNC routers and vinyl cutters. All perform a similar job, but each one is suited to machining different materials and different sheet sizes.

A CNC lathe is used for producing cylindrically-shaped parts, directly from a CAD drawing.

The electronic system in many prototypes is built on a PCB. Designing the PCB copper track pattern can be quite tricky as the components need to be laid out so that the tracks do not cross over each other. PCB design software uses an **autorouting** function to achieve this. The PCBs in modern electronic appliances such as computers and mobile phones are so complex that they could not possibly be designed without the aid of PCB design software.

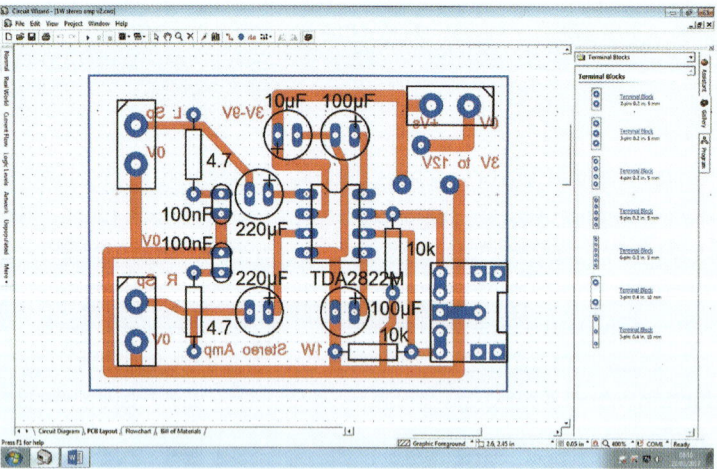

Figure 6.52 A PCB track pattern

Once the PCB design is complete, the software will print out the track pattern artwork on to a translucent film, which is then used to produce the actual PCB. Alternatively, the software can output to a CNC engraver which will create the track pattern directly onto a sheet of copper coated board by removing the unwanted copper.

During the designing stages of an engineered project, a custom-designed part is sometimes needed, such as a mechanical linkage, or a motor bracket. Such parts can be manufactured by hand in the workshop using machine tools and hand tools, but the advent of rapid prototyping has meant that a usable part can be designed using CAD software and then produced in a matter of minutes or hours using a 3D printer.

Jigs and devices to control repeat activities

During manufacturing, when the same task needs to be carried out more than once, it is important to consider how to achieve repeatability. A **jig** or a **fixture** is a device which is made specifically for a certain manufacturing task. Figure 6.54 shows the principle of a sawing jig which will guide the saw so that the tube is always cut to the same length. The drilling fixture in Figure 6.55 is clamped to the table of a bench drill. It will then hold the strips of wood in exactly the right place while they are drilled. Fixtures can also be used to hold materials in position while they are glued or welded together.

Templates are useful for repeated marking out of shapes onto materials which are then cut out. When bending materials to shape, the material is bent around a **former** to ensure that the correct shape or bend angle is achieved.

Figure 6.53 PCB engraving

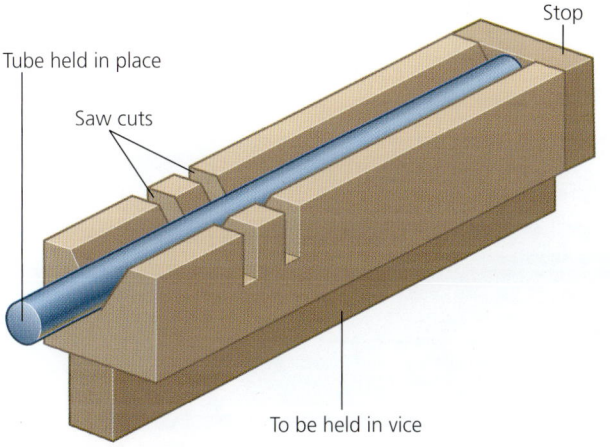

Figure 6.54 A sawing jig

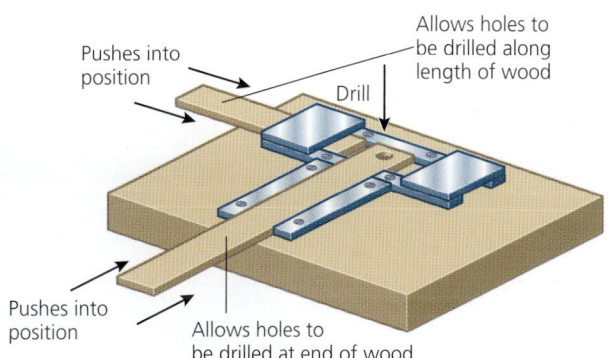

Figure 6.55 A drilling fixture

6.6 Specialist techniques and processes that can be used to shape, fabricate, construct a high-quality prototype

Wastage/addition

Marking out

Marking-out tools are very basic pieces of equipment. As a minimum you will need:

- a steel rule to measure length
- a try-square or engineer's square to mark right angles
- a method of making a mark on the material, such as a pencil, fine line marker pen or a scriber.

Other instruments such as a compass, protractor, mitre-square, etc. are useful for marking more complex shapes.

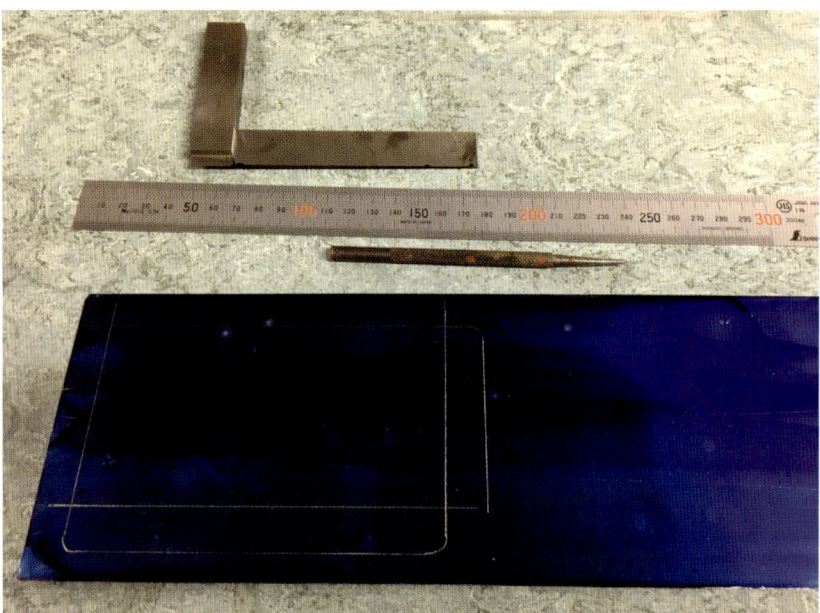

Figure 6.56 Marking-out tools

Holding and cutting

The bench vice is the first choice for holding materials while they are being cut. However, it is frequently necessary to vary the holding method depending on the material and the type of cut being made. A bench hook, clamped into a vice, can be used to support timber while it is being cut. G-cramps can be used to hold a material firmly against a workbench so that it can be cut or processed.

The choice of saw depends on the material and whether the cut is straight or curved.

Hand cutting tools:

- Tenon saw – a general purpose wood saw for straight cuts.
- Coping saw – a thin blade saw for curved cuts in wood or polymer.
- Hacksaw – for cuts through metal. A junior hacksaw has a shorter, thinner blade which produces finer cuts.
- Tin snips – for cutting thin sheet metal. Similar to a pair of scissors.
- Nibbler (or notcher) – for cutting sheet metal. These can be hand-held or bench mounted. Bench shears perform a similar task.

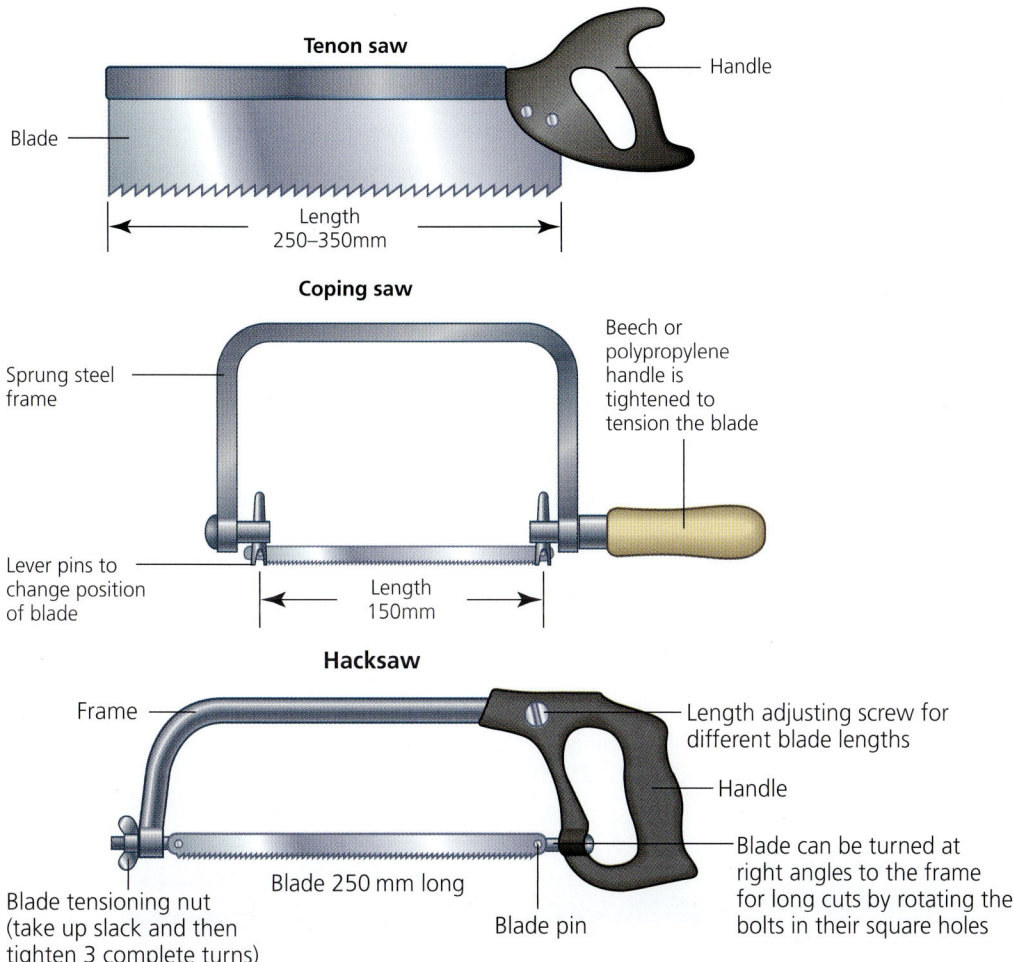

Tenon saw

Handle

Blade

Length
250–350mm

Coping saw

Beech or
polypropylene
handle is
tightened to
tension the blade

Sprung steel
frame

Lever pins to
change position
of blade

Length
150mm

Hacksaw

Frame

Length adjusting screw for
different blade lengths

Handle

Blade can be turned at
right angles to the frame
for long cuts by rotating the
bolts in their square holes

Blade tensioning nut
(take up slack and then
tighten 3 complete turns)

Blade 250 mm long

Blade pin

Figure 6.57 Tenon saw, coping saw and hacksaw

Machine cutting tools:

● Scroll saw (or fretsaw) – bench mounted with a thin reciprocating blade for making curved cuts in wood or polymers.
● Bandsaw – a larger machine with a continuous moving blade for straight and curved cuts in most materials.

Shaping

Files are used to remove material. They can be used on wood, metal or polymer. Files are named according to their shape, size, and cut (coarseness). Information about files can be found in Chapter 9.

The flat file can be used on flat and convex edges. For filing a concave edge, a half-round or rat-tail file must be used.

Smaller files, known as needle files, are useful for intricate work. The coarsest files, for removing material quickly, are rough or bastard cut. Second cut are medium files for general purpose work, and smooth files are for final finishing.

A sanding machine can also be used for shaping wood and polymer.

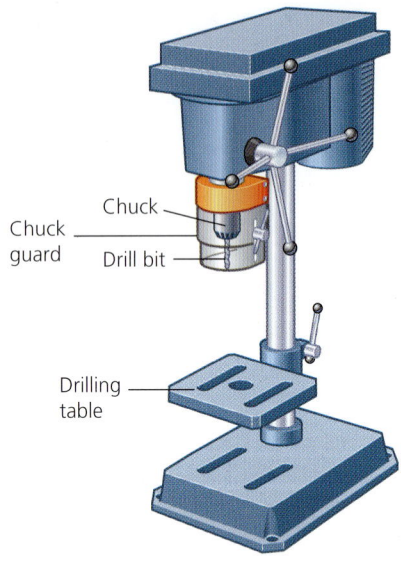

Chuck guard

Chuck

Drill bit

Drilling table

Figure 6.58 Bench drill

Drilling

The battery-operated cordless drill is widely used in workshops. Its keyless chuck means that drill bits can be quickly changed. Clamp your work when using a cordless drill, and make sure that the drill is **always** switched to 'forwards', so that the chuck rotates clockwise. You should **never** switch to reverse when drilling.

For more accurate drilling, or for larger holes, the pillar drill (bench drill) will be used. Work should be clamped to the drilling table where possible, and the depth of the hole can be set by adjusting a stop on the drill. A chuck key is usually required to open/close the chuck when changing drill bits. A safety guard around the chuck reduces the chance of the operator's hair getting caught in the spinning chuck.

For drilling holes straight through, a piece of scrap wood is needed under the material. Large diameter holes should first be drilled with a smaller pilot drill, and then drilled out with the final size drill.

Various drill bits are available:

- Twist drills are the most used bits for general purpose drilling.
- Forstner bits drill a flat-bottomed hole.
- Flat bits are useful for large holes in wood.
- Hole saws are useful for cutting very large diameter holes up to about 75 mm.
- A cone cutter drills holes which get wider the further the cutter is pushed into the work.

Jigs and formers

See Section 6.5.

Deforming/reforming

Bending polymers

Thermoforming polymers such as HIPS or acrylic become soft when heated. They can then be bent into shape around a former and held in place while they cool, after which they will hold their new shape.

Line bending involves heating a narrow strip of a thermoforming polymer, such as acrylic (PMMA), using a strip heater machine. The polymer can then be bent to the required angle around a former.

Drape forming is used for larger curves. A sheet of a thermoforming polymer, such as high-impact polystyrene (HIPPS), is heated in an oven. Once soft, it is removed (wearing heatproof gloves) and then draped around a former. A piece of cloth is used to pull the tightly against the former until it cools.

Vacuum forming

Thin sheets of HIPS (or acrylic) can be formed into complex shapes by vacuum forming. A former of the required shape is made from any material which is resilient to the heat of the forming process. The shape of the former needs careful thought in order that it will easily release from the moulded polymer, so it can be reused. The edges of the former are tapered towards the top with a draft angle, and sharp corners are rounded-off so they do not puncture the softened polymer sheet. For deep 'draws', vent holes may need to be drilled through the former.

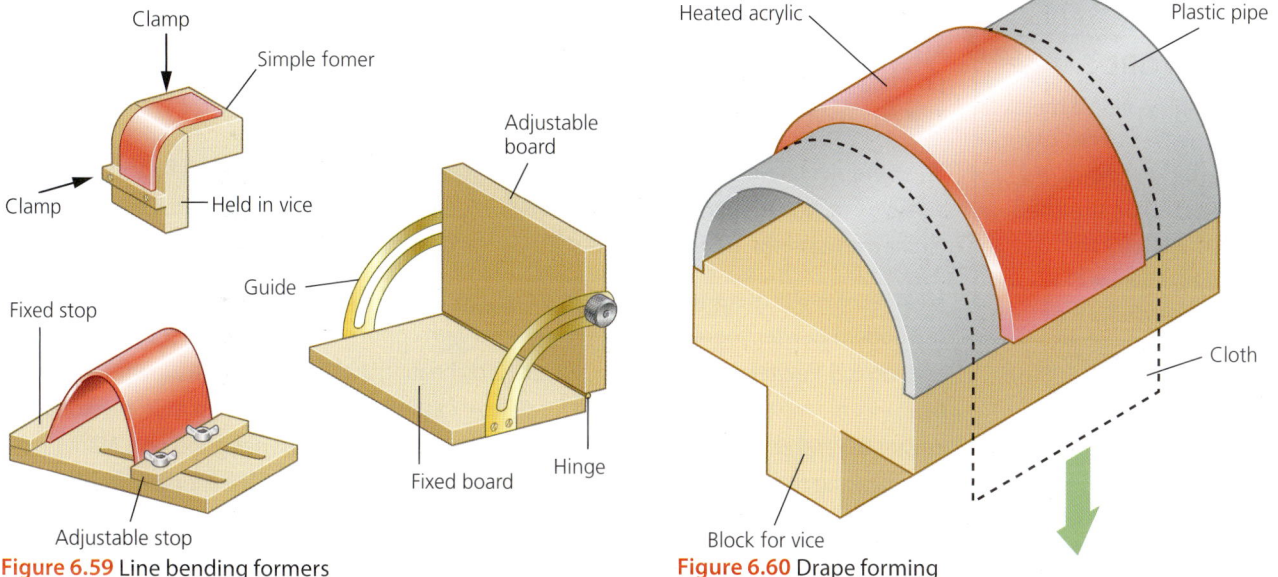

Figure 6.59 Line bending formers

Figure 6.60 Drape forming

The process is described in Figure 6.62. Once the polymer sheet is hot and soft, the former is raised and an air pump is switched on which removes the air underneath the sheet. The air pressure on top of the sheet then presses the soft polymer around the former. Once cool, the former is removed and the polymer form is cut out from the sheet.

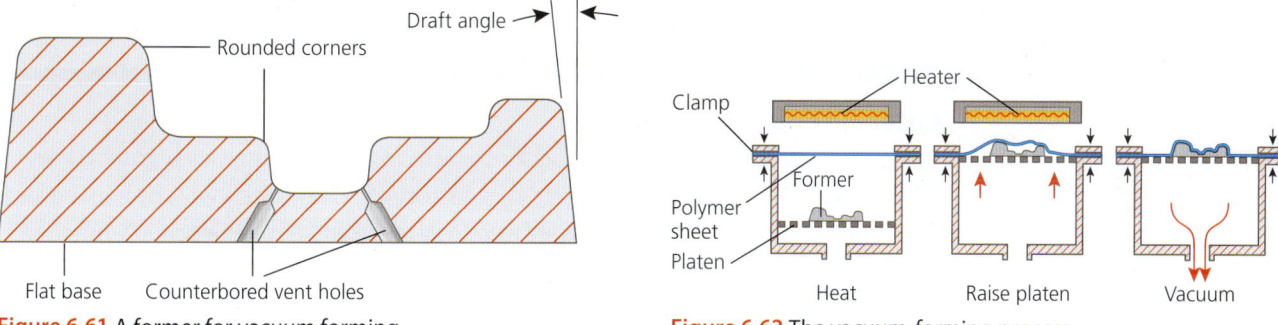

Figure 6.61 A former for vacuum forming

Figure 6.62 The vacuum-forming process

Hot/cold working of metals

Many designs require thin metal sheets to be folded (bent) into shape. Small sheets can be folded in a bench vice, using a hammer to get a sharp bend. Many types of metal folding tools are available, and many school workshops have a bench-mounted sheet-metal working machine which can accurately fold sheet metal to a desired angle. Some of these machines can also cut and punch holes, and press-roll the metal sheets to create smooth curves.

Bending metal can cause it to become hard and brittle. For single folds in thin sheets, this is not normally a problem, but when thicker bars are bent there is a risk that the bar will crack on the bend. This can be eliminated by heating the metal and bending it while hot. The heat **anneals** the metal which increases its **ductility** (elasticity). Once bent, the metal is allowed to cool naturally.

Figure 6.63 A metal folding machine

Casting

Metals will melt into a liquid state if heated to a high temperature. Once molten, they can be poured into moulds and allowed to cool, after which the solid metal part can be removed. This process is called casting.

Brass and steel have a very high melting point (1000°C and above) and this is far too high to achieve in schools. Aluminium melts at 660°C, and some schools have the equipment to make aluminium castings. However, this is still a dangerously high temperature.

Pewter is a useful metal for casting in schools. Traditionally, pewter is an **alloy** of tin and lead (in modern pewter, the lead has been replaced with copper and antimony – see RoHS in Section 6.2). Pewter will melt at around 230°C by heating it in a ladle using a blowtorch, or in an electric melting pot. The mould for pewter casting can be made from MDF, plywood, plaster of Paris, or even cardboard. In school, such moulds are often designed on CAD software and then cut using a CNC milling machine or a laser cutter. The mould is made in two halves which are clamped together.

After the casting is removed, the sprue (the piece where the mould was filled) is cut off with a hacksaw, and the casting is finished with files and wet and dry paper to achieve a smooth, shiny surface.

Turning

A lathe is used for producing cylindrical parts. The material is clamped in a chuck and rotated at speed. Cutting tools are then applied to the surface of the rotating material to produce the desired shape. Components such as drive shafts, wheels, collars, knobs, etc. can all be produced on a lathe. On a metal lathe, the cutting tools are clamped in a tool stock and moved using hand wheels. On a wood lathe, the cutting tools are normally hand-held.

Laser cutting

Laser cutters are 2D manufacturing machines which cut and engrave a variety of thin sheet materials such as polymers, wood sheets, card, textiles, etc. Laser cutters work by burning and vapourising the material. Laser cutters are extremely useful and popular in schools, but they require many adjustments if good results are to be achieved:

- The laser power and speed of cut needs to be matched to the thickness and type of material.
- The laser beam needs to be focussed onto the top surface of the material.
- The sheet material must be completely flat across its entire surface.
- The mirror system which directs the laser beam onto the material must be kept clean and aligned.

There is no requirement to clamp the material while it is being cut. A laser cutter produces a very good finished edge when cutting most polymers.

3D printing

3D printing opens unique design opportunities and solves some of the problems with other forms of manufacture. A 3D printed design starts with a 3D CAD model. The printer then builds up the 3D object by depositing several 2D layers. The printing material is usually polymer, but can also be metal, ceramic or even food.

KEY WORDS

Anneal: heating a metal to increase its elasticity.

Ductile: the ability of a material to be stretched out.

Alloy: a mixture of two or more metals.

Figure 6.64 Pewter casting

3D printing technology can produce sophisticated parts in hours for very little cost. This is useful when developing prototype parts, but it is also ideal for creating bespoke, one-off designs.

Assembly and components

Temporary material joining methods

Nuts, bolts and screws

These components are used to mechanically hold two parts together.

When using a nut and bolt, a **clearance hole** is drilled through both parts. The bolt slides through the parts and the nut is screwed on and tightened to squeeze the parts together. A washer is often used under the nut to spread the pressure over a greater area. Bolts are labelled according to their diameter and length, e.g. an M6 25 bolt is 6 mm diameter and 25 mm long. A 6 mm drill would be used to produce a clearance hole for this bolt.

Self-tapping screws can cut their own thread into sheet metal. The first metal part is drilled with a clearance hole so that the screw thread passes through. The second part is drilled with a pilot hole of suitable diameter so that the screw cuts its way into the hole.

Wood screws are used in a similar way to self-tapping screws. A **pilot hole** is essential to avoid splitting the wood when the screw is inserted.

Permanent material joining methods

Pop rivets

Pop rivets are a quick and easy method of mechanically joining two sheet materials. A clearance hole is drilled through both sheets, then a pop rivet gun is used to insert the rivet and pull the sheets together.

Adhesives

Adhesives provide a permanent chemical bond between two surfaces. It is important to select the correct adhesive for the materials being used. For adhesives to work effectively, the surfaces must be clean, and the joint must be clamped until the adhesive sets hard.

Adhesives can be used to bond like or unlike materials, providing the correct adhesive is used. Some polymers are difficult to join with adhesives.

> **KEY WORDS**
>
> **Clearance hole**: a hole large enough for a screw to slide through.
>
> **Pilot hole**: a hole into which a screw cuts its own thread.

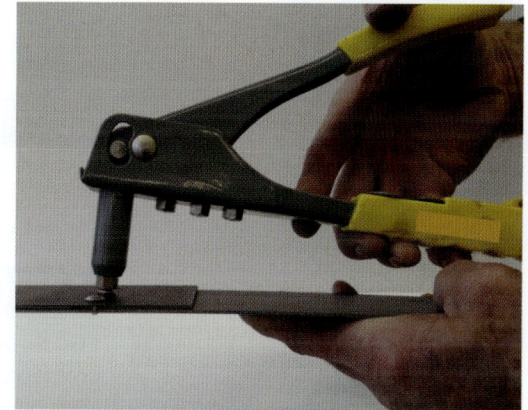

Figure 6.65 Using a pop rivet gun

Adhesive	Application
PVA	For wood and card.
Gorilla Glue®	Similar to PVA, but containing resin which allows its use on a variety of materials. Sets quicker than PVA.
Hot melt	Used with a glue gun. General purpose adhesive, but messy and rarely achieves a strong bond.
Contact adhesive	A thin layer is spread on each surface and allowed to dry. When the surfaces are brought into contact, the bond is instant. Useful on a variety of materials.
Tensol	A solvent which is used to 'weld' the surface of certain polymers, especially acrylic.
Epoxy resin	A two-part adhesive. When mixed, the adhesive sets hard after a few minutes. Exceptionally strong and will bond to most materials.

Table 6.2 Types of adhesive and their uses

Soldering

Soldering is the main method used to mechanically attach components to a circuit board. Poor soldering or failure of a solder joint is by far the most common cause of faults in electronic systems.

Solder was traditionally an alloy of lead and tin, but the RoHS directive (see Section 6.2) has resulted in most solder now being lead-free, containing tin, copper and silver.

Soldering for small-scale electronics construction will be carried out by hand using a soldering iron. The hot end of the soldering iron is called the bit, and this will be shaped down to a small size in order to direct the heat to precisely where it is needed. The solder will be in the form of a thin wire with a core of flux, which is a cleaning chemical needed to ensure that the solder binds effectively to both parts of the joint. Poor solder joints can occur for a number of reasons, including:

- the joint not being hot enough for the solder to flow completely around the joint
- dirt or oxidisation on the metals, or a dirty soldering iron bit
- the joint moving before the solder solidifies
- not feeding in fresh solder wire – trying to transfer hot solder from the iron onto the joint.

A careful visual inspection must be made after every joint is made. Bad joints must be corrected or they are likely to cause problems later on during testing.

Figure 6.66 Brazing

Brazing and welding

Brazing is similar to soldering, but done at a higher temperature using a blowtorch. It can join different metals which have different melting points, such as steel, aluminium, copper and brass. A filler metal is melted into the join and allowed to cool, when it solidifies and bonds the metals together.

Welding is the strongest way of joining like metals together. Welding melts the metals themselves and fuses them together, making them a single piece.

Activity

Go through your school workshop and identify every tool, machine and material covered in Section 6.6. Taking photographs might be useful. You will have used most of the equipment you identify, so refresh your memory on how each piece is used.

KEY POINTS
- Accurate marking-out of materials is crucial before cutting.
- Various hand and machine tools are used for cutting, shaping and drilling different materials.
- Various methods can be used to deform/reform polymers.
- Metals are more ductile when deformed while hot.
- Metals can be cast into shape.
- Turning on a lathe is used to create cylindrical parts.
- Laser cutting and 3D printing are two CAM processes which open up unique design opportunities.
- Temporary joining of materials can be achieved using nuts, bolts and screws.
- Permanent joins can be made using rivets, adhesives, soldering, brazing and welding.

6.7 Appropriate surface treatments and finishes that can be applied for functional and aesthetic purposes

Surface finishes applied to electronic devices for functional or aesthetic purposes

Previous sections of this chapter have covered methods of using materials and casings to provide protection for electronic systems, including the consideration of environmental conditions and waterproofing. We also looked at the importance of aesthetics when choosing the material for manufacturing a case.

Some materials are **self-finishing**, meaning that they do not require any additional surface finishes. Most polymers fall in this category. Acrylic and HIPS both have a high-quality finished surface which will resist water.

Steel will require some form of finish to protect it from rusting, which occurs due to a combination of moisture and oxygen. If aesthetics are not important, then a thin film of oil, spread over the steel surface with a rag, could offer sufficient protection. A better finish for steel would be to paint it. Painting involves cleaning the steel, then applying a coat of **primer** paint, followed by two or more final coats of the desired colour. Paint can be applied by brush or sprayed on.

Aluminium and brass do not require protection from moisture as they do not rust. However, they will still **oxidise**, which causes the metal to lose some of its aesthetic appeal. For this reason, these metals are often polished to a shine and then a coat of clear lacquer is applied. The lacquer protects from oxidation but allows the natural colour of the metal to show through. A particularly attractive finish is achieved by brushing aluminium with a fine wire brush, followed by a coat of lacquer, as seen in Figure 6.39.

Woods require a finish to be applied if they are going to be used outdoors or exposed to moisture. Wood can have a preservative applied, which is a chemical treatment to delay biological decay. Paint can also be applied to wood. The wood first needs to be sanded smooth, and then a primer coat is applied. Further coats are used, ending with the desired colour. The wood needs to be lightly sanded between coats to ensure a good aesthetic finish.

Powder and polymer coating of metals

Powder-coating is an alternative to painting a metal surface. The metal is first thoroughly cleaned, usually by shot-blasting. A dry, coloured powder, made from polyurethane, polyester, epoxy or acrylic polymer, is then sprayed onto the surface of the metal part. The metal and the paint gun are given an opposite electrical charge so that the particles of powder are attracted to and stick to the metal in an even layer.

The powder-coated part is then baked in an oven at 200°C until the polymer powder melts, **fuses** and forms an even, smooth coating. Once it has cooled, the coating is extremely durable and has a very good aesthetic finish.

KEY WORDS

Self-finishing: a surface which requires no further treatment to protect it or improve its appearance.

Primer: the first coat of paint, designed to bond to the surface.

Oxidise: a chemical reaction with the air which changes the surface of the material.

Fuse: the melting and joining of powder particles into an even layer.

Figure 6.67 Powder-coating an alloy wheel

Figure 6.68 A dip-coated spanner

Powder-coating is used extensively on domestic appliances such as washing machines and fridges, on bicycle frames and car alloy wheels.

Dip-coating is a similar process to powder-coating. A **fluidised bath** of coloured polymer powder is used. In this 'bath', air is gently blown through the polymer powder to make it look and behave like a fluid. The metal is heated to around 350°C and then the hot metal is plunged into the fluidised powder bath. The polymer melts and fuses to the hot metal.

The metal part is removed from the bath and allowed to cool, leaving a durable and attractive polymer coating which also protects the metal. Tool handles are sometimes dip-coated to provide a non-slip finish.

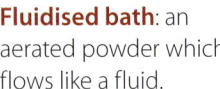

KEY WORD

Fluidised bath: an aerated powder which flows like a fluid.

Activity

Find and photograph examples of powder-coated and dip-coated products around your home or in the school workshop.

KEY POINTS
- Some materials are self-finished and require no further surface treatment.
- Some materials require finishing to protect them from oxidation or degradation.
- Finishes for metals include oil, paint or lacquer.
- Woods can be chemically treated with preservative, then painted.
- Metals can be powder- or polymer-coated in a range of colours.

Know it

1 a Draw a system diagram for a burglar alarm which sounds a siren for 15 seconds when a light beam is broken. Then draw a full circuit diagram, calculating all the relevant components values.

  b An industrial garden shredder requires a drive system to transfer the rotational output of an engine to the shredding mechanism through a distance of 600 mm. A velocity ratio of 3 is required from the mechanism. Sketch two possible designs for such a system.

  c Describe two ways in which a designer can make a product more able to be recycled at the end of its life.

2 Explain the techniques used by manufacturers to miniaturise electronic products.

3 Describe three factors which influence the extent a member in a structure will bend when subject to a force. Describe ways in which a framework can be made more rigid.

4 Draw a pinout for a 14-pin DIL package, labelling the pin numbers and indicating how pin 1 is identified.

5 Describe the key differences between batch production and mass production.

6 Describe how to accurately mark out a 100 × 150 mm rectangle on a sheet of plywood. Describe how this rectangle could then be cut out.

7 Describe how to apply a suitable finish to steel which will be used outdoors.

8 List three stock forms of polymer available in your school's D&T department.

9 Describe three processes for shaping polymers in your school's D&T department.

10 Explain where the following adhesives could be used: PVA, Tensol, Epoxy resin.

Chapter 7
Paper and boards

Learning objectives

By the end of this chapter you should have developed a knowledge and understanding of:

- the physical and working properties of a range of papers and boards
- the sources and origins of paper, board and laminated boards
- the processes used to extract paper and board into a useable form

- the ecological, social and ethical issues associated with processing paper and board
- the life cycle, recycling, reuse and disposal of paper and board
- how and why papers and boards can be reinforced to withstand external forces and stresses.

7.1 Sources, origins, physical and working properties of paper and boards and their ecological and social footprint

Sources

The first paper was made in China around 100 AD from fibres of tree bark mixed in water. This mixture, known as 'pulp', was then drained, spread out onto bamboo-framed matting before being pressed down into a thin layer and dried out in the sun. It was later discovered that 'lignin', which is the natural glue that holds the wood's fibres together, could be broken down more easily if plants with long cellulose fibres were used. This meant the fibres could be made into a finer pulp which made better-quality paper.

Paper

Paper making by hand
- Take some sheets of old used paper (cartridge paper, newspaper, etc).
- Cut or rip up the paper into small pieces (approx. 2 cm squares).
- Soak the paper overnight in a bucket of water.
- Fill a kitchen/food blender with clean water.
- Add a few pieces of the soaked paper and blend a little at a time, then add more paper.
- Continue blending until the mixture has become a pulp that looks like wallpaper paste, then pour into a tray.
- Using a mould and deckle (two wooden frames with a fine mesh screen) scoop up some pulp.
- Shake to spread out the pulp evenly across the screen, then leave to let the excess water drain out.
- Remove the deckle from the mould, then transfer the wet sheet from the mould to a flat, absorbent surface such as paper towels.
- Place another paper towel and a sponge on top.
- Press gently to begin with, then gradually increase the pressure using a rolling pin or similar object to flatten and squeeze out as much moisture as possible.
- Alternatively, place a board on top and then add weights or stand on top.
- Remove and leave to fully dry out in a warm environment.

The mechanical pulping process

The methods used to make paper today are essentially the same or very similar to the original method, but mechanical methods are used to separate the wood fibres. Using large tanks, known as pulpers, the raw wood chippings are soaked in up to 100 times their weight of water and then pulverised with large steel rotor blades. The finished pulp is then pumped into a paper machine where it is sprayed onto large sheets of thin mesh and pressed through a series of rollers into paper.

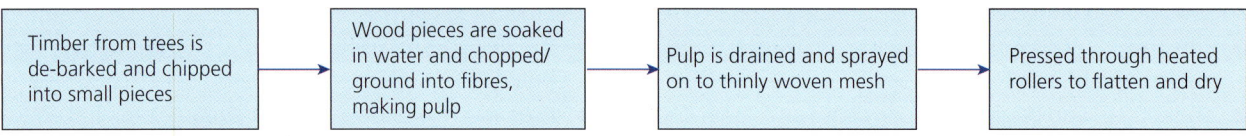

Figure 7.1 The mechanical pulping process

Mechanically pulped paper is suitable for paper products that use 'bulk' grades of paper, such as newspaper and toilet tissue. However, because of the damage done to the fibres in the grinding process, it has a low strength. It will tear relatively easily and disintegrate quickly when wet. The mechanical process also means that a large amount of lignin remains in the pulp mixture which can lead to the paper 'yellowing' over time or when exposed to bright light.

The chemical pulping process

The chemical pulping process uses chemicals such as caustic soda and sodium sulphate to help break down the wood pieces and chemically remove the lignin. This separates the fibres without damaging them and creates a much stronger pulp. Other fibres, such as cotton and linen, are then added to the pulp mixture to improve or change the texture – this is called 'blending'. Chemicals such as bleaching agents, dyes, and fillers are then also added to give the paper a specific colour, or property. The pulp is then dried, pressed and formed into rolls of paper in the same way as before. Chemically pulped paper is generally of a much higher quality and can be bleached or coloured to a much brighter finish. Specialist coatings can also be added to the paper once it has been formed into sheets, such as glossy or shiny finishes.

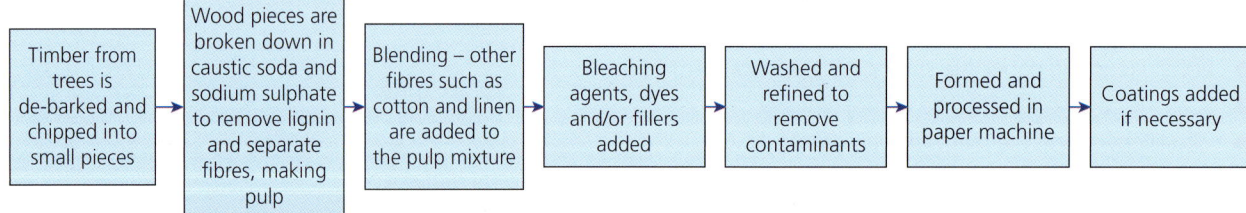

Figure 7.2 The chemical pulping process

Recycled paper

It takes around 12 average sized trees to make 1 tonne of newspaper, and around 24 trees to make 1 tonne of copier paper. Recycled paper was created to reduce the number of trees needed to make paper and therefore lessen the environmental impact of paper production.

Paper cannot be recycled indefinitely as the fibres get shorter and weaker every time they are recycled. After around five or six times, the fibres usually become too short and weak to be of use and will not pulp adequately. To maintain the quality and strength of recycled paper, many manufacturers use a mixture of recycled paper and new virgin wood chippings to make the pulp (see Table 7.1). This cuts down on the amount of trees needed by about 60–80 per cent.

Pulping process	% recycled paper	% virgin
Mechanical pulping	55%	45%
Chemical pulping	77%	23%

Table 7.1 Amount of recycled paper used in making paper

Common name	Weight (gsm)	Properties/working characteristics	Uses
Layout paper	50	Bright white, smooth, lightweight (thin) so slightly transparent and inexpensive	Sketching and developing design ideas Tracing parts of designs
Copier paper	80	Bright white, smooth, medium weight, widely available	Printing and photocopying
Cartridge paper	80–140	Textured surface with creamy colour	Drawing with pencil, crayons, pastels, water colour paints, inks and gouache
Bleed-proof paper	80–140	Bright white, smooth surface, stops marker 'bleed'	Drawing with marker pens
Sugar paper	100	Available in wide range of colours, inexpensive, rough surface	Mounting and display work

Table 7.2 Physical and working properties of paper

Figure 7.3 Corrugated cardboard

Boards

Card

Cardboard is made in a number of different ways. One method is by sandwiching and pasting multiple layers of paper together to make a thick paper. Another method is to press together the layers of wet pulp used for making paper together into a thicker layer. By layering either sheets of paper or pulp together, card of various different thicknesses can be produced.

Corrugated card

Corrugated cardboard is made by passing paper through a corrugation machine to form three layers. The centre layer is treated with high pressure steam to heat soften the fibres. The paper is then pressed into the required thickness and shape by crimping to give it a wavy shape. The two outer layers of paper are then glued on each side of the wavy centre layer. After the corrugator has heated, glued, and pressed the paper together to form the corrugated cardboard, it is cut into large pieces or 'blanks' which then go to other machines for printing, cutting, and gluing together.

Figure 7.4 A typical corrugator is around 90 metres long, roughly the length of a football field.

Double-wall corrugated card is made in the same way but has an additional wavy and flat layer added to make it even more **rigid** and give extra protection.

Board sheets

Mounting board is a rigid type of card with a thickness of around 1.4 mm (1400 **microns**) and a smooth surface. It is available in different colours, but white and black are the most commonly available and used colours. Mounting board is often used for picture framing mounts and architectural modelling.

Common name	Thickness (microns)	Properties/working characteristics	Uses
Card	180–300	Available in a wide range of colours, sizes and finishes Easy to fold, cut and print onto	Greetings cards, paperback book covers, etc. as well as simple modelling.
Cardboard	300 upwards	Available in a wide range of sizes and finishes Easy to fold, cut and print onto	General retail packaging, such as food, toys, etc., design modelling
Corrugated cardboard	3000 upwards	Lightweight yet strong Difficult to fold Good heat insulator	Pizza boxes, shoe boxes, larger product packaging (e.g. electrical goods)
Mounting board	1400	Smooth and rigid Good fade resistance	Borders and mounts for picture frames

Table 7.3 Physical and working properties of card

Laminated layers

Foam board and Styrofoam

Foam board and Styrofoam™ are slightly different types of expanded polystyrene foam. Expanded polystyrene foam is made from small pellets of polymer (around 1 mm in diameter) that are heated to around 200°C, allowing the gas in the polymer to escape and air to enter. The air entering the polymer expands the polymer to up to 40 times its original size. The enlarged polymer balls are then fused together using heat to create large blocks which can be cut into sheets or other required shapes. Foam board uses foam sandwiched between two outer layers of paper or thin card.

For more information on the sources and origins of expanded polystyrene foam please see Chapter 10.

Corriflute

Corriflute is a trade name for corrugated polypropylene polymer. It is similar to corrugated card in appearance but manufactured in one piece by extrusion instead of constructed in layers. To make Corriflute the molten polypropylene is drawn through a former that moulds the polymer into the corrugated shape required.

For more information on polypropylene see Chapter 10.

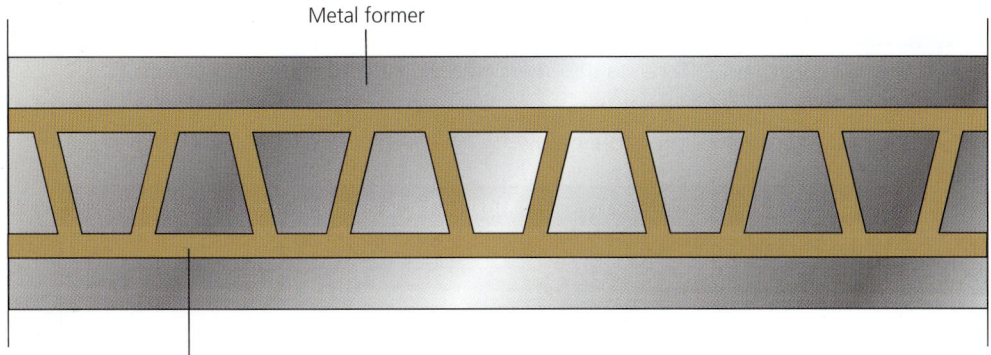

Metal former

Polymer is drawn through voids in the former to form the required shapes

Figure 7.5 Section through Corriflute

Foamex

Foamex is a tradename for polyvinylchloride (PVC) foam. It is a lightweight material and has good insulation properties similar to Styrofoam, but is more robust and can be printed onto easily. PVC foam sheet is available in a range of different colours and is easy to cut and join to other materials. It is resistant to water and many chemicals so is often used for outdoor displays and signs. For information on PVC see Chapter 10.

PVC foam is made by mixing two chemicals (diisocyanates and polyols) which react fully with each other and 'foam'. Pigments for colour and other additives are added during the mixing stage. The mixture is then poured onto a moving conveyor belt where it starts to 'foam', forming one long continuous block of foam.

Common name	Properties/working characteristics	Uses
Foam board	Smooth and rigid Very lightweight and easy to cut.	Point-of-sale displays, ceiling-hung signs in supermarkets, architectural modelling
Styrofoam	Light blue colour Easy to cut, sand and shape Water resistant Good heat and sound insulator	3D moulds for vacuum forming and GRP, wall insulation in caravans, boats, etc.
Corriflute	Wide range of colours Waterproof Easy to cut Rigid and lightweight	Outdoor signs, packaging and modelling
Foamex	Lightweight Good insulation properties Easy to print on Water resistant	Outdoor displays and signs

Table 7.4 Properties of types of board

Activity

1 Explain the main difference between mechanical and chemical pulping processes.

2 Copy and complete the table below.

Product	Most suitable material	Reason for choice
House 'For Sale' sign		
Scale model of a building		
Former to make a plastic blister pack		
Greetings card		
Packing for a flatscreen television		

3 Draw a section through foamboard, corrugated cardboard and Corriflute.

Ecological and social footprint

Paper and card

If waste paper is not recycled it ends up in landfill sites, which are bad for the environment in numerous ways. As well as trees, thousands of gallons of water and kilowatts of energy are needed. By recycling paper, natural resources and energy can be reduced along with greenhouse gas emissions from the manufacturing process and space in landfill sites.

The two main materials used in the manufacture of paper and card are wood pulp and recycled paper. The use of trees for wood pulp requires harvesting of many acres of forestland. However, most trees come from **managed forests**, managed by the **Forest Stewardship Council (FSC)** or the paper manufacturers themselves. This ensures that one or more trees are replanted for every one felled and ensures a continuing supply of wood.

Paper manufacturing can be a source of both air and water pollution. However, the use of recycled paper reduces the demand for fresh pulp, which in turn lowers the amount of energy needed to produce the pulp along with the amount of air and water pollution produced during manufacture. Recycled paper produces 73 per cent less air pollution than if it was made from raw materials. Large quantities of water are used in the papermaking process, but this is reused, or returned to the water source.

Bleaching agents, dyes and additives are used in the manufacturing process. Hydrogen peroxide and sodium hydrosulphite are the most common bleaching agents and can be harmful to the environment. Hydrogen peroxide is highly corrosive, especially when concentrated, but even domestic-strength solutions can cause irritation to the eyes, and skin. Inhaling can cause severe breathing problems. Hydrogen peroxide has also been classified as carcinogenic.

KEY WORDS

Managed forest: a forest where new trees are planted whenever one is cut down.

Forest Stewardship Council (FSC): organisation that promotes environmentally appropriate, socially beneficial, and economically viable management of the world's forests.

Life cycle: the stages a product goes through from beginning (extraction of raw materials) to end (disposal).

Lignin, which is a waste product extracted during the pulping process, can be burned as a fuel substitute, and in some manufacturing plants the burning of bark and other residues can often be used to supply power or steam to local firms or energy suppliers.

Laminated boards

Laminated boards, such as Styrofoam, PVC foam and Corriflute, are much harder to recycle because they are made of polymers, which need to be sorted, cleaned and chipped before being melted down into useable granules. The recycling process can also use lots of energy, which does further environmental damage. Foam board needs to have the two outer layers of paper separating from the foam core before it can be recycled, which can be a difficult and time-consuming process. For this reason, foam board usually ends up in landfill.

The ecological, social and ethical issues associated with processing the polymer elements in laminated layers are covered in Chapter 10.

Life cycle

After they are discarded, paper and cardboard do not stay in the environment for long. Because of their fibrous construction and susceptibility to moisture they will decompose quickly. Paper products take only 2–4 weeks to decompose, and cardboard around 2 months. Laminated layers take much longer to decompose as they contain or are made up of polymers which can resist chemical attacks. Styrofoam can take around 50 years to decompose and PVC can take up to 500 years.

Because paper and cardboard are made almost entirely of natural materials, they do not release any harmful chemicals during decomposition. Laminated layers that contain Styrofoam or PVC can release toxic chemicals, such as trichloroethane and methylene chloride.

The majority of paper and cardboard products we use (approximately 70 per cent) are recycled back into new paper. However, as we have seen, paper fibres can only be recycled so many times. They are then either left to decompose or burned as a fuel source. A small percentage of paper and card cannot be recycled and ends up in landfill.

Food packaging is the most common type of paper and card that is not recycled. This is because the paper used often becomes contaminated by grease, oil and other liquids that are absorbed into the fibres of the paper. When this occurs, the paper cannot be recycled as the fibres cannot be separated from the grease and oils, which get into the pulp mixture during the recycling process. Later in the process, the oil separates and causes problems with bleaching and washing the paper. When the water is squeezed out of the pulp, the oil residue creates dark marks and holes that make the paper a very low quality, or in some cases unsuitable for any use.

Pizza boxes are a classic example of how grease can contaminate paper and card. Oil from the cheese and grease from meat runs down into the cardboard meaning it cannot be recycled.

Figure 7.6 Used pizza boxes cannot be recycled

Figure 7.7 Composting bin

In cases like this, where paper or card cannot be recycled, they do not need to go into landfill. An alternative is for them to be composted using a composting bin. Food soaked paper and cardboard can be composted with no ill effects. Composting is a natural process that not only reduces the amount of paper put into landfill, but also benefits the environment by creating new soil that is rich in minerals.

Activity

1   Draw the life-cycle diagram of a cardboard coffee cup.
2   Why is food packaging often difficult to recycle?
3   Why can paper only be recycled a limited number of times?
4   Why is composting good for the environment?

KEY POINTS
- Paper can only be recycled so many times.
- The higher the content of recycled paper in a product the lower the quality.
- Contaminated paper cannot be recycled.

7.2 The way in which the selection of materials or components is influenced by a range of factors

Requirements or personal preference of the client

Specific products often require a certain type of material with requirements such that only one material is suitable. Often products are designed with a specific material already in mind, due to the personal preferences of the designer, based on their experience of using this material.

Properties of the material

The main influence on selection of material will be the properties and characteristics of the material. When selecting papers and boards the following properties need to be considered:

- Surface finishes – these can affect strength, rigidity and a gloss (shiny) or matt finish. Many products require a shiny finish, for example food packaging.
- Absorbency – the lower the absorbency of the material the less 'bleed' it produces, which gives a much crisper and higher-quality image when printed onto. Printer paper needs to have a very low absorbency, whereas toilet paper needs to be highly absorbent.
- Colour – many products have information, images or corporate branding printed onto them. This often requires a specific colour paper to be used.
- Texture – the rougher the texture the better the material is to draw or paint on. Copier paper needs to be smooth to give clear printing and move through machinery, whereas cartridge paper used by artists has a rougher finish.
- Flexibility/rigidity – some products require the material to be flexible so it can bend or curve around something, whereas others require a rigid, stiff material that will remain straight under stress.
- Water resistance – surface coatings and lamination can be applied to paper products to improve their resistance. Certain outdoor applications require boards such as Corriflute, which are completely waterproof.

Type of printing process

Modern printing methods allow printing to be applied to a wide range of materials and different shaped products. However, traditional mass production printing methods, such as flexography and lithography, which use rollers, cannot print onto thicker materials such as corrugated card, foam board or Corriflute.

Cost

It is in a manufacturer's best interests to try to keep manufacturing costs as low as possible in order to maximise profit while making the product as cheap to buy as possible. The easiest way of achieving this is to purchase materials as cheaply as possible and to not use materials of a higher specification than necessary.

Scales of production

One-off products are usually hand-made by craftsmen. Batch-produced products often have a small team with different specific skills who carry out a specific part in the manufacturing process. Mass-produced products may use production lines with human and/or automated assembly. The type of method used for production, and in turn the materials used, will be affected by the number of products being made.

Availability

While the vast majority of paper and board is freely available, some products may require sizes, colours or textures that are non-standard and have to be made to order. Speciality materials take longer to produce and are made in more limited quantities which can delay production of products as well as increase costs significantly. Wherever possible the designer will therefore try to use standard materials and sizes.

Environmental influences

Deforestation

Paper production requires large areas of forest to be felled, which can take years to grow back and leads to **deforestation** in many areas worldwide. This has led to an increase in endangered forests and the many species of animals who inhabit them. Many paper manufacturers have reduced this danger by using trees from managed forests, such as those run by the Forest Stewardship Council (FSC).

Water and energy consumption

Paper making uses a great deal of water, which often comes from local supplies. This can lower the water table of the area and cause problems such as increased water temperature and sedimentation, and may affect local wildlife. To reduce their consumption, many paper mills now recycle up to 90 per cent of the water used in the process. Paper-making machines also use large amounts of electricity.

Chemicals and solvents

The paper-making process uses a range of toxic solvents and chlorine compounds to remove the lignin from the pulp, to bleach and colour the paper, and in the coatings used to improve strength, absorbency, etc. However, the use of chemicals has been reduced by many pulp and paper mills, choosing to use unbleached paper for products that do not need to be white in colour can improve the carbon footprint and reduce costs.

Air pollution

Pulp and paper mills produce carbon dioxide and other pollutants that can cause damage to the ozone layer, acid rain and contribute to global warming.

Solid waste

Once paper fibres become too short or weak to be recycled they form a sludge which is either disposed of into landfill or can be dried out and burned as a fuel.

Social, cultural and ethical issues

We live in a diverse society where even small communities are made up of people from a range of different **cultures** who may have different beliefs, different ways of life and different traditions. What one person may take as perfectly ordinary could be considered offensive and insulting by another person from a different culture.

When designing any kind of graphic product, social, cultural and ethical issues must also be considered. Imagery, symbols and even certain colours can cause offence to people, which can lead to conflict between the manufacturer or brand and a particular sector of society.

It is important that graphical imagery on products does not offend in any way. Therefore, designers must be aware of the beliefs and needs of minority groups and take care how they portray individuals or groups of people on products.

Designers must also take great care when selecting and using photographs or images of people on their products. Using a person of a particular race on a product can sometimes portray them in a negative light or stereotypical manner, which can be extremely offensive. It is important that careful thought goes into selecting images and consideration of how an image may represent a minority group.

Designers must also consider different social attitudes across the world. What is socially acceptable to people of the western world may not be in other countries. In some cultures certain animals are considered sacred. In other cultures there are different beliefs and attitudes regarding revealing clothing and keeping certain parts of the body covered at all times.

Responsibilities of designers

Globalisation has meant that many products are produced in developing countries where labour rates and materials are much cheaper.

In the western world there are strict health and safety rules regarding the buildings, machinery and safety of workers, and laws that protect the rights and welfare of all workers. However, this is not the case in many developing countries, and this can lead to **exploitation**. Exploitation is when workers are forced to work:

- in unsafe, unhealthy or dangerous conditions
- for extremely long hours without sufficient breaks
- without correct protective equipment
- for low pay rates that do not reflect a fair wage.

KEY WORD

Exploitation: treating someone unfairly in order to benefit from their work.

Designers have a responsibility to ensure that products they are involved in will not be manufactured in this way and to 'refuse' to design products for companies who exploit their workers.

Organisations such as Fairtrade ensure that workers are not exploited in this way. As consumers we can also support the rights of workers by refusing to purchase goods from manufacturers that are not approved by these organisations.

Estimating the true costs of a prototype or product

The price of producing a prototype or final product will vary depending on factors such as:

- the quantity required
- the size and complexity of the product
- the materials and processes used to make it
- the production time
- the price and availability of any manufactured components.

The costs of paper and boards reduce the more you purchase. Therefore, when designing a product and planning the manufacture of a model or prototype, it is essential that designers carefully consider and calculate the amount of material they will need. For example, if you need just over three sheets of A1 foam board, it may be cheaper to buy seven sheets of A2 than four A1-sized sheets.

Another consideration is that the cost per mm² of all sheet materials, including papers and boards, will decrease as the sheet size increases. In most cases it is more economical to buy a large size sheet and cut it down into smaller sheets yourself than buying them ready cut. However, larger sheets are more difficult to transport, so the designer must also factor in transport and delivery costs.

Buying materials from countries on the other side of the world can often be cheaper than buying in your own country. The designer has a responsibility to think about the effects of globalisation and local economies when deciding where to purchase products.

Activity

A designer needs seven pieces of A4-sized foamboard to make a prototype product. One A4 sheet costs £0.45. A pack of 10 A4 sheets costs £3.00. An A1 sheet costs £2.75. Calculate the cheapest way of purchasing enough material for the prototype.

KEY POINTS
- There are many factors that can influence the cost of a product.
- Fairtrade products are made by unexploited workers.
- Certain colours, symbols and signs can be offensive to other cultures.

KEY WORDS

Force: something pushing or pulling on an object.

Structure: object constructed from several parts.

7.3 The impact of forces and stress on materials and objects and the ways in which they can be reinforced and stiffened

The structural integrity of a product or object is its ability to hold together under a **force** or load, including its own weight, without bending or breaking. If an object has structural integrity it will perform its function without failing for as long as it was designed to do so. If the object does not hold together because it has been stressed more than it can withstand, it is known as structural failure. This could be a part of the object's **structure** or the whole thing.

As a thin sheet material, paper can appear to have little structural integrity. However, its structural integrity can in fact be greatly increased in various ways.

Folding

Folding a sheet of paper or thin card turns it from a flat sheet that will bend and flex easily into a structure. The fold creates a rigid section within the paper that can support its own weight and additional weight.

By folding the paper a number of times, the paper's or card's structural integrity can be further increased.

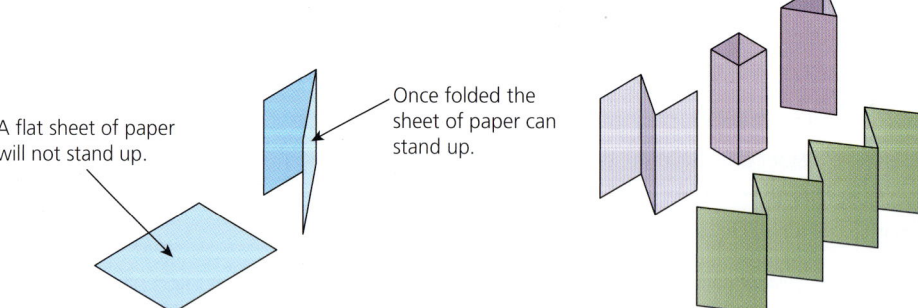

A flat sheet of paper will not stand up.

Once folded the sheet of paper can stand up.

Figure 7.8 Effect of folding paper

Figure 7.9 Effect of folding paper a number of times

Curving and bending paper and card

As well as folding, paper and card can be bent into curved shapes, such as cylinders, which have excellent strength and structural stability.

The wavy centre section of corrugated card gives it its rigidity and strength. A standard cardboard box with four vertical folded corners will be able to withstand and hold the weight of an average sized human. The structural integrity provided by the box shape means that many can be stacked on top of one another without collapsing. The triangulated shapes in the centre of Corriflute work in the same way.

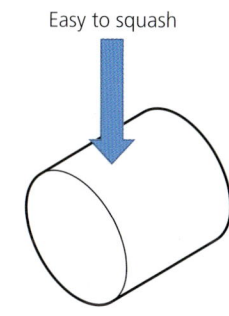

Difficult to squash   Easy to squash

Figure 7.10 Cylinders have strength and structural stability.

Figure 7.11 Stacked cardboard boxes in a factory or warehouse

Stiffening papers and boards

Materials like corrugated card, foam board, Corriflute and Styrofoam are stiff and rigid, unlike thinner card and paper, which is flexible and easy to bend. Thin card and paper can be stiffened by:

- sticking together several sheets to increase thickness
- adding ribs to give extra strength in one direction – ribs can be made from thicker card, other boards or even thin softwood (sets used in theatres often use cardboard shapes that are **reinforced** and stiffened using thin softwood)
- laminating (encasing the paper in thin sheet plastic).

Structural integrity of card

The structural integrity of cardboard can also be increased by shaping it into a structure. Cardboard egg boxes are an excellent example of this. When the card is manufactured, the pulp is sprayed onto a dimpled mould. The shape of the carton not only supports each individual egg and isolates it from the other eggs, the structure created helps to absorb shock and protect the eggs against breakage. This type of structure is called a '**monocoque**' structure meaning 'single structural skin'. Monocoque structures are commonly used in boat hull design and monocoque chassis are used on many modern vehicles.

KEY WORDS

Reinforcement: extra material added to increase strength.

Monocoque: structural system where loads are supported through an object's external skin.

Figure 7.12 Cardboard egg boxes are an excellent example of increased structural integrity.

Structural integrity can also be increased by reinforcing one material with another. Foam board is made up of a thin layer of foam sandwiched between two layers of paper or thin card. On their own, the sheets of paper and foam would have very little structural integrity or strength. If stood on their edge they would collapse or fall over like a sheet of paper. However, by joining the materials together they gain structural integrity. The foam board inside allows the outer paper layers to stand on their edge and not bend as easily. The paper outer layers spread any load across the foam instead of it being concentrated in one place.

Activity

1   Cut some strips of different paper and thin card approximately 4 cm wide by 30 cm in length.

    Place the card and paper strips on the edge of a desk so that they overhang by around 25 cm and place a weight on top to hold each one firmly on the desk.

    Place a 1p coin on the overhanging end and measure the deflection of each strip (how much they bend). Continue adding coins until each one bends so much they fall off.

    Now fold each strip in half lengthways down the centre of the strip. Repeat the exercise and notice how much stronger each strip has become.

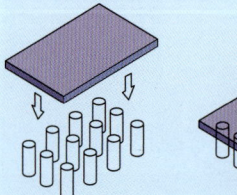
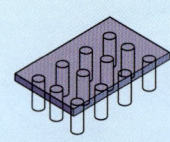

Figure 7.13 A board being placed on toilet rolls

2   Collect around ten toilet roll or kitchen roll tubes. Place the tubes on the floor together and place a sheet of MDF or plywood on top of them.

    Gently stand on the structure – it should take your weight. Remove two of the central toilet/kitchen rolls and repeat the exercise. Progressively remove more tubes and repeat the tests until the structure collapses.

3   Cut down a toilet roll so that it is the same length as its diameter. Try to squash the tube one way then the other.

KEY POINTS
- Simple structures found in nature can be extremely strong.
- The structural integrity of materials can be changed, depending on how they are shaped.

7.4 Stock forms, types and sizes in order to calculate and determine the quantity of materials or components required

Paper and board sizes

Paper and board is available in standard-sized sheets ranging from A10, which is approximately the size of a postage stamp, through to 4A0 which is larger than a king-size bed sheet. For full details of paper sizes see Chapter 5, Section 5.2.

Laminated board sizes

Foam board

Like paper and cardboard, foam board is available in the standard-sheet sizes ranging from A4 to A0. Many suppliers also stock standard imperial sizes up to 8 ft × 4 ft (2440 mm × 1220 mm) which is a standard commercial size for many other materials, such as MDF, plywood and plasterboard. Foam board is available in thicknesses of 3 mm, 5 mm or 10 mm. The standard colours available are white, black or black/grey (one side black, one side grey).

Corriflute

Corriflute is available in a range of sizes, but typical sheet sizes are:

- 450 mm × 600 mm
- 600 mm × 900 mm
- 900 mm × 1200 mm.

It is also available from specialist suppliers in standard imperial sizes:

- 8 ft × 4 ft (2440 mm × 1220 mm)
- 8 ft × 6f t (2440 mm × 1830 mm).

Corriflute is available in thicknesses of 2 mm to 10 mm and comes in a range of different colours.

PVC foam

PVC foam is available in standard paper sizes and larger sizes, typically:

- 10 ft × 4 ft (3050 mm × 1220 mm)
- 10 ft × 5 ft (3050 mm × 1530 mm)
- 10 ft × 7 ft (3050 mm × 2030 mm)

It is available in thicknesses of 1, 2, 3, 4, 5, 6, 8, 10, 13, 15, 19 and 25 mm and a wide range of standard and special designer colours with gloss or matt finishes.

Styrofoam

Styrofoam™ is available in sheet form or in blocks. Sheet thicknesses available range from 5 mm up to 165 mm through increments of 5 or 10 mm. Thicknesses above 165 mm are considered a block rather than a sheet. Sheet sizes range from 600 mm × 300 mm up to over 3 m × 1.5 m, depending on the supplier.

KEY WORD

Ream: pack of 500 sheets.

Calculating costs

To calculate the costs of a product, the designer must first work out the size of the product and the minimum sheet size they can cut the product from. If the product is made up of numerous pieces, they must calculate the most cost-effective way of getting all these pieces from standard-sized sheets.

Products such as flyers, posters and business cards are produced on standard-sized sheets of paper and/or card which can be bought in various numbers. For example, a **ream** (500 sheets) of blank white A4 paper can be purchased from any stationery supplier.

To calculate the cost of 3D products made from card or paper, the product must be opened up into its

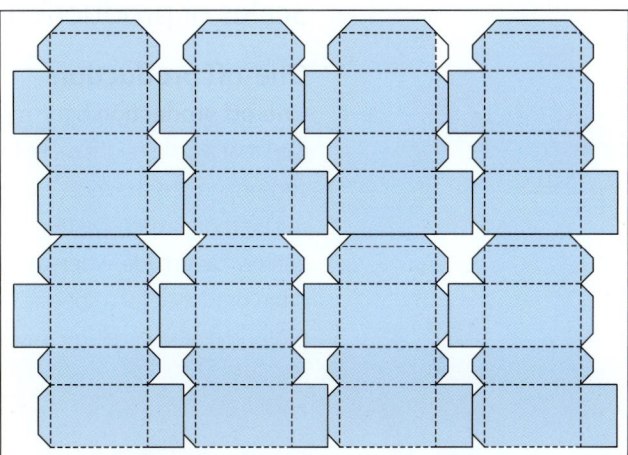

Figure 7.14 Maximising space using tessellation

development (net) and measured. The designer can then calculate the size of sheet material needed to make each item. Depending on the number required and the sheet sizes available, the designer must try to fit as many nets as possible onto each sheet in order to maximise space and minimise waste. This is known as **tessellation**.

Once the designer knows how many items they can get from each sheet it is simple to calculate the number of sheets required and multiply this by the cost per sheet.

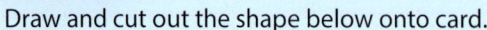

Activity

Draw and cut out the shape below onto card.

Using the shape as a template, draw around it onto a sheet of A3 paper.

Arrange the template so that you can get as many on the page as possible (tessellation).

In a small group have a competition to see who can get the most items from one sheet pf A3 paper.

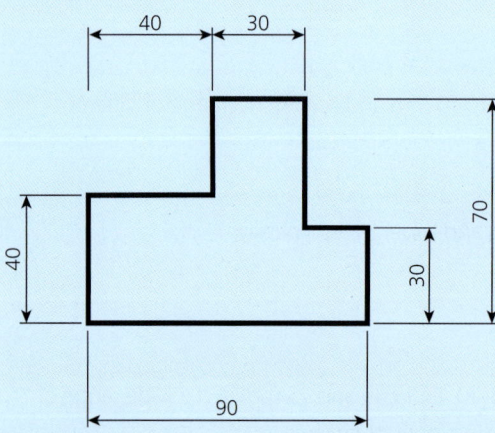

Figure 7.15 Shape template

7.5 Alternative processes that can be used to manufacture products to different scales of production

Scales of production

One-off production

One-off production is the making of a single product, for example a handmade birthday card that a child might make for their parent. One-off products are labour-intensive and time consuming. It is the most expensive way of producing an item, and usually the final product will be more expensive than if it was mass- or batch-produced. Some one-off products are entirely handmade, whereas others can use automated processes. One-off products are often produced for a specific client's requirements or needs. Often designers create a one-off prototype of their design to show what it will look like or how it will function.

Batch production

Batch production is where a limited number of an item is produced in one go. Batch production has the ability to produce similar products with slight variations, such as changes to text or colour. For printed products on paper and card, digital printing is the most cost-effective production method as it allows variations to be easily made, such as enlargement and reduction, cropping, rotating, etc. Digital printing is ideal for personalised printing, such as party invitations or company name badges, as the main design will stay the same but the name can be easily changed and another copy printed.

Digital printers are inexpensive to buy, readily available and many people have them for household use. The **cost per sheet** of printing using a digital printer is high compared to other types of commercial printing, but because there are no set up costs and only a limited number of printouts are needed they are the best option for small print runs.

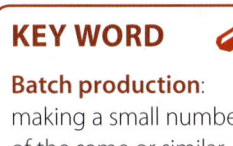

Figure 7.16 A batch of party invitations could be produced using a digital printer.

Screen printing is another method of printing suitable for batch production. Screen printing is used for creating repeating patterns or designs, such as on wallpaper or fabrics.

Screen printing uses a porous fabric mesh screen stretched over a wooden frame, called the screen. The screen is the exact size of the pattern or design required. The lightest colour is printed first by masking off the parts of the screen that are not in that colour on the design. This creates a stencil of the coloured parts to be printed. The frame is then laid onto the paper or fabric, a small quantity of ink is added and a squeegee is used to spread the ink evenly over the whole of the screen. The ink is pushed through the mesh by the squeegee in the un-masked areas onto the paper or fabric below. The screen is then moved to the next position and the process is repeated.

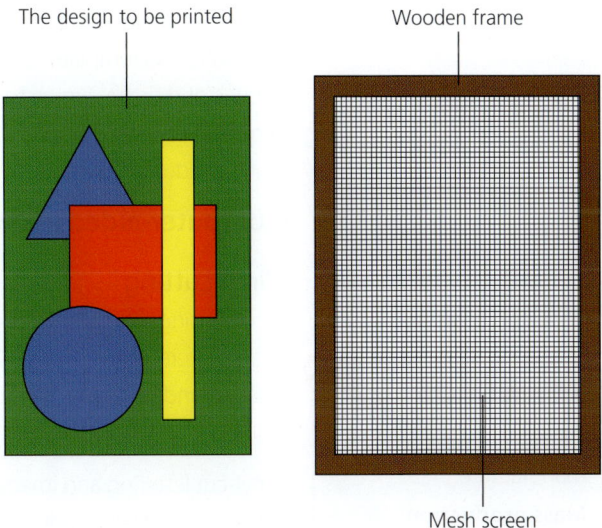

The design to be printed

Wooden frame

Mesh screen

Figure 7.17 The screen is made to the same size as the design.

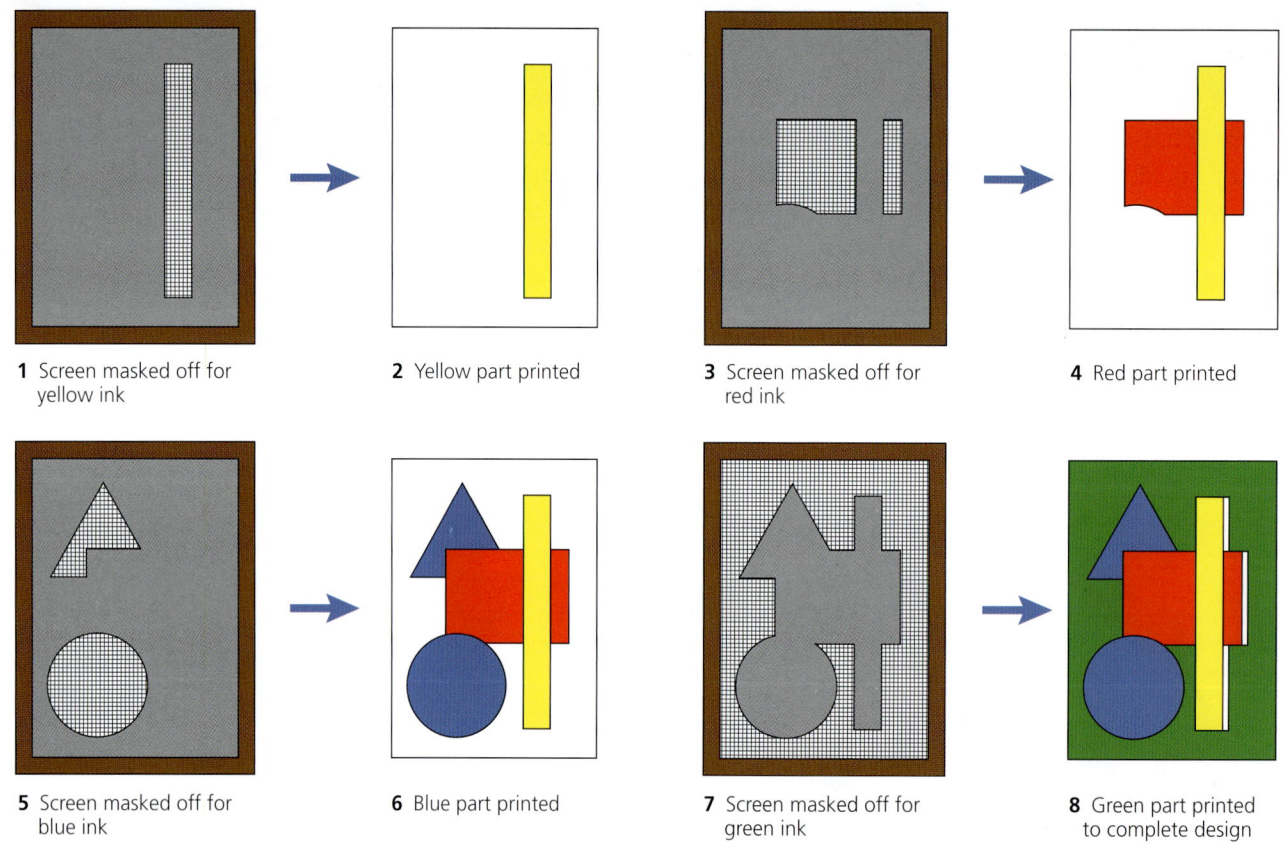

1 Screen masked off for yellow ink	**2** Yellow part printed
3 Screen masked off for red ink	**4** Red part printed
5 Screen masked off for blue ink	**6** Blue part printed
7 Screen masked off for green ink	**8** Green part printed to complete design

Figure 7.18 The screen-printing process

Once the lightest colour has been printed across the whole area required, the screen is washed and masked up for the next colour. The process is repeated until all the colours have been printed.

Stencils and templates

Stencils and templates can also be used for batch production. If multiple numbers of the same part are required, it can be drawn out once onto card and cut out to create a cardboard template. This template can then be laid onto the material required and drawn around, then moved and drawn around again and again until the required number is reached. Using a template ensures that every piece is exactly the same and saves the time of drawing each part out individually. To reduce waste, tessellation should be used.

Computer-aided manufacturing (CAM)

Vinyl cutting

Vinyl cutting is frequently used in sign making and display work. The material is available in many different sizes, from A4 size up to A0. The most common uses are for creating logos, designs and text to stick onto packaging, point-of-sale displays, etc. where they cannot be printed.

Vinyl-cut lettering and images are often used on the sides of cars, buses and lorries. The advantages of using vinyl graphics instead of painting or sign writing onto the vehicle is that they can be removed relatively easily by applying a little heat to soften the vinyl and peeling them off.

KEY WORDS

CAM: Computer-aided manufacture.

Mass production: making large quantities of an item.

Large-scale (mass) production

Offset lithography

When large numbers of graphic products are required then commercial printing methods are the best option. Offset lithography is one of the most common forms of commercial printing used today. The process uses four ink colours: cyan, magenta, yellow and black (called the key). These are often shortened to CMYK. These four colours can be overlaid to create others, for example printing cyan on top of yellow creates green.

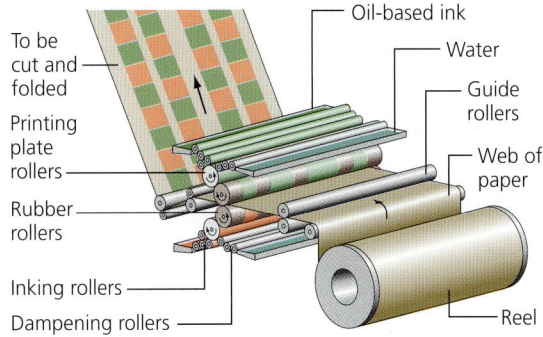

Figure 7.19 Offset lithography printing

The initial setting of the print run is the most expensive part of the process as it requires an image setter to produce films for each of the four colours of the artwork. These are then used to produce a set of printing plates.

The principal of offset lithography is that oil and water do not mix (oil will separate from water). The image on the plate is set to attract the ink but repel water, whereas the non-image parts of the plate attract moisture and repel the ink. The plate is kept wet during the printing process so that the ink will only stick to the areas required.

Flexography

Flexography uses water-based rather than oil-based inks, which allows a wider range of different inks to be used. The water-based inks dry much faster so the process is much quicker, and although the print quality is not as good, the costs are significantly cheaper. It is largely used for printing on packaging, such as corrugated cardboard boxes, cartons, sweet wrappers and plastic carrier bags where the quality of print is not as important.

Like offset lithography, the four colours CMYK are printed one at a time. A flexible printing plate is mounted onto the plate cylinder, and the material to be printed is pressed against it by the impression cylinder. Ink is transferred to the printing plate from an ink pan via two rollers (fountain roller and anilox roller).

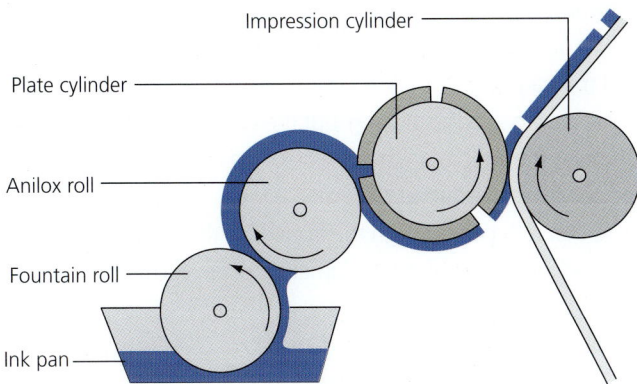

Figure 7.20 Flexography printing

Pre-press

Once a design has been drawn on paper or produced on a software program, it must go through the pre-press stages before it is ready to be printed.

The first stage is the checking of the file or image to make sure:

- the fonts shown are all correct and included
- it has the correct format and resolution
- the colours are set up correctly.

The layout of the page is then checked to ensure it fits on the page and in the correct position. Registration marks are printed on the edge of the page, outside the area of the design and are used to accurately line up the different letterpress plates for multi-colour printing jobs. There are different marks, such as bulls-eye targets, plate information, and crop marks. The crop marks show where the paper will be trimmed after printing is completed. The registration marks are trimmed off during this process.

Commercial printing processes use a **colour separation** printing process. This process prints the four CMYK colours onto the same page. As the sheets of paper run through the printing press, each coloured plate transfers an image in one of the four colours on to the paper. The colours are applied as tiny dots which combine to produce the full-colour design.

Once all the checks have been made, a 'proof' of the document is created. A proof is a prototype of how the finished item will look when it is printed. This is then sent to the client for them to check and give their final approval. If the printed product is a book or magazine that requires binding or folding, a physical proof showing how it will be constructed, folded, etc. will be made.

Once the proof has been approved, the item is ready to be produced. If it is digitally printed, the file is transferred electronically to the press and printed. If it is to be printed on an offset press, the printing plates that transfer the inked images to the paper are produced and then the item can be printed.

Binding methods

Documents and graphic products with approximately ten pages or less can be printed in a larger format and stapled together down the centre to create a booklet.

When a document has more pages than this there are different binding methods used commercially for books, magazines and other large publications. The majority of publications are sewn together using different techniques, depending on the number of pages required:

- **Saddle stitching** is the most common and least expensive method. It works in a similar way to stapling in that a thin wire goes through the outside spine and is then bent flat on the inside centre fold to grip all the pages.
- **Loop stitching** works in a similar way to saddle stitching, but the wire is threaded through to create loops along the external spine which can then be held in a ring binder. This method allows extra pages to be added at a later date.
- **Side or stab stitching** uses wire that is forced through the front of all the pages then folded flat. A covering section along the edge of the document is often added to cover the wires.
- **Sewn binding** is similar to saddle stitching, but uses thread instead of wire. The document is stitched all the way down the spine with one continuous thread.

Where a document has a large number of pages, such as a novel or hardback book, the book will be bound in stages. The number of pages will be divided up into small sections called signatures, and each signature will be joined together using one of the above methods. The separately bound signatures are then joined together using one of the methods below:

- Perfect binding is where the signatures are glued together into a wrap-around cover.
- Tape binding is similar to perfect binding, but uses an adhesive tape that is wrapped around the signatures to hold them all in place.
- Case binding involves gluing the signatures to end papers which are then glued to the spine of the book cover. This is most commonly used for hardback books.

Ring or comb binding is when holes are punched along the edges of the pages and a spiral ring or plastic comb binder is inserted that holds the pages loosely together. The advantages of this type of binding is that pages can be folded all the way back without damage to the spine. This method is commonly used on road atlases.

Plastic spines are u-shaped lengths of plastic that can be forced apart so that they grip the pages placed between. They are easy to fit but can become loose over time.

Stud binding (also known as screw or post binding) is a very secure method of joining pages. Holes are drilled through all the pages then a stud is pushed through and an end cap fitted. Using this method requires a wide enough margin on the left-hand edge of the page for the studs and means this area of the page is unable to be seen after binding.

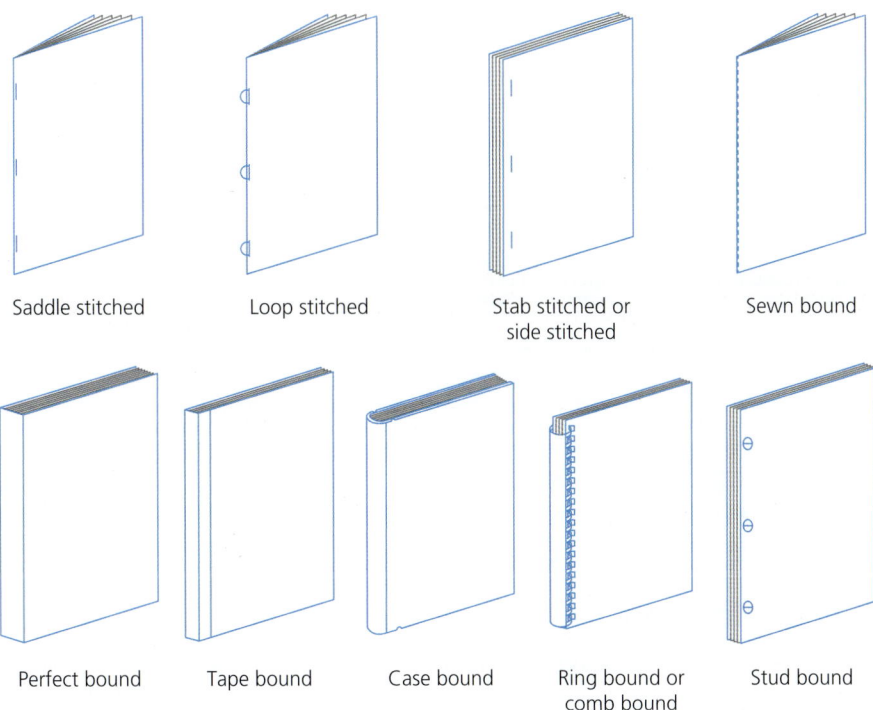

| Saddle stitched | Loop stitched | Stab stitched or side stitched | Sewn bound |

| Perfect bound | Tape bound | Case bound | Ring bound or comb bound | Stud bound |

Figure 7.21 Different binding methods

Activity

Collect some old magazines or books. Look carefully at the spine and try to identify the type of binding method used.

Get some blue (to represent cyan), red (to represent magenta) and yellow paint.

Mix small amounts of each to try and make the whole colour spectrum (red, orange, yellow, green, blue, violet).

Now try to make other colours, such as brown and grey, using the same three initial colours.

KEY POINT
- The larger the quantity of production, the cheaper the unit cost.

7.6 Specialist techniques and processes that can be used to shape, fabricate, construct a high-quality prototype

Marking out

Before a design can be cut it must be marked out. Pencil or pens can be used to mark out on paper, card and foam board. Styrofoam, Corriflute and PVC foam can be marked with a thin permanent marker, but this can leave a mark on the material. A chinagraph pencil or non-permanent marker can also be used, but lines drawn with these can be smudged easily.

Wastage/addition

Wasting is the process of shaping material by cutting away unwanted parts to leave the desired shape. The material that is removed (the waste) may be thrown away, recycled or saved for use on something else, depending on its size and shape. Shaping by wasting does not just apply to papers and boards. It is a shaping method used on all types of materials.

Cutting

Scissors and craft knives are the most obvious and best choice for cutting paper and card. When using a craft knife, a safety rule and cutting mat should also be used to ensure a clean cut and reduce the likelihood of injury.

Foam board, PVC foam and Corriflute are too thick to be cut with scissors, so must be cut using a craft knife. Styrofoam can be cut using a craft knife, but only up to a thickness of around 10 mm as this is around the size of a normal craft knife blade. Thicker Styrofoam can be cut using a serrated edged knife (such as a bread knife), bandsaw, hacksaw blade or hot wire cutter. Once the bulk of the material has been removed, final shaping can be done by sanding and smoothing with files and abrasive paper.

Laser cutters are now a common feature in many schools. A laser cutter can be used to cut any 2D shape out of card, PVC foam, foam board or Corriflute. Intricate shapes are much easier and quicker to cut using a laser cutter. However, as the laser 'burns' through the material the edges of paper and card can be left with slight scorch marks. Depending on the material being cut, care must be taken to ensure the correct settings and laser speed have been selected.

Deforming/reforming

Deforming is the process of changing the shape of a material. This can be by applying force, heat or moisture, depending on the material.

Folding

Folding is the most common way of deforming paper and thin card. Paper and thin card can be folded easily by hand. Scoring the material first using a blunt knife blade or other dull pointed object will help fold thicker card and ensure a clean, sharp crease.

Foam board can be folded by cutting through the foam in one of two ways:

- Hinge cutting is where the foam board is cut part-way through so that the bottom layer of card acts as a hinge so the card can be folded backwards.
- Vee cutting is where a v-shaped cut is made in the foam board and the material removed. This allows the foam board to be folded inwards and gives a clean, tidy fold.

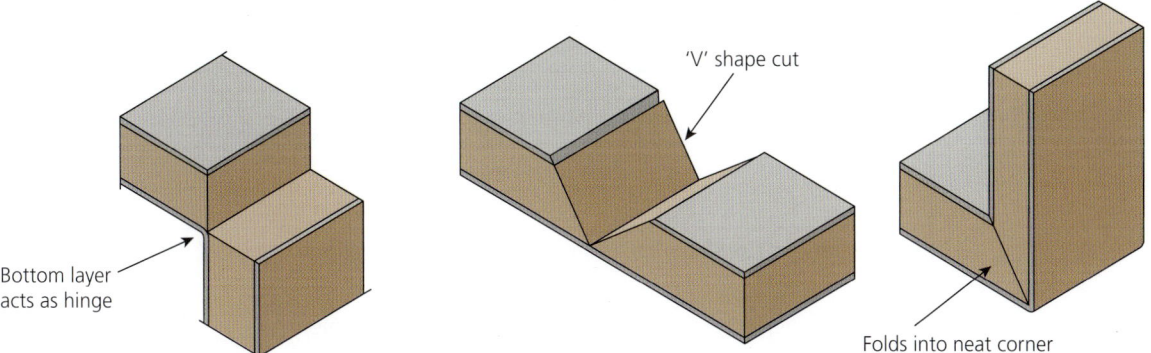

Bottom layer acts as hinge

'V' shape cut

Folds into neat corner

Figure 7.22 Hinge cutting   **Figure 7.23** Vee cutting

PVC foam cannot be folded unless it is cut part-way through, in a similar way to foam board. Similarly, Corriflute is not easily folded, but this can be done by cutting a section of material away from the top layer between the flutes, allowing the material to be folded backwards or forwards. Styrofoam cannot be folded.

Adhesives

There are a range of different adhesives available for papers and boards. Different glues are suitable for different products and purposes. See Table 7.5 for details of the properties of different adhesives.

Adhesive	Medium	Properties
Glue stick	Paper and thin card	Easy to apply, inexpensive and mess free Only strong enough for paper and very thin card Can unstick over time, pieces can break off making surface lumpy Quick setting
Spray glue	Paper and thin card	Gives a light even coating Can be permanent or temporary fixing Quick setting Can be messy
PVA glue	Thicker card, corrugated cardboard, foam board, Styrofoam	Dries clear Only a thin layer required Inexpensive Can be watered down
Hot-glue gun	Thick card, Corriflute	Quick setting Can burn material and user Can melt material Cool melt versions available Coloured glue sticks available

Adhesive	Medium	Properties
Cyanoacrylate glue (superglue)	Corriflute, PVC foam	Quick setting Very strong bond Short shelf life (1 year approx.) Can melt material (foam board/Styrofoam)
Polystyrene cement	Corriflute, PVC foam	Dries quickly Clear finish
Contact adhesive	Corriflute, PVC foam	Must be applied to both surfaces Needs to partly set before joining Instant bond Does not require clamping
Epoxy resin	Corriflute, PVC foam	Needs to be mixed with hardener Very strong bond Gives off strong fumes

Table 7.5 Properties of adhesives

Staples

Staples are thin strips of u-shaped metal which are used in a stapler. The stapler is closed around the sheets of material and staples are forced through the paper and then bent to hold the pieces together. Staples come in different sizes and strengths, from light duty ones that can be used to join a few sheets of paper through to heavy duty staples which can pierce thick card as well as wood and MDF.

Plastic rivets

Plastic rivets, also known as clic rivets, can be used to secure thicker boards, including Corriflute and foam board, together. There are many different types and designs of plastic rivet, but the majority have a sleeve which is pushed through a hole in the materials being joined together. An inner section is then fitted inside the sleeve which covers one end and pushes open the other end, locking the sheets together.

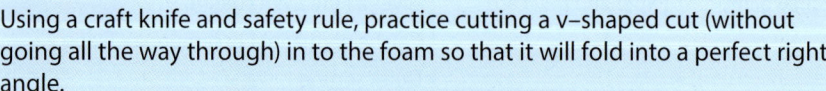

Activity

Take some foam board.

Using a craft knife and safety rule, practice cutting a v–shaped cut (without going all the way through) in to the foam so that it will fold into a perfect right angle.

Use PVA glue and pins to hold it in position until the glue dries.

Once perfected, try making a simple model house using the same method.

Figure 7.24 A clic rivet

KEY POINTS
- Solvent-based adhesives can melt certain types of board.
- Epoxy resins must be mixed and applied in a well-ventilated area, as when inhaled, epoxy fumes can affect the nose, throat and lungs.

7.7 Appropriate surface treatments and finishes that can be applied for functional and aesthetic purposes

Paper

The properties and aesthetics of paper and board can be altered and improved by applying different surface treatments. A range of different coatings can be applied to improve the **opacity**, lightness, surface smoothness, **lustre** and colour-absorption ability of paper.

Some types of **coating** are applied during the making process, while it is in the paper-making machine. Other types are applied separately, after the paper has been produced.

Cast coatings are applied after the paper has been produced. One or both sides of the paper is coated with china clay, chalk, starch, latex and other chemicals. The wet coated paper is then pressed or rolled against a polished, hot, metal drum creating a finish so smooth, reflective and shiny that it can seem almost mirror-like. Cast-coated paper also holds ink well and produces sharper, brighter images when printed on.

Super calendering

Super calendering gives paper an even smoother paper surface. The paper passes through a series of rollers with alternately hard and soft surfaces. The pressure on the paper creates a smoother and thinner paper with a very high lustre surface. Super-calendered paper is primarily used for glossy magazines and high-quality colour printing.

> **KEY WORDS**
>
> **Opacity**: the quality of lacking transparency or translucence.
>
> **Lustre**: a gentle shine or soft glow.
>
> **Coating**: an additional outer layer added to paper.

Type of paper	Properties	Used for
Cast-coated	Provides the highest gloss surface of all coated papers and boards	Labels, covers, cartons and cards
Lightweight coated	A thin, coated paper, which can be as light as 40 g/m2	Magazines, brochures and catalogues
Silk- or silk-matt-finished	Smooth, matt surface High readability and high image quality	Product booklets and brochures
Calendered or glossy	Glazed shiny surface – can be coated and/or uncoated	Colour printing
Machine-finished	Smooth on both sides No additional coatings applied after leaving the paper-making machine	Booklets and brochures
Machine-coated	Coating applied while it is still on the paper machine	All types of coloured print
Matt-finished	Slightly rough surface prevents light from being reflected Can be both coated and uncoated	Art prints and other high-quality print work.

Table 7.6 Types of paper finish

Card and board finishes

Varnish

Varnish coatings are a thin coating of matt, silk or gloss varnish that can be applied to paper and card products to enhance their look and feel. Most graphic products use spirit varnish, which is alcohol based and dries quickly, unlike traditional oil-based varnishes. The coating also adds additional protection and makes the paper or card last longer. A varnished card has a high-shine finish and feels like plastic to the touch.

Spot UV varnish is a special varnish that is applied to the printing surface, then cured or hardened by **UV light** during the printing process. Spot varnish is only used on certain areas of the paper or card. The varnish makes the area coated shinier and clearer than the surrounding uncoated areas, making the coated parts stand out.

Figure 7.25 A business card with embossing and debossing

Embossing and debossing

Embossing and debossing give paper and card a three-dimensional image that can be seen and felt. Embossing creates a raised area on the paper or card that stands out slightly. Debossing has the opposite effect and creates a sunken or lowered area. Using both techniques can create stunning visual effects.

The embossing and debossing process uses two metal formers (a male and a female) in the shape of the design required that fit together perfectly. The card is placed between the two formers and heat and pressure are applied. This squeezes and deforms the fibres of the material into the shape of the formers.

Laminating

The coating processes applied to paper are sometimes called laminates, but they actually use spray-on methods that are completed during or straight after the paper-making process.

The other form of laminating is usually applied to finished documents, such as menus, posters, signs, identity badges and other printed documents to:

- improve their strength and resistance to bending, creasing or ripping
- waterproof the document, allowing it be wiped clean and prevent it smudging or going soggy
- improve the appearance, making the document shiny
- increase the lifespan of the printed document.

Laminating involves applying a film of clear plastic between 1.2 and 1.8 mm thick to either one or both sides of paper or thin card. There are three methods of laminating a document:

- pouch lamination
- thermal or hot lamination
- cold lamination.

Pouch lamination uses thin clear plastic pouches which are available to fit standard paper sizes, such as A3 and A4. The pouches are coated on the inside with a thin layer of heat-activated glue. The document is placed inside the film pouch, which is slightly larger than the paper, before being fed through a laminating machine. Inside the machine, the pouch is heated and pressed between rollers. The heat activates the glue which seals the pouch together as it is pressed through the rollers encasing the document inside it.

Pouch laminators can only do one document at a time, so are ideal for small-volume items. Laminating pouches and laminating machines are reasonably cheap to purchase and are readily available in schools.

Thermal or hot lamination

Where large volumes of laminated documents are required, commercial lamination methods will be needed. Thermal lamination uses rolls of thin, heat-sensitive polymer film. This method is also known as encapsulation. There are different types of film available with different properties:

- BOPP/OPP (polypropylene) film has good resistance to water, chemicals and cracking, excellent transparency, and can be recycled. It is commonly used for write-on/wipe-off products, such as calendars, labels, etc.
- PET (polyester) film has all the benefits of BOPP/OPP with improved gloss, scratch resistance and durability. It is commonly used for book covers and documents that have undergone foil application.
- Nylon film is considerably more expensive than other film due to the high temperatures needed for it to laminate, but it has a high chemical, mechanical and abrasion resistance. It will also absorb moisture in a similar way to the paper, which prevents the documents curling. It is commonly used for soft covers, such as paperback books.

As well as clear laminating films, metallic colours such as gold and silver are available. Holographic films and iridescent films that shift and change colour as they catch the light can be used to give interesting effects to the printed documents being laminated.

Cold laminating

Cold laminating is done when only one side of the paper or card is to be coated. Many cold lamination machines are inexpensive, hand-operated machines that do not require any type of power. The lack of heat makes them ideal for documents that can be damaged by heat, such as photographs.

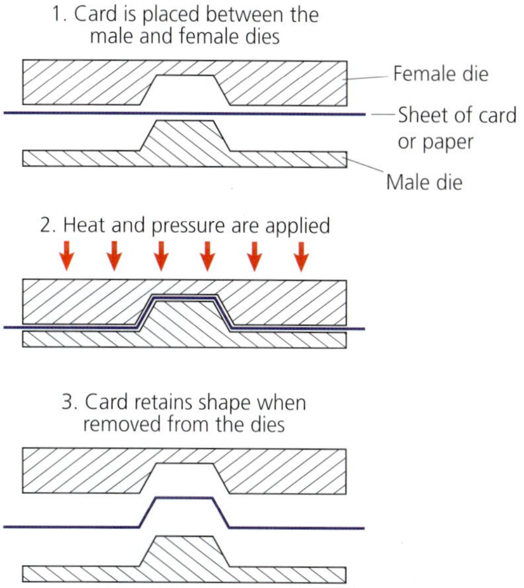

Cold lamination uses film which has a thin coating of pressure sensitive adhesive applied to one side. The film is placed over the document and passed through the machine's rollers, which press down and smooth out the adhesive, sticking the film firmly to the document. It can then be trimmed to size if necessary.

Cold lamination is mainly used in the sign-making industry. By adjusting the pressure applied by the rollers, cold lamination can also be used on other graphic products, such as foam board and PVC foam. It is also used in other areas of industry, such as coating sheets of glass, or as a protective coating for stainless steel, aluminium and acrylic.

Other laminated layers, such as Corriflute and PVC foam, which are polymers, can have additional surface finishes applied to them.

1. Card is placed between the male and female dies

Female die

Sheet of card or paper

Male die

2. Heat and pressure are applied

3. Card retains shape when removed from the dies

Figure 7.26 A The embossing process

Figure 7.27 A laminating machine producing a document

Chapter 8
Natural and manufactured timber

Learning objectives

By the end of this chapter you should have developed a knowledge and understanding of:

- the sources and origins of natural and manufactured timber
- their physical and working properties
- their ecological and social footprint
- how to select natural and manufactured timber based on function, aesthetics, cost, and environmental, social, cultural and ethical factors

- how forces and stress affect natural and manufactured timber
- the stock forms of natural and manufactured timber
- how the scale of production affects the manufacturing technique
- specialist techniques and processes
- the different surface finishes that can be applied to natural and manufactured timbers.

8.1 Sources, origins, physical and working properties of natural and manufactured timbers and their ecological and social footprint

Figure 8.1 Logging machinery

Primary sources

Trees are our primary source of timber-based materials and are grown in forests throughout the world. Britain was once covered in forests, but now, mainly due to the needs of agriculture, we import most of the timber we use. Softwoods come mainly from the cool northern parts of Europe, Canada and Russia. Hardwoods are grown in central Europe, West Africa, Central and South America. Whether you are using a **natural timber** such as pine or oak, or a manufactured board such as plywood or MDF, they all started life as a tree.

The time it takes for a tree to reach an age when it can be cut down (felled) and used commercially as timber varies depending upon the type of wood. A pine tree grows relatively quickly, only taking around 30 years to be commercially useable, whereas exotic hardwood trees can take considerably longer.

Once a tree reaches maturity it can then be felled. This is a mechanised process involving sophisticated logging machinery. The tractor carries a special adapter that can cut the tree, strip off the branches and slice the logs into manageable lengths. This operation is carried out by the driver from the comfort of their cabin in minutes. The logs are then transported to the saw mill where they are converted into useable planks.

Seasoning

Newly converted timber contains a lot of moisture and is known as 'green' timber. This makes the wood difficult to work – it is very difficult to saw or plane. It will twist, warp and split if left in this state. It is also open to rotting and is vulnerable to insect attack.

WJEC EDUQAS GCSE (9–1) Design and Technology

The high moisture content needs to be reduced by a process known as **seasoning**. There are two different methods of seasoning:

- Air seasoning – **planks** are stacked inside a building that has a roof but is open on all sides, allowing air to circulate around the boards. As the air flows around the stack it will slowly dry out the planks. This is a relatively cost-effective process, but takes a considerably longer time than kiln seasoning – it can take around a year to season a 25 mm thick plank of wood.
- Kiln seasoning – **timber** is mounted onto a trolley that is wheeled into a kiln The kiln is fully enclosed and has steam fed into it. As the moisture content of the steam is reduced it dries out the timber. This is significantly quicker than air seasoning but has a higher financial and environmental cost.

KEY WORDS

Seasoning: reducing the moisture content of timber.

Finish: an applied coating to a material in order to protect or improve aesthetics.

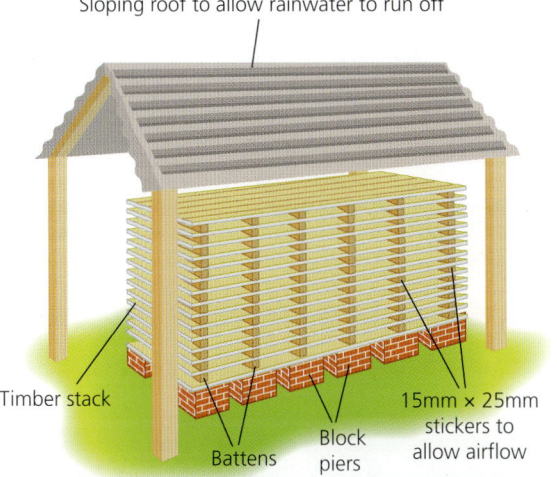

Figure 8.2 Air seasoning

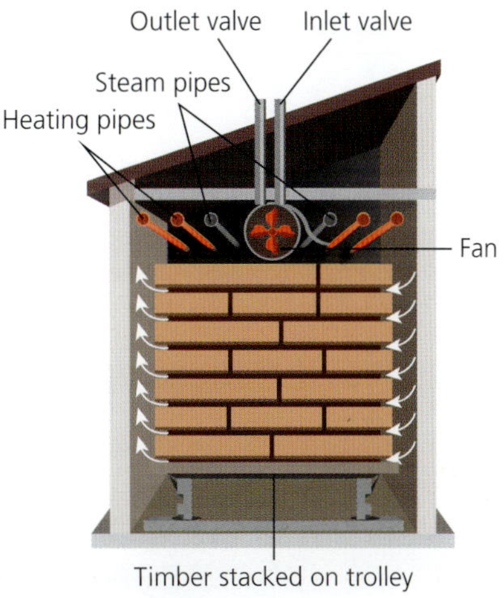

Sloping roof to allow rainwater to run off

Timber stack

Battens

Block piers

15mm × 25mm stickers to allow airflow

Outlet valve   Inlet valve

Steam pipes

Heating pipes

Fan

Timber stacked on trolley

Figure 8.3 Kiln seasoning

Defects in timber

If timber is left unseasoned it can case a number of defects.

- **Shrinkage** occurs when the newly felled timber is not seasoned correctly. The wood will dry out in an uncontrolled way and it will then twist, warp, cup and/or bow. This will cause problems if it used to manufacture products.
- **Splits** occur in the ends of the timber if the drying out of the timber is not controlled.
- **Shakes** are cracks in the timber that are a result of uncontrolled drying out of the timber. Thunder shakes can happen when a felled tree hits the ground or even during a thunderstorm!
- **Knots** form in timber where a branch has grown out of the tree trunk. Knots can cause several problems; they can weaken the timber, cause the timber to decay and can release resin which ruins the surface **finish** of the wood.
- **Fungal attack** – if timber is left unseasoned it can be attacked by fungus that will infect the timber, cause disease and ruin the wood.

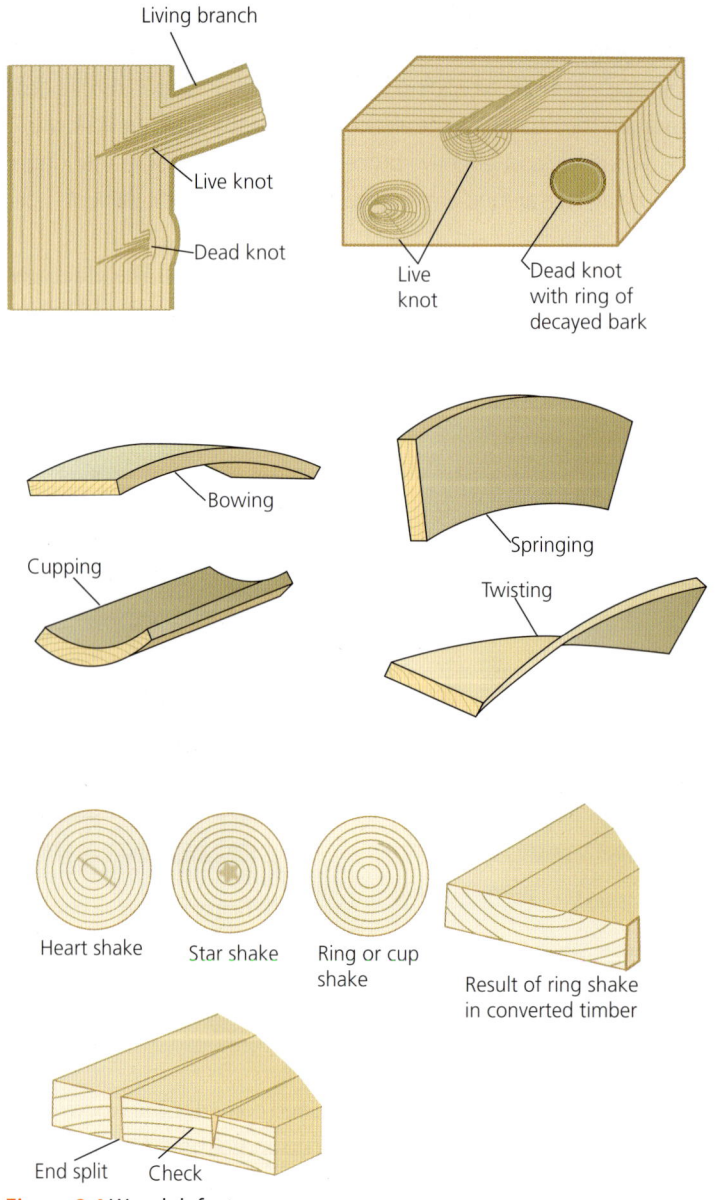

Figure 8.4 Wood defects

Types of natural timber

Natural timber is categorised in to two groups; hardwoods and softwoods (see Tables 8.1 and 8.2).

Hardwood	Properties	Common uses
Jelutong	A close grain timber with a pale colour Medium hardness and toughness Easily worked	Pattern making
Beech	A hard, strong, close-grained timber with a light brown colour with distinctive flecks of brown Prone to warping and splitting Can be difficult to work	Furniture, children's toys, workshop tool handles and bench tops

Hardwood	Properties	Common uses
Mahogany	A strong and durable timber with a deep reddish colour Available in wide planks Fairly easy to work but can have interlocking grain	Good-quality furniture, panelling and veneers
Oak	A hard, tough, durable, open grained timber Can be finished to a high standard	Timber-framed buildings, high-quality furniture, flooring
Balsa	A very lightweight, soft and easily worked timber Pale in colour but weak and not very durable	Model making, floats and rafts

Table 8.1 Hardwoods

Softwood	Properties	Common uses
Western red cedar	Very resistant to weathering and decay Has a light reddish-brown colour with a close, straight grain Easily worked	Fencing, fence posts and cladding
Scots pine	A straight-grained, light yellow-coloured timber Soft and easy to work Can be quite knotty	Interior joinery and furniture, window frames
Parana pine	Has a very distinctive open, straight grain Contains few knots and is strong and durable	Internal joinery and staircases

Table 8.2 Softwoods

Manufactured timber

Manufactured boards are commercially produced sheets of timber that offer advantages over natural timber:

- They are available in much larger sheets than solid timber (2440 mm × 1220 mm).
- They have consistent properties throughout the board.
- They are more stable than natural timbers, meaning they are less likely to warp, shrink or twist.
- They can make use of lower-grade timber, so can have environmental benefits.
- They can be faced with a veneer or a laminate to improve their aesthetic appearance.
- Due to their consistent quality, they are well suited to CNC machining and volume production.

Manufactured boards fall into two categories. **Laminated** boards are produced by gluing large sheets or veneers together and **compressed boards**, as the name suggests, are manufactured by gluing particles, chips or flakes together under pressure.

KEY WORDS

Veneer: a very thin section of natural timber.

Manufactured boards: sheets of timber that have been commercially produced.

Laminated: layers of wood glued together.

SECTION 2 IN-DEPTH KNOWLEDGE AND UNDERSTANDING

143

Medium-density fibreboard (MDF)

MDF is a compressed board that is manufactured from fine fibres of wood combined with a synthetic adhesive (usually formaldehyde resin). The MDF pulp is compressed between two heated plates where the adhesive bonds the fibres together. MDF makes use of low-grade softwood and hardwood timber, along with the waste created from other wood manufacture processing. Care should be taken to limit the dust produced when working with MDF, as it can cause respiratory issues due to the size of the fine particles.

The surface of MDF boards is smooth, which makes it easy to apply a high-quality paint finish. The edges of the board are fibrous and so need additional sealing before painting. The MDF pulp is compressed to $\frac{1}{40}$ of its original thickness, which is why MDF is denser than other manufactured boards.

In addition to standard board, MDF is also available in a range of specialist versions, including moisture-resistant board, fire-resistant board and flexible MDF. Flexible MDF has a series of small grooves, known as kerfs, cut into one side of the material, which allows the board to bend around a radius. This particular form of MDF is often used in shop-fitting applications.

MDF is also commonly faced with a veneer to improve its aesthetics. Common veneered or faced boards include oak-faced, ash-faced and beech-faced. Faced MDF can be single or double sided and adhesive veneer edging tape of the corresponding material can be applied with an iron or edge banding machine to improve the aesthetic of the otherwise exposed MDF edge.

Common uses of MDF include flat-pack furniture, decorative mouldings and shop interiors.

Plywood

Plywood is a laminated board made of several veneers of wood glued on top of each other. Each layer is laid at a 90° angle to the last, so that the grain alternates in direction. The number of layers is always an odd number and the two outside surfaces always have the grain running in the same direction. This arrangement of layers gives plywood a consistent strength across the whole board. The adhesive used to produce plywood is a formaldehyde resin.

Where the plywood is going to be visible in use, it is common to find that the outside veneers are made from a more expensive wood, such as birch or oak. Due to the very nature of the material, veneer-faced boards will differ in appearance from one to the next. While impossible to specify its appearance, timber merchants will use a plywood grading system to help with appropriate selection. 'A grade' plywood will be blemish-free and of high quality, whereas 'D grade' plywood will have knots and repair patches visible.

One of the advantages of plywood over other manufactured boards is its stiffness. This means that it is hard to bend into other shapes. You will however often see plywood in bent forms. In these cases, the glued veneers will have been compressed in a shaped mould as they dried.

You can clearly see the alternating plywood layers in the laminated skateboard in Figure 8.7, where the alternate grain provides a stiff, strong board.

Most plywood is manufactured with interior applications in mind, although it is also available in weatherproof and marine versions, where the adhesive and types of wood veneers are selected to be more suitable for exterior use. Common uses of plywood include laminated flooring, roofing, and furniture.

Figure 8.5 Medium-density fibreboard

Figure 8.6 The application of veneered MDF edging strip

Figure 8.7 Maple ply skateboard

Chipboard

Chipboard, sometimes referred to as 'particle board', is a manufactured board that is made up of large flakes or chips of timber glued together under pressure. Chipboard is cheaper to produce than MDF and plywood, but is not as strong or durable. It is commonly used in applications where cost is a more important factor than strength or aesthetics. It can be faced with a laminate or polymer film, as the unfinished surface is usually rough. Many popular chipboard applications have been superseded by MDF. Common uses of chipboard include kitchen work surfaces, kitchen cupboards and flooring.

Figure 8.8 Chipboard

Hardboard

Hardboard is a very low-cost board often used as a backing for products such as wardrobes and for drawer bottoms. It is made from wood pulp that has been compressed and heated to produce a tough board with one smooth surface and one meshed surface.

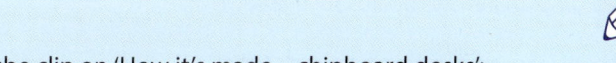

Activity

Watch the following YouTube clip on 'How it's made – chipboard desks':
www youtube.com/watch?v=GBrgZihZhjs

Identify six key stages in the production of chipboard.

Deforestation

Deforestation happens when trees are cut down and they are not replanted. This is a key concern in the manufacture of wooden products. Hardwoods take many years to re-grow and have to be managed carefully. Deforestation has a huge effect on animals and people. If there are fewer trees and less vegetation in the forests, wild animals have fewer places to live and populations decrease. Indigenous people also have fewer places to hunt and less food to eat. The Amazon alone is losing 200 000 acres of rainforest every year. Fertile soil is washed away by the rain if tree roots are not there to bind it together. This results in the silting up of rivers, leading to villages becoming uninhabitable.

Trees are said to be the lungs of the world, as they absorb carbon dioxide and give out oxygen. With fewer trees there is a greater build-up of carbon dioxide in the atmosphere, leading to greater effects of global warming.

Social footprint

The felling of trees for timber leaves a social footprint. Roads may need to be laid to gain access to the forest; this may mean disturbing towns and villages. Workers will be employed directly in the forest and in the service industries. This may provide work opportunities for local people, but specialist forest workers may need to be brought in, meaning that they may need to relocate. Working in the forest can involve performing potentially dangerous activities and workers should receive the correct training and be provided with the appropriate equipment to ensure their safety.

A greener world

Although timber is a renewable product, it is important that we understand the negative effect that the processing, use and disposal of timber can have on the environment. As a society we must reduce the amount of waste we create and aim to reuse and recycle timber products.

KEY WORD

Deforestation: large areas of trees cut down by logging.

Figure 8.9 Forest Stewardship Council (FSC) logo

Figure 8.10 Old railway sleepers used in a garden

KEY WORD

FSC: Forest Stewardship Council.

As trees are a renewable resource, it is vital that we only use timber that comes from managed forests. The **Forest Stewardship Council® (FSC®)** is an international, non-governmental organisation dedicated to the promotion of responsible forest management worldwide. FSC helps take care of forests and the people and wildlife who call them home. The FSC labels can be found on forest products that are responsibly sourced.

Timber can be reused in order to reduce the amount of trees that are cut down. Examples of this are in the building industry, where beams and structural pieces of material may be reused as products such as floorboards. Old railway sleepers are also often used in landscape gardening. FSC Recycled and FSC Mix products can contain verified reclaimed timber.

It is important in the manufacture of all products for materials to be easily separated. If materials are permanently joined it is difficult to sort them into different groups, and so temporary fixings, such as screws, are used so that products can be dismantled and the parts recycled according to their material type. When timber is recycled, it is possible to use it to make other manmade boards such as MDF.

Life cycle of timber products

Designers and manufacturers who use timber should be aware of the life cycle of the products they make. Figure 8.11 shows the typical life cycle of a wooden product from the planting of a tree to the product's final disposal or recycling.

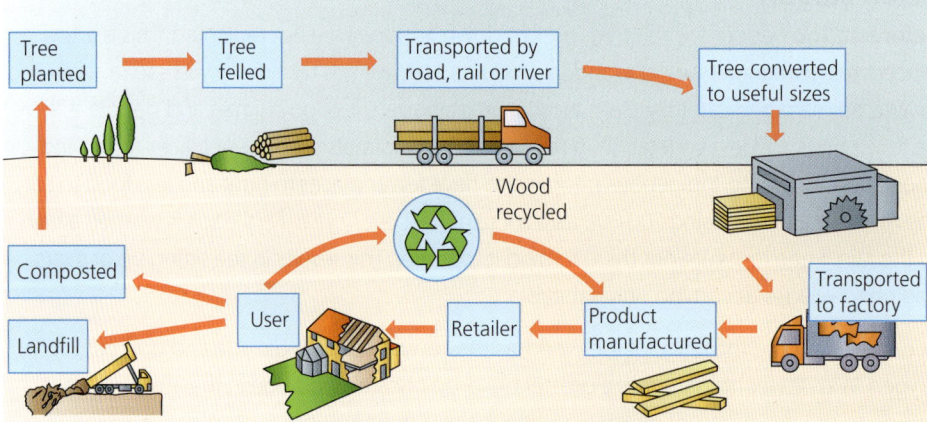

Figure 8.11 Life cycle of a wooden product

Activity

Visit the FSC website (www.fsc-uk.org/en-uk). Navigate to 'Resources' where you will find lots of activities, such as an e-magazine, fact sheets and competitions.

KEY POINTS
- Natural timber is classified into two categories: hardwoods and softwoods.
- Natural timber should be seasoned to remove excessive moisture.
- Unseasoned natural timber is prone to defects.
- Manufactured boards have the advantage of being available in large sheets and have a smooth flat surface.
- The FSC ensures that timber is produced in an ethical, moral, social and environmentally sensitive way.

8.2 The way in which the selection of materials or components is influenced by a range of factors

Functionality

There are many opportunities for using wood when designing and making prototypes. Wood is typically used when making items of furniture and for providing structure to a design. The properties of wood vary considerably. Balsa, for instance, is light in weight, soft and relatively weak, but is very easy to work, which makes it ideal for use as a modelling material. Teak is a strong hardwood and contains a natural oil that makes it an excellent choice for use in garden furniture. Oak is a very strong material that has a very decorative grain known as 'figuring', which makes it suitable for manufacturing high-quality furniture.

Aesthetics

Different types of timber are available in a wide variety of colours. Sycamore is a very pale cream coloured timber, mahogany has a deep red colour and ebony is very black. Burr walnut is a special timber that has very distinctive markings and is used by high-quality car manufacturers to make their dashboards. Bird's eye maple is a hardwood that is used by manufacturers of musical instruments to make bass guitars.

The colour of timber can be easily changed by staining or by painting. Timber can be given a varnish finish, which will give it a matt, satin, or a shiny **gloss** look.

Timber is relatively easy to shape into interesting and unique forms by sawing, planing and sanding. Very creative curved forms can be produced by **laminating** and **steam bending**.

Environmental factors

Natural timber is considered to be the most environmentally friendly material as it is renewable, reuseable, recyclable, and has a less negative impact on the environment when being processed from a tree to its stock form. Manufactured boards are less environmentally friendly, as they have undergone additional processes that involve using extra energy and adhesives. Some manufactured boards, such as MDF, also produces fine particles of dust when being machined/sanded. This fine dust can be harmful if inhaled and has been linked with cancer. Using good-quality materials and finishes can extend a product's life so that fewer replacements need to be made.

Availability

Timber is a readily available material that comes in a wide variety of stock forms, such as planks, boards, strips, dowel and mouldings. Some timbers, like oak, are slow growing, whereas bamboo grows very quickly, so more will be available in a given length of time. If managed sensitively we will never run out of timber.

Solid wood is sold in a number of different states:

- rough sawn
- **PSE** (planed square edge)
- **PAR** (planed all round).

For more information, see Section 8.4 'Stock forms'.

Figure 8.12 Wooden chair with curved, shaped back

KEY WORDS

Functionality: how well a product fits its purpose.

Aesthetics: how a product looks.

Gloss: a shiny surface finish with high lustre.

Laminating: a method of bending wood by slicing into thin veneers and gluing back together.

Steam bending: a method of bending wood by steaming, bending and cooling.

Availability: how easy it is to obtain a material.

PSE: planed square edge.

PAR: planed all round.

Cost

The price of wood can vary considerably. Rough-sawn softwoods are relatively inexpensive as there is a plentiful amount of softwood forests found throughout the world. They are relatively quick to grow and can be processed into useable timber faster than hardwoods. Softwoods are therefore very useful where large amounts of timber are required, such as in the construction industry.

Hardwoods, such as teak, oak and ash can be quite expensive as they are slow growing, are found in remote parts of the world and are less abundant. They take much longer to process into useable timber and are used to make more expensive products, such as bespoke furniture. Balsa is surprisingly expensive, but that reflects the amount of cutting to size and transportation required, and the small amounts it is usually purchased in.

Manufactured boards, such as MDF, are inexpensive as they are manufactured in large quantities from general inferior-quality or recycled timber. This makes them suitable for the flat-pack furniture industry. Special manufactured boards, such as marine plywood, are much more costly as they are produced using adhesives that are more expensive and are manufactured in smaller quantities.

The true cost of timber products

The initial price of the timber will affect the end price of a product, but these are often only a small percentage of the costs. Traditional woodworking skills are time consuming and are carried out by skilled workers who will demand a high wage. Most timber-based products will also require a finish to be applied; this will involve an additional cost. Specialist finishes, such as French polishing, are time consuming and also need to be carried out by a skilled craftsperson.

Social factors

Developments in the production of manufactured boards and automated machining processes have influenced how we buy products such as furniture. Previously, furniture would be handed down through generations of a family and there was little opportunity to buy new products. Today, flat-pack furniture is readily available and more affordable, allowing people to change the look of their home on a regular basis.

Figure 8.13 A Japanese dining table and chairs

Cultural factors

Designers of timber products need to investigate the traditions of the cultural group that the product is being made for so that the design is suitable for their needs and fits in with their beliefs of what is good or bad design. Many products are basically the same in all cultures, but the colour or way they are decorated may have specific meanings. Also, some products are very different – for example, Japanese families traditionally sit on the floor to eat their meals, so the design of dining furniture for Japan is unlike that in the western world.

Ethical factors

The use of materials and energy can have a big impact on people's lives, and we all have a responsibility to use them carefully and avoid waste. Careful and economical use of materials and the prevention or reduction of pollution during manufacture can help to keep a safe environment which does not impact unfairly on people's lives. When products are made in countries where labour is cheap, people are sometimes exploited and pollution may be less strictly controlled than in the UK.

Deforestation can lead to global warming and to certain species of animals and plants becoming extinct. Making sure that those operating machinery and working with hazardous materials are adequately protected and kept safe is an ethical necessity in today's world. Making sure that products are fit for purpose and disposed of carefully at the end of their life is also important in protecting people and the world.

Biodiversity

Forests are a very biodiverse environment. This means that not only are forests an area where trees are grown, but they also provide a habitat for many types of plants and wildlife. Many types of animal, birds, insects, grasses and flowers live within the forest and rely on them for their existence. Some of these species are now endangered and they, and their forest environment, must be protected or they will become extinct.

Activity

Figure 8.14 Softwood stool

Figure 8.15 Hardwood stool

Study the pictures of the two stools.

Evaluate the suitability of the material used in terms of:

- functionality
- availability
- cost
- aesthetics
- environmental factors.

KEY POINTS

- The properties of a timber directly affect the function of a timber-based product.
- Natural timber is available in a wide variety of colours and grain styles.
- Natural timber is generally considered to be an environmentally friendly material, but some manufactured boards contain adhesives that mean they are hard to recycle.
- Timber is a readily available product that comes in a variety of regular sections and sizes.
- The cost of timber varies, but the true cost must be taken into consideration.

Figure 8.16 A roof truss

8.3 The impact of forces and stress on materials and objects and the ways in which they can be reinforced and stiffened

Forces and stress

Timber can be used to give structure and strength to many wooden products. Think of a wooden chair; the legs must be strong enough to take the weight of the chair plus the weight of the person who will sit on it. The legs must have good **compressive strength**. Compressive strength is the ability of timber to resist being squeezed. The back of the chair must be strong enough to take the force of someone leaning back against it. The back must have good **bending strength**. Bending strength is the ability of the timber to resist being bent.

Different types of timber have different strengths and weaknesses. Oak is a particularly strong timber that can be used for the manufacture of beams in the construction of buildings. Beech is another strong timber that is used to make the benches that you use in the workshop.

Scots pine is often used to construct roof trusses. The timber is relatively lightweight and has good compressive strength enabling it to take the weight of the roof.

The strength of timber is also influenced by its cross-section. A thicker piece of timber is going to be stronger than a thin cross-section of timber.

Defects in timber will also negatively affect the strength of timber; knots will almost certainly weaken timber and must be positioned so they do not compromise the structure.

Reinforcing and stiffening

Laminated timber beams are an example of an engineered wood product. They are manufactured from layers of parallel timber laminations, normally of softwoods like pine or spruce, although hardwoods can be used. The sawn timbers are selected for strength before being glued together with the grain running in line with the laminates. Knots reduce the strength of timber so they are evenly distributed throughout. This means the beams are able to withstand high stresses.

Manufactured boards, such as plywood, are much stiffer than natural timbers. Plywood is a laminated board made up several veneers of wood glued on top of each other. Each layer is laid at a 90° angle to the last, so that the grain alternates in direction. The number of layers

Figure 8.17 Laminated timber beams above a Crossrail station in London

Figure 8.18 The structure of plywood

is always an odd number and the two outside surfaces always have the grain running in the same direction. This arrangement of layers gives plywood a consistent strength across the whole board. By adding more and more layers the strength of the plywood is significantly increased.

The cross-sectional area of natural timber has a direct effect on its strength. Natural timber floor joists support the first floor of your house and need to be very strong. They are much deeper than they are wide; usually around 300 mm deep and 50 mm wide.

Joining and fixing

The method of fixing timber products together will affect the strength of the product. Nailing is a quick and economical method of fixing two pieces of wood together, but on its own offers little strength. Screwing timbers together offers greater strength and has the advantage of being a non-permanent fixing that can be taken apart if necessary.

A butt joint is the simplest of joining methods, but is weak in comparison to a dovetail joint, which has the advantage of interlocking the wood.

Adding a glue, such as PVA, to a wood joint significantly improves its strength and gives the reassurance of a permanent fixing.

Activity

Gather together strips of different types of natural timber (30 mm × 50 mm × 3 mm would be ideal) and a similar-sized piece of 3 mm plywood.

Support each strip at the end and add weights to the middle.

Use a ruler to record how much each strip bends and record in a table similar to the one below.

Material	Weight	Amount of bend
Scots pine		
Mahogany		
Oak		
Plywood		

KEY POINTS

- The stiffness and strength of a timber is affected by the type of timber and its cross-section.
- Natural timbers can be strengthened by laminating.
- Manufactured boards, such as plywood, gain extra strength by alternating their grain direction between layers.
- The method used to fix or join timber has a direct effect on its strength.

8.4 Stock forms, types and sizes in order to calculate and determine the quantity of materials or components required

Materials are supplied in many common shapes and forms. It is important that you are aware of these stock forms when designing and planning your projects and when selecting the most appropriate material for use. The use of an appropriate stock form will keep down material costs and avoid the need for any additional machining or processing before use. Standard stock forms and sizes are cheaper than special or bespoke sizes, because they are processed in large quantities.

Natural timber

Natural timbers (hardwoods and softwoods) are generally supplied in planks, boards, strips and squares. These generally come rough-sawn straight from the sawmill, but it is common for the timber merchant to then **plane** the wood to give it a smooth surface. This can either be planed both sides (**PBS**) or planed all round (PAR), also referred to as planed square edge (PSE). It is worth remembering that the planing process removes around 3 mm off each side of the plank, therefore timber advertised as nominally PAR 100 mm² would actually be 94 mm². Planed timber is more expensive than rough-sawn, but it provides you with a more accurately sized material.

KEY WORDS

Planing: smoothing the surface of rough sawn-timber on one or more sides using a plane.

PBS: planed both sides.

Dowel: a cylindrical timber moulding of consistent cross-section.

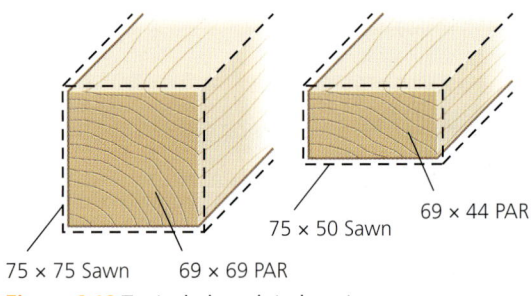

75 × 75 Sawn   69 × 69 PAR

75 × 50 Sawn

69 × 44 PAR

Figure 8.19 Typical planed timber sizes

Timber is also available in a variety of shapes and decorative mouldings. These can be used in many products, but are commonly found in framing applications and architraves. They are manufactured using a spindle moulder and a series of specialised cutters. The waste timber removed can be used in the production of manufactured boards.

The most common timber moulding shape is **dowel**. It is supplied in a range of sizes from 2 mm diameter up to 75 mm diameter and can come in lengths up to 2400 mm.

All of these timber stock forms are available in both hardwood and softwood, depending on the intended application.

Timber can also be supplied as large thin sheets known as **veneers**. They are commonly used to face the external surfaces of manufactured boards such as plywood and MDF. Veneers can also be layered up, glued together and clamped in a shaped former to form curve-shaped products.

Figure 8.20 Timber mouldings

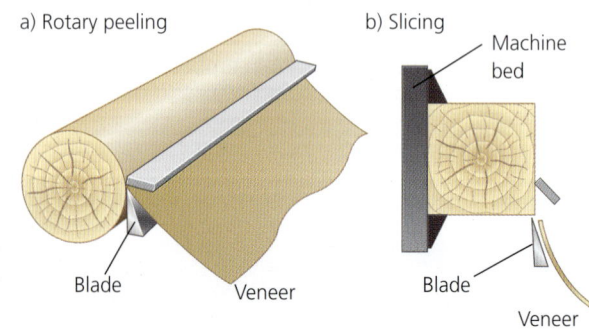

a) Rotary peeling

b) Slicing

Machine bed

Blade   Veneer

Blade

Veneer

Figure 8.21 Producing timber veneers

Veneer is available in a variety of thicknesses and can either be manufactured by rotary peeling, which is then used for plywoods, or slicing, which is more decorative and used in furniture. Rare hardwood trees are often processed into veneers, as it is one of the most efficient **conversion** processes, using as much of the original trunk as possible.

Manufactured boards

Manufactured boards are readily available in large standard-sized sheets of 2440 × 1220 mm. They are also available in a variety of thicknesses ranging from 3 mm up to 38 mm. The thickness of plywood and MDF generally increases in 3 mm increments (6 mm, 9 mm, and so on) whereas chipboard and hardboard come in a more limited range of thicknesses. Flexible plywood is one of the thinnest manufactured boards available at 1.2 mm, and MDF kitchen work surfaces one of the thickest at 38 mm.

Most manufactured boards are flat, smooth and are far less prone to the problems of twisting, warping and splitting than natural timbers. Unlike natural timber, most manufactured boards do not need any additional machining or **preparation** before they can be worked with.

Calculating the costs involved in the design of timber products

When designing a product from timber it is important to consider the costs associated with all elements of its manufacture. This includes the initial purchase of the rough-sawn timber and the costs associated with machining the material to the desired size before shaping and fabrication can take place. It is not sufficient to simply calculate the cost of the individual elements, as there will have been waste material produced throughout the manufacture. With some materials, such as metals and polymers, this waste material can be recycled or reused, reducing the overall cost of the item, but this is harder to achieve with timber-based products.

Depending on the type of product, a manufacturer may also have to take into consideration the cost of fixtures and fittings, such as cam locks, hinges or handles.

Table 8.3 compares the costs of two timber-based products that have been manufactured in different ways.

Figure 8.22 MDF storage unit versus bespoke oak dining table

	MDF storage unit	Bespoke oak dining table
Materials	Constructed from MDF, delivered to the workshop by a local supplier	Manufactured from oak selected from the timber yard by the designer
Fabrication	CNC-routered panels that are joined using PVA adhesive	Hardwood planks that are planed all round and biscuit-jointed together using a resin-based adhesive; shaped by hand with a profile
Components	Drawer sliders	Screws have been used to join the legs
Finish	Surface preparation by hand before being sprayed with a cellulose paint	Surface preparation by hand before receiving several layers of polyurethane oil
Assembly	Sold as a one-piece product with no customer assembly needed	Transported in parts and assembled by the customer at home
Delivery	Transported to the distribution centres and stores by road, rail and sea; shipped assembled in corrugated cardboard and expanded polystyrene packaging	Delivered by road direct to the customer's home; transported in parts and assembled on delivery

Table 8.3 Cost implications of different products

The MDF storage unit is a cheaper product than the bespoke piece of furniture primarily due to the significantly lower costs associated with using manufactured timber and the scale of manufacture that is possible when using CNC machinery to cut and shape component parts. Automated production, although costly to establish, will quickly produce significant savings over manual workers. A company that is batch producing an item is also likely to have greater purchasing power than a lone manufacturer. This means that they can buy components and materials in bulk.

> **Activity**
>
> Think about the projects and products that you have manufactured over your GCSE course. Can you identify the original stock forms of timber that were used?

> **KEY POINTS**
> - The common sizes, shapes and profiles that timber is supplied in are known as stock sizes.
> - When calculating the cost of timber products, do not forget to consider planing the rough-sawn material, processing costs, components and surface finish.

8.5 Alternative processes that can be used to manufacture products to different scales of production

> **KEY WORDS**
>
> **One-off production**: one product is made.
>
> **Batch production**: several identical products are made.

One-off production

One-off production gives the advantage of manufacturing bespoke timber products following the exact requirements of the client. You can use exotic timbers and work to high tolerances using highly skilled woodworkers. The disadvantage is that the products are generally very expensive, very labour intensive, take a long time to produce and are difficult to repeat.

Batch production

Batch production has the advantage of manufacturing a limited range of identical timber products. This means that materials can be purchased in bulk, which reduces the overall cost of manufacture. The time taken to make the product is reduced as machinery, tools and equipment can be set up ready for manufacture. The skill level of the labour force is reduced as many can work as machine operators. Product efficiency increases as all aspects of the work speed up. Products can be produced to exactly the same sizes and tolerances. The disadvantage is that you lose the unique element of one-off production.

The use of jigs

A **jig** is a device that is specially made to perform a specific part of the manufacturing process. Jigs are extremely useful when the process has to be carried out multiple times. They can be used when cutting, drilling, sawing, and gluing. They have a number of very important advantages:

- They speed up the manufacturing process.
- They reduce the risk of human error.
- The reduce the unit cost of a part.
- They make the process safer to carry out.
- They increase the accuracy of the process.
- They increase the consistency of the process.
- They reduce wastage.

It should be noted that there are disadvantages of using jigs:

- They are only cost effective when large numbers of similar parts are required.
- They increase the initial cost of the part.
- They require a high level of skill to produce.

Mass production

Mass production is the manufacture of timber products in large quantities. This typically uses a production line where individual parts are manufactured in sub-assemblies and then come together for final assembly and finishing. Specialist machinery is often used, but the skills required to operate the equipment and assemble the product are low, meaning that the workforce is largely unskilled and can be reorganised quickly when the product changes. Using standardised components and unskilled labour allows the cost of the specialised equipment to be offset, resulting in a large number of cheap products.

Continuous flow production

Continuous flow production is where timber products are made continuously for 24 hours per day, seven days per week. Highly specialised equipment and extensive use of computer-aided machinery (CAM) is used to manufacture the timber products. This requires a large initial investment and is only cost effective when very high numbers of the same timber product are made for long periods of time. The whole process of continuous flow production can be fully automated, meaning that workers become deskilled and are involved in servicing and maintenance rather than making.

Issues with high-volume production

High-volume production creates a number of issues. Workers become deskilled and there is less employment as the machines take over manufacture. Timber products become very similar and lose their uniqueness. More energy is need to power factories, creating greater pollution for our planet.

KEY WORDS

Jig: a device used to assist the manufacture of timber products.

Mass production: many products are made, with extensive use of machinery and manufacturing aids.

Continuous flow production: products are made 24/7, making use of computer-aided machines (CAM).

Activity

Watch the following YouTube clip on 'How it's made – dining chairs': www.youtube.com/watch?v=1M5I47Bq5vM

Identify all the specialist machines that are used in the production of the dining chairs.

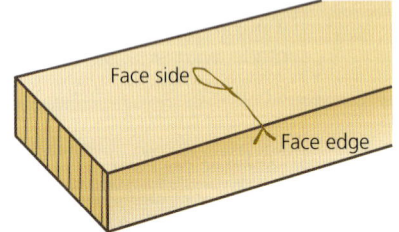

Figure 8.23 Face side and face edge marks

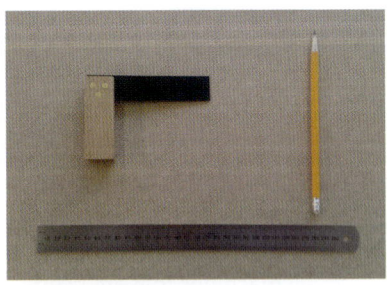

Figure 8.24 A pencil, steel rule and a try square

Wastage/addition

Marking out

If you are **marking out** a length of timber, you should start by planing a surface flat, and ensuring that one edge is square and at 90° to the surface. These surfaces are usually referred to as '**face side**' and '**face edge**'. These will give you an accurate datum or reference point from which to measure and mark out your timber. Care should be taken to mark out material lightly, as any marks will need to be removed before applying a surface finish.

When marking out a shape on a piece of board, consider the placement of the design on the material available. There is little point in marking out a shape in the centre of a large board when it will fit comfortably in the corner.

Where possible, try to choose the smallest piece of material that is suitable for the relevant design, and if marking out several items, try to **tessellate** your designs as efficiently as possible. Tessellation involves marking out your shape to make best use of the material available to you. This may mean that you have to rotate your design in order to fit more on to your available material.

Marking out tools

A soft-leaded pencil is the best tool for marking out on wood as it is easy to see and will not score the surface of the wood. A steel ruler is durable within the workshop environment and is less likely to snap or break. A try square will produce an accurate 90° line and will improve the accuracy of your work.

Top tips: make sure that your try square is pushed up tight against the side of your wood or you will not get an accurate 90° line. Always read a rule by having your eye directly over the measurement or you will get an inaccurate reading.

A **marking knife** can be used instead of a pencil. It has the advantage of producing a thin cut line that reduces tearing and acts as a guide when sawing or chiselling wood.

A **mitre square** looks similar to a try square, but is set to an angle of 45°. It can be used to measure an angle of 45° and can also check an angle of 45°. This angle is particularly important when producing a mitre joint in wood. Check out the skirting boards around the bottom of walls in your house or the corners of a picture frame and you will see a mitre joint. A **sliding bevel** performs the same function as a mitre square, but can be set at any angle. This is particularly useful when you have a series of more complex angles to cut, such as cutting the rails to fit into a wooden staircase.

Figure 8.25 A mitre square

Figure 8.26 A sliding bevel

A **marking gauge** is used to mark a line parallel to an edge. It is particularly useful to a joiner when fitting a hinge. Initially, it can be difficult to use but with practice it can save time when multiple lines need to be marked at exactly the same distance. A mortise gauge belongs to the same family of tools as the marking gauge. The **mortise gauge** has two spurs and therefore will produce two parallel lines to an edge. When marking out a mortise and tenon joint it will ensure that both the mortise hole and the tenon are marked out to the same size, increasing the accuracy of the joint.

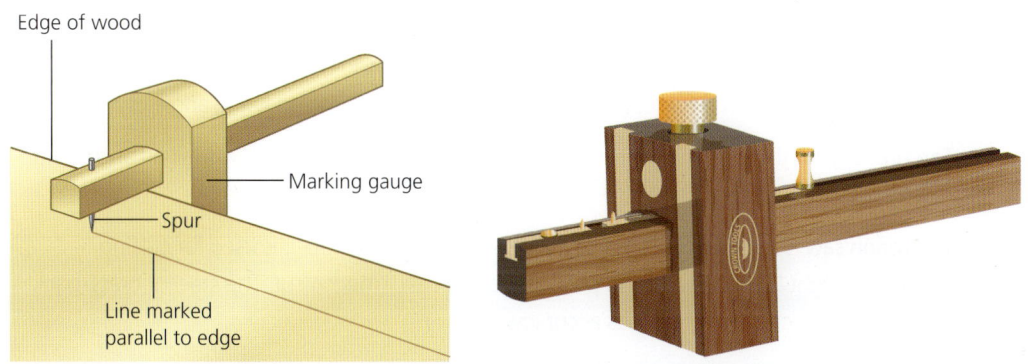

Figure 8.27 A marking gauge

Figure 8.28 A mortise gauge

Compasses are used to create a circle or an arc on wood.

A **template** consists of a profile shape of a part that is to be manufactured. They are often used for irregular shapes where it would be difficult to mark out the profile directly onto the material. Simple templates can be made from paper and could be a printed out as a CAD drawing. They are usually stuck down onto the material and then the shape can be cut out following the profile. Paper templates are generally only used as part of a one-off production.

When a batch of identical profile shapes are needed, the template may be made from a durable material. Drawing around a cardboard template would enable a number of shapes to be produced. If a larger volume of identical shapes is required then the template may be made from MDF, or even aluminium.

Measuring tools

A 300 mm **rule** is the most popular measuring device, but they are also available in 150 mm (pocket size) and in 600 mm and 1000 mm sizes for measuring longer lengths. A steel **tape** measure consists of a coiled steel tape, enclosed in a casing, which is spring loaded for

KEY WORD

Template: a 2D shape that aids cutting out a shape.

Figure 8.29 Sawing with a handsaw

quick retraction. It is used where very long lengths need to be measured and is available in sizes from 5 m to 20 m. When using a rule or a tape measure you should always make sure that your eye is directly over the measurement. If your head is slightly to one side then you will get an inaccurate reading. This is called a parallax error. Another frequent error is to forget to allow for the body of the rule when measuring between uprights such as a window.

Sawing wood

The handsaw is used for cutting thick pieces or large sheets of wood. It cuts relatively quickly, but produces a coarse, rough edge and is generally not as accurate as a 'backed' saw such as the tenon saw.

When sawing with a handsaw it is essential to have your work firmly clamped down. In Figure 8.29 you can see that the plank of wood has been clamped to the woodwork bench using a G-clamp.

Top tip: place a scrap piece of wood between the clamp and the wood to prevent bruising.

Notice the hand positions: the right hand if you are right-handed (or the left if you are left-handed) is positioned through the handle with the index (trigger) finger pointing outwards, this helps to control the saw. The other hand is placed over the top of the handle to provide power for the sawing action. The full length of the saw should be used at a sawing angle of around 45°.

Top tip: support the wood as you are coming to the end of the cut or it will fall off and could leave you with a large splinter.

The **tenon saw** is the most commonly used saw in the workshop. It is used for cutting accurate straight lines in wood and produces a relatively smooth cut. The steel or brass 'back' keeps the blade stiff and gives it its accuracy.

Figure 8.30 A brass-backed tenon saw

Figure 8.31 Sawing with a tenon saw using a G-clamp

The work piece can be clamped to the woodworking bench as with the handsaw or it can be held in the woodworking vice, or even held in a bench hook for smaller cuts.

Top tip: you can start a saw cut by dragging the saw backwards three times. This will produce a 'nick' in the wood that will allow you to check that you are about to begin sawing in the correct position. It will also provide a guide for the saw and prevent it from skidding over the surface of your wood.

The **coping saw** is used for cutting curves in wood. It can cut quite fine, intricate cuts but is not easy to control and takes practice to be able to use it accurately. The blades are thin and easily broken, but the design of the saw allows the blades to be quickly changed.

Top tip: the blade in the coping saw should face backwards as this keeps it in tension when sawing.

Shaping wood

One of the easiest ways to shape wood is by using a surform or wood rasp. These are both similar to a file but have much coarser teeth. Files can be used to shape wood but will become clogged quite quickly.

Top tip: if you do use a file to shape wood be sure to keep a file card handy. This will help you keep the file clean.

The **disc sander** is a very effective way of quickly shaping or smoothing wood. It consists of a wheel that is covered with abrasive paper that spins around removing waste wood. You must ensure that you follow all the relevant safety precautions when using this machine. In particular, you should be wearing an apron and safety glasses and ensure that guards are fitted and that the dust extraction system is switched on.

The **linisher and belt sander** works in a similar way to the disc sander but produces a flat surface.

Top tip: make sure that the grain on your wood is facing in the same direction as the direction of the linisher/belt sander.

A **plane** works in a similar way to a chisel in that it slices away thin shavings of wood. All planing should be done in the same direction as the flow of the grain or the surface will tear. End grain can be planed but must have a waste piece clamped to the end, or it should be planed from the ends to the middle; this will prevent the ends from splitting.

There are two main types of plane, as well as a wide variety of special planes.

The **jack plane** is a general-purpose plane used to flatten and smooth the surface and the edges of wood.

The **smoothing plane** is used on small wooden parts or for final cleaning of wooden surfaces.

Figure 8.35 shows four different types of special plane and the type of cut that they produce.

Figure 8.32 A coping saw

Figure 8.33 A surform

Figure 8.34 Cleaning a file

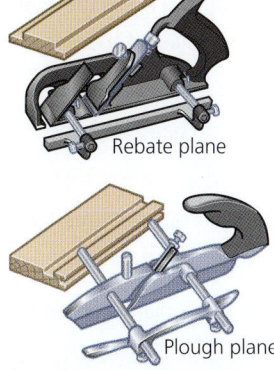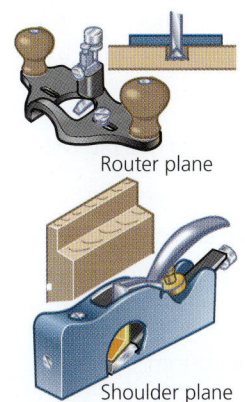
Rebate plane

Router plane

Plough plane

Shoulder plane

Figure 8.35 Special planes

Figure 8.36 Using a chisel to cut a housing joint

Chiselling is used for shaping wood and for producing a variety of wood joints. Your work should be firmly held in a vice or G-clamped to the workbench, with your hands always behind the cutting edge. Horizontal paring will produce a flat horizontal surface while vertical paring will produce a flat vertical surface. Paring involves pushing the chisel through the wood.

Drilling

Drill bits will produce a round hole in your wood. Drill bits come in various sizes and you can get specialist drills that will produce quite large holes. It is important to be able to select the most suitable type of drill bit and to be able to use it safely, accurately and efficiently. Wear the correct **PPE** (personal protective equipment) and make sure your work is firmly held.

A **bench** or **pillar drill** is an essential piece of workshop machinery. Its speed can be changed to suit the size of drill bit and the type of material being drilled. In general, a large drill bit and hard materials require a slow speed while small drill bits and soft materials need a fast drill speed. The bench/pillar drill is normally fitted with a depth-stop so that holes can be drilled to a predetermined depth, and it has numerous safety devices including a chuck guard and an emergency stop button.

KEY WORD

PPE: the range of protective equipment or clothing worn when working with a material.

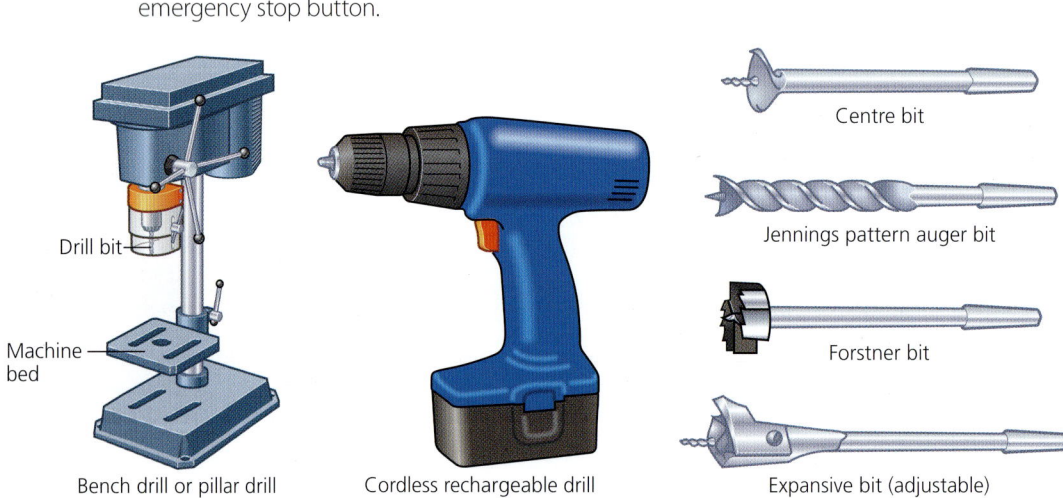

Figure 8.37 A bench drill   **Figure 8.38** A cordless drill   **Figure 8.39** A selection of drill bits

Cordless drills are popular with tradespeople as they do not need to be connected to a power source and can therefore be used in remote locations. As well as drilling holes they can be also used as a power screwdriver. You can even set the torque (turning force) of the drill so that small screws do not receive too much power.

Twist drills are the most popular type of **drill bit**. They are made from hardened and tempered high-carbon steel.

Countersink bits are used to open the top of a pre-drilled hole to accept a countersunk screw. This makes the screw level or slightly recessed below the surface of the material.

Flat bits are used for drilling holes in wood. They are available in larger diameters and, as the name suggests, leave a flat bottom.

Figure 8.40 Using a Forstner bit

A Forstner bit will produce a large, clean hole with a flat bottom. The drill produces a lot of torque (turning force) and therefore it is essential that the work is firmly clamped down or the work piece will spin out of your hands.

A hole saw will also produce a large hole, but the finished hole will not be as clean and it will cut all the way through the material. The drill will produce a lot of torque and therefore it is essential that the work is firmly clamped down.

Top tip: ensure that there is a scrap piece of wood underneath your wood so that the hole saw can drill all the way through or continue drilling until the pilot drill emerges and then reverse the work.

A drilling jig will ensure that a series of holes are drilled in exactly the same place every time. This speeds up the manufacturing process, reduces human error, make the process safer to carry out and increases the accuracy and consistency of the process.

Figure 8.41 Using a hole saw

Deforming/reforming

Joining wood
We classify the joining of material into two categories.
- Temporary joints are joints that can be taken apart, such as screws and nuts and bolts.
- Permanent joints are joints that cannot be taken apart, such as glued joints.

Wood is a very versatile material and can be joined in a variety of ways. There are three main categories of joints.

Different **carcase or box joints** have their own advantages and disadvantages. A butt joint is relatively easy to produce, but is not the strongest joint. A comb or finger joint requires a higher degree of skill to produce, but is far superior in strength. Aesthetically, the mitre joint looks attractive, while a nail joint looks inferior. The lap joint is a simple method of joining wood that gives greater strength and accuracy than a butt joint. A housing joint is typically used to join a shelf into a bookcase. A dovetail is one of the hardest joints, requiring

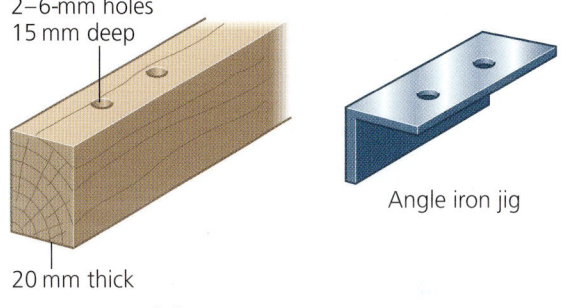

Figure 8.42 A drilling jig

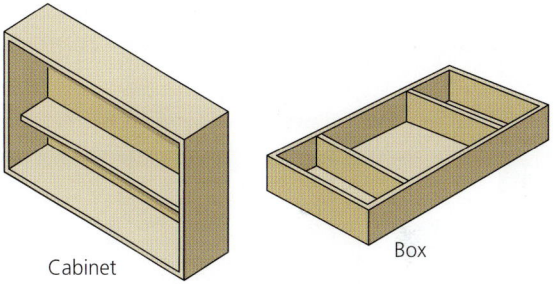

Figure 8.43 Carcase or box construction

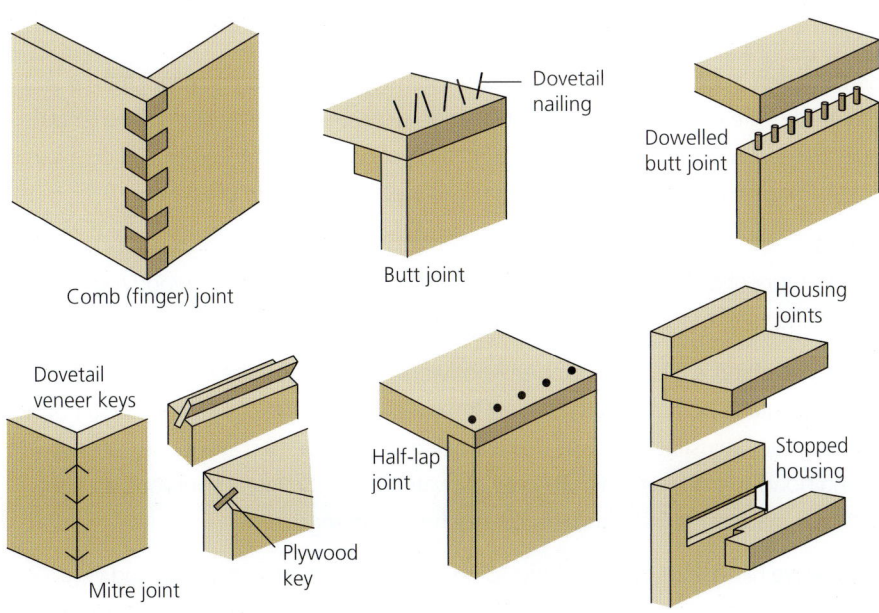

Figure 8.44 Carcase or box joints

a high level of skill to cut by hand. Dovetails are typically found on expensive furniture as part of a drawer construction.

Stool joints should be used when you need to connect a leg to a rail, such as on stools, tables and chairs. The dowel joint is a relatively simple joint that involves joining wooden pieces together with dowels, which are cylindrical connecting pieces of hardwood that are inserted into a pre-drilled hole and glued in place. The mortise and tenon joint is a more complex joint that gives greater strength due to the increase in surface area of the joint. This joint consists of a rectangular section of wood that is cut from the rail (the tenon) and a rectangular hole (the mortise) that has been chiselled out of the leg. The tenon is inserted into the mortise hole and glued into place. A bridle joint is slightly easier to produce than a mortise and tenon join, but is not as strong and is also has the disadvantage of being visible.

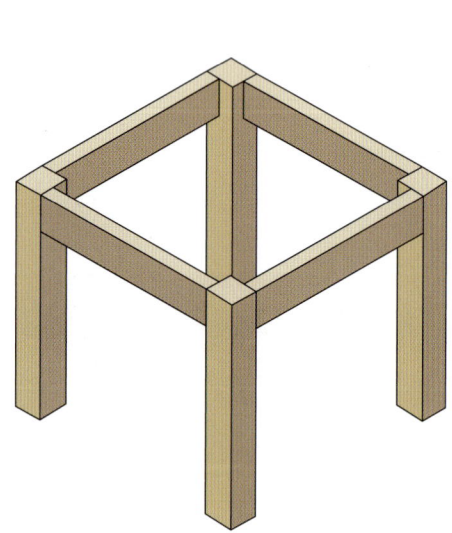

Figure 8.45 Stool construction

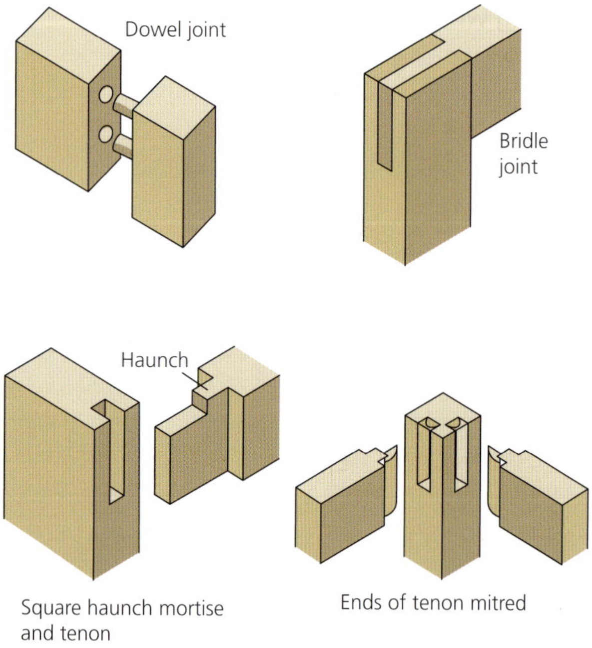

Figure 8.46 Stool joints

Frame construction is used to produce panels, door frames, window frames, mirror frames and picture frames. For greater strength in door and window construction, the mortise and tenon joint would be used. A halving joint is a simpler method of producing the corner joint on a frame and a cross-halving joint can be used where crossrails meet in the centre of a frame.

Adhesives

There are a number of different types of adhesives that can be used to glue wood together. Before any gluing takes place, all surfaces should be free from dust and dirt.

PVA (polyvinyl acetate) is the most popular woodworking glue. It can be used straight from the bottle and requires no further preparation. It has a good amount of slip time (the amount of time you have for adjusting the parts that are being glued together) and it dries clear, giving a very strong bond. It is available in both exterior (waterproof) and interior versions. Its main disadvantage is that it takes 24 hours before it reaches full strength.

Contact adhesive has the advantage of providing an almost instant joint. It is spread very thinly over both surfaces of the wood then left to dry for several minutes. It is then pushed together providing a quick joint. Its main disadvantages are that it is not as strong as PVA, does

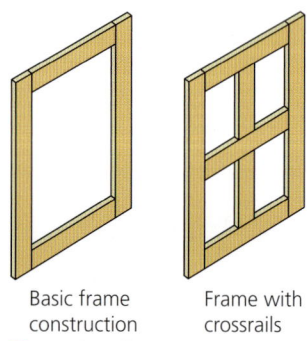

Basic frame construction

Frame with crossrails

Figure 8.47 Frame construction

not dry clear and has a number of health and safety issues – it is an irritant to the eyes and skin, and is highly flammable.

Epoxy resin is a strong, waterproof, two-part adhesive that can glue dissimilar materials together. Equal amounts of glue and hardener are first mixed together and then applied to the surface of the materials to be joined. The joint will usually need to be clamped together until the epoxy resin sets.

Screws

Wood screws are effective in joining two pieces of timber together or for joining another material to a wooden structure. They can also be removed easily to dismantle the parts. They normally have one or two teeth that spiral around their shank; turning them winds them into the wood. There are hundreds of types of screws with special features for particular functions, but Figure 8.49 shows one of the most common types. Note the cross head (Pozidriv®) that allows it to be driven easily with a cordless screwdriver.

Wood screws have different designs of heads and there are specially designed screwdrivers and screwdriver bits for each. The two most common are Pozidriv and slotted.

Screws also have different shaped heads depending on the application that they are going to be used for.

The countersunk screw is by far the most popular type of screw used. It has the advantage of being able to be fitted so it sits flush (level) or lower than the surface of the wooden pieces being joined. Where the thickness of the wood does not allow it to be countersunk a round headed screw would be used. This type of screw sits above the surface.

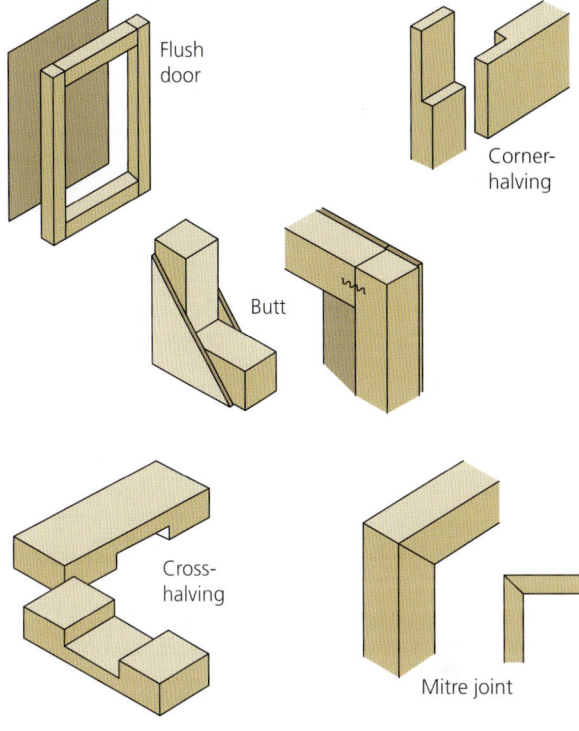

Flush door

Corner-halving

Butt

Cross-halving

Mitre joint

Figure 8.48 Frame joints

Figure 8.49 A modern woodscrew

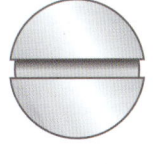
Straight slot

Phillips

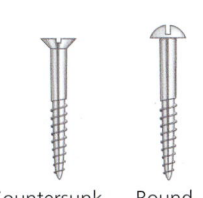
Pozidriv

Figure 8.50 Common screwdriver slots

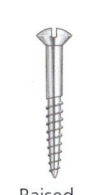
Countersunk   Round   Raised   Twinfast   Coach

Figure 8.51 Common screw heads

Traditionally, you would go through the following stages to fit a wood screw to join two pieces of wood.

1 Drill a pilot hole through the top layer of wood and into the base wood. The diameter should be the size of the core of the screw.
2 Drill a clearance hole slightly larger than the shank of the screw (outside diameter).
3 Countersink the top of the hole to make a recess for the head of the screw to sit in.

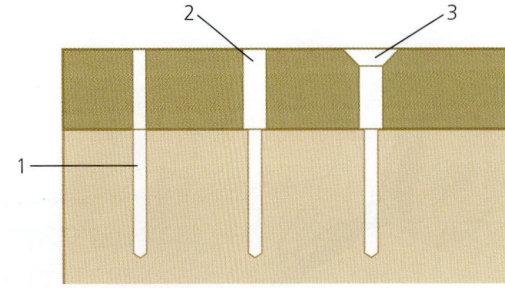

Figure 8.52 Joining two pieces of timber

This can be a time-consuming process, but modern screws have special features that reduce or avoid the need to go through the stages listed above. The TurboGold screw in Figure 8.53 is a good example of an efficient modern design.

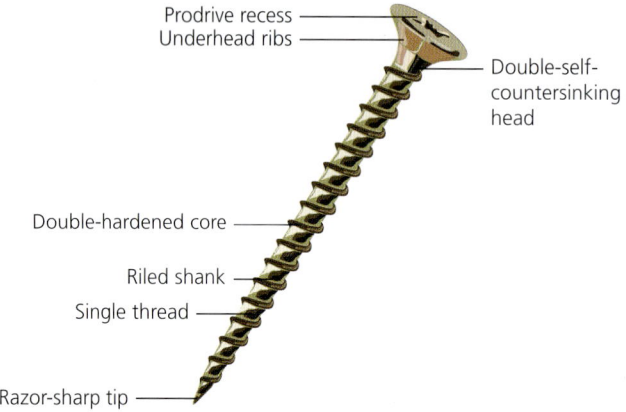

Prodrive recess
Underhead ribs
Double-self-countersinking head
Double-hardened core
Riled shank
Single thread
Razor-sharp tip

Figure 8.53 A TurboGold screw

Woodscrews made from steel are usually zinc-coated to prevent corrosion. Where greater resistance to moisture is needed, brass or stainless steel screws are normally used.

Knock-down (KD) fittings

Many retailers sell furniture unassembled in cardboard boxes, often known as 'flat-pack furniture'. The advantage of this sort of furniture is that it is much more compact and therefore easier and cheaper to transport. The disadvantage is that it needs to be assembled by the customer.

Manufacturers have developed a wide range of components especially to allow for ease of assembly and adjustment with a few basic tools. Typically, a screwdriver and Allen key are all that are needed to join all the parts together.

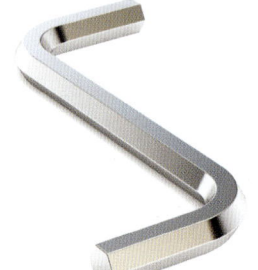

Figure 8.54 Allen key

An Allen key is a small hexagonal shaped tool that can be used with socket heads or hex head fixings. Allen keys are available in a wide range of sizes and are useful as they have a greater contact area with the fixing than a traditional screwdriver head, so are less likely to slip. The shape of the Allen key also allows the user to access hard-to-reach fixings.

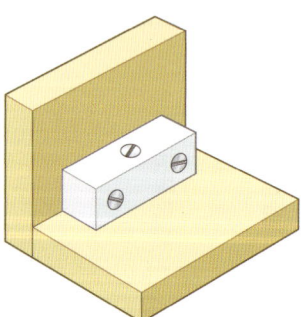

Figure 8.55 Corner block

Corner blocks are a simple way to join two boards together at 90° to each other. They are often used to join parts of a cabinet. The block fits in the corner, between the two parts, and three screws are driven in; one into the shelf and two into the side of the cabinet. Although they are easy to use, they are less attractive than other methods because they are very visible. The limited thickness of the material being joined can also cause difficulties with screw length.

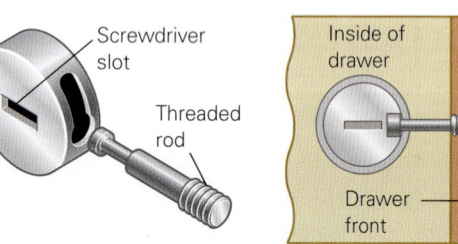

Screwdriver slot
Threaded rod

Figure 8.56 Cam lock

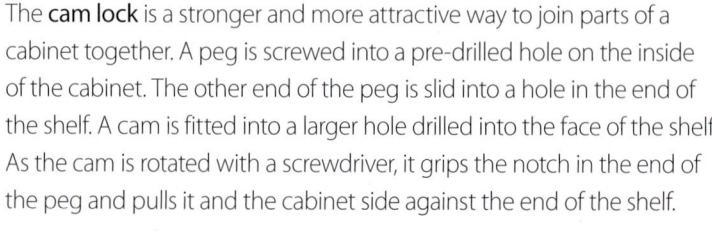

Inside of drawer
Drawer front

The **cam lock** is a stronger and more attractive way to join parts of a cabinet together. A peg is screwed into a pre-drilled hole on the inside of the cabinet. The other end of the peg is slid into a hole in the end of the shelf. A cam is fitted into a larger hole drilled into the face of the shelf. As the cam is rotated with a screwdriver, it grips the notch in the end of the peg and pulls it and the cabinet side against the end of the shelf.

A scan fitting is also known as a 'cross dowel and bolt' or a 'captive barrel nut and bolt'. This is another way of joining two parts together at 90°. More often, it is used to join a table leg to its rail, or a bed headboard to the bed frame. An aluminium barrel is fitted into a pre-drilled hole in the side of the frame. An Allen screw is passed through a hole in the leg, into a hole in the end of the frame. Care must be taken to align the threaded hole in the aluminium barrel with the Allen screw. Tightening the Allen screw pulls the leg onto the end of the frame.

A corner plate is a swift way to join the top of a table leg to the frame under the table top. The diagram in Figure 8.58 is of an upturned table. The plate is screwed onto the two parts of the frame, and the leg is pulled tight against the frame parts by tightening the nut on the studding fitted to the table leg.

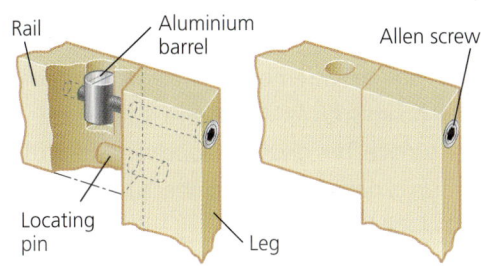
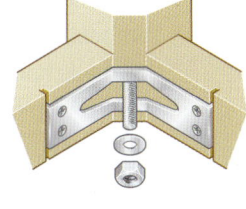

Figure 8.57 Scan fitting

Figure 8.58 Corner plate

Laminating and steam bending

Complex bends in wood can be achieved by a process known as laminating. It is important to choose a suitable type of wood to laminate; it needs to be a close-grained hardwood such as beech. A furniture maker will use lamination to produce unusual and interesting curved pieces of furniture.

Firstly, a former needs to be produced. This is additional work that will take time, money, resources and skill. Because of these factors, lamination is only usually undertaken when batches of products are required. The former will be made from a durable material, such as multi-ply, and clamped together using G-clamps or wedges.

The wood is firstly sawn into veneers. As the veneers are thin they will easily bend round the former. Each veneer should be slightly longer and wider than the final product to allow for finishing. The veneers will be glued and clamped into the former and left until dry. Once dry the lamination is removed from the former and trimmed and finished.

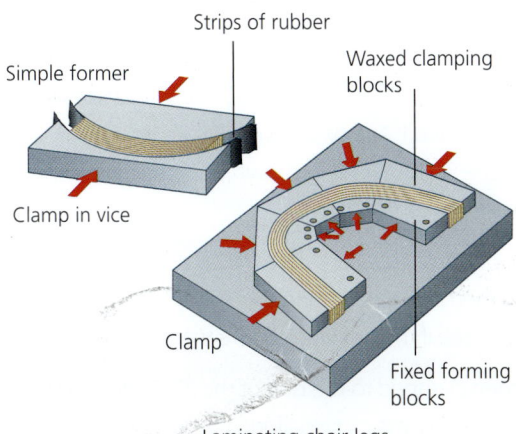

Figure 8.59 The process of laminating

Figure 8.60 A laminated chair

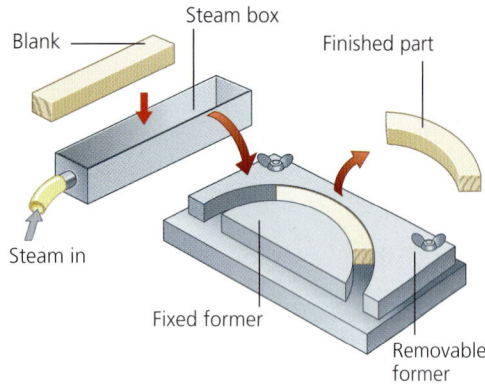

Blank — Steam box — Finished part — Steam in — Fixed former — Removable former

Figure 8.61 The process of steam bending

Steam bending allows a solid piece of wood to be bent. Again, selection of the type of wood is important; it needs to be a strong wood such as oak, ash or beech. As with lamination, a former needs to be produced, making this method only really suitable for batch production.

The wood is firstly steamed in a steam box. Typically, this will take a few hours to make the wood pliable enough for it to be bent into the former. It is then clamped into position and left to fully dry. Once dry it can be removed from the former and trimmed and finished.

Veneering

Veneers of wood can also be used as a way of enhancing the appearance of timber. In industry, mass production self-assembly furniture would initially be made from a manufactured board such as MDF, then a real-wood veneer would be glued to the surface. This gives the appearance that the furniture has been made from an expensive natural timber such as oak. This considerably reduces the cost of the furniture.

Veneering can be easily done in the school workshop by taking a manufactured board, a real-wood veneer and gluing them together with either contact adhesive or PVA.

Computer-aided manufacture (CAM)

Laser cutting

The laser cutter can cut timber-based materials into thin sections of up to 3 mm. There are a number of manufactured boards that are specially produced to work with the laser and will cut with minimal discolouration due to burning. The laser is very effective at etching onto the surface of wood and produces an accurately burned image similar to that achieved by pyrography, which is the burning of an image into the surface of a material, usually done with a hot tool similar to a soldering iron. When etching, the laser cutter can work from a CAD drawn image but can also work from an imported image. Monochrome line drawings can be downloaded from the internet and work very well.

Figure 8.62 Laser-cut wooden coasters

The 3D router

The 3D router is capable of machining 3D products from timber-based materials. Most types of wood can be machined, but close-grained hardwood produces the best results. Many manufactured boards can be used, but chipboard would not be recommended due to its open, brittle nature. Modelling polymers such as PVC foam sheet work extremely well with the 3D router, producing high-quality models with a very good surface finish.

The 3D router requires a CAD drawing to be produced. At a basic level this can be a 2D image using relatively simple 2D CAD software, but the 3D router really shows its capability when used with sophisticated 3D CAD software.

The CAD image shown in Figure 8.63 is for a portable speaker system to be used with a mobile phone. Having drawn the image, it is then processed using the 3D router's dedicated software, and a computer simulation checks to see if the drawing can be manufactured.

A suitably sized piece of PVC foam sheet is then clamped to the bed of the 3D router and the correct cutting tool is fitted. As the cutting tool spins, it is moved along the x, y and z axes, powered by three stepper motors that are controlled by a computer. The combination of the three directional movement means that virtually any 3D image can be produced.

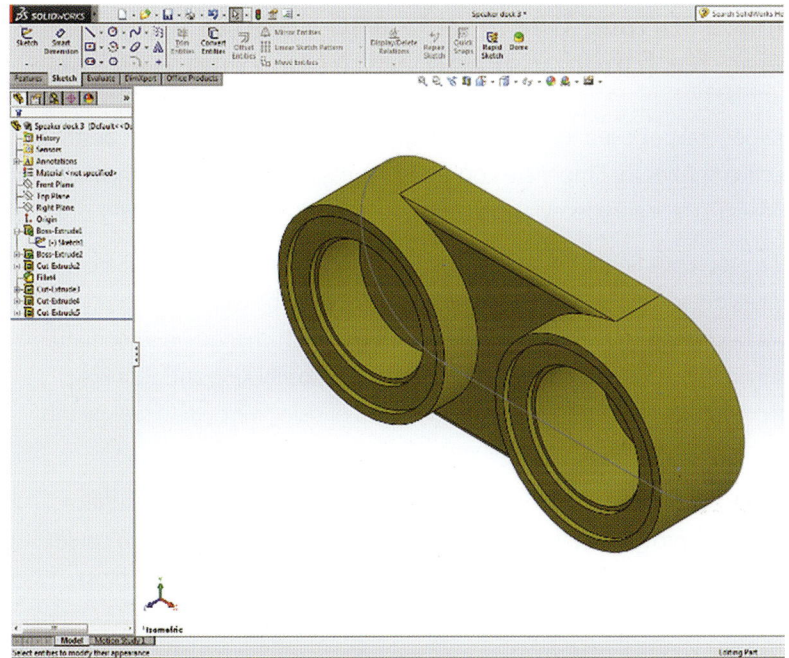

Figure 8.63 A CAD image of a portable speaker system

Figure 8.64 Machining a PVC foam model

Figure 8.65 Finished portable speaker system

If the designer/client is happy with the model then the process can be repeated with a timber-based material. Figure 8.65 shows the finished design machined from mahogany.

This process can then be repeated many times to produce accurate, consistent outcomes. As more products are produced the unit cost of each product is reduced.

Activity

Your work desk at home is no doubt cluttered with pens, pencils, rulers and other items of stationery that you use every day. Use 2D or 3D CAD software to produce yourself a desk tidy that consists of a block of wood that has several holes, slots and recesses machined into it to hold specific items of stationery.

You should then machine this out on the 3D router.

You can even develop your design to hold other items, such as your smartphone, tablet, loose change, etc.

If you do not have access to CAD/CAM equipment then you can do this by traditional methods.

Mark out where you want the holes and recesses on a block of wood and use a combination of drilling and chiselling to produce the holes and recesses.

KEY POINTS
- Accurate marking out is essential if you are to achieve a quality product.
- Jigs and templates will speed up the making process and help achieve consistency.
- There are many saws that will cut wood and it is important to be able to match the saw to the process.
- Chisels and planes help to shape and smooth wood.
- Disc sanders, belt sanders and linishers will mechanically smooth wooden surfaces.
- Wood can be bent by kerfing, steam bending and laminating.

8.7 Appropriate surface treatments and finishes that can be applied for functional and aesthetic purposes

Surface finishes are generally applied to a material to either protect it or enhance its aesthetic appearance. Protective finishes for timber are applied to increase the durability of the material, to protect it from insect attack and decay, and to improve its resistance to weathering.

The application of a protective finish is especially important in timber products that are going to be used outside, as they are more likely to be exposed to the elements. The cycle of a timber product becoming wet and then drying out, along with changes in temperature and exposure to sunlight, quickly damages the surface, leading to cracking and shrinking. The application of preservatives or specific external varieties of paint will help to reduce this degradation, and increase the timber's durability.

It is rare that a finish for timber is applied to perform a purely protective role. Most surface finishes are also used to improve or alter the aesthetic appearance of a product. This could involve changing the colour of a timber by painting or staining, or applying a clear gloss varnish or oil to enhance the timber's natural colouration and grain.

It is uncommon for a timber product to be used without some kind of surface finish or treatment having been applied, but cedar is one timber that is often found unfinished in outdoor applications, such as building cladding. Cedar has natural oils that help protect it against damage from the elements, and it naturally resists insect attack.

Figure 8.66 A modern cedar-clad building

Surface preparation

Before applying a finish to a timber surface, it is important to get the surface smooth and flat. Any imperfections in the surface, such as scratches and dents, are often accentuated by the application of a finish. If you are using a clear finish, such as varnish or oil, it is also very important to remove all pencil and pen markings from the surfaces. The preparation of the timber surface is described in Section 8.8, below.

Finishes for timber

When choosing a finish for timber, it is important to think of the effect that you want to achieve, the environment in which is going to be used, and what sort of timber it is going to be used on. If you are using natural timber or plywood with an attractive outer layer, you may want to use a finish which allows you to see the natural grain pattern of the timber. You may want a completely clear finish, or one that changes the colour of the timber while still showing the grain pattern. With these finishes, and fully coloured finishes, you will also need to decide whether you want a matt, silk or shiny finish.

Stain

Stains are applied to enhance or change the colour of the natural timber. Many are variations of the brown, red and black colours of hardwoods, so a softwood can be stained to mimic a hardwood. Sometimes bright colours are used (for example, for children's toys). It is important to apply the stain evenly, with a cloth or brush, and it is worth testing it first on some scrap materials. The stain itself does not give much protection to the timber; it is mainly used to change the colour. It will need an additional clear finish such as varnish or wax applied over it to give protection. Alternatively, you can buy varnishes which have coloured stains in them. These are more difficult to apply evenly, as each layer of varnish will intensify the colour change, so coats need to be applied very evenly.

Figure 8.67 Modern preservatives have excellent water repelling properties

Preservatives

These products are applied to wood to help it repel water and moisture and in some cases resist insect attack. Traditionally, a brown product called Creosote was used, typically on sheds and fences. In recent years, manufacturers have developed an attractive range of **preservative** colours, which are easy to apply with a brush and repel water really effectively.

Commercially, preservatives can be added to timber through a process known as tanalising. Here, the timber is placed in a sealed chamber where the preservative is pumped in under pressure, forcing the preservative liquid to penetrate the outer cells of the timber. The level of penetration and therefore level of protection achieved can be adjusted by altering the pressure and time. You can see in Figure 8.68 how the preservative has penetrated the outer layer of the timber decking section.

Figure 8.68 Tanalised wooden decking

Preservatives that are applied to timber products before they are sold will not last indefinitely and are quickly degraded by the elements. Therefore, it is common to have to reapply preservatives throughout the life of the product, and a range of preservative paints are available. These are generally applied by brush or can be sprayed onto large objects such as fences.

Varnish

Varnish can achieve a similar look to polish, but gives better protection to the surface. This is particularly so of modern polyurethane and acrylic varnishes. Like polish, the varnish needs to be built up in thin layers, with each layer drying thoroughly before sanding. The final coat can have wax applied to it to achieve an even higher-quality finish.

Oils

Oils are applied to enhance the natural oils already in the woods. They are applied with a cloth and can be built up in layers. The oil soaks into the timber, enhancing the timber's ability to repel moisture, without creating a layer on top of the wood that would flake off in time. Teak oil is excellent for oily hardwoods like teak and is widely used on yachts. Danish oil, which is mainly linseed oil, is excellent for lighter-coloured

Figure 8.69 Re-oiling some teak garden furniture

woods and is used both indoors and outdoors. Beech worktops are often treated with Danish oil. Oiled timber products often need recoating periodically.

Polishes

Polishes protect the timber and enhance the natural pattern and colour of the timber. A shellac polish can be used to create a deep, high-quality finish; this process is often referred to as French polishing. It is used on high-quality furniture pieces. As with many timber finishes, the most effective way to create a hard-wearing finish is to slowly build up the coating in thin layers.

Figure 8.70 Acrylic paints on a plywood toy for a child

Paints

Painting gives a solid colour finish to the surface of the wood; you cannot see the wood grain through it, if the surface is flat. You will need to build up the paint in layers, starting with a coat of primer to seal the wood, then a layer of undercoat, followed by at least one coat of top coat. The finish may be matt, silk or gloss, giving different levels of reflection of light. The paint surface needs to be rubbed down with fine glass paper between each coat of paint to help ensure a smooth finish. If the wood has knots, these need to be treated with knotting before applying the primer, to stop any sap bleeding through the paint finish.

When choosing paint for wood, oil-based paints are generally tougher and more durable, but take longer to dry. Acrylic paints usually dry quicker and are often non-toxic, making them suitable, for example, for a child's toy.

Paint can also be applied from an aerosol spray can or, for larger areas, with a roller. Emulsion paint, designed for house walls, is often more suitable for brush application on large surfaces.

Commercially produced spray finishes can be applied to timber using specialised spray equipment that runs off a compressor. The quality of finish that can be achieved commercially is generally better than that achievable by brush or roller. The paint used can be water- or solvent-based. The appropriate personal protective equipment (PPE) that the operator would wear would depend on the type of paint being used. You can see that extraction and respiration equipment are hugely important in a spray paint environment. Developments in technology have meant that timbers can now also be powder-coated (see below). It is common to find MDF furniture and kitchen doors finished in this way.

Activity

Identify and list the health and safety measures that should be taken at each stage when spraying a piece of timber in a school environment.

KEY POINTS

- Stains and paints can change the colour and appearance of a timber.
- Oils are generally applied to provide a protective finish.
- The finish of varnishes and paints can be matt, satin or gloss.
- Remember to consider the end of use of a timber product when selecting the appropriate material, fixings and finishes.

8.8 Designing and making principles for natural and manufactured timber

Choosing a manufacturing method

We have covered a wide variety of timber manufacturing processes and have learnt about the correct use of tools and machinery, but what decisions need to be considered when choosing the most appropriate manufacturing method for a prototype?

When working with softwoods and hardwoods it is important to consider the intended end use of the product; this will help determine the variety of materials chosen, the strength and type of the joints or fixings used and the manufacturing process chosen.

Where a traditional timber outcome is required, such as a dining room table or chair, you may choose to use traditional cutting, shaping and joining techniques. There is nothing to say that the outcome has to be traditional, but many wood joints such as dowel joints and mitres are excellent ways to create strong timber products.

Where more organic shapes may be required, then laminating and steam bending may provide you with a reliable method to create curves and bends in timber. Traditional two-part laminating moulds may have limitations with the size of object to be made, but vacuum-bag systems and polyurethane foam moulds allow for greater creativity. When these are used in commercial products, the mould is cut using a CNC hot wire system, thus achieving accuracy. In school workshops you are more likely to shape mould using a bandsaw and sander, or in some cases a CNC router.

Figure 8.71 Plywood laminated balance bike

Manufactured boards, such as MDF and plywood, are ideal materials to machine accurately using a CNC router. The large flat smooth surface can be easily clamped down using a vacuum bed, which speeds up the manufacturing process by removing the need for mechanical clamps. These manufactured boards are also easy to join and assemble using knock-down fittings, as seen in flat-pack furniture.

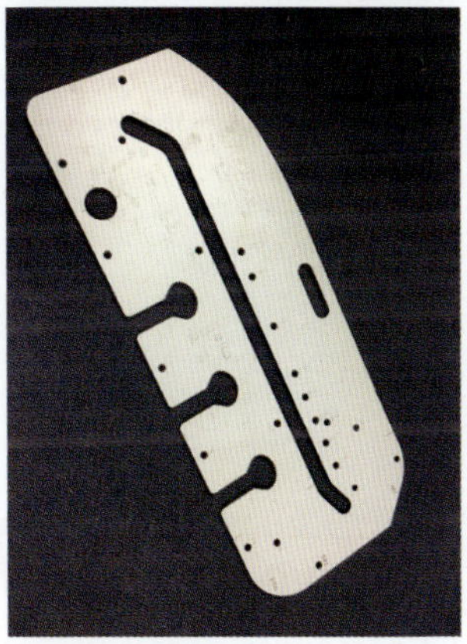

If you do not have access to a CNC router, then a handheld router could be used to create accurate shapes in timber. If you are looking to create a channel or a profile along a length of material, then the use of a router table may be suitable. Otherwise, you could produce a template that the router could follow. For common shapes it may be possible to use a pre-made router template such as the ones used by kitchen fitters.

Finishes

Protective finishes for timber are applied to increase the durability of the material, to protect it from insect attack and decay, and to improve its resistance to weathering. Most surface finishes are also used to improve or alter the aesthetic appearance of a product. The different finishes available, and reasons for choosing each one, were explained in Section 8.7, above.

Figure 8.72 Kitchen fitter's jig

Preparation

With all surface finishes, the success and quality of the final finish is directly related to the preparation that has taken place on the material beforehand. It is important to sand down the wood to provide a clean, smooth surface.

To sand down the surface of natural timbers and the edges of manufactured boards, a sharp, finely set, smoothing plane is most efficient. On curved surfaces, or on the faces of manufactured boards, abrasive paper or glasspaper is best.

Figure 8.73 Preparing a timber surface with abrasive paper

Figure 8.74 A cellulose varnish being applied to a softwood floor by hand. The varnish both accentuates the natural grain pattern and protects the timber from wear, increasing its durability.

The higher the grit rating, the less coarse the glasspaper. You will need to start with coarse glasspaper (60 or 80 grit) and work your way through to fine glasspaper (400). If the surface has a natural grain pattern on it, it is important to sand in the direction of the grain. To help get a surface flat, wrap the glasspaper round a cork or wood block.

To sand the end grain of a piece of natural timber, a disc sander is very effective. You will then need to remove the scratches left by the sander by using fine glasspaper wrapped around a block.

Dust will need to be cleaned from the surface thoroughly before starting to apply the finish.

Knots are found in timber, particularly in softwoods, as branches are located along the length of the tree trunk. Knots can be an attractive feature, but can also cause issues when preparing and finishing a timber. Knots are naturally resinous and sometimes need sealing before a finish is applied.

Sanding the surface of a timber is a sufficient level of preparation for finishes that are designed to soak into the surface of the timber, such as stains and oils. Where a surface finish such as paint is to be used, it is good practice to apply a primer to the timber to help seal the surface and help the paint adhere to the timber properly.

Application

Application to small products or pieces of furniture is most commonly undertaken by hand using a brush or roller if painting. On larger items or products manufactured on a commercial scale, varnishes and paints can be applied by spraying. Some preservatives used in fencing and fence posts can be applied by dipping the pieces or by pressure treating, where a preservative is forced under pressure into the outside cell layer of timber.

Some preservatives can cause problems with the timber at the end of its useful life, as they can prevent the material from naturally degrading.

Activity

Using a small piece of flat-pack furniture, such as a child's Ikea chair, undertake a disassembly task to identify the methods of construction used.

KEY WORD

Coarseness: a measure of the rough texture found on abrasive papers.

KEY POINTS

- When sanding timber it is important to always go with the grain.
- The **coarseness** of glasspaper is measured in grit. The lower the number, the more coarse the paper.
- Most finishes are not permanent and will degrade through wear and weathering. Most need regular reapplication to maintain their durability.

Know it

1 Explain the following terms: datum line, face edge, face side.
2 Identify and describe the different types of saw used to cut wood.
3 List the advantages and disadvantages of using a cordless drill.
4 List the stock forms and sizes of different types of wood and manufactured boards.
5 Explain how to laminate wood.
6 Justify why a veneer may be used to face an MDF board rather than use a natural timber.

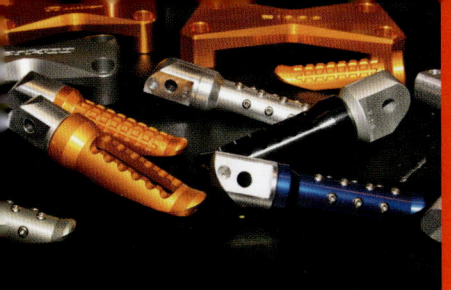

Chapter 9
Ferrous and non-ferrous metals

Learning objectives

By the end of this chapter you should have developed a knowledge and understanding of:

- the sources and origins of ferrous and non-ferrous metals
- their physical and working properties
- their ecological and social footprint
- how to select ferrous and non-ferrous metals based on function, aesthetics, cost , and environmental, social, cultural and ethical factors

- how forces and stress affect ferrous and non-ferrous metals
- the stock forms of ferrous and non-ferrous metals
- how the scale of production affects the manufacturing technique
- specialist techniques and processes
- the different surface finishes that can be applied to ferrous and non-ferrous metals.

9.1 Sources, origins, physical and working properties of ferrous and non-ferrous metals and their ecological and social footprint

Metals can be categorised into three groups: ferrous metals, non-ferrous metals and alloys.

Ferrous metals

All ferrous metals contain iron and when alloyed (mixed) with carbon they produce steel. Steel is our most abundant metal and is generally used for its strength. Iron is magnetic, which is a useful property when it comes to sorting out metals when recycling. However, the carbon content of steel means that it is prone to corrosion, in the form of rust, when exposed to moisture and oxygen.

Their properties, such as hardness and malleability, are directly related to their carbon content. For example, the more carbon that is found in steel, the harder and less malleable the steel becomes.

Ferrous metal	Composition	Properties	Common uses
Cast iron	Iron and 3.5% carbon	Hard surface but has a brittle soft core Strong compressive strength Poor resistance to corrosion 1200°C melting point Good electrical and thermal conductivity Cheap	Vices, car brake discs, cylinder blocks, manhole covers
Mild steel	Iron and 0.15%–0.35% carbon	Good tensile strength, tough, malleable Poor resistance to corrosion 1500°C melting point Good electrical and thermal conductivity Cheap	Car bodies, nuts, bolts and screws, RSJs and girders

Ferrous metal	Composition	Properties	Common uses
Medium-carbon steel	Iron and 0.35%–0.7% carbon	Good tensile strength Tougher and harder than mild steel Poor resistance to corrosion 1500°C melting point Good electrical and thermal conductivity	Gardening tools and springs
High-carbon steel	Iron and 0.70–1.4% carbon	Hard but also brittle Less tough, malleable or ductile than medium-carbon steel Poor resistance to corrosion 1500°C melting point Good electrical and thermal conductivity	Screwdrivers, chisels, taps and dies

Table 9.1 Common ferrous metals

KEY WORDS

Annealing: A heat treatment process that softens steel.

Hardening: A heat treatment process that hardens steel.

Tempering: A heat treatment process that removes the brittleness from hardened steel.

Heat treatment of ferrous metals

The properties of ferrous metals can be altered by the use of heat.

Annealing involves heating the metal to red heat and then allowing it to cool very slowly. Burying it in sand is good way of slowing down the cooling time. This makes the metal as soft as possible.

To **harden** ferrous metal, you must heat it to red heat (red heat is when the metal turns red in colour) and then cool it as quickly as possible. This is normally done by quenching it in water.

Hardened ferrous metals will become brittle. The brittleness is reduced by **tempering** the steel. This involves heating the steel to a known temperature and then allowing it to cool naturally.

Case hardening is one way of hardening just the surface of the ferrous metal. The metal is first heated to red heat and then placed in a high-carbon compound where it soaks up some of the carbon. This carbon-rich coating can then be hardened by heat treatment.

Non-ferrous metals

Non-ferrous metals differ from ferrous metals in that they do not contain iron. The lack of iron means that non-ferrous metals do not rust. Most of them are also not magnetic, which means that they are suitable for electronic devices and wiring.

Non-ferrous metal	Composition	Properties	Common uses
Aluminium	Pure metal	Lightweight, soft, ductile and malleable A good conductor of heat and electricity Corrosion resistant 660°C melting point	Aircraft bodies, high-end car chassis, cans, cooking pans, bike frames
Copper	Pure metal	Extremely ductile and malleable An excellent conductor of heat and electricity Easily soldered and corrosion resistant 1084°C melting point	Plumbing fittings, hot water tanks, electrical wire

Non-ferrous metal	Composition	Properties	Common uses
Silver	Pure metal	A soft, precious metal that is extremely resistant to corrosion An excellent conductor of heat and electricity 961°C melting point Expensive	Often used as jewellery

Table 9.2 Common non-ferrous metals

Heat treatment of non-ferrous metals

The properties of non-ferrous metals can also be altered by the use of heat, for example by annealing and hardening in a similar way to ferrous metals. The main difference is that hardening and annealing non-ferrous metals happens at a much lower temperature.

Alloys

The mechanical and physical properties of pure metals can be significantly altered by alloying them with other metals. An alloy is a metal that is produced by combining two or more elements together to produce a new metal. Alloys can also be categorised as ferrous alloys or non-ferrous alloys, depending on the main pure metal that they contain.

Alloy	Composition	Properties	Common uses
Stainless steel – ferrous alloy	Alloy of steel also including chromium (18%), nickel (8%) and magnesium (8%)	Hard and tough Excellent resistance to corrosion 1510°C melting point Good electrical and thermal conductivity	Sinks, cutlery, surgical equipment, homewares
High-speed steel – ferrous alloy	A medium-carbon alloy that also contains tungsten, chromium and vanadium	Very hard Resistant to friction Can only sharpened by grinding 1540°C melting point Good electrical and thermal conductivity	Lathe cutting tools, drills, milling cutters
High-tensile steel – ferrous alloy	A low-carbon steel that also contains chromium and molybdenum	A steel with a very high yield strength 1540°C melting point	Used to reinforce concrete
Brass – non-ferrous alloy	Alloy of copper (65%) and zinc (35%)	Strong and ductile Casts well Corrosion resistant 930°C melting point Conductor of heat and electricity	Castings, forgings, taps, wood screws
Bronze – non-ferrous alloy	Copper 80–90%, tin, aluminium, phosphorous and/or nickel in varying amounts	Reddish-yellow in colour Harder than brass Corrosion resistant 1200°C–1600°C melting point	Castings, bearings and gears

Recycling metals

Most metals can be recycled by collecting them, melting them down and reusing them to make other metal products. Recycling metal can save as much as 95% of the total energy used to manufacture metal products from the original source.

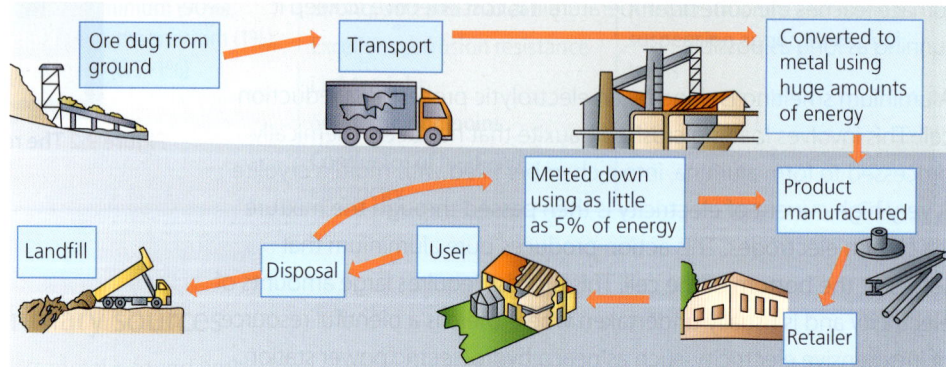

Figure 9.4 Life cycle of metal products

Figure 9.4 shows the typical life cycle of metal products. Ore is extracted from the Earth's crust and transported to the smelting plant where it is converted into metal. It is then transported to the manufacturer who makes metal products, and then on to the user. At the end of the product's life it should be recycled or, as a last resort, go to landfill.

Activity

1   Watch the following YouTube clip on 'How does recycling work?': www.youtube.com/watch?v=qAGCI0-pQ3E

    Produce a flowchart to show how a fridge is recycled.

2   Watch the following YouTube clip on 'How stuff works: recycling aluminium': www.youtube.com/watch?v=AOpGhAdQFEY

    Write down ten key facts that you have learned from the video.

KEY POINTS

- Ferrous metals contain iron and are used to produce cast iron and steel.
- Non-ferrous metals do not contain iron and do not rust.
- An alloy is a mixture of different metals designed to change the properties of the original material.
- The properties of metals can be improved by heat treatment.
- Metal is found embedded in rock in the Earth's crust and is known as ore.
- Metal is extracted from ore by the process of smelting.
- Extracting and processing metal from ore has both ecological and social issues.

9.2 The way in which the selection of materials or components is influenced by a range of factors

Aesthetics and functionality

The **functional** and **aesthetic** properties of ferrous and non-ferrous metals are detailed in Table 9.4.

Metal	Aesthetics	Functionality
Aluminium (duralumin)	Easily cast into unique shapes, can be polished to a mirror like finish or be coloured with a vivid finish known as anodising	Excellent strength to weight ratio, easy to cut, weld and join by various methods, good resistance to corrosion
Copper	Easy to shape by beating, has a reddish-brown finish that can be highly polished. Has the unique feature of going green when left outdoors and unprotected	Easily worked, good conductor of heat and electricity, malleable, ductile and easily joined by soldering
Brass	Easily cast into unique shapes, has a yellowy-brown colour that can be highly polished	A harder, more durable material than copper, a good conductor of heat and electricity
Bronze	Often used by sculptors to cast into works of art, has a deep reddish-brown colour that can be highly polished	A hard, durable material that is very resistant to corrosion
Pewter	Very easily cast into shape due to its low melting point	Soft metal with a relatively low strength
Silver	Can be polished to a high-quality finish, widely used in the manufacture of elegant jewellery	A hard, durable metal that can be easily joined by soldering, excellent resistance to corrosion, expensive
Cast iron	Nearly always cast in to a variety of shapes, rusts if unprotected	A hard, durable, strong, heavy metal
Mild steel	Can easily be worked into shape, rusts if left unprotected, can receive a wide variety of finishes/platings/coatings	Tough, durable, strong and malleable, relatively easy to work
Medium-carbon steel	Harder to work into shape than mild steel, will gain rust if left unprotected but can accept a variety of finishes	Very tough, durable and strong

Table 9.4 Functional and aesthetic properties of ferrous and non-ferrous metals

Environmental factors

Metals can be considered to be environmentally friendly, as they are durable. This means that they are less likely to break and will last longer, so there will be less need to use raw materials. Metals are reusable; when they have finished their life as one product the metal can be reused as something else. Metals are infinitely recyclable and can be collected and melted down to be used again.

However, metals are a finite resource, and when we have used this natural resource there is no more. The processing and manufacturing of metals use further natural resources and leads to pollution of the atmosphere that will lead to the formation of greenhouse gases and contribute to global warming.

Availability

Most common metals are readily available in a wide variety of stock forms such as bar, rod, strip, sheet, tube angle and channel. Metal can sold by length, width, thickness (gauge) and weight. Metals that are to be cast are sold in blocks known as ingots.

Cost

The **cost** of metals varies quite considerably.

KEY WORDS

Functionality: the selection of a metal based on its mechanical and physical properties.

Aesthetics: the selection of a metal based on how it looks.

Environmental factors: the selection of a metal based on its impact on the environment.

Availability: the selection of a metal based on its availability in a particular size/quantity.

Cost: the selection of a metal based on its initial purchase cost and true cost of processing and finishing.

- Common ferrous metals, such as mild steel, are relatively inexpensive as they are produced in very high quantities and there is a plentiful supply of the raw material.
- Non-ferrous metals, such as aluminium, are more expensive as they require a more complex process to extract the metal from its ore.
- Semi-precious metals, such as copper and brass, are more expensive as they require further processing and are not produced in such high volumes.
- Precious metals, such as gold and silver, are very expensive as they are much rarer and require even more sophisticated processing.

The production of metal products is a major cost. Producing metal products requires factories to be built, machinery to be purchased and a labour force to be trained and employed. However, metal products are suitable for high-volume production, which reduces the individual unit cost.

Social factors

Modern manufacturing techniques have enabled metal products to be efficiently and cost-effectively manufactured for the mass market. For example, the car is a complex machine that makes extensive use of metal, but is now available, and affordable, in a wide range of styles to suit the needs and preferences of the user.

Cultural factors

Metal products need to be produced sensitively to meet the requirements of the particular cultural groups that the product is being made for. The design must meet their needs, and fit in with their beliefs of what is good or bad design. Metal jewellery is an example of how products can be designed for a particular cultural group.

Ethical factors

The sourcing of metal ore can have a major impact on the environment; **open cast mining** can leave scars on the landscape and strip the land of fertile soil. The processing of metals will use large amounts of power and cause air pollution, leading to the build-up of greenhouse gases and contributing to global warming. Designers and manufacturers must aim to reduce the negative impact of processing metals.

Manufacturers have an obligation to ensure that their employees, who may be operating machinery and working with hazardous materials, are adequately protected and kept safe. They should ensure that workers are paid at least the minimum wage to prevent them falling into the poverty trap.

Making sure that products are fit for purpose and disposed of carefully at the end of their life is also important in protecting people and the world. The ELVD (End of Life Vehicles Directive) is a European directive aimed at ensuring that vehicles are correctly dealt with at the end of their usable life.

Activity

Evaluate the suitability of aluminium in the production of a soft drink can. Use the following headings to help structure your answer.
- functionality
- availability
- cost
- aesthetics
- environmental factors

9.3 The impact of forces and stress on materials and objects and the ways in which they can be reinforced and stiffened

Metal is the perfect material to use when a design has to withstand large amounts of force and stress. Metal has excellent **compressive**, **tensional**, **torsional** and **bending strength**.

Steel is an excellent construction material as it has great compressive and bending strength. Large buildings, such as warehouses, make use of the I beam to support the roof. This gives a large unhindered space that is free from posts and supports.

The cross-section of metal is very important to its strength. The I-shaped beam has been shown to be a very efficient way of supporting bending and shear loads.

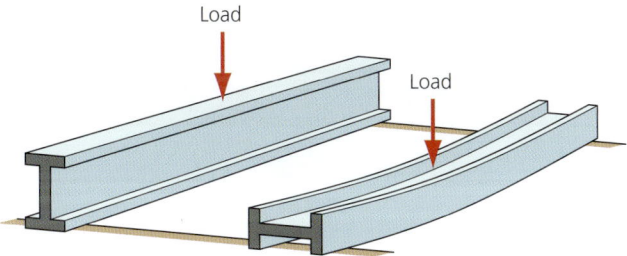

Figure 9.5 The strength of the I beam

Hollow tubing and box sections of steel offer great strength, but because they are hollow they are relatively lightweight.

High-tensile steel has great tensile strength and can be used to hold up bridge roadways, such as the Millau suspension bridge.

Figure 9.6 Millau suspension bridge

Softer metals, such as lead, are malleable and can withstand being beaten into shape without cracking. Have a look at where a chimney enters the roof of a house. The silver metal around the chimney is made from lead and has been beaten into shape.

Copper is a ductile metal and can withstand being drawn out into fine wire. Most of the electrical cables in your house are made from copper.

Improving the properties of metals by hardening and tempering

High-carbon steel can be made even harder by a heat treatment process known as hardening. The steel is heated with a brazing torch, in a brazing hearth, until it is red hot. It is then quickly cooled in water, which has the effect of hardening the steel.

Unfortunately, the hardening process also makes the steel brittle. To remove the brittleness the steel must once again be heated, but this time to a specific temperature between 230 and 300°C.

Figure 9.7 shows what temperature you should heat the metal to for the desired hardness.

Colour	Temp. °C	Hardness	Typical uses
Light straw	230	Hardest	Lathe tools, scrapers
Dark straw	245		Drills, taps and dies, punches
Orange/brown	260		Hammer heads, plane irons
Light purple	270		Scissors, knives
Dark purple	280		Saws, chisels, axes
Blue	300	Toughest	Springs, spinners, vice jaws

Figure 9.7 Tempering colours and temperature.

Activity

1 Take four pieces of different types of metal. Make sure each is the same size and thickness (100 mm × 20 mm × 1 mm). Place each piece of metal half way up in a vice, and attempt to bend it over to a 90° angle. You may need to use a hammer on some metals.

Record your findings in the following table.

Metal	How easy was it to bend (easy, hard, needed a hammer)?
Aluminium	
Mild steel	
Copper	
Pewter	

2 Gently heat a piece of mild steel using a brazing torch on the brazing hearth. Make sure you are wearing the correct protective clothing. Watch carefully as its temperature rises from 230–300°C. Record what happens to the mild steel as it moves through this temperature range. Produce a coloured chart to help describe this process.

9.4 Stock forms, types and sizes in order to calculate and determine the quantity of materials or components required

Common forms

Metals are supplied in various stock forms, and the wide range of available forms differs, depending on the specific metal used. For example, aluminium and steel can be purchased in a variety of forms such as rod, square rod, hexagonal rod, strip, sheet, square and round tube, angle and channel (see Chapter 5, Figure 5.10). It is especially important to plan what you are making while considering stock sizes of metals, as they are lot harder to machine to a specific shape than timber. In most cases it will be more sensible, more cost effective and less time consuming to adjust your design slightly than to try to machine the metal to a bespoke size.

These stock forms are generally **extrusions** (a long length of material with a standard cross-section) but can also be rolled and shaped out of larger metal sections known as **billets**. In the case of steel tubes, they are rolled and then welded to form a hollow cross-section. The stock forms are available in different widths and diameters, as well as different wall thicknesses. They are also usually supplied in shorter lengths to aid storage and delivery.

You will find that many metal suppliers still list the dimensions of metals in imperial measurements. You will often see metal sheets, or the wall thickness of an extrusion or tube, expressed as Standard Wire Gauge or **SWG**. SWG is a well-established unit of measurement where 12 SWG, for example, is equivalent to 2.642 mm and 16 SWG is equivalent to 1.626 mm. The larger the value, the smaller the metric equivalent.

In addition to flat sheets, metal is also available in a wide range of perforated or pressed patterns.

Calculating the cost of metals

Metals are sourced from all over the world. Although there is a significant amount of steel manufacturing left in the UK, most of our aluminium is imported, and as with any imported goods, the cost can change significantly, based on supply and demand.

It is possible to reduce the costs associated with the manufacture of metal products in several ways. A less expensive material could be used, but metals are often chosen for their application due to their working properties and it is likely that there will be a reduction in performance or durability if a less appropriate, cheaper material is used.

It is also feasible to plate or coat a cheaper base metal with a more expensive option. This can be done to save money, but also to improve a material's aesthetic. This process is called electroplating, and is commonly found on jewellery where a copper base material may have been plated in gold or silver. The plating process will not last indefinitely and may need to be repeated as the coating wears.

The last consideration about cost is related to how the product is manufactured or fabricated. As we have already discussed, the use of a stock size or profile of material will help reduce unnecessary machining costs, but this is not always possible.

The aluminium block in Figure 9.9 could be manufactured in a variety of ways.

- It could be machined away from a large block or billet by the process of wasting, using a milling machine, or even cut out carefully using a series of cuts with a hacksaw. This would provide an accurate shape and it would have the advantage of being a one-piece component with no joining or fixing. However, there would be significant waste, all of which would need to be factored into the costing of the final component.
- The other option would be to fabricate the component from two pieces and join the smaller block to the base. This could be done either by a mechanical fixing from below, such as a machine screw or, depending on the application, the join could be completed by using an adhesive such as epoxy resin. For a more permanent joint the block could be welded. If these two pieces were from bars that were a stock size, the cost of manufacturing the component could be significantly less.

Figure 9.8 Perforated metal sheet

Figure 9.9 Aluminium block

Activity

Which of the two manufacturing options for the aluminium block do you think would be the most cost effective? Present your arguments using up-to-date costings.

9.5 Alternative processes that can be used to manufacture products to different scales of production

There are four main types of production used in manufacturing: one-off (or prototype), batch, mass and continuous. Costs, time, skill needed, efficiency of production and design considerations change as the number of products made increases.

A product that is going to be changed each year, such as a mountain bike, would be made using batch production. This would mean that possibly a few thousand bikes would be made, then the design would change before another batch of a few thousand would be made. However, if you were making nuts, bolts and metal fasteners then you would need to make them in very large quantities and you would use 'continuous flow production'.

One-off production

One-off production gives the advantage of manufacturing metal products following the exact requirements of the client. You can use precious metals, such as gold and silver, and work to high tolerances using highly skilled metalworkers. The disadvantage is that the products are generally very expensive, very labour intensive, take a long time to produce and are difficult to repeat. Metal sculptures are a typical example of one-off production.

Batch production

Batch production has the advantage of manufacturing a limited range of identical metal products. This means that materials can be purchased in bulk, which reduces the overall cost of manufacture. The time taken to make the product is reduced, as machinery, tools and equipment can be set up ready for manufacture. The skill level of the labour force is reduced, as many can work as machine operators. Product efficiency increases, as all aspects of the work speed up. Products can be produced to exactly the same sizes and tolerances. The disadvantage is that you lose the unique element of one-off production. The aluminium frame of a mountain bike would be produced in batches.

The use of jigs

As the scale of production increases, the use of production aids becomes necessary. Jigs are specially made devices that can be used to assist in the production process. Jigs are typically used when drilling a series of identical holes in a component or to hold metal parts together while they are fixed together by welding or brazing.

For more information on jigs see the next section on 'Specialist techniques'.

Mass production

Mass production is the manufacture of metal products in large quantities. This typically uses a production line where individual metal parts are manufactured in sub-assemblies and then come together for final assembly and finishing. Specialist machinery is often used, but the skills required to operate the equipment and assemble the product are low, meaning that the workforce is largely unskilled and can be reorganised quickly when the product changes. Using standardised components and unskilled labour allows the cost of the specialised equipment to be offset, resulting in a large number of cheap products. Cars are an excellent example of a mass-produced metal-based product.

Continuous flow production

Continuous flow production is where metal products are made continuously for 24 hours per day, seven days per week. Highly specialised equipment and extensive use of computer-aided machinery (CAM) is used to manufacture the products. Computer-aided machinery such as the CNC milling machine and CNC lathe can perform all the operations of turning and milling, but can perform these tasks autonomously, at high speed, with great accuracy and consistency. This requires a large initial investment and is only cost effective when very high numbers of the same product are made for long periods of time. The whole process of continuous flow production can be fully automated, meaning that workers become deskilled and are involved in servicing and maintenance rather that making. Aluminium drinks cans are produced by continuous flow production due to the very high demand for soft drinks.

Issues with high-volume production

High-volume production creates a number of issues. Metalworkers become deskilled and there is less employment as the machines take over manufacture. Metal products become very similar and lose their individual uniqueness. More energy is need to power factories, creating greater pollution for our planet.

9.6 Specialist techniques and processes that can be used to shape, fabricate, construct a high-quality prototype

Metals are much harder and tougher materials than wood, and therefore it is particularly important to ensure that marking out is carried out with great accuracy, as mistakes are difficult to rectify.

Wastage/addition

Marking out

Marking out on metal requires a different set of tools to timber. A pencil would not show up on most metals, therefore a scriber is used instead. The scriber will produce a fine line that scratches the surface of the metal. The metal can be coated with a layer of marking-out fluid which makes the lines easier to see. Marking-out fluid is a thin paint, specially formulated to be quick drying. It can be removed at a later date by rubbing with an abrasive paper, such as an 'emery cloth'. An engineer's square, when used with a scriber, will produce an accurate 90° line when marking out; it can also be used to check a 90° corner. A ball pein hammer has two faces – the flat face is used for general hammering, but the ball face is particularly useful when spreading a rivet during the riveting process.

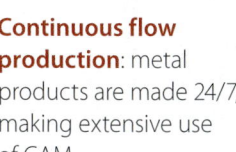

Figure 9.10 Marking-out tools for metal: a scriber, metal rule, ball pein hammer, centre punch and an engineer's square

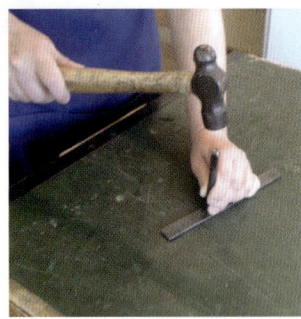

Figure 9.11 Centre punching metal

When drilling a hole in metal, it is essential to have an indent marked into the metal to prevent the drill from skidding. This is produced by making a dot with the point of the punch by hitting it with a hammer into the metal.

Odd-leg callipers are used to mark a line parallel to an edge.

Outside callipers are used to measure/check the outside diameter of round bar/rod. They are typically used when turning steel bar on a metal-working lathe.

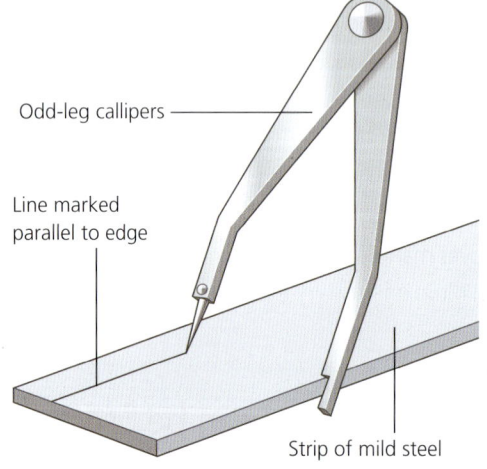

Odd-leg callipers

Line marked parallel to edge

Strip of mild steel

Figure 9.12 A pair of odd-leg callipers

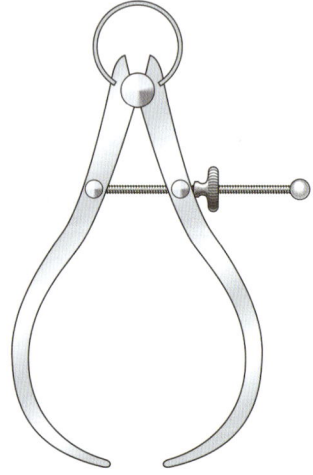

Figure 9.13 A pair of outside callipers

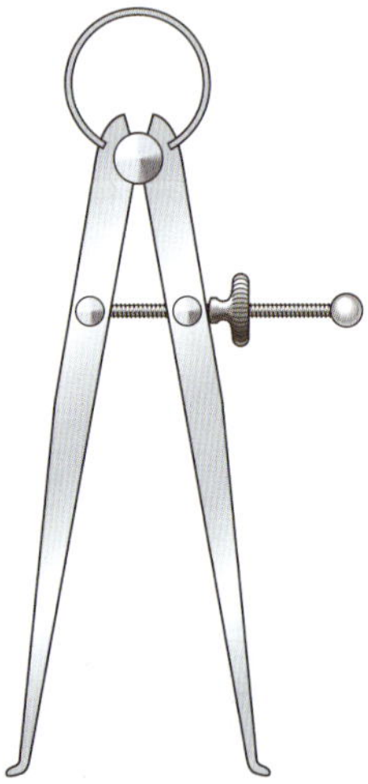

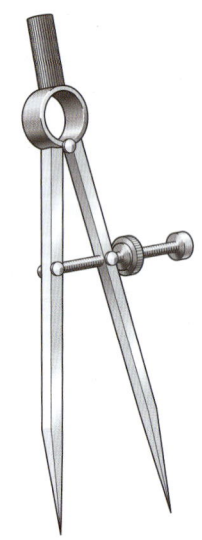

Figure 9.14 A pair of inside callipers

Inside callipers are used to measure/check the inside diameter of a hole.

A pair of dividers is used to mark out a circle or an arc on metal. It is useful to first use a dot punch to locate the centre of the circle or arc when working on metal; this will increase the accuracy and will prevent the dividers from skidding and scratching the surface.

The surface plate is a very smooth, flat and accurate surface to work from. The scribing block firmly holds the scriber at a predetermined height, the angle plate ensures that the work piece is held at 90° to the surface plate and vee blocks will steadily hold a round bar. This combination of equipment increases the accuracy of marking out.

A micrometer is a very accurate tool used for measuring small distances from 0 to 50 mm. Larger micrometers are available, but the 0–50 mm is the most common. It utilises a very fine screwthread with a pitch of 0.5 mm. Take hold of a 300 mm ruler and place your thumbnails either side of a millimetre, now try and imagine dividing that space into one hundred. That is how accurately a digital micrometer can measure!

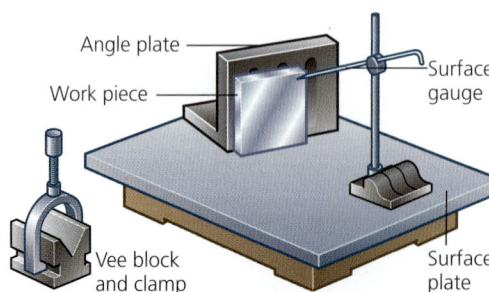

Angle plate

Work piece

Surface gauge

Vee block and clamp

Surface plate

Figure 9.16 A surface plate with scribing block and vee blocks

0.06065

Figure 9.17 A digital micrometer

Figure 9.15 A pair of dividers

A digital vernier calliper is another very accurate measuring tool that can measure to an accuracy of one hundredth of a millimetre. It can measure outside dimensions, inside dimensions and depths. Digital vernier callipers normally measure from 0 to 150 mm.

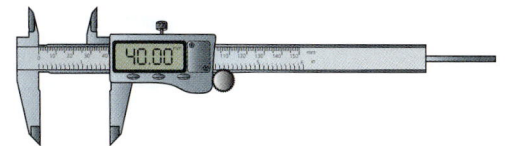

Figure 9.18 A digital vernier calliper

Tools, equipment and processes

The next stage in the manufacturing process is normally cutting out the shape. The type of tool you use will be determined by the material you are using, the profile of the shape and the number of components required. It is important to choose the correct tool and to be able to use it safely, accurately and efficiently.

Sawing

The **hacksaw** is the most popular saw for sawing metal. The hardened and tempered high-carbon steel blade is held in a tubular steel frame and tensioned with a wing nut. The handle is usually made from die cast aluminium with a powder-coated finish.

Figure 9.19 A hacksaw

The metal to be sawn is generally held in a metalworking vice. It is important to position your metal carefully in the vice, making sure that the cut is as close to the side of the vice as possible.

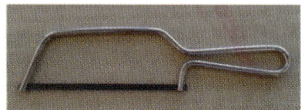

Figure 9.20 A junior hacksaw

Your right hand (if you are right handed) is positioned through the handle with the index (trigger) finger pointing outwards, this helps to control the saw. The other hand is placed on the curve of the frame and provides power and direction. The full length of the saw should be used.

As the name suggests, the **junior hacksaw** is a smaller version of the hacksaw. The hardened and tempered high-carbon steel blade is held in a sprung steel frame that can be compressed to allow a worn blade to be quickly changed.

A **piercing saw** has a very thin hardened and tempered steel blade. The blade is held in a steel frame and tensioned by moving the handle assembly along the frame. As the blade is very fine and delicate it is easily snapped, however small lengths of blade can be easily accommodated in between the blade clamps.

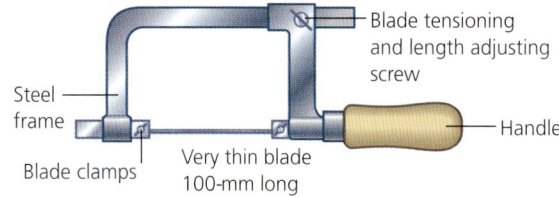

Blade tensioning and length adjusting screw

Steel frame

Handle

Blade clamps

Very thin blade 100-mm long

Figure 9.21 A piercing saw

Filing

Filing is the process of final shaping and smoothing of a material once it has already been cut to shape. There are two basic techniques of filing: **cross filing** and **draw filing**.

Cross filing removes the most material and involves pushing the file across the material. You should aim to use the full length of the file and slide along the edge of the material as you push forward. The file does not cut on the backward stroke so save yourself some time and energy by bringing it back in thin air.

Draw filing is used to smooth the edge or surface of the material. You hold the blade of a smooth file in both hands and draw it forwards and backwards along the surface. You can also wrap a piece of abrasive paper, such as an emery cloth or wet and dry paper, around the file for an even smoother finish.

KEY WORDS

Cross filing: a method of shaping metal.

Draw filing: a method of smoothing the edge of metal.

A **tapping hole** is a hole that is drilled before a screwthread is produced inside it. This is a smaller hole than the actual screwthread (for example, an M8 screwthread requires a 6.8 mm tapping hole to be drilled).

A **clearance hole** is a hole that is drilled larger than the actual size of the bolt to allow it to slip through. A clearance hole for an M8 bolt would be 8.5 mm.

A **countersunk hole** is a hole that has been drilled with a countersink bit ready to accept a countersunk headed setscrew.

A **counterbored hole** is a hole that has been enlarged to accept the head of a bolt. A counterbored hole for an M8 bolt could be 12 mm.

Deforming/reforming

Metal can be joined in a number of permanent and non-permanent ways.

Non-permanent methods of joining metal

A non-permanent method of joining is a method that can be taken apart. This is particularly useful for maintenance as it means that parts that are broken or worn out can be replaced.

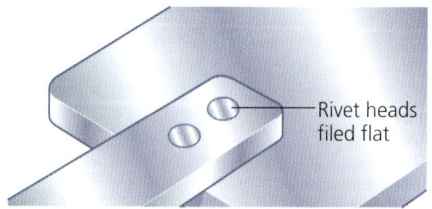

Figure 9.29 The riveting process

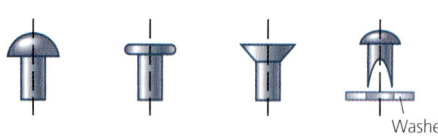

Figure 9.30 Types of rivet

Rivets

Riveting is a widely used technique for joining metals. It has the advantage that it does not normally require heat, which can make metals bend and distort (particularly thin sheets). Also, the equipment used for riveting is simpler, cheaper and safer to use.

When riveting, you have to drill a hole through both sheets of metal to be joined and then pass a rivet with the same diameter through the hole. The head of the rivet butts up against one side of the sheets and the other side is hammered over to hold the second sheet against the first (round- or snap-head rivets). For a neater finish, countersunk rivets can be used. Both metals to be joined need to be countersunk, and then the rivet is filed flat with the surface of the metal. Flat head rivets are used for joining materials that are too thin to countersink. Bifurcated rivets are used to join soft materials such as fabric and leather.

If you cannot access the back of the hole through the materials (for example, when riveting a panel on the outside of a closed box), you can use a special rivet called a pop rivet. This rivet is hollow with a pin through it. A pop rivet gun is used to pull the pin into the rivet from the back, squeezing the back of the rivet against the material to be joined. When it is squeezed right against the surface, the pin breaks off. This process is also known as blind riveting.

Nuts and bolts

A nut and bolt can be used to join together two materials. A hole is drilled through both and then a bolt with the corresponding diameter is passed through the holes. A nut can then be screwed onto the bolt. Care should be taken to choose a bolt that is long enough for the nut to completely screw on the bolt, but short enough so that the bolt does not stick out too far. The bolt and nut are most commonly made with a hexagonal head which can be tightened with a spanner, but can also have an Allen key or socket head.

Machine screws

A machine screw (machine bolt) is designed to fasten an object to an existing tapped hole in a metal surface; there is usually no need for the use of a nut. They are normally referred to by their width and length (e.g. M12 × 50 mm).

Bolts and machine screws are available with a range of heads, designed for different situations, and fitted using different tools. Figure 9.32 shows common varieties.

Nuts

Figure 9.33 shows common types of nut, most tightened with a spanner, but the wing nut can be tightened by hand using the two metal 'wings' on the side. The nylon insert lock nut has a ring of nylon in one end that is slightly smaller than the screw thread. This grips the thread of the bolt and the friction stops the nut from undoing through vibration. An example of its use is on a folding push chair for toddlers. The trade name for them is a 'nyloc' nut. A dome nut is used where a more decorative finish is required or if the exposed end of the bolt needs to be covered for safety reasons. When you use a security shear nut, the end snaps off as it tightens, leaving a conical nut that is almost impossible to undo. You would use this where you do not want people to be able to undo the nut.

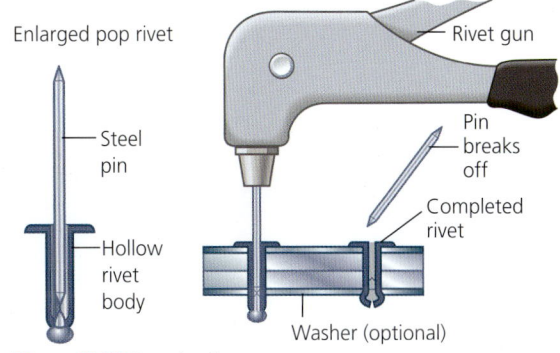

Figure 9.31 Pop riveting

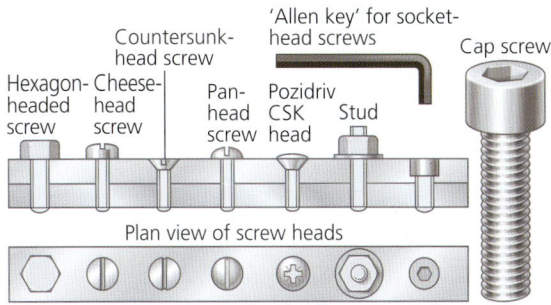

Figure 9.32 Types of machine screw

Figure 9.33 Types of nut

Washers

When using a nut, bolt or machine screw, it is common to use a washer to spread the load across a larger area. A plain washer is usually slightly bigger in diameter than the head of the bolt. If the materials being joined are quite soft, then a larger washer called a penny washer is used. If the parts are subject to vibration, a lock washer can be used between the face of the nut and a plain washer.

Figure 9.34 Types of washer

Permanent methods of joining metal

As all these processes involve the use of heat, it is essential that you wear the correct PPE and observe all safety procedures.

Soft soldering is commonly used when manufacturing electrical circuits and when plumbing with copper pipework. As with all soldering processes, it is essential that the joint is perfectly clean before the parts are soldered together, as any dirt will prevent the

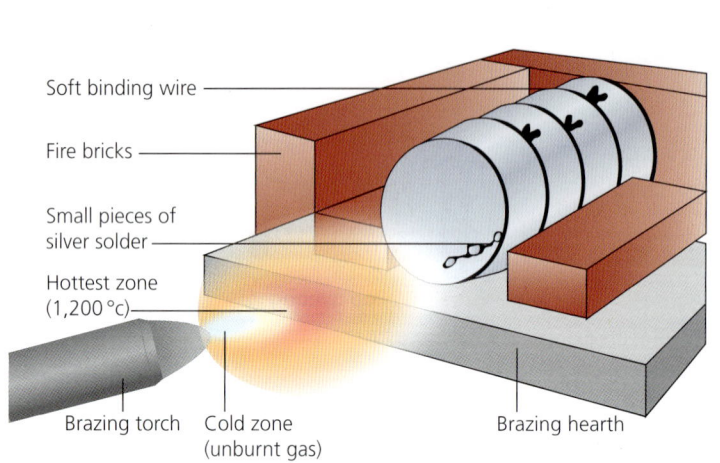

Soft binding wire

Fire bricks

Small pieces of silver solder

Hottest zone (1,200 °c)

Brazing torch Cold zone (unburnt gas) Brazing hearth

Figure 9.35 The hard-soldering process

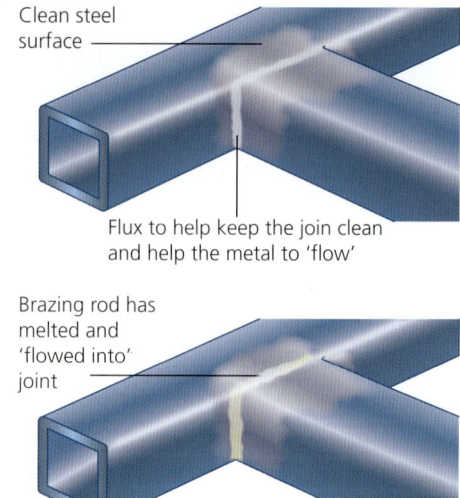

Clean steel surface

Flux to help keep the join clean and help the metal to 'flow'

Brazing rod has melted and 'flowed into' joint

Figure 9.36 Brazing

solder from bonding to the metal. When joining electrical components to a circuit board, a soldering iron is used to heat the joint and soft solder is used as the bonding metal. The solder contains a flux that keeps the joint clean and helps the solder to flow into the joint.

When joining copper pipework, a blow torch is used to heat the metal and a paste flux is applied to help the solder flow.

Hard soldering is a similar process to soft soldering, but is used for joining precious metal together. The heat is applied using a blow torch or brazing torch and the solder is an alloy of silver, copper and zinc.

Brazing is a method of joining steel parts together. This time, heat is applied with a brazing torch in a brazing hearth. The flux (borax) is applied to the cleaned joint before heating – the flux will prevent the steel from oxidising during heating and will help the brass to flow into the joint. Once the steel is red hot, the brazing rod (brass) is introduced. It will then melt and flow into the joint.

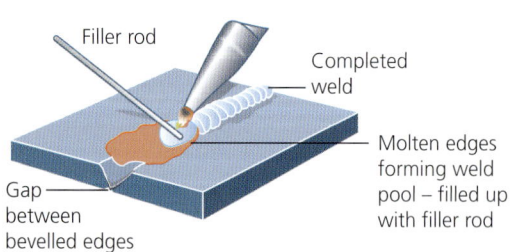

Filler rod

Completed weld

Molten edges forming weld pool – filled up with filler rod

Gap between bevelled edges

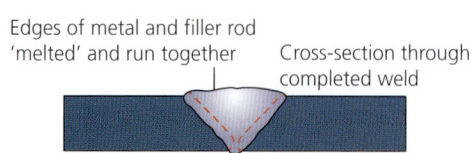

Edges of metal and filler rod 'melted' and run together

Cross-section through completed weld

Figure 9.37 Oxyacetylene welding

Welding is a very strong method of permanently joining metals together. It differs from soldering in that it uses the same metal as that used to produce the joint. There are a number of methods of welding that use either gas, electricity or a mixture of gas and electricity to generate the heat.

Most welded joints require the metal to be prepared by forming a v-gap between the two pieces of metal that are to be joined.

Oxyacetylene welding uses a mixture of oxygen and acetylene gases to produce a very hot flame (3500°C). The flame will melt both sides of the v-cut, and at this time the filler rod (copper-coated steel) is introduced where it will also melt and fill the v-gap.

Electric arc welding uses a low voltage, high current of electricity down a flux-coated filler rod. As the electricity jumps across the gap between the filler rod and the joint it produces a very high temperature arc that instantly melts both sides of the v-gap and the filler rod.

Epoxy resin is a strong, waterproof, two-part adhesive that can glue metal parts together. Equal amounts of glue and hardener are first mixed and then applied to the surface of the metal surfaces to be joined. The joint will usually need to be clamped together until the epoxy resin sets.

Machining
Centre lathe

The **centre lathe** is a very useful workshop machine. It is used to make circular components from metal or polymer bar. Various stock forms can be held in the chuck while it spins around. A cutting tool can then be used to perform a variety of **turning** operations.

Knife tools can be used to face off the end of a bar. Facing off a bar involves moving the tool across the end of the bar and produces a flat, smooth 90° surface.

Round-nose tools can be used to parallel turn along the length of the bar. Parallel turning involves sliding the tool along the length of the bar and produces a smooth parallel surface. Round-nose tools can also be used to taper turn. Taper turning involves setting the compound slide to a predetermined angle and then sliding the tool along an angled path that produces a taper.

Parting tools are used to produce an undercut or to cut off the end of a machined component.

Milling machines

Milling machines are used to carry out a range of machining operations in metal or polymers. They can be used to cut slots, grooves, machine edges and smooth large surface areas.

Small work pieces can be held in a machine vice that is bolted down onto the milling machine table. Larger pieces of work are bolted directly to the table.

These machines are often used with automatic feeds. This ensures that the correct speed of cut is maintained, giving an accurate surface finish. Due to the large amount of work that the machine can do, the process will generate lots of heat. The heat needs to be controlled by applying coolant or the tool will become damaged and the surface finish will be poor.

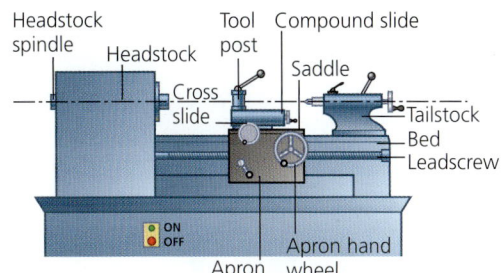
Figure 9.38 Centre lathe

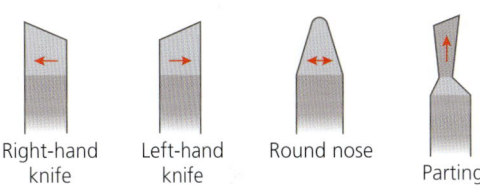
Figure 9.39 A selection of lathe tools

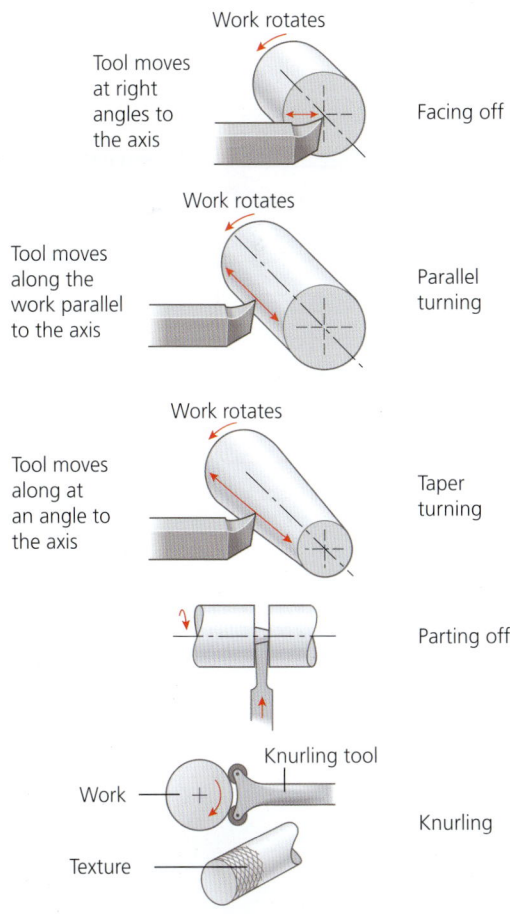
Figure 9.40 Lathe operations

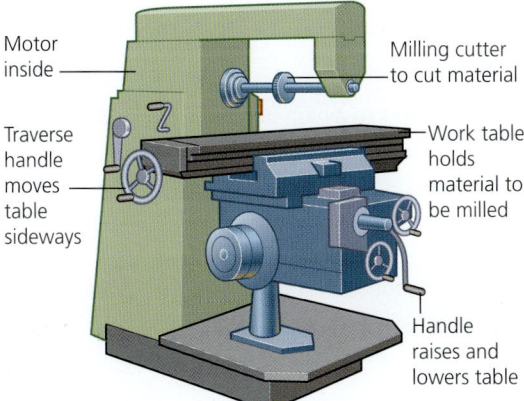
Figure 9.41 Horizontal milling machine

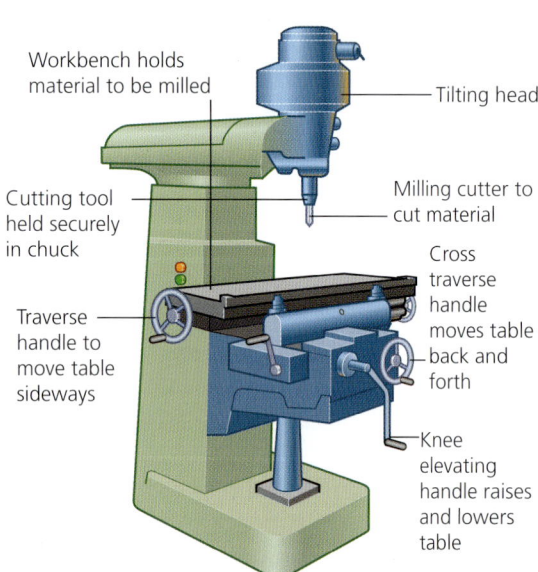

Workbench holds material to be milled

Tilting head

Cutting tool held securely in chuck

Milling cutter to cut material

Cross traverse handle moves table back and forth

Traverse handle to move table sideways

Knee elevating handle raises and lowers table

Figure 9.42 Vertical milling machine

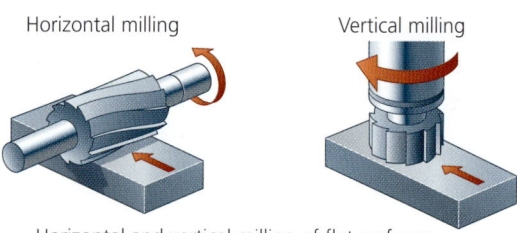

Horizontal milling

Vertical milling

Horizontal and vertical milling of flat surfaces

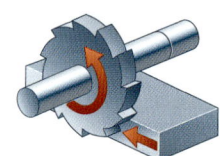
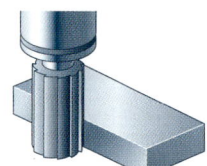

Horizontal and vertical milling of vertical surfaces – the horizontal machine is using a side and face cutter which cuts on its side and on its diameter

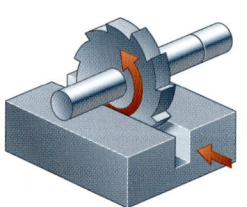
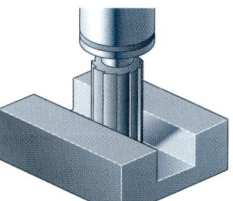

Horizontal and vertical milling of slots

Figure 9.43 Milling operations

Computer-aided manufacture (CAM)

CNC lathe

A CNC lathe can perform all the operations of a 'traditional' centre lathe, such as parallel turning, facing off, taper turning and screw cutting, but the processes are controlled by a computer. Sophisticated CNC lathes can even perform their own tool changes, and this significantly speeds up the manufacturing process. A CNC lathe can be used to manufacture components from most metals and polymers.

A CNC lathe works from a CAD drawing. Once the drawing is completed it is then run through the machine's own dedicated software program, which turns the drawing into machine code (information that controls the lathe), and then it runs a simulation to see if the component can be made. A blank piece of metal or polymer is then fastened into the lathe and the manufacturing process can begin.

The advantages of using a CNC lathe are that it can work to a high degree of tolerance, it can produce components far quicker than by traditional methods, it consistently produces identical components and, because it is totally enclosed, it is safer to operate.

CNC milling machine

As with a CNC lathe, a CNC milling machine will carry out all the operations of a 'traditional' milling machine, such as cutting slots, grooves, machining edges and smoothing large surface areas, but once again these processes are controlled by a computer. It has the same advantages as a CNC lathe: it machines to a high level of accuracy, is faster and is consistent. It works from a CAD drawing that is processed into machine code and runs this through a simulation before actual machining takes place.

Figure 9.44 A CNC lathe

Laser cutter

You may have a laser cutter in the school workshop and you might use it to cut and engrave acrylic (PMMA) and thin sections of timber and manufactured boards. In industry, much more powerful lasers are used to cut and engrave sheet metals. First, a CAD drawing is produced of the profile of the component to be manufactured. Then dedicated machine software converts the CAD drawing into machine code and sets the speed and strength of the cutting power once the material and its thickness have been entered. This process is significantly quicker than other machining processes and it has the advantage of being able to cut very intricate shapes and leaves a high-quality edge finish.

Plasma cutter

A plasma cutter works in a similar way to a laser cutter, but it can cut through much thicker sheet metal and heavy metal plate. The cutting medium is a high-velocity ionised gas that burns its way through the metal.

Activity

With a partner, each make a key fob using two different metals.

Choose from mild steel, aluminium, copper or brass.

The process:

- Draw out a shape for a key fob (30 mm × 30 mm max.)
- Cut out the paper template and stick it to a blank sheet of metal (30 mm × 30 mm).
- Cut out the shape using a hacksaw.
- Cross-file the key fob to get an accurate shape.
- Draw-file the key fob to smooth the edges.
- Mark out and centre punch a hole.
- Drill the hole with a 4 mm drill bit.
- Polish the key fob with metal polish.

Evaluate how the different metals affect the production of the key fob and the quality of the final product.

KEY POINTS

- The shape of metals can be altered by wasting. This involves the removal of metal using a variety of tools and equipment, such as saws, files and drills.
- The shape of metals can also be altered by addition. This means joining metals together by processes such as bolting, screwing, riveting, soldering and welding.
- Computer-aided manufacture (CAM) uses CNC machines to shape metal by turning, milling and cutting. CAM is quick, accurate, consistent but expensive to set up.

9.7 Appropriate surface treatments and finishes that can be applied for functional and aesthetic purposes

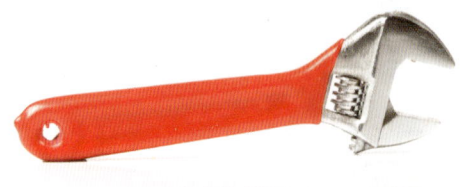

Dip coating

The **dip-coating** process provides a thin layer of polyethylene over the surface of the metal. The part to be coated is cleaned and then heated to 200°C before being dipped in a fluidised (air blown through it) bath of polyethylene powder for a few seconds. The heat makes the powder stick to the metal and fuse together to give a smooth, shiny, colourful surface that protects the metal. Handles of tools are often dip coated to give better grip on the tool.

Powder coating

Powder coating is a commercial finishing process. The item being coated is electrostatically charged and the paint is applied in a powder form. The powder is attracted to the charged object where it forms an even layer. The object then passes through an oven, where the paint cures and hardens. Powder coating provides a more durable finish than other painting methods and it can be used with a variety of metals.

Figure 9.46 Powder coating

Galvanising

Galvanising gives excellent protection from rusting to steel parts. The steel is dipped into a bath of molten zinc, giving the surface a bright grey colour. It is used in many products used outdoors (for example, steel gates and fencing). The zinc is more reactive than the metal that it is coating, and therefore corrodes at a quicker rate than the steel. This means that the steel is protected from corrosion for a period of time while the zinc coating degrades first. In reality, this means the base metal is protected temporarily. In this application, the zinc can be referred to as a sacrificial anode, corroding at faster rate than the steel, protecting the base metal.

Figure 9.47 A galvanising tank

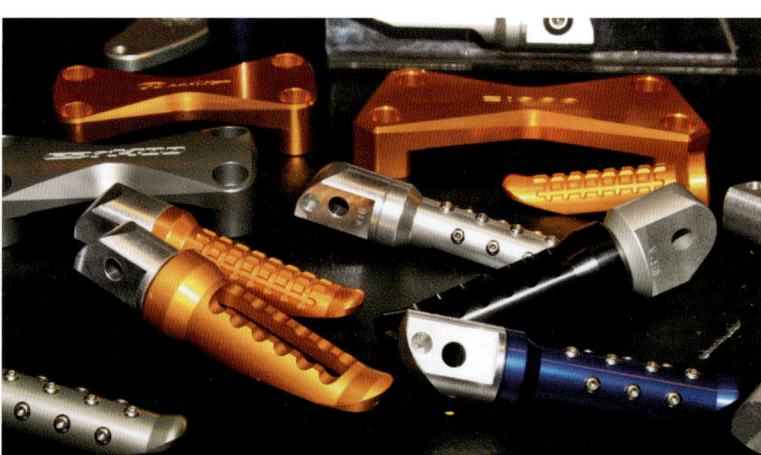

Figure 9.48 A range of anodised bike components

Anodising

Anodising is an electrolysis process where aluminium parts are dipped in a chemical bath and an electrical current is passed through the product being anodised. This causes the surface of the aluminium to oxidise, forming a hard surface which is resistant to wear and scratches. Coloured dyes can be added during the process, giving the surfaces an attractive shiny metallic finish.

Enamelling

Enamelling is a method of finishing metal, most commonly associated with decorative jewellery, but can also be used as a finish on some kitchen appliances, baths and homeware. Enamelling involves coating a metal with powdered glass and subsequently firing in a kiln or high-temperature oven. When heated to the region of 850°c, the glass particles melt and fuse together, and when they cool they provide a hard-wearing surface finish. As with most hard materials, the enamel finish can be quite brittle, occasionally chipping or cracking if the base metal is too flexible.

Oil finishing black steel

This is more commonly referred to as 'blackening', and relates to the process of coating a ferrous metal with a substance called black oxide. The black oxide is resistant to corrosion, and as such it protects the metal component from rusting. It can be applied by either a hot or cold process, although the hot process uses a variety of harmful chemicals, so the cold application process is becoming more common. The cold process involves the metal component, usually low-carbon steel, being dipped in a series of baths of solution ranging from an alkaline cleaner, through the black oxide substrate and finally a sealant bath.

One of the advantages of the blacking process is that the surface coating is extremely thin, so the overall size of the component is barely affected by the surface finish. This makes it ideal in applications where the dimensional accuracy of the final piece is important. It is often found as a finish on engine parts, tool holders and architectural metal work.

Painting

Metals can be painted in the same way as timber, usually applying a **primer**, undercoat and topcoat, either by brush or by spraying. Like timber, metals need to be well prepared. All grease and dirt need to be removed and rough surfaces need to be made smooth with a grinder, file and emery cloth. Before painting, dents and holes need to be filled with

Figure 9.49 Enamelled mug

Figure 9.50 Paint being applied by hand

appropriate filler. This is particularly important when spraying, as the thin layers of paint tend to accentuate blemishes. 90% of the work is in the preparation for spraying. The primer can then be applied, which provides a smooth surface for the following coats to adhere to. Primers can sometimes be red in colour where they have had zinc added. The zinc adds a level of corrosion protection to the metal (usually steel).

Activity

Identify five products in the workshop that have been dip coated.

KEY POINTS
- Preparation of the metal is a very important factor in the successful application of a surface finish.
- Powder coating provides an even, durable surface finish.

9.8 Designing and making principles for ferrous and non-ferrous metals

Choosing a method to make a prototype

Metals are generally harder to work with than timbers and polymers due to their hardness. This is especially true if shaping and cutting metal by hand. The advantage of using metal in the manufacture of products is that more accurate tolerances can be achieved and there are a wide variety of manufacturing processes that can be used, particularly in commercial manufacture.

In a school workshop you are probably going to shape and cut metal using a range of hand tools, such as files and hacksaws; achieving accuracy with these kinds of tools is challenging. If you have access to metal-specific band saws, centre lathes and milling machines, both the quality and accuracy of your work can increase.

Sheet-metal manufacture can be undertaken in school workshops where shapes and developments can be cut out using tin snips and saws, but accuracy and quality will increase with the use of guillotines and sheet-metal folding equipment. In some schools you will start to see plasma cutting machines, which are capable of cutting quickly through metal. These can be handheld, and in some cases operated by computer in a similar way to a laser cutter or CNC router.

Choosing a finish

As you have already been introduced to the physical properties of metals, you should remember that corrosion and oxidisation are two major factors to consider when thinking about an appropriate surface finish for metal. Corrosion (rust) and oxidisation occur when the material reacts with oxygen, so the application of a surface finish that provides an impermeable coating on the metal will prevent corrosion and oxidisation.

As with timbers, the application of a finish to most metals also influences the aesthetic appearance of the product. Most ferrous metals can be painted or polymer coated in a wide range of colours. Metals such as aluminium can also be painted, but often aluminium products are anodised to protect the surface from corrosion.

Ferrous metals can also be chrome plated, which is an electro-plating process. The chrome plating provides a hard, protective coating with excellent aesthetic qualities. Where protection is more important than the aesthetic appearance, ferrous metals can be galvanised.

Galvanising protects the metal by coating it in a zinc layer that is more reactive than the base metal. Galvanising is used in road barriers and lamp posts. Ferrous metals cannot be anodised.

Preparation

Metal must be completely clean and grease free before applying any surface finish, otherwise the finish being applied may not adhere correctly. Abrasive papers can be used to prepare metal surfaces for the application of a finish, and in large objects or when a large volume is being produced, more industrial methods such as sand blasting or bead blasting can be used. Here, small abrasive particles of sand or glass are fired under pressure at the surface of metal to remove any dirt or grease. This is an effective way of efficiently preparing large surface areas.

When applying a paint finish, most metals will benefit from a primer being applied beforehand. This primer will help the topcoat adhere to the metal.

Figure 9.51 The aluminium torch has been anodised to help protect the surface from oxidising, while at the same time providing an attractive aesthetic finish.

Application

The application of a surface finish to small metal objects or products can usually be achieved with cellulose aerosol sprays. As the scale and volume increase, processes such as powder coating are more commonly used. It is important when using any spray paint with metal that you follow the relevant health and safety procedures. PPE should be worn in the form of goggles and possibly a respirator. All spraying should take place in a well-ventilated area and the paints should be stored according to the **COSHH** regulations.

Activity

Your bike is probably made mostly from metal. Investigate the range of surface finishes that have been applied and identify whether the finish is aesthetic, functional or both.

KEY POINTS
- Metals are hard to work with to achieve precise accuracy when using hand tools.
- Corrosion in ferrous metals is known as rust.
- Anodising can be used to provide an aesthetic protective finish to aluminium.
- Ferrous metals cannot be anodised.

Know it

1 Explain the difference between a ferrous and a non-ferrous metal. Give examples of each.
2 Name two different metal alloys and give examples of their use.
3 Name two permanent and two non-permanent methods of joining metal.
4 Why is it cheaper for a manufacturer to use a stock size of metal when producing a metal component?
5 What is an extrusion? What other materials as well as metals are available as extrusions?
6 Explain how production aids, such as drilling jigs, affect the manufacture of metal-based products.
7 Discuss the effects on the environment of sourcing, processing, manufacturing and using metal-based products.

Chapter 10
Thermosetting and thermoforming polymers

Learning objectives

By the end of this chapter you should have developed a knowledge and understanding of:

- the sources and origins of thermosetting and thermoforming polymers
- their physical and working properties
- their ecological and social footprint
- how to select thermosetting and thermoforming polymers based on function, aesthetics, cost, and environmental, social, cultural and ethical factors

- how forces and stress affect thermosetting and thermoforming polymers
- the stock forms of thermosetting and thermoforming polymers
- how the scale of production affects the manufacturing technique
- specialist techniques and processes
- the different surface finishes that can be applied to thermosetting and thermoforming polymers.

10.1 Sources, origins, physical and working properties of thermosetting and thermoforming polymers and their ecological and social footprint

Primary sources

KEY WORDS

Synthetic polymers: polymers that come from crude oil.

Natural polymers: polymers that come from plant products.

Fractional distillation: the processing of crude oil to produce naptha.

Most polymers are obtained from crude oil and are known as **synthetic polymers**. Deposits of crude oil are distributed throughout the world, but by far the biggest reserves can be found in the Middle East and in Central and South America. Crude oil is a finite, non-renewable resource and we are slowly running out of it. It is therefore essential that, wherever possible, polymers are recycled and reused. There are a few polymers that are sourced from plants; these are known as **natural polymers** (biopolymers). Natural polymers have the advantage of being renewable.

Synthetic polymers

Crude oil is found deep under the Earth's crust in 'oil fields'. The oil fields are quite often in very remote locations, such as in the middle of the sea, in the middle of a desert or even in frozen wastelands. A seismic test, which is a controlled underground explosion, is carried out and by analysing the results geologists can make a prediction as to whether crude oil is present. Exploratory bore holes are then drilled into the ground to see if the oil is commercially accessible. If it is, the crude oil now needs to be pumped to the surface and transported to an oil refinery where it can be made into various oil-based products. Transportation is normally carried out by pumping the crude oil across vast areas of land in pipelines and across oceans in huge oil tankers.

Crude oil in its raw state is of very little use. It consists of a mixture of hydrocarbons, with each hydrocarbon having a different weight. The lightest of the hydrocarbons are gases, such as liquid petroleum gas (LPG) which can be used to fuel cars. The heaviest are thick tar-like substances, such as bitumen which can be used in road surfacing.

The first part of transforming crude oil into these useful petrochemical products is to break it down by a process known as **fractional distillation**. During this process the crude oil is heated up until it becomes a gas. It then vents off through a tall column and as it cools it condenses into different petrochemical products. Many of these products you will be familiar with, such as gas, petrol and oil, but it is one specific petrochemical product that is used to make polymers: naphtha.

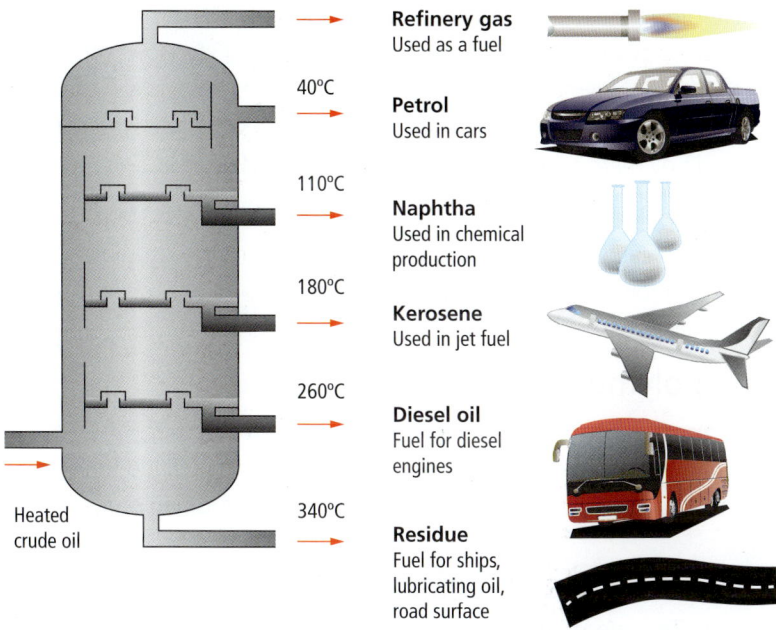

Figure 10.1 Fractional distillation

Cracking

Naphtha is made up of a mixture of hydrocarbons and needs to undergo another process known as **'cracking'** before we can begin to use it to manufacture polymers. The naphtha is once again heated to break it down further into individual hydrocarbons, such as ethylene, propylene and butylene. These are the building blocks for the manufacture of the polymers that we are familiar with, and we refer to them as 'monomers'.

Polymerisation

The process of **polymerisation** takes place in a polymerisation reactor and involves a chemical reaction that links the monomers together into polymer chains. Different monomers linked together in different ways give each polymer its unique properties. The monomer ethylene is polymerised to make the polymer we know as polyethylene (PE) and the monomer propylene is polymerised to make the polymer polypropylene (PP).

A simple monomer

The structure of the polymer polyethylene

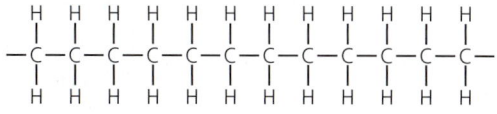

Figure 10.2 Monomers and polymers

KEY WORDS

Cracking: the processing of naptha to produce a monomer.
Polymerisation: the blending of different monomers to produce a certain polymer.

Natural polymers (biopolymers)

Biopolymers differ from synthetic polymers in that they are manufactured from plant materials, such as sugar beet and corn starch. Because plant material can be grown, it means that the raw building block for producing biopolymers is renewable and **biodegradable**. Therefore, in theory, we should have an endless supply of polymers that do not have a negative environmental impact at the end of their life. However, at present, the production of biopolymers is more expensive and takes longer than that of petrochemical-based polymers. Biopolymers also do not have the same impact resistance as petrochemical-based polymers, and they are not as resilient to chemicals.

Polylactic acid (PLA) is a biopolymer that is produced from corn starch. The corn starch undergoes a chemical fermentation process that changes the corn starch into a usable biopolymer that has similar properties to acrylonitrile butadiene styrene (ABS). You may be using this in your 3D printer!

Thermoforming polymers

Thermoforming polymers differ from thermosetting polymers in that they can be softened by heating many times. Once softened they can then be shaped and formed using a wide variety of processes. We will look at the various thermoforming processes later in this chapter.

The majority of everyday plastic products that we use are likely to be made from thermoforming polymers. They are ideally suited to high-volume production methods, making thermoforming polymer products very cost effective.

Thermoforming polymer	Properties	Common uses
Acrylic (PMMA)	Hard Excellent optical quality Good resistance to weathering Scratches easily and can be brittle Excellent thermal and electrical insulator Good polymerity when heated	Car-light units, bath tubs, shop signage and displays
High-density polythene (HDPE)	Hard and stiff Excellent chemical resistance Excellent thermal and electrical insulator Good tensile strength Good polymerity when heated	Washing up bowls, buckets, milk crates, bottles and pipes
Low-density polythene (LDPE)	Flexible and tough Waterproof and suitable for all moulding techniques Excellent thermal and electrical insulator Good polymerity when heated	Polymer bags and refuse sacks
Polyvinyl chloride (PVC)	Hard and tough Good chemical and weather resistance Low cost Can be rigid or flexible Excellent thermal and electrical insulator Good polymerity when heated Good tensile strength	Pipes, guttering, window frames

Thermoforming polymer	Properties	Common uses
Polypropylene (PP)	Tough Good heat and chemical resistance Lightweight Fatigue resistant Excellent thermal and electrical insulator Good polymerity when heated Good tensile strength	Toys, DVD and Blu-ray cases, food packaging film, bottle caps and medical equipment
Polycarbonate (PC)	Tough, durable and impact resistant Good resistance to scratching Excellent thermal and electrical insulator Good polymerity when heated	Safety glasses, safety helmets
Extruded polystyrene foam (XPS) Styrofoam™	Lightweight Easy to work Good thermal insulation	Thermal insulation barriers in the construction industry, modelling material
Expanded polystyrene (EPS)	Lightweight Easy to mould Good impact resistance Excellent thermal insulator	Packaging, disposable cups and plates
Nylon	Hard, tough, resistant to wear A low coefficient of friction Excellent thermal and electrical insulator	Bearings, gears, curtain rail fittings and clothing

Table 10.1 Properties and uses of thermoforming polymers

Car-indicator lenses are made from acrylic (PMMA). This is an ideal material as it has a hard, shiny waterproof surface. It has excellent optical qualities and it can be easily coloured with the introduction of a coloured pigment. It is available in transparent, translucent and opaque forms.

Thermosetting polymers

Once a **thermosetting polymer** has been initially shaped or formed by heat, it cannot be reheated or reformed. This makes them excellent thermal insulators, but also means that thermosetting polymers cannot be recycled.

Figure 10.3 Car-indicator lens made from acrylic (PMMA)

Thermosetting polymer	Properties	Common uses
Epoxy resin	Excellent thermal and electrical insulator Good chemical and wear resistance Can be brittle	Adhesives such as Araldite®, PCB component encapsulation
Melamine formaldehyde (MF)	Stiff, hard and strong Excellent resistance to heat, scratching and staining Excellent thermal and electrical insulator	Kitchen work-surface laminates, tableware
Urea formaldehyde (UF)	Stiff and hard Excellent thermal and electrical insulator	Electrical fittings, toilet seats, adhesive used in MDF

Table 10.2 Properties and uses of thermosetting polymers

KEY POINTS
- Polymers are categorised as thermoforming or thermosetting.
- Most polymers are sourced from crude oil.
- Natural polymers are sourced from vegetable products, such as corn starch.
- Crude oil must undergo fractional distillation and cracking to produce the basic building block of all synthetic polymers.
- There can be a serious ecological penalty to pay if the sourcing and processing of polymers is not carefully regulated.

10.2 The way in which the selection of materials or components is influenced by a range of factors

Functionality

Polymers have a number of inherent properties that a designer should be aware of before selecting a material.

- One of the main reasons for selecting thermoforming polymers is due to their ability to be moulded with the use of heat. This allows you to produce a wide variety of interesting shapes with relative ease.
- Many polymers have a natural high-gloss finish, which means there is no need to apply a finishing coat.
- They can be obtained in a wide variety of colours, and therefore do not need to be painted or stained.
- They do not corrode, therefore they do not need to be protected from water.
- They are a good thermal insulator.
- They are a good electrical insulator.
- They can be very tough and durable.
- They are available in transparent, translucent and opaque forms.
- They are unaffected by many chemicals. However, they can be affected by solvents.
- Thermoset polymers are unaffected by heat once they have been moulded.

Figure 10.8 Wheelie bin: one of the many functional uses of polymers

Aesthetics

Polymers can be relatively easily coloured with the use of coloured pigments, making them an ideal choice where colour is essential, such as when manufacturing children's toys. Polymers can be easily moulded, making them an excellent choice for products that contain intricate shapes. Polymers are available in transparent and translucent form making them an ideal substitute for clear and coloured glass.

Environmental factors

Figure 10.9 Children's brightly coloured plastic toys

Synthetic polymers come from crude oil, and therefore the use of polymers is generally considered not to be environmentally friendly. However, a number of polymers are very tough and durable, meaning they are less likely to break, and therefore they will last longer. This type of polymer is more environmentally friendly as there will be less need to use raw materials.

Many polymer products can be reused. Plastic drinks bottles should be reused instead of being thrown away or recycled after their first use. Most thermoforming polymers are infinitely recyclable and can be collected and reused used time and time again. Thermosetting polymers are very difficult to recycle, making them the least environmentally friendly polymer.

The processing and manufacturing of polymers uses further natural resources and leads to pollution of the atmosphere that will lead to the formation of greenhouse gases and contribute to global warming.

Natural polymers (biopolymers) come from natural renewable resources, and are themselves renewable, making them the most environmentally friendly polymer.

Availability

Polymers are **available** in a more limited range of stock forms than other material groups. For more details see Section 10.4.

Cost

Polymers are considered to be expensive when compared to most metal- and timber-based materials. However, due to their suitability for volume production, the **cost** of polymer-based products is generally low. This is because processes such as injection moulding and blow moulding are mechanised processes that require relatively low energy, use a small workforce and produce products at a high volume.

Social factors

The development of different types of polymers, and advances in manufacturing techniques, have led to a vast increase in the number of affordable, polymer-based products that are available today. This can be considered an advantage as we have more choice of products that are specifically targeted to our specific needs. However, this can also be a disadvantage in that people can feel pressured into buying products.

For example, the video games mouse and keyboard in Figure 10.10 have been designed specifically for the gaming market; they look stylish and offer additional features, but would a video games player feel pressured into paying extra for them?

Cultural factors

Designers must take into account the needs, beliefs and tastes of different cultures when designing polymer products. Polymer products need to be produced sensitively to meet the requirements of the particular cultural groups that the product is being made for. As our society becomes more and more multicultural, designers must look to produce designs that encompass all cultures, especially when polymer products are being manufactured in high volumes for the mass market.

KEY WORDS

Function: how a material is expected to perform.

Aesthetics: The visual qualities of a material.

Environmental factors: how the material affects the environment during sourcing, processing, manufacture, use and final disposal.

Availability: what shape, form a material is and how easy it is to access.

Cost: what the financial cost of a material is relative to other materials.

Figure 10.10 Video games mouse and keyboard

Ethical factors

The use of synthetic polymers can have a big impact on the world that we live in. It is important to be aware of the issues and reduce the negative consequences of using synthetic polymers. The sourcing and processing of polymers can lead to environmental damage and global warming. The unregulated use of polymers will eventually mean we will run out of crude oil. The uncontrolled disposal of polymers will pollute our oceans.

Polymer products are now clearly labelled with the type of polymer to make recycling easier. Councils all over the country promote plastic recycling.

Designers and manufacturers of polymer products are now looking to use more natural polymers (biopolymers). Natural polymers are renewable, biodegradable and environmentally friendly.

The low cost of labour in third world countries attracts manufacturers of polymer products to set up huge factories to mass produce everyday products. However, when manufacturers see profits as their driving goal it can lead to the mistreatment of employees, who may receive a low wage, forcing them into poverty and exposing them to hazardous working conditions.

Activity

Collect a number of 'regular' plastic shopping bags and a number of 'biodegradable' plastic shopping bags.

Carry out a number of tests and produce a report on their suitability.

Use the following headings to help structure your answer.

- Functionality – how much shopping can you fit in? What weight can they hold? How comfortable are they to carry?
- Aesthetics – How do they differ in appearance? Why?
- Environmental factors – What polymer are they manufactured from? Is the polymer renewable, recyclable and/or biodegradable?

KEY POINTS

- The properties of a polymer should be carefully matched to the intended use of the product

10.3 The impact of forces and stress on materials and objects and the ways in which they can be reinforced and stiffened

The majority of polymers are man-made, and as such chemical engineers have been able to fine-tune the properties of polymers more than any other material group. This has led to the development of polymers with excellent toughness and durability, chemical resistance and electrical insulation along with the ability to handle extremes of temperatures.

The office chair in Figure 10.11 is a modern replica of a design classic from the 1950s. Once manufactured in fibreglass, this replica has been produced by injection moulding the shell of the chair from high-density polythene (HDPE). HDPE is tough and lightweight, meaning that it can be easily moved around an office and that it will comfortably handle the wear and tear of day-to-day use. It also has the ability to have pigment added to it, meaning that it can be produced in a wide variety of colours. As a thermoforming polymer it can be easily injection-moulded, which is suitable for large-scale production.

Figure 10.11 Thermoforming polymer seat

Thermoset polymers are less common than thermoforming polymers, but they do possess some properties that make them ideal for applications where resistance to heat and electrical insulation are vital. Thermoset polymers are generally considered to be less resistant to stress than thermoforming polymers and certain thermosets can be brittle. Urea formaldehyde is a thermoset polymer which is used in the manufacture of electrical plugs and sockets, along with smoke alarm covers. It is a hard material that does not soften when exposed to heat, so if there were an electrical error with an appliance, the plug would not melt, protecting the user from electrocution. As a good electrical insulator, it is also suitable to be plugged in and removed from the socket without risking any harm to the user.

Cross-sectional area

The stock form of a polymer can have an effect on its strength. Solid forms, such as round and square bars, have good resistance to force and stress, but are quite dense. Round and square tubes are hollow, and although they lose some strength, they are significantly lighter. Most polymer products are moulded into shape and therefore the strength of the product is influenced by the design. Ribs, webs and supporting structures can be moulded into the product to give it extra strength and rigidity.

Strengthening by laminating with fibres

Carbon fibre reinforced polymer

Carbon fibre reinforced polymer (CFRP) is a composite of carbon fibre strands woven together and encased in a thermosetting polymer resin. The resin, which is lightweight and rigid, encases the carbon fibre strands, which have a high tensile strength, to create a high-performance engineering material. CFRP is instantly recognisable due to its woven appearance.

Figure 10.12 CFRP matting

CFRP is now a common material used in the manufacture of both racing bikes and mountain bikes. Its strength-to-weight ratio and stiffness, along with the ability to produce streamlined shapes, makes it the material of choice for these high-end products. Common uses of CFRP include Formula 1 components, high-performance sports equipment and applications in the aerospace industry.

Glass-reinforced plastic

Glass-reinforced plastic (GRP) is a composite of glass fibres and polyester resin. It is a more common composite polymer than CFRP due to its lower cost and more accessible manufacturing methods. The polyester resin makes GRP tough and lightweight, with the glass fibres providing rigidity. GRP has a less attractive surface than CFRP so is usually seen with a 'gel coat' finish. When the plastic resin has set or cured it is impossible to reverse the process so composite materials are not recyclable.

KEY WORDS

Carbon fibre reinforced polymer (CFRP): a thermoforming polymer reinforced with carbon fibre.

Glass-reinforced plastic (GRP): a thermoforming polymer reinforced with glass fibres.

Figure 10.13 CFRP tennis racket

Figure 10.14 A jet ski made from GRP

The modification of properties for specific purposes

There are a number of additives than can be blended with polymers to enhance certain properties.

- **Plasticisers** are added to polymers to enhance the flexibility of the polymer; phthalate esters are added to polyvinyl chloride (PVC) when used for cables.
- **Stabilisers** can be added that resist UV degradation; UV stabilisers are added to polyvinyl chloride (PVC) when used for polymer window frames.

KEY WORDS

Plasticisers: give flexibility to polymers.

Stabilisers: added to polymers to reduce UV degradation and brittleness.

Extrusion: a length of material with a consistent cross-section.

Activity

Watch this three-minute YouTube clip, which will show you how carbon fibre is used in the manufacture of the Formula 1 racing car: www.youtube.com/watch?v=X6addl525lc

KEY POINTS

- The physical, mechanical and aesthetic properties of a polymer can be altered in a number of ways to enhance the material.

10.4 Stock forms, types and sizes in order to calculate and determine the quantity of materials or components required

Polymers are available in a more limited range of stock forms than other material groups. Most polymers that you will encounter in school or college will come in sheet form, although **extrusions**, such as tube and rod, are available.

Common forms

Standard sheets of acrylic are usually 1200 × 500 mm or 1200 × 600 mm and are most commonly 3 mm in thickness. Other thicknesses are available, but the choice of colour becomes more limited in the less common sizes. High-Impact Polystyrene (HIPS) can also be supplied in large sheets but is usually then processed down into smaller sizes for use in vacuum formers.

As with metals, polymers are readily available in extrusions of different shapes and profiles including rod, tube, square and angle section. Extruded polymer sections are used in the construction of the frame of UPVC double glazing.

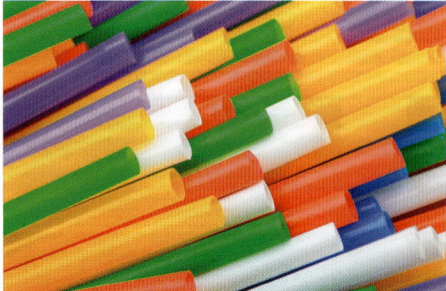

Figure 10.15 Polymer extrusions

Figure 10.16 Polymer granules

Figure 10.17 Plastazote foam flooring

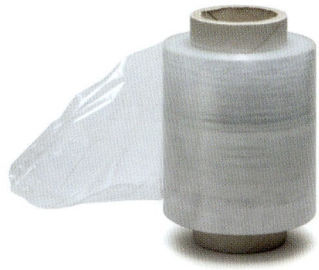

Figure 10.18 PVC film

Figure 10.19 PLA filament

Other stock forms of polymers include granules or pellets, which may be used in processes such as injection moulding, and powders that may be used in fluidising tanks to polymer-coat small metal parts.

Thermoset polymers are also generally found in powder form, but due to the compression moulding manufacturing process it is unlikely that you will come across them in a school environment.

Other forms of polymer that are readily available are films and foams. These vary in thickness and material, depending on the intended application.

Foams are categorised into two groups: open cell and closed cell. In open-cell foams the structure of the material has gaps in between the cells that are occupied by air. Open-cell foams are generally soft and sponge-like in texture and have a lower density than closed-cell foams.

Plastazote® foam is an example of an open-cell foam. It is trademarked, although the material itself is polyethylene foam. It is available in a variety of thicknesses and densities. It is often used in protective packaging, swimming pool floats and safety mattings in gyms and nurseries.

Closed-cell foams have no spaces between the cells and therefore no spaces for air to occupy. This means that closed-cell foams are more dense than open-cell foams. They are good insulators of heat, sound and are water resistant.

Polymer film is also available in a variety of thicknesses. PVC is a popular material that is supplied in film form and can be easily vacuum formed for use in food packaging.

More recently, one of the most common stock forms of polymer that you will come across in school is the **filament** that is used in 3D printing. This is usually supplied on a reel and varies in diameter, depending on the brand of 3D printer being used.

In addition to the rigid stock forms of polymers available, there is also a range of liquid polymers. These are rarely used in their liquid form, but instead harden when exposed to air or, in some cases, when exposed to a chemical catalyst. Liquid silicon can be used to create moulds for pewter casting as it can be poured around a shape or former, and its resistance to heat means that small-scale manufacture is possible. Other liquid polymers include casting resin, which can be used in GRP manufacture or for producing decorative jewellery and components. Here, the resin is combined with a hardener or catalyst to help it set into a solid state.

KEY WORD

Filament: the extruded material that is used in a 3D printer.

All of these polymer stock forms are available in a wide range of colours; one of the main advantages of polymers is their ability to be coloured by the addition of a pigment.

Calculating material costs

When you work with polymers in school you will probably be fabricating a product or component from a bigger sheet of source material. When it comes to costing your project or trying to work out the most efficient method of manufacture, you must remember to factor in the waste material that you have created. This cost can be limited by sensible material management, such as tessellating designs on a sheet before laser cutting. It may also be possible to select different variations of material. For example, acrylic comes in cast and extruded varieties. Cast acrylic is better to laser cut, but more expensive than its extruded equivalent.

Laser cutters are now commonplace in schools with many machines having large bed sizes in excess of 500 mm². This capability to cut large pieces of material means that material management is an important consideration to minimise and reduce waste and unnecessary cost. If small cutting jobs are necessary, then it is good practice to source an appropriate sized piece of material, but one-off jobs tend to be fairly wasteful. It is much more efficient to use a larger piece of material and layout as many designs as possible on it.

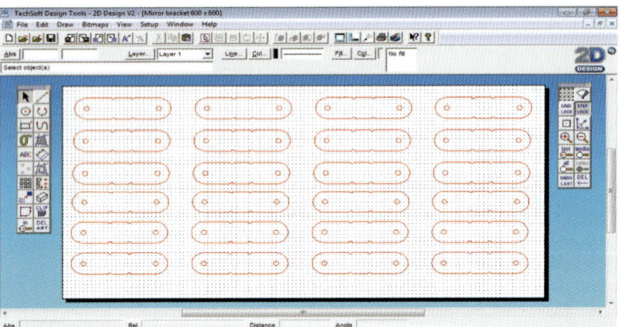

Figure 10.20 Wasteful arrangement of designs

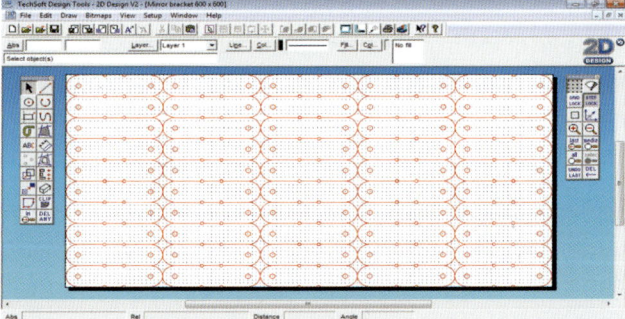

Figure 10.21 Efficient tessellated designs

Figures 10.20 and 10.21 show screenshots of two files that are set up for manufacture on a laser cutter. The material in both examples is the same dimension, but 10.20 has 24 nets arranged on the work piece, whereas 10.21 has 50. This illustrates the importance of tessellation and of planning the layout of your work to make the most efficient use of the material you choose.

Activity

Explore the range of polymer sheet material that you have in school. Find out what thickness the material is supposed to be and then, using a vernier calliper, measure the material. Is there any difference? Often polymer sheets can be slightly larger or thinner than advertised. What impact could this have when in use?

KEY POINTS

- The majority of polymers that you will come in to contact with in school will be thermoforming polymers.
- Thermoforming polymers can be heated, shaped and then harden when cool. This process can be repeated indefinitely.

10.5 Alternative processes that can be used to manufacture products to different scales of production

One-off production

A one-off product is a unique, bespoke product that is made for a specific purpose. The advantage of manufacturing polymer products by one-off production is that the product can be manufactured to the exact requirements of the client. You can use expensive polymer composites such as carbon fibre and work to high tolerances using highly skilled workers. The car bodies of Formula 1 racing cars are made by this method. The disadvantage is that the products are generally very expensive, very labour intensive and take a long time to produce.

Batch production

Batch production involves the manufacture of a small number of identical products. The advantage of manufacturing polymer products in limited quantities is that you are able to produce a batch of identical products. This means that raw materials can be purchased in bulk, which reduces the overall cost of manufacture. The time taken to make the product is reduced, as machinery, tools and equipment can be set up ready for manufacture. The skill level of the labour force is reduced, as many can work as machine operators. Product efficiency increases, as all aspects of the work speed up. Products can be produced to exactly the same sizes and tolerances. As only a small batch is being produced, it allows the design to be changed after a short period of time so that improvements can be made or the style can be changed. The disadvantage is that you lose the unique element of one-off production.

The use of jigs

A **jig** is a device that is specially made to perform a specific part of the manufacturing process. Jigs are extremely useful when the process has to be carried out multiple times. They can be used when cutting, drilling, sawing, and gluing. They have a number of very important advantages:

- They speed up the manufacturing process.
- They reduce the risk of human error.
- They reduce the unit cost of a part.
- They make the process safer to carry out.
- They increase the accuracy of the process.
- They increase the consistency of the process.
- They reduce wastage.

It should be noted that there are disadvantages of using jigs:

- They are only cost effective when large numbers of similar parts are required.
- They increase the initial cost of the part.
- They require a high level of skill to produce.

High-volume production

Polymer products are ideally suited to high-volume production as they are relatively easy to mould and form into shape by machines. Due to their very high demand, polymer products such as water bottles, margarine tubs, yoghurt pots, pens, and containers for household cleaning products are now made by continuous flow production, where manufacture never stops and machines run 24 hours a day, 7 days a week.

KEY WORDS

One-off production: one product is made.

Batch production: several identical products are made.

Jigs: a mechanical device to aid production.

High-volume production: many products are made, making extensive use of machinery and manufacturing aids.

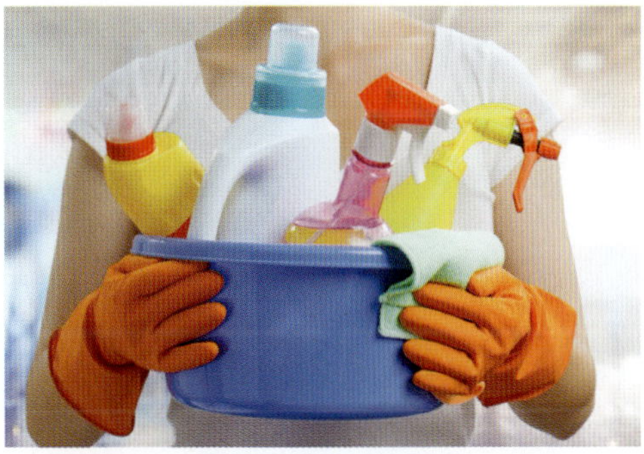

Figure 10.22 Everyday cleaning products in polymer containers

High-volume production has a number of **advantages**:

- raw materials can be bought in bulk
- machines are used to make the products
- the size of the workforce is significantly reduced
- the unit cost of a product is much cheaper
- products are identical and accurately produced.

However, there are a number of **disadvantages** in using high-volume production:

- products lose their unique appearance
- employment opportunities are lost
- the workforce becomes less skilled
- the machines require more energy.

Computer-aided manufacture (CAM)

Highly specialised equipment and extensive use of computer-aided machinery (CAM) is used to manufacture polymer products in high volumes. This requires a large initial investment in new factories and state-of-the-art machines. It is only cost effective when very high numbers of the same polymer products are being made for long periods.

There are a number of processes that are used to manufacture polymer products in high volumes. These are:

- blow moulding
- injection moulding
- vacuum forming
- press forming
- compression moulding.

All these processes use the same principles of manufacturing.

- The polymer is heated and becomes soft and pliable.
- The polymer is then blown, sucked, drawn or pressed into a die or mould.
- The polymer takes the form of the die or mould.
- The polymer is then cooled.
- The product is removed from the die or mould and then trimmed and finished.

Activity

You have been asked to produce a design for a school key fob that is going to be given away as batch of around 100 key fobs to next year's new intake.

- Use a suitable CAD program, such as 2D Design, to produce your idea.
- Use the laser cutter to produce a one-off to show to your teacher.

If successful, your design will be produced as a batch of around 100 at the open evening.

10.6 Specialist techniques and processes that can be used to shape, fabricate, construct a high-quality prototype

Wastage/addition

Marking out on polymers

A spirit-based pen is suitable for polymers as it will mark the surface without scratching it. A plastic ruler is also useful – a metal rule could damage the shiny surface of the polymer.

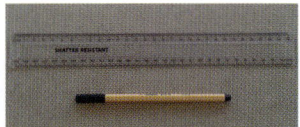

Figure 10.23 Spirit-based pen, plastic ruler

Top tip: if the polymer comes with a protective coating, keep it on as long as possible to prevent it becoming scratched.

Many of the marking-out tools used on wood and metal can also be used on polymer-based materials. Polymers are ideally suited to the use of paper templates as they give the polymer an extra protective layer.

A laser cutter can etch lines on to the surface of polymer. This is particularly useful when bending acrylic.

Holding polymers

Polymer sheet can be held in a similar way to timber and metal, by placing it into a vice or clamping it with a G-clamp, but extra protection is needed to prevent the high-quality surface of the polymer being marked. It is good practice to leave any protective coatings/films on the polymer as long as possible.

Sawing polymers

Polymers such as acrylic (PMMA) are ideal for cutting on a laser cutter. However, if a laser is not available or the design does not allow one to be used, then polymers can be cut by a saw or, if the polymer is thin and soft enough, by a knife. Most of the metalworking and woodworking saws, such as a coping saw and hacksaw, can be used to cut polymers.

Top tip: when holding your work in a metal vice you can protect the polymer by wrapping it in a paper towel. It is also advisable to keep it as low down in the vice as possible to prevent snapping.

A coping saw will cut all polymers, but it is not a very accurate tool. It will wander and does not cut a straight and true line. It is able to cut around tight corners. Always cut away from the shape you are cutting. The lever pins allow you to quickly change the position of blade.

The scroll saw is a mechanised version of a coping saw. It is very versatile as it can be fitted with a range of different blades, allowing it to cut wood, metal or polymers. It allows you to concentrate on following the shape of the part you are cutting.

The **hacksaw** is the most popular saw for sawing metal, but is also very effective at sawing polymers.

Shaping polymers

Polymers can be easily shaped using metalworking files. For more information on files and filling techniques see Chapter 9.

Disc sander

A **disc sander** is a very useful, time-saving machine. It will quickly and accurately clean, shape and true the edges of polymer. The disc sander does have a number of health and safety issues that must be taken into consideration. The sander will remove skin just as easily as it will remove polymer, and therefore you must not get your fingers near the disc. The disc spins at a high speed, and so all loose clothing and hair must be tied away. It also produces high volumes of dust, so it is essential that it is fitted with dust extraction equipment and that the user is wearing safety glasses/goggles.

Figure 10.24 A disc sander

Drilling polymers

Polymers can be easily drilled with regular metalworking drill bits and hole saws. They can be drilled with a handheld cordless drill, but for greater accuracy, you should use a pillar drill.

Pillar drill

A pillar drill can be used to drill holes in polymers. The speed of the pillar drill can be altered to match that of the drill and the material it is drilling into. As polymers are a soft material they generally require a fast speed setting. Many polymer shapes are flat and non-uniform, and therefore it is good practice to clamp them down to the drilling table with a specialised drill clamp or a G-clamp. Make sure that you are wearing the correct PPE at all times and follow all the relevant safety procedures.

Figure 10.25 A cordless drill

Cordless drill

The cordless drill is not as accurate as a pillar drill and does not have the same power. However, it is convenient and can be taken to the job and used in remote locations.

Drill bits

Twist drills are the most popular type of drill bit. They are made from hardened and tempered high-carbon steel.

Top tip: it is a good idea to place tape over the area to be drilled to prevent the point of the drill from slipping across the surface.

Hole saw

A hole saw will produce a large hole in your polymer. The drill will produce a lot of torque and therefore it is essential that the work is firmly clamped down. Figure 10.26 shows a hole saw being used.

Figure 10.26 Using a hole saw

Top tip: ensure that there is a scrap piece of wood underneath your polymer, so that the hole saw can drill all the way through or continue drilling until the pilot drill emerges, and then reverse the work.

Forming polymers

Thermoforming polymers can easily be formed into shape by a number of different methods.

Line bending is one of the simplest methods of forming a polymer sheet; acrylic is by far the most common material formed by this method in the school workshop. The **strip heater** consists of a hot wire that is used to heat the acrylic to a temperature of around 160°C. At this temperature the acrylic becomes pliable and can be bent into shape. The heat can be regulated to accommodate varying thicknesses of acrylic and varying bends. Care should be taken not to overheat the acrylic as it will blister, and you must remember that you are using hot materials and equipment.

Figure 10.27 A strip heater

Jigs and formers are often used when bending acrylic to ensure that accurate and consistent shapes are obtained.

An oven can be used to soften a thermoforming polymer until it is soft and pliable. It can then be carefully removed from the oven and bent around a pre-prepared former. Again, remember to use the correct PPE (personal protective equipment) when handling hot material.

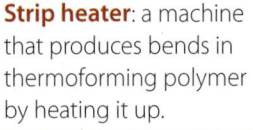

KEY WORD

Strip heater: a machine that produces bends in thermoforming polymer by heating it up.

Types of hole

- A **pilot hole** is drilled before a screw is screwed directly into polymer. The pilot hole will be just smaller than the size of the screw. A pilot hole can also be used before a large hole is drilled into polymer. This prevents the build-up of excessive heat that could melt the polymer.
- A **clearance hole** is a hole that is drilled larger than the actual size of the bolt. This allows the threaded part of the bolt to slip through the component being fastened. A clearance hole for an M8 bolt would be 8.5 mm.
- A **tapping hole** is a hole that is drilled before a screwthread is produced. This is a smaller hole than the actual screwthread (for example, an M8 screwthread requires a 6.8 mm tapping hole to be drilled).
- A **countersunk hole** is a hole that has been drilled with a countersink bit ready to accept a countersunk headed setscrew.
- A **counterbored hole** is a hole that has been enlarged to accept the head of a bolt. A counterbored hole for an M8 bolt could be 12 mm.

Deforming/reforming

Joining polymers: temporary methods

Nuts, bolts, set screws and washers

Polymers can be treated like metal and bolted together using nuts, bolts, set screws and washers. These tend to have larger heads than conventional bolts to allow the pressure to be distributed over a wider surface area.

Nuts and bolts can also be made from polymer. Nylon is commonly used for the nuts and bolts that fix your number plate to your car. The have the advantage of being completely waterproof, corrosion resistant and can be coloured to blend in with the number plate.

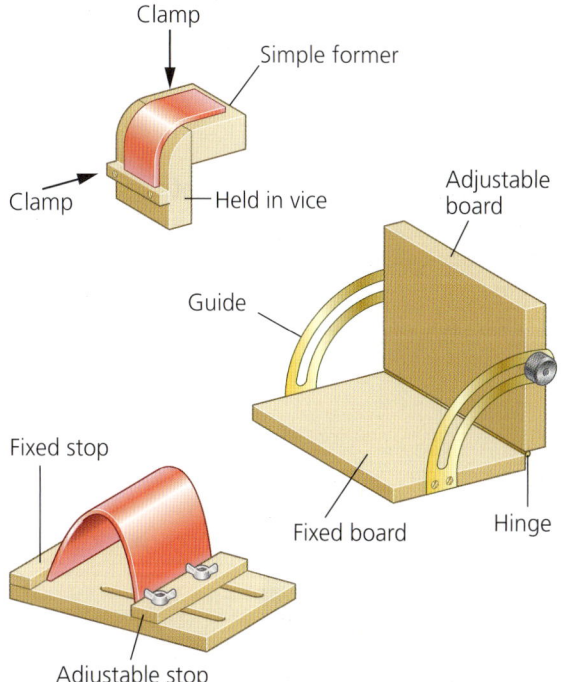

Figure 10.28 A selection of line-bending jigs

Figure 10.29 Large-headed bolts and washers

Figure 10.30 Nylon nuts and bolts

Self-tapping screws

Polymers can also be screwed together using self-tapping screws. The self-tapping screw does not require a screwthread to be made as it has a hardened screwthread that allows it to cut its own thread through soft materials such as polymers.

Figure 10.31 Self-tapping screws

Panel trim fixings

The automotive industry makes extensive use of panel trim fixings. These purpose made fixings hold together the polymer panels in your car. They can be removed quickly and easily to allow for maintenance and are very inexpensive.

Rivets

Polymer can be riveted together using a number of different riveting techniques. The traditional process of riveting can be used to fasten sheets of polymer together, but only with aluminium rivets. Steel rivets would be too hard, require too much hammering and would most likely crack the polymer. See Chapter 9 for more details on the traditional riveting technique.

Pop rivets are made from aluminium and are hollow. They require only a limited amount of force to apply, and therefore this makes them ideal for fastening polymer sheets together. They also have the advantage of being able to fasten sheets together 'blind' (when you cannot gain access to the rear). See Chapter 9 for more details on the pop riveting technique.

Hinges

Polymer hinges can be used with similar materials, but equally may be suitable for use with metals and woods. The properties of the polymer may be better suited to the application than a metal equivalent (for example they may be lighter in weight and will not corrode). One advantage of using a polymer hinge with a polymer fabrication is that you can use an adhesive to join the two items together instead of having to add nuts and bolts or similar fixings.

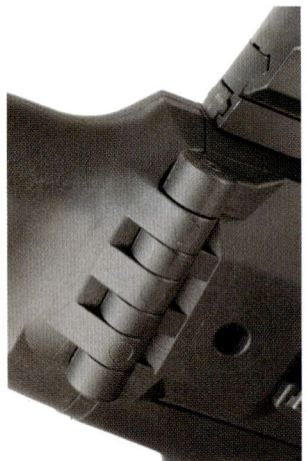

Figure 10.32 Polymer hinge

Catches

Catches are used as a closing for doors, drawers and lids. There have a number of different types of catches including a ball catch, spring catch and a magnetic catch.

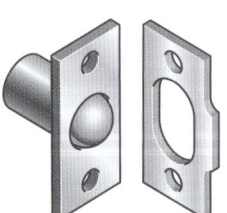

Figure 10.33 Ball catch

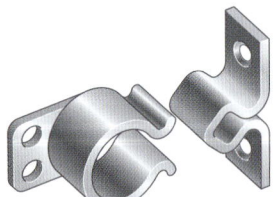

Figure 10.34 Spring catch

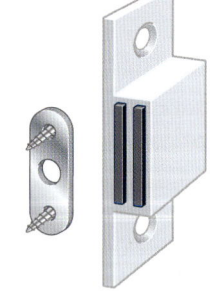

Figure 10.35 Magnetic catch

Permanent methods of joining polymers

Polymers can be glued, riveted and welded together to form a permanent joint.

Polymers can be glued with a variety of **adhesives**, but there are a number of specific glues that are specially formulated for use with certain polymers.

Tensol cement (dichloromethane and methyl methacrylate) is a clear solvent that gives a very effective bond when used with acrylic (PMMA). It melts the surfaces and fuses them together. It has a number of health and safety issues, and you must wear the correct PPE before using it and ensure that you follow all the relevant health and safety procedures.

Welding can also be used to permanently join polymers. Within the school workshop the only convenient method of welding polymers is by solvent welding. This is achieved by using a solvent adhesive such as Tensol cement. The surfaces of the polymer should be free from dust or dirt and the solvent cement applied with a spatula. The two surfaces are then pressed and held together. The solvent will melt the two surfaces and they will fuse together forming a welded joint.

Commercial methods of welding thermoforming polymers include the use of a hot-air gun to melt the two surfaces or by using hot metal clamps to form a seal on thin polymer sheets.

Centre lathe

You may well have used a centre lathe for machining metal components, but it is equally as good at machining polymers. It is used to make circular components from various sections of polymer bar. Various stock forms can be held in the chuck while it spins around. A cutting tool can then be used to perform a variety of turning operations.

See Chapter 9 for more details on using a lathe.

Milling machine

Again, you may have used milling machines to carry out a range of machining operations in metal, but it will perform the same operations in polymer. They can be used to cut slots, grooves, machine edges and smooth large surface areas.

Small workpieces can be held in a machine vice that is bolted down onto the milling machine table. Larger pieces of work are bolted directly to the table.

These machines are often used with automatic feeds. This ensures that the correct speed of cut is maintained, giving an accurate surface finish.

See Chapter 9 for more details on using a milling machine.

Computer-aided manufacture

Computer-aided manufacture (CAM) is now the leading method of production within the industrial world. CAM involves the manufacturing of products and components by machines that are controlled by computer. We are rapidly approaching a time when whole products will be produced by CAM, with very little, if any, direct human input.

The advantages of CAM are very compelling when compared to traditional methods of manufacture. CAM is far quicker, more consistent and works with greater accuracy than traditional methods. The disadvantages of CAM are that the initial set-up costs are high as machines are expensive to buy, they have a high energy cost, and it can lead to a market flooded with similar products that lack individuality.

CAM requires a computer-aided design (CAD) drawing of the component to be produced. From the CAD drawing, special software will convert the drawing into machine code that will inform the machine how to cut/form the component. Most CAM operations involve the control of two or three motors to accurately move the tools to cut/form the component. These motors are known as **stepper motors** and, unlike normal electrical motors that spin at high speeds, can be very accurately controlled to index (turn) around to a specific angle. By controlling the tool in a combination of three axes, known as the **x, y and z axes**, any shape can be cut/formed.

Figure 10.36 A vinyl cutter

Figure 10.37 A laser cutter

Vinyl cutters

A vinyl cutter consists of a very sharp blade that is controlled by two stepper or servo motors that run along the x and y axes. By combining the two movements, the vinyl cutter can produce very accurate and consistent replications of 2D CAD images. Typical applications of vinyl cutters are cutting out lettering and signs in self-adhesive vinyl, or cutting card for use in modelling or packaging. Sophisticated vinyl cutters incorporate printing facilities and allow a complete coloured 2D product to be produced in one operation. The house number on many wheelie bins was probably produced in this way.

Laser cutters

Laser cutters work on the same principle as vinyl cutters. They work from 2D CAD images and are controlled by two stepper or servo motors that run along the x and y axes. Again, the combination of these two movements allows the tool to produce very accurate and consistent replications of the 2D CAD drawing. Laser cutters found in school workshops use a laser beam as their tool and are typically used to cut through relatively thin acrylic (PMMA). They can also be used as an engraving tool on any thickness of material.

Having loaded a CAD drawing on to a computer, the laser cutter requires the image to be processed into machine code; the speed and strength of the laser also needs to be set to match the material being machined. The laser beam is then focused on to the surface of the material and the cutting/engraving process can begin. Laser cutting can give off toxic fumes so it is essential to have an air extraction/filter system fitted. Looking directly at the laser can harm your eyesight and therefore must be avoided.

3D router

A 3D router can be used to accurately machine polymers. It uses a router bit as its cutting tool and, by combining the movement of three stepper motors, it can travel along the x, y and z axes to produce 3D components.

CNC milling machine

A **CNC milling machine** is very similar to a 3D router and will machine an accurate 3D component. CNC milling machines can machine polymers as well as much harder materials, such as low-carbon steel and aluminium. Again, the material is clamped to the bed of the machine or held in a vice and the correct milling cutter is fitted to the motor. A CAD drawing is uploaded to the computer and the dedicated machine software converts this information into machine code. The CNC milling machine will then machine the material.

CNC lathe

A CNC lathe performs all the operations of a centre lathe, but it is controlled by computer. It can be fitted with a variety of lathe cutting tools, enabling it to parallel turn, taper turn, face off, part off, drill and even produce external screw threads. As with the centre lathe, it can be used to machine a wide variety of metals and polymers.

The machining process:

1 The blank material is fitted into the lathe chuck.
2 The correct tools are fitted and calibrated.
3 The CAD drawing is uploaded to the computer.
4 The dedicated software converts the information into machine code, taking into account the type of material being machined.
5 The CNC lathe will then begin the machining process.

Blow moulding

Blow moulding can also be done in the school workshop to form a dome shape. The process is a relatively simple one that is done on a vacuum-forming machine.

Firstly, a clamping ring needs to be produced. This consists of a sheet of material, such as 3 mm plywood, that has had a hole cut into it that is the same size as the diameter of the dome. It is clamped onto the vacuum former together with a sheet of thermoforming polymer, such as high-impact polystyrene (HIPS). The HIPS is then heated until soft and then blown into a dome shape. If your design requires a flat base on your dome then a restrictor can used. A restrictor is a flat piece of material that the blown dome will come into contact with while it is still warm. Once cool, the dome can be removed from the vacuum former and trimmed.

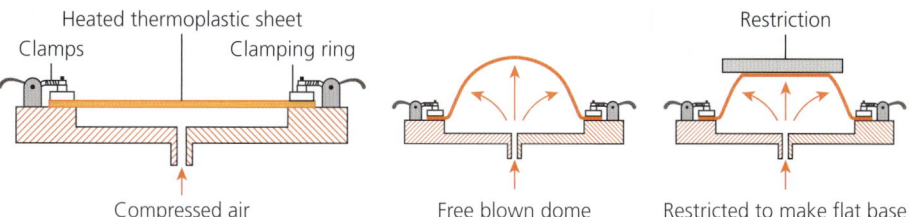

Figure 10.38 Blow moulding

Vacuum forming

Vacuum forming is used to produce 3D complex shapes in a thermoforming polymer sheet. High-impact polystyrene (HIPS) sheet is the most popular material used for vacuum forming in the school workshop. Before a vacuum-formed product can be made, a mould must be produced.

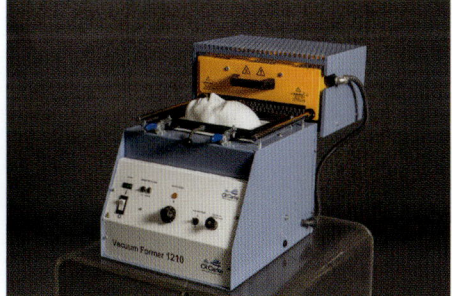

Figure 10.39 A vacuum-forming machine

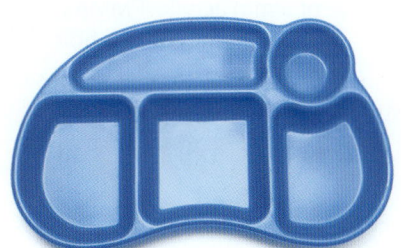

Figure 10.40 A vacuum-formed product

> ### KEY WORDS
>
> **Blow moulding**: a method of shaping thermoforming polymer by heating it and blowing it into shape.
>
> **Vacuum forming**: a method of shaping thermoforming polymer by heating it and sucking it around a mould.

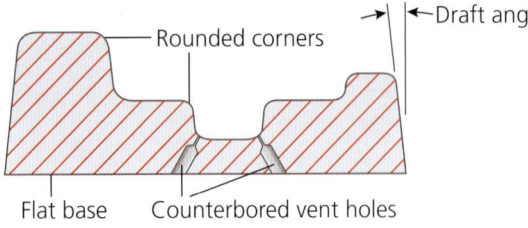

Figure 10.41 A cross-section through a mould used for vacuum forming

The accuracy and finish of the mould for vacuum forming is very important, as any imperfections will show up on every product it produces. There are certain key features of a mould.

- It should have sloping sides (usually around 5°) to ensure the HIPS sheet can be removed.
- It should have rounded corners to prevent the HIPS sheet from thinning on the corner and possibly splitting.
- It should have vent holes drilled to allow the air to be removed from inset sections.
- It should have a smooth surface.

The vacuum-forming process:

- Once the mould is ready, it is placed on the platen (table) of the vacuum former and lowered into the machine.
- A sheet of HIPS is then clamped over the top of the machine and heat is applied.
- After a short time, the HIPS sheet will become soft. Care should be taken not to overheat the HIPS sheet, as it will not form properly and webbing may occur.
- The mould is then raised up into the hot HIPS sheet and immediately the air is sucked out of the machine by turning on the vacuum pump.
- Once formed, the sheet should be allowed to cool then removed from the vacuum former and trimmed.
- Deeper moulds may require the soft HIPS sheet to be blown into a dome before the mould is raised. This gives an even thickness of material around the taller mould.
- See Chapter 6 Figure 6.62 for a diagram of the process.

> ## KEY WORD
>
> **Press forming**: a method of shaping thermoforming polymer by heating it and pressing it between two halves of a mould.

Press forming

Press forming produces similar 3D outcomes to vacuum forming, but is used with simpler shapes in thicker thermoforming polymer sheets, such as 3 mm acrylic.

The press-forming mould comprises of two parts: a 'yoke' and a 'plug'. The acrylic sheet should be heated up in an oven to make it soft and pliable. It is then placed between the yoke and the plug, and the two parts of the mould are than pressed together. The mould may feature guide pins to ensure that the two parts accurately align with each other. Once cool, the acrylic sheet can then be removed and trimmed.

Figure 10.42 A press-forming mould

Activity

Draw a simple-shaped paper template to be used to produce a pendant. Glue it onto a piece of 3 mm acrylic (PMMA), then shape it using saws and files. Clean and polish the edges, then drill a 4 mm hole through it and fit a piece of cord.

You could produce smaller shapes to be cut, shaped and polished and glued onto the surface of your first piece.

10.7 Appropriate surface treatments and finishes that can be applied for functional and aesthetic purposes

Most polymers are self-coloured; this means that they are made in a range of colours and you would choose the most appropriate colour for parts as you make a project. Most polymers are also quite resistant to wear and decay, so you do not normally need to apply a protective finish to polymers.

Figure 10.43 Polishing mop

Polishing

Polymer surfaces are often smooth and highly polished. If you cut a sheet of polymer, either using hand tools or with a laser cutter, you will normally need to make the edge smooth with a file and/or abrasive papers before polishing on a buffing machine.

Flame polishing can also be used to finish the edges of polymers. In this process the edge of the polymer is exposed to a naked flame, which melts the outside surface. This can provide a high-quality finish.

Printing

Decoration, texture and detail can be added to polymer products by various printing techniques. Pad printing or **screen printing** can be used to transfer a chosen image or design. It is possible to print on flat or curved surfaces.

Vinyl decals

In applications where screen printing is not a viable process, you will often find that **vinyl** decals are applied to polymer products. These can either be screen-printed images that are then cut out and applied in a similar way to a sticker or can be individual text or shapes that have been cut out using a CNC knife cutter.

Textured finishes

Textured finishes are often seen on polymer products, but in most cases these are not technically a finish. Instead it is more likely that they have been created by the addition of a vinyl pattern, or more commonly are a result of the moulding process used to manufacture them. As thermoforming polymers are moulded, they will pick up any detail on the inside of the mould used. This can be used to provide a matt surface finish, as seen on a phone case, or could also be used to emboss a logo, etc.

> **KEY WORDS**
>
> **Screen printing**: a printing process for adding detail or text to polymer products.
>
> **Vinyl**: a self-adhesive polymer, available in a range of colours, suitable for CNC knife cutting.

Figure 10.44 Vinyl decal logo

Activity

Use the internet to investigate how vinyl decals are applied to vehicles and explore how the vinyl wrapping of entire car panels is increasing the possibilities of applying finishes to polymers.

KEY POINTS
- Most polymers are self-finished and only require edges to be polished.
- Working through the stages of abrasive paper and then polishing will give you a high-quality finish.
- Vinyl designs can be easily created on a CNC knife cutting machine.

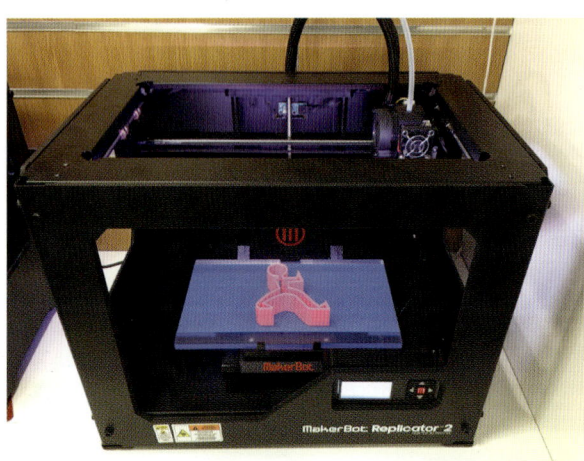

Figure 10.45 In this popular construction kit you can see how polymers can have different aesthetic finishes including textured surfaces and screen-printed detail.

10.8 Designing and making principles for thermosetting and thermoforming polymers

Choosing a method to make a prototype

Thermoforming polymers, such as acrylic and high-impact polystyrene, are the most common varieties used in schools and colleges. They can be cut and shaped using similar hand tools to timbers and are slightly easier to finish to a high standard than metals.

The most accurate way to shape and cut polymer in a school or college environment is by the use of a laser cutter. Intricate designs can be cut out and engraved in a range of thermopolymer polymers.

The use of CNC machinery in manufacture is a reliable way to achieve accurate, high-quality results. 3D printing is now a common method of producing high-quality intricate parts. Most 3D printers use PLA filament, but some can also use ABS to produce a more durable print due to ABS being tougher than PLA.

Thermoforming polymers can be moulded and formed with the addition of heat. In a school or college workshop, vacuum forming and plug-and-yoke press forming are two frequently used ways to create accurate polymer products. As with all moulding processes, the outcome can only be as good as the original mould used to produce it; any blemish or defect found on the surface of the mould will be transferred to each and every moulding. The use of heat when shaping polymers is the primary health and safety consideration. Heatproof gloves should always be used when using an oven to heat the polymer before moulding.

Thermoforming polymers can be joined together with a variety of adhesives, but it is important when using chemical adhesives such as liquid solvent cement, that the gluing surface area is as large as possible. It is also important to consider whether the joint is going to be visible, as often the solvent adhesives will mark the surface or leave a white residue.

Figure 10.46 3D printing in PLA

Choosing a finish

Most polymers require no surface finish and are often referred to as self-finishing. Polymers can, however, be coloured by the addition of a pigment. The pigment is usually added to the polymer before it is moulded, where it combines with the polymer to create a material that is coloured from its core through to its outer surface. This means that the colour will never wear off and small scratches are masked and hard to notice.

Polymers can also be painted. They would go through the familiar preparation process of being rubbed down with abrasive papers in order to provide a smooth, dirt-free surface and then have a polymer-specific primer applied. Care needs to be taken when applying a spray finish to a polymer, as the chemicals in some paints can react with the surface of the polymer.

Other aesthetic surface finishes can be applied to polymers by a series of printing processes or by the application of transfers. These tend to use the colour of the polymer as the background and then logos or decals can be added in a contrasting colour. This process is commonly found in packaging such as carrier bags and carbonated drinks lids.

Figure 10.47 Polymer car bumpers are painted to match the colour of the main metal panels of the car.

Activity 🖊

Using a polymer project with which you are familiar, produce a stage-by-stage diagram highlighting the techniques used throughout its shaping, fabrication, construction and assembly.

KEY POINTS 🎯
- The most common polymers that you use in schools are thermoforming polymers.
- 3D printing and vacuum forming both use heat to shape and form thermoforming polymers.
- Pigments can be added to polymers before the initial moulding process takes place.
- Polymers are the same colour from their core through to their surface.
- Thermoforming polymers can be easily recycled.

Know it

1 Name a suitable thermoforming polymer that could be used to make the ice cream tub.
2 State three properties of the polymer you have named in Question 1 that make it suitable for the ice cream tub.
3 Give three reasons why vacuum forming has been used to manufacture the ice cream tub.
4 Use notes and sketches to describe the process of vacuum forming.
5 Why is it important to measure the thickness of a polymer material before using on a laser cutter?
6 Name five common stock forms of thermoforming polymer.
7 It is important that designers consider the world we live in and the needs of future generations. Evaluate how designers can lessen the impact on our environment when designing new polymer products such as food packaging.

Figure 10.48 Ice cream tub

Chapter 11
Natural, synthetic, blended and mixed fibres, and woven, non-woven and knitted textiles

Learning objectives

By the end of this chapter you should have developed a knowledge and understanding of:

- the sources of and working properties of textiles
- the main construction methods used to manufacture textile fabrics and how this affects their potential use
- how fabrics can be combined to improve functionality
- the ecological and social footprint of textile fabrics and industry
- the processes used for finishing and adding surface treatments to materials for specific purposes
- the impact forces and stresses have on a range of fabrics and products
- how and why specific fabrics need to be reinforced
- the processes that can be used to ensure structural integrity in fabrics
- the range of stock forms that are readily available when selecting fabrics
- the range of standardised components for use with fabrics
- the scale and methods used for manufacturing
- how manufacturing systems are organised
- the methods of ensuring accuracy and efficiency in manufacturing
- the processes and techniques used to produce toiles and prototypes
- the tools and equipment used in the construction of textile products
- surface treatments that can be applied to textile fabrics for functional and aesthetic purposes.

11.1 Sources, origins, physical and working properties of fibres and fabrics and their ecological and social footprint

Choosing the right material for the products you want to make is vital if you want a successful outcome. The way a material behaves and what it can be used for depends on a number of factors:

- the source of the fibre and its unique set of properties
- the way the fibre has been spun or twisted to make a yarn
- how the yarns have been used to construct the material, including how materials can be joined for different purposes
- special finishes that can be applied to improve the material's natural properties and characteristics.

Woven, non-woven and knitted textiles

Fabrics are constructed using a range of different methods, depending on their intended use. The two main methods of **fabric construction** are weaving and knitting. Both of these have subtypes.

Woven fabric construction

Weaving was originally done on wooden looms. These days it is mainly done on industrial machinery, although traditional methods are still in use, usually in smaller independent woollen mills where more traditional or bespoke designer pieces can be created.

Woven fabrics are produced using **warp** and **weft** yarns. The warp yarn is usually the stronger of the two and runs vertically down the length of the fabric. This is known as the **straight grain** and runs parallel to the edge of the fabric. The **selvedge** is the factory-finished edge of

> **KEY WORDS**
>
> **Fabric construction**: the way a fabric has been made – for example, knitted or woven.
>
> **Warp**: yarns that run along the length of fabric.
>
> **Weft**: yarns that run across the fabric.
>
> **Straight grain**: indicates the strength of the fabric in line with warp yarns.
>
> **Selvedge**: the sealed edge of the fabric.

the fabric roll. The selvedge prevents the fabric from fraying or unravelling. Weft yarns run horizontally across the fabric, which is also known as the cross grain.

The warp yarns are wound on to the loom in parallel rows and are threaded through frames containing plastic, wooden or metal strips. These frames are known as heddles. The heddles lift the warp yarns upwards, allowing a shuttle to be passed through, carrying the weft yarn. The heddles are then lowered, trapping the weft yarn in between the warp yarns. Different heddles are used to lift alternate warp yarns with each pass of the shuttle. This results in the interlocking of the warp and weft yarns, creating a fabric. Weaving patterns are achieved by setting up several heddles to lift different warp yarns at different times, although this is a time-consuming process. Computerised looms allow the creation of complex weave patterns quickly and efficiently.

Plain weave

A plain weave is the simplest and most widely used weave structure and it is very versatile. Various weights of fabric can be produced by altering the spacing of the warp and weft yarns or by using coarse, fine or textured yarns or combinations of thicknesses. Stripes, checks and texture can be created by alternating the warp and weft yarns with different coloured or fancy yarns. The stability of the fabric can be altered, depending on how closely packed the yarns are.

Muslin is a common example of a lightweight plain weave fabric with quite a loose weave. Calico is a common example of a medium to heavyweight plain weave fabric which is more stable because the yarns are closer together. Ripstop nylon, a tightly woven fabric, is an example where different thicknesses of yarn are used at regular intervals in the warp and weft yarns. The woven fabric is reinforced by the varying thicknesses of yarn.

A tight weave can also make fabrics windproof. A kite, for example, needs to resist the wind in order to fly. A very tight weave will make the nylon fabric windproof and the strength of nylon yarns will resist tearing when under pressure. The combination of a tight weave and the fibre's properties make it an ideal fabric for kites.

Twill weave

A twill weave is easily recognised by the lines which run diagonally across the fabric. It is formed by crossing over the warp and weft yarns. Variations in the weave include herringbone and chevron. The structure of the twill weave allows it to drape quite well. Twill weave produces a heavier fabric than a plain weave, making it stronger and more durable. For this reason, twill weaves are often used in products that need to resist heavy wear and tear, such as denim jeans and canvas bags. Twill weaves are sometimes selected for aesthetic reasons.

Satin weave

A satin weave is easily identifiable by its smooth, shiny, lustrous appearance, which is created by the 'floating yarns' on the surface of the fabric – the weft yarns are woven under one warp yarn, then over a minimum of three warp yarns. This results in a larger surface area, which reflects light, giving a shiny finish. Satin weaves are the weakest of the three types of weave and can be snagged easily, due to the structure of the floating yarns.

Figure 11.1 A traditional woven fabric from Melin Tregwynt woollen mill, Pembrokeshire

Figure 11.2 A plain weave structure

Figure 11.3 A twill weave structure

Figure 11.4 A satin weave structure

Pile weave

Pile weave fabrics have a raised surface formed either by tufts or loops that stand up. They are formed as a result of having an additional warp thread or an additional weft thread woven into the fabric. The main fabric is called the ground, and the additional yarn forms a loop. This can be left as it is, as in terry towelling, or it can be cut, as in velvet. Pile weave fabrics tend to be quite hard wearing because of the thickness created by the extra loop of yarn. Extra care is needed when working with pile weave fabrics, as they have a directional surface. It is important that all pattern pieces are laid in the same direction so that an even colour is achieved. Shading occurs when pattern pieces are laid in different directions.

Activity

You will need strips of paper (1 cm width) in two colours and adhesive tape.

1 Line up ten strips of paper (of one colour) vertically, side by side. Place a strip of tape across the top to secure them.

2 Use the diagrams above as guides to help you create the three types of weave.

Figure 11.5 The surface of a pile weave fabric

Non-woven fabrics

Non-woven textiles are made from a web of fibres which can either be stitched together or bonded by heat or adhesives. They are created directly from fibres, which makes them economical to use. Some fibres are short and have crimp (wavy texture) which causes the fibres to tangle together.

Bonded fabrics

Bonded fabrics are made directly from fibres rather than from yarns. They are manufactured by laying out a 'web' of synthetic fibres, then applying pressure and heat or adhesives to bond the fibres together. Some bonded fabrics are stitched to hold the fibres together and add more strength to the fabric.

Bonded fabrics are often used in disposable textiles, such as wet wipes, tea bags, surgical masks, dressings and nappies. These fabrics lose their strength and structure once wet, so they are usually only suitable for one use. Some bonded fabrics are used to reinforce or strengthen other fabrics.

Felted fabrics

KEY WORD

Appliqué: stitching different shaped pieces of fabric in a particular design onto a different base fabric.

Felted fabrics are non-woven fabrics that are produced by applying moisture, heat, pressure and friction to a web of staple fibres, which cause them to bind together. The most commonly used fibres in this process are wool and acrylic. The fabric will be denser and stronger the more it is worked – this also causes some shrinkage. Felt is quite a weak fabric and will easily stretch out of shape, particularly when wet. It is however easy to cut and will not fray along the edges. Felt is often used for crafts, decorative purposes such as **appliqué**, and is historically applied to the surface of pool and snooker tables. Felt is also used for cushioning and insulating various products.

Figure 11.6 A non-woven fabric structure

Figure 11.7 The principles of making felt can easily be adapted for a school-based project or at home.

Knitted fabrics

There are two types of knitted fabric – weft knit and warp knit. Knits are created by a series of interlocking loops of yarn. The loops in the construction of knitted fabric trap air, which means they are generally warmer to wear than woven fabrics. Knitted fabrics have different characteristics to woven fabrics, which determine what they can be used for.

Weft knit fabric

Weft knit fabric is comprised of a single continuous yarn, and is constructed in horizontal rows of interlocking loops. Weft knits are often produced by hand using knitting needles. Patterns can be created using needles singularly or all together. Weft knits can also be manufactured on a larger scale using automated knitting machines. These machines can knit a flat length or a tube of fabric – tubes are very useful in the production of socks. Weft knits may snag and can unravel if part of the yarn is damaged, cut or pulled. Weft knits stretch easily but can also lose shape. Weft knit fabrics have an obvious right and wrong side. They are used for a wide range of knitwear, accessories and home furnishings.

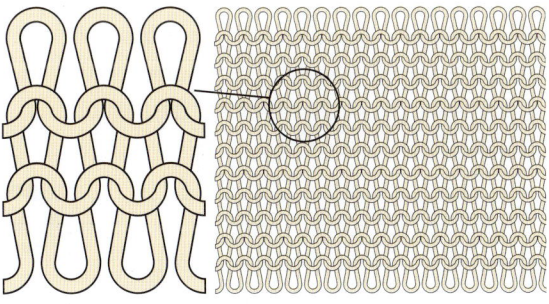

Figure 11.8 The weft knitting structure has a series of loops made from a single yarn that interlocks horizontally.

Warp knit fabric

Warp knit fabric has a more complicated structure than weft knit fabric. Warp knits are made from multiple yarns that interlock vertically along the length of fabric. Warp knits do not run or unravel and are more flexible than weft knits, making them suitable for leisurewear, sportswear and swimwear. Warp knit fabrics have some stretch, but hold their shape well. They are easier to work with and do not unravel when cut, meaning they can be cut to shape when making products. Warp knits are identical on both sides. They can only be completed on automated machines.

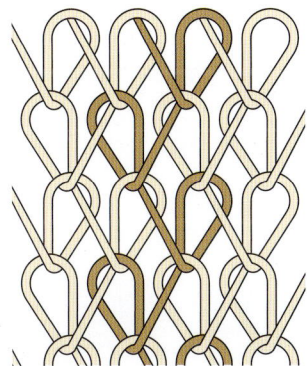

Figure 11.9 The warp knitting structure has a series of loops that interlock vertically.

Activity

Collect a range of fabric samples that show different fabric structures. Sort the samples under the following headings:

- Woven
  - Plain
  - Twill
  - Satin
  - Pile
- Non-woven
  - Bonded
  - Felted
- Knitted
  - Weft knit
  - Warp knit

Name some textile products that you would expect to see made from each of the fabric structures. Give reasons for your choices. You could also collect pictures of products made from each of the samples. Present your work neatly and keep as a revision aid.

Fabric specification

When you choose fabrics for your practical tasks you have to consider the end use or main **function** of the product. You need to consider the properties of the fibres in the fabric, as discussed in Chapter 5, and the method of construction. A designer will work to a **fabric specification** and consider the physical and working properties of fibres and method of construction for the fabrics carefully before selecting an appropriate material to use.

Table 11.1 shows the fabric properties required for a bath towel.

What does it need to do?	Properties required
Be soft next to the skin	Good **handle**
Soak up moisture to aid drying	Absorbent
Keep us warm	Insulating
Be easy to care for	Crease-resistant
Withstand regular use	Durable

Table 11.1 The fabric properties required for bath towels

Most towels are made from cotton which is **absorbent**. The construction of the fabric for a bath towel is usually a pile weave. The additional surface area created by the loops in the pile weave increases the towel's ability to absorb moisture. The loops in a pile weave also trap air, which would increase the towel's ability to keep the user warm. The fabric construction and fibre content are equally important in supporting the function of the towel.

KEY POINTS

- Make sure you know the different types of fabric construction as this affects what the fabrics can be used for.
- All fibres once spun into yarns can be knitted and/or woven into fabrics. Designers have to consider the fibre source as well as the fabric's construction method when choosing fabrics. A woven cotton fabric will have different characteristics to a knitted cotton fabric as well as some similarities!

Fibres

Fibres are the raw materials used in all textile fabrics. They either come from a natural source or are manufactured. In Chapter 5 you looked at the source and classification of different fibre types along with a description of each fibre's properties and what they could be used for. Fibre blends bring together different fibre types to improve functionality, cost or appearance.

Mix/blend	Benefits from fibre 1	Benefits from fibre 2
1 Polyester 2 Cotton	Strength, durability, crease resistance, stain resistance, low cost	Handle, absorbency, cool to wear, strength, durability, drape, anti-static
1 Cotton 2 Elastane	Good handle, absorbency, cool to wear, strength, drape, anti-static	Crease resistance, stretch/elasticity, snap-back, flexibility
1 Acrylic 2 Wool	Quick-drying, strength, durable, resistance to chemicals, low cost	Insulation, good elasticity, crease resistance, absorbency, drape, anti-static
1 Silk 2 Viscose	Strength, smooth soft texture, absorbent, lustre, can be both warm and cool to wear, creases easily, expensive	High absorbency, drapes well, soft, lustrous, anti-static, inexpensive
1 Cotton 2 Wool	Handle, absorbency, cool to wear, strength, drape, anti-static	Insulation, crease resistance, absorbency, drape, anti-static
1 Hemp 2 Cotton	Stronger than cotton, breathable, resistant to mildew, anti-microbial and UV resistant, resistant to abrasion/very durable, easy to care for, creases easily/poor elasticity, not as soft as other fibres	Good handle, absorbency, cool to wear, strength, drapes well
1 Hemp 2 Silk	Stronger than cotton, breathable, resistant to mildew, anti-microbial and UV resistant, resistant to abrasion/very durable, easy to care for, creases easily/poor elasticity, not as soft as other fibres	Strength, smooth soft texture, absorbent, lustre, both warm and cool to wear, creases easily, expensive

Table 11.2 Some common fibre blends and mixes with combined benefits

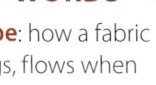

KEY WORDS

Drape: how a fabric hangs, flows when handled.

Monomer: a molecule that can be bonded to others to form a polymer.

Filament: a very fine slender thread.

Fibres are made from chemical units called polymers, which are formed from much smaller single units called **monomers**, which link together to form long chains. Some polymers occur naturally, for example plants (cotton) and animals (wool). Others are as a result of a chemical reaction – for example polyester.

There are two main fibre types:

- long continuous **filaments** – for example polyester, nylon, acrylic, polypropylene, silk
- short staple fibres – for example cotton, linen (flax), wool.

Silk is the only natural continuous filament.

The shape of the fibres affects how it feels or the handle (softness) and its lustre (shine). Fibres also have different thicknesses, from extremely smooth and fine, as in a microfibre, to quite coarse in texture like some wool fibres that have a natural crimp and scales.

Spinning

Spinning is the process of twisting fibres together to make a yarn. Individually fibres are quite weak but when spun into yarns take on additional properties. Fibres are normally spun in two ways:

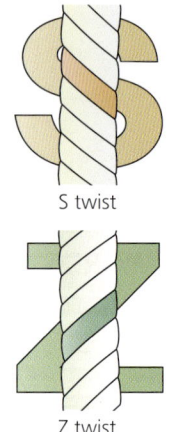

- S twist (anticlockwise)
- Z twist (clockwise).

Figure 11.10 Spinning yarns: S twist and Z twist

The process of spinning will affect the end use of the yarn. The tighter the twist, the more air is squeezed out and the fibres will be closer together. This prevents air being trapped, so the resultant yarn will be strong and fine, but will not be warm. If the twist is quite loose, the opposite happens – a warmer yarn because it will allow air to become trapped, but a much weaker yarn. Multiple yarns can be twisted together for different effects.

Fancy yarns

Different effects can also be achieved through varying the spinning process. Textured or novelty yarns have irregular surfaces with bumps, knots and varying thicknesses. The resultant yarns are more interesting, but can be more difficult to work with. They can be used in knitting and weaving to create texture and surface interest on the fabrics. Chenille and bouclé are two common fancy yarns.

Figure 11.11 Chenille yarn

Figure 11.12 Knitted fabric using bouclé yarn creates an interesting texture

Fibre	Structure	Description
Cotton	Cotton fibre longitudinal view Cross-section Mature Immature	Short staple fibres, slightly twisted with a smooth surface which prevents air being trapped. Inner cavity allows moisture to be absorbed. Cotton is a poor insulator, but has good absorbency.
Linen	Linen fibre (flax) cross-section Cross-section of linen fibre bundle	Short staple fibres, with a smooth surface which prevent air being trapped. It has a slight shiny lustre which prevents soiling. The structure, with cavities like cotton, makes it highly absorbent. Linen is a poor insulator, but has good absorbency.

Fibre	Structure	Description
Silk	Cross-section	Silk is the only natural long continuous filament. It is made up of two long protein bundles closely packed together. Silk is very absorbent, with the ability to absorb a third of its weight of water vapour, making it very cool to wear.
Wool	Round Cross-section	Wool fibres have a natural crimp (wavy) and are coated with scales. The crimp allows air to be trapped, so it is a good insulator. However, if the fibres get wet the scales can hook together. This can cause shrinkage. The natural grease in the fibres makes wool water repellent.
Polyester		One of the most versatile fibres with a wide range of uses. It can be engineered for different purposes. It is a long flat filament that does not hold water, so it has poor absorbency. It can be crimped in the manufacturing process, which allows it to trap some air and improve its insulation properties.

Table 11.3 Structure and descriptions of fibre types

Activity

Cut a selection of different yarns to the same length for comparisons. Study the yarns. How do they differ? Do they feel different to each other? Can you untwist any, what does this tell you?

Can you identify any short staple yarns or filament yarns? How are they different? Use a magnifying glass and draw what you see.

Glue your samples onto paper, make notes on your findings. Retain the information for revision or to support you in your non-examined asessment.

Laminated and coated fabrics

Two or more fabrics can be joined together through a process called **lamination**. This process combines the performance characteristics of all the fabrics to make a superior fabric. One method is to use an adhesive to hold the layers together. A different method is to heat either a polymer film or a layer of foam and press it onto the fabric it is to be joined to. Neoprene and silicone rubber are often laminated with other materials to increase their functionality.

Gore-Tex is an example of a laminated fabric which has a **hydrophilic membrane** as one of the inner layers. The structure of the laminated fabric with the combined properties allows moisture (from perspiration) to escape but the fabric repels the wind and rain. When used in active wear it is a means of controlling body temperature. Permatex is very similar to Gore-Tex. It is a weatherproof, breathable membrane used as linings and outer fabrics for high-performance clothing, footwear, industrial wear and sportswear.

KEY WORDS

Lamination: process of joining materials together with heat or adhesives.

Hydrophilic membrane: ability to repel and release moisture.

Quilting: process of layering three materials together and stitching through to improve its characteristics.

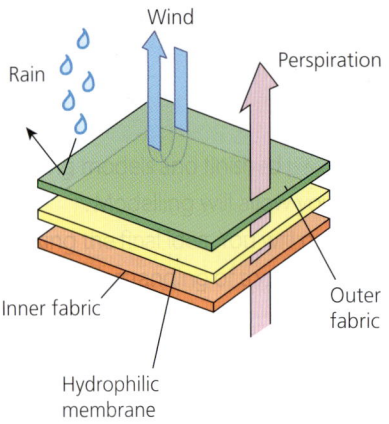

Rain

Wind

Perspiration

Inner fabric

Outer fabric

Hydrophilic membrane

Figure 11.14 Gore-Tex is an example of a laminated fabric and is widely used for high-performance clothing.

Figure 11.15 A PVC-coated cotton cosmetic purse. Combined properties improve the functionality of the fabric: The PVC coating makes the product waterproof, the inner layer of woven cotton is stable and strong.

A coated fabric has a polymer, usually polyurethane or polyvinylchloride (PVC), applied to it which is then fixed in an oven. The most well-known coated fabrics are PVC coated cotton and faux leather. Coated textiles have a wide range of uses and can be engineered to withstand the most challenging of uses. They are widely used throughout the fashion and textile industry for items such as table cloths, aprons, waterproof clothing, bags and accessories.

The processes of laminating and coating fabrics improve the functionality of the combined fabrics.

Figure 11.16 A quilted winter jacket. The middle layer consists of a mixture of polyester wadding and duck down. The outer layer is lightweight and showerproof. The combined properties of the fabric used makes this a highly effective lightweight warm winter jacket.

Quilting

There are many different forms of **quilting**. English quilting consists of three layers of fabrics with a layer of polyester wadding sandwiched between a more decorative or aesthetically pleasing top layer and a cheaper plain layer underneath. The essence of quilting is to stitch through the three layers to hold them together. Quilting can be done for a number of reasons:

1 Insulation: the three layers trap air which will keep the user warm. Examples include quilted jackets and accessories for colder weather, bedding and thermal bottle carriers. The inner padding can be a different fibre type and thickness, depending on what is required from the end product. Different types of fabrics can be quilted together to further increase thermal qualities.

2 Decorative reasons: detailing to add surface interest to a wide range of products, particularly soft furnishings. Other types of decorative quilting include Trapunto and Italian.

Trapunto quilting is a decorative technique that adds another dimension, almost a 3D effect to fabrics. It consists of two layers of fabric with designs stitched through the layers. A slit is made in the under layer of fabric inside the stitched area which is then padded out from underneath creating a puffy raised surface area.

Italian quilting also creates a raised effect. Again, two layers of fabric are needed. Two parallel rows of stitches are sewn to create a channel, then a cord is inserted into the channel to create a raised pattern. Some really creative work is possible by varying and mixing fabric types and quilting methods.

3 Functional reasons: used to reinforce parts of clothing, for example on workwear and sportswear where added protection is needed (extra padding for knees, elbows or shoulders). Quilting can also be seen on accessories and in interior design.

Ecological and social footprint

The textile products we use and the clothes we wear have an ecological and social footprint. The ecological footprint is a measure of the impact human activity has on the environment, as discussed in Chapter 1; it includes the production of fibre crops and the processing and manufacture of textile fabrics and products. The production of a simple cotton t-shirt can generate tonnes of CO_2.

In some countries, workers are exploited, often working long hours in poor conditions on very low salaries. In the textiles industry there have also been several cases of child labour. Many of these issues are directly linked to more wealthy societies' demand for more products at a much cheaper price.

Ecological impact of natural cellulose fibres

Natural fibre crops, such as cotton and linen, are intensively farmed on vast areas of land in order to keep up with global demand. As well as using significant amounts of water, farmers use toxic **pesticides** which safeguard the crops against pests, and fertilisers to promote growth but which damage the **ecosystem**. Chemicals soak through the soil and into water sources, killing wildlife and contaminating drinking water. These chemicals also strip the soil of nutrients, reducing crop quality and eventually making the land unusable.

Natural crops can be farmed organically using natural fertilisers and pesticides. Although this reduces the impact, this type of farming still requires a substantial amount of water. It is estimated that approximately 2700 litres of water are required to produce enough cotton for a single t-shirt.

Ecological impact of natural protein fibres

The farming of livestock for wool production has a lower ecological impact compared to the farming of fibre crops. The land used for the rearing of livestock is often unsuitable for crops, but livestock can damage the land by overgrazing. On large wool farms, the number of sheep can exceed 300 000. Livestock are protected from mites and ticks by immersing them in chemical dips which contain **insecticides**. These dips contaminate soil and water sources. Livestock can also produce large amounts of the greenhouse gas methane.

Figure 11.17 Overgrazing with large flocks of sheep can damage the soil.

Silk is a highly renewable resource with little ecological impact. The production of silk in captivity, however, is heavily criticised by animal welfare activists. The breeding of silkworms in captivity has led to the demise of the *Bombyx mori* moth in the wild, and captive moths have evolved to be blind and unable to fly. These moths live only for a few days and in this time lay up to 500 eggs.

Transportation and processing

There are few countries where fibre production is local to its manufacturers. Transportation of raw fibres causes air pollution and uses a significant amount of non-renewable resources, which adds to our carbon footprint.

The processing of synthetic fibres uses **finite resources** such as oil and coal. High levels of energy and chemicals are used in the extraction and processing of these resources. It also produces contaminated waste. Greenhouse gas emissions from factories cause air pollution and add to the depletion of the ozone layer. Additionally, there is significant water pollution in local areas around factory sites as many factories do not follow rules and guidelines when disposing of waste water, due to cost implications.

Synthetic fibres are non-biodegradable – polyester would take up to 450 years to break down in the environment. However, they are **recyclable** and this practice is going from strength to strength within the industry.

Plastic waste is created by the unnecessary over-packaging of textile products. When garments are delivered to a retail store, each item is covered in a plastic garment bag that is immediately disposed of. The purpose of these bags is to protect garments from moisture and dust in transit. The same garments are also placed inside cardboard boxes and covered in an extra layer of plastic wrap before shipping.

Biodiversity

Biodiversity refers to the balance of a wide variety of different creatures and species living side by side in the world or in a particular habitat. The land used to grow textile fibre crops, water used in crop production, pollution caused by manufacturing methods and the disposal of textile waste all impact on the world's ecosystem. The habitats of many small creatures are adversely affected or even destroyed, consequently biodiversity is affected.

Social and ethical issues

Working conditions

The treatment of garment workers in the textile industry has been under scrutiny for years, and although some steps have been taken to improve conditions for employees, it is still one of the most exploitative industries. In many countries, such as Bangladesh and Cambodia, garment workers are subjected to long hours, low pay and often work in dangerous conditions. Children as young as six have been found working in factories, despite local laws to prevent child labour. Garment workers in developing countries do not have union rights, and those who attempt to take a stand for themselves and their colleagues are often met with violence.

Figure 11.18 Employees work long hours for little money, and often in poor working conditions.

The demand for **fast fashion** has risen dramatically in recent years. Many people consider it acceptable to buy an item of clothing at rock-bottom price, wear it once and quickly dispose of it. This **throwaway culture** drives down retail prices, and as a result, manufacturing costs are cut in order to maintain profitability.

In developing countries, those who live and work near the textile industry are also affected by the contamination of the land and water supplies. Skin conditions, lung problems, jaundice and cancers affect the workers and their families following possible exposure to toxic chemicals used in the production and processing of textiles.

Responsible textile manufacturers consider the health, safety and well-being of their workers and those who live nearby by putting appropriate measures in place to protect them.

Figure 11.19 Waste water from factories pollutes local drinking water sources.

Life cycle

Natural fibres are **biodegradable** and most will decompose naturally in the environment within six months. They will still release CO_2 during decomposition, and natural fibres treated with dyes and chemicals will release these into the ground. Synthetic, polymer-based fibres take between 450 and 1000 years to break down. During this time the fibres will release toxic and greenhouse gases into the atmosphere.

Recycling, reuse and disposal

Most fibres and fabrics can be easily recycled. It is vital that we do this in order to protect the environment and our resources as the textile industry is continuing to grow. There are three types of recycling:

- **Primary recycling** means reusing the material or product without changing it in any way and often for the same purpose, for example giving clothing to charity shops or handing clothing down to younger siblings.
- **Secondary recycling** means the material or product is reused with some modification, but without reprocessing it. A good example would be cutting a pair of jeans to create shorts. This type of recycling makes good use of old clothing or household textiles that cannot go to clothing banks.
- **Tertiary recycling** is when materials are broken down to their original state and made into brand new products. An example of this process is the use of plastic bottles to make polyester fleece. Polyester fibres are **thermoforming** and can therefore be cleaned,

KEY WORDS

Fast fashion: a recent trend involving the quick transfer of new collections from the catwalk into stores. Fast fashion is often on trend, low quality and low in price.

Throwaway culture: the rise of fast fashion has made clothing far more affordable for consumers. The incredibly low prices in some high-street stores have resulted in a throwaway culture, meaning that consumers do not feel the need to keep clothing that is no longer in fashion, and happily dispose of it.

Biodegradable: the ability of a material, substance or object to break down naturally in the environment through the action of microorganisms, thereby avoiding pollution.

Thermoforming fibre: a synthetic fibre that can become plastic when heated and harden on cooling – a process that can be repeated.

Figure 11.20 A man's shirt has been upcycled to a versatile top.

shredded, melted down and re-formed into new fabrics. Natural fibres can be shredded, bleached and spun into new yarns, or used for padding and insulation applications in the building industry.

Tertiary recycling is beneficial to the environment in many ways. It does, however, use toxic chemicals and energy in the cleaning, sorting and processing of recycled fibres.

It is estimated that 350 000 tonnes of used clothing goes into landfill in the UK each year. Most of this could have been used again. However, fibres cannot withstand endless recycling and it is inevitable that some will eventually need go to landfill at the end of their useful life.

Activity

When the life cycle of a product or material is analysed, the path it takes from its origins (fibre source), through the stages of manufacture, its useful life and final disposal is studied. In particular we need to look at the impact it has already had on the environment during its useful life and may have in the future.

1   Choose any textile product. Look at the stages it has gone through during its life so far, and where it is likely to end up in the future. List what happens to it during its life; this could include processes applied during manufacture or washing and ironing. Consider where it will end up. What is the impact on the environment? Think about its carbon and ecological footprint.

2   Consider each stage. How could its impact be reduced?

3   What could happen to it instead of going to landfill? Redesign a new product from the existing one. Add notes to explain your thoughts.

KEY POINTS

- The construction method used to make textile fabrics gives each type a distinctive set of characteristics which affects what it can be used for.
- When choosing textile fabrics for a product, you should consider the source of fibre, the construction of the fabric and any finishes that have been applied.
- Fabrics can be joined together in processes such as laminating, coating and quilting to improve their functionality.
- The textile industry has a major detrimental impact on the environment. Product designers should try to find alternative fibre sources or manufacturing processes to lessen the impact.

11.2 The way in which the selection of materials or components is influenced by a range of factors

Fabric finishes

Finishes can be added to improve aesthetics, comfort or function. These finishes can be applied mechanically, chemically or biologically. The **applied finishes** will also need to be considered when choosing fabrics for textile products, alongside fibre source and the construction of the fabric.

Surface decoration

Surface decoration techniques can be used to improve the aesthetics of a product, by adding colour, **texture** and pattern. These include dyeing, printing, painting, and embellishments including embroidery and appliqué. These will be looked at in more detail later in the chapter.

Mechanical or physical finishes

Brushing

Brushing involves passing wire brushes over the surface of the fabric to raise the fibres to produce a soft, fluffy surface, improving its appearance. Brushing is commonly used on fleece and flannel fabrics, but the process can weaken the structure of the weave. The raised surface also improves the functionality of the fabric by increasing its ability to trap air and in so doing enhances **insulation**.

Calendering

Calendering involves pressing the fabric using heated rollers to give it a smoother, more lustrous surface, enhancing the aesthetic qualities of the fabric. This is often used on upholstery fabrics to give them a flat surface and sheen, but it does not always give a permanent finish. A different effect, called moiré, can also be achieved through calendering. It adds a wavy, watered effect to the fabric – usually silk.

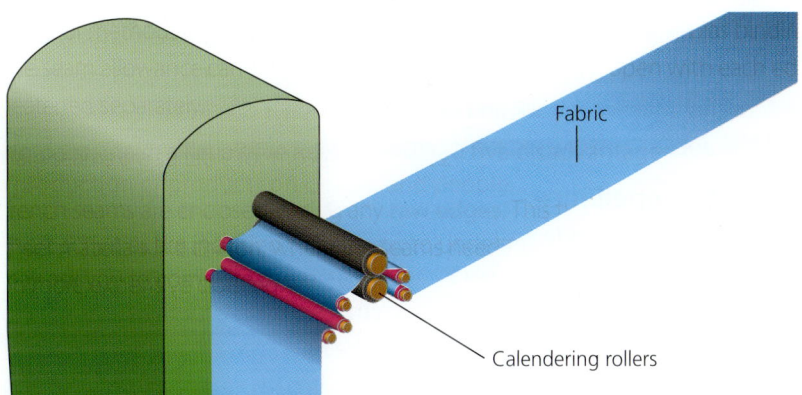

Fabric

Calendering rollers

Figure 11.21 Calendering involves passing the fabric through heated rollers.

Glazing

Glazing is a similar process to calendaring giving fabrics a smooth, lustrous look. In this process stiffeners or resins are also applied to the fabrics, which makes the finish more permanent.

Embossing

Embossing produces a slightly raised pattern on the surface of the fabric. The fabric is passed through engraved rollers, and heat and pressure is applied, which leave an imprint of the pattern in the fabric.

Chemical finishes

Mercerising

Mercerising uses caustic soda to cause the fibres in the fabric to swell up. The result is a more lustrous, stronger fabric, but it only works for cellulose fibres. It improves the uptake of dye, giving a deeper and more even colour. It improves the aesthetic qualities of the fabric.

KEY WORDS

Surface decoration: techniques to add detail, such as pattern to fabrics.

Texture: a raised surface that adds to the feel and handle of a fabric.

Insulation: a means of adding warmth and keeping warm.

Crease resistance

Crease-resistant finishes are applied in the form of a resin coating. This resin reduces absorbency and stiffens the fibres so the fabric is easier to care for, reducing the need for ironing. Treated fabrics will also dry more quickly. The functionality of the fabric is improved at the expense of its ability to absorb moisture.

Flame resistance

Flame-resistant finishes, such as Proban®, are applied to the surface of fabrics as a liquid coating; when dry, this is durable and long lasting. These types of finishes are applied to products in high-risk areas, such as soft furnishings in hotels, and in public areas, such as stage curtains in theatres. They are also widely used in children's sleepwear, bedding and other home furnishings.

Bleaching

Bleaching is the most common chemical finish. It removes any natural colour and prepares fabric well for dyeing and printing. The result of this finish is an even, consistent colour.

Stain resistance

A stain-resistant finish can be applied to any textile fabric, but is particularly useful in furnishing fabric and carpet. Teflon™ and Scotchguard™ fabric protectors are now widely used throughout the textile industry, particularly clothing and home furnishing, without affecting the fabric's natural qualities.

Anti-static

A chemical-based product is applied to the fabric to prevent the build-up of electrostatic charge, also known as static electricity. It is usually applied to synthetic fabrics and silk, and prevents the fabrics clinging to the body. It is also applied to some synthetic carpets.

Water repellence

Fabrics can be made water repellent by spraying them with silicone. However, this is not considered a permanent finish. Applying a fluorochemical resin to the fabric is a more effective method, making it water repellent and wind resistant. The finish can be applied to many textile products including all-weather wear, bags, tents and shoes. Teflon and Scotchguard are both examples of water-repellent finishes. Some fabrics are coated with PVC, PVA or wax in order to repel moisture.

Figure 11.22 Teflon and Scotchguard can both be used to protect the tent from the elements – in this case rain. A woven nylon fabric has been used for the tent. When nylon is woven in a very tight weave it makes the fabric wind resistant.

Shrink resistance

Some fabrics, such as wool, can shrink if not washed with care. The scales of the wool fibres will lock together causing the wool to shrink in size. Wool can be made shrink resistant by treating it with a chlorine-based chemical which smooths out the scales on the fibre. This process prevents them locking together if washed incorrectly. It also means wool can be machine washed. Other fabrics, such as cotton, are also prone to shrinkage. In this case, wet fabrics are compressed into the size they would be after shrinking and then dried in the compressed state so no more shrinking can occur.

Moth proofing

Animal fibres found in wool are particularly susceptible to attack by moths who feed off the keratin found in the wool fibre. The applied finish simply aims to repel the moth without affecting the quality of the fabric.

Biological finishes

Stonewashing

Stonewashing is most commonly used in the production of denim jeans, giving a distressed look. Manufacturers achieve this effect by adding stones to industrial washing machines, along with the jeans. The result is a faded, 'worn out' pair of jeans.

Responsibilities of designers and manufacturers

Many of the finishes outlined in this section include the use of energy and water as well as chemicals and toxins which are hazardous to the environment and could impact on the health of textile workers. Chemical finishes can also affect the sustainability of fabrics at the end of their life. Natural fabrics, such as cotton, are biodegradable; however if finishes have been applied they are not able to biodegrade safely. Chemical traces will inevitably damage the delicate ecosystems and impact on biodiversity, as discussed earlier in this chapter and in Chapter 1.

The textile industry, which includes designers and manufacturers, is trying to reform and improve itself. Research continues into fabric technology that could eliminate the need for applied chemical finishes. New finishing chemicals are being developed that are reusable, do not require the use of water and are biodegradable.

Designers and manufacturers today are more environmentally aware than ever before. Many make discerning choices about the materials they use and the processes needed for manufacture. Stella McCartney is one such designer, leading the way in sustainable fashion design without compromising on style.

Activity

For each of the products listed, choose a finish that would either enhance the fabric used for the product, its aesthetic qualities or improve its functionality. Give a reason for your answer and state whether the finish is chemical or mechanical.

Product	Finish and reason	Type of finish
Rucksack		
School skirt		
Cotton pyjamas		
Nylon jacket		
Upholstery fabric		
Linen trousers		

KEY POINTS

- Applied finishes can be mechanical, chemical or biological.
- Finishes are applied to improve the fabric's functional, aesthetic or physical properties.
- Some finishes can affect a fabric's ability to fully degrade on disposal.

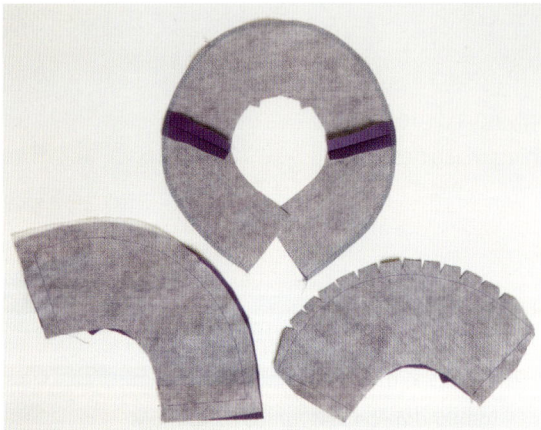

Figure 11.23 Interfacing can be ironed on (fusible) or sewn into place.

Figure 11.24 Interlining provides insulation and structure.

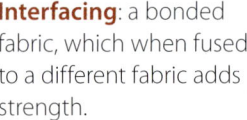

KEY WORDS

Interfacing: a bonded fabric, which when fused to a different fabric adds strength.

Appliqué: a decorative feature made by stitching one fabric shape onto a different fabric to create pattern.

Stabilise: make more rigid and stronger, prevents movement.

Lining: a layer of fabric in the same shape as the outer layer which adds supports and conceals the construction processes.

11.3 The impact of forces and stress on materials and objects and the ways in which they can be reinforced and stiffened

Structural integrity

Most fabrics have a natural drape, depending on the yarn used and type of weave. Fabrics can also be quite fluid. While this can be beneficial to designers, in many ways products need more structure to improve aesthetics and/or their function. There are a number of methods used to reinforce and strengthen materials, such as laminating, bonding and quilting, as discussed on pages 233–234.

Design considerations

Some methods used in the construction of seams are much stronger than others. A hot air balloon when filled to capacity with hot air is subjected to extreme pressure when travelling at height and speed. The seams would be double-stitched to add strength and to withstand the applied forces. Likewise, heavy-duty workwear needs to be strong and durable – often a twill weave fabric would be used, but seams would be double-stitched for strength.

A loaded rucksack used by campers, for example, will be subjected to heavy loads and will need to withstand wear and tear during use. While the fabric used needs to be strong and durable and the components quite robust, the structure of the rucksack also needs to be supported. In many heavy-duty rucksacks, aluminium or carbon fibre frames are used to support the structural integrity of the bag and also to help distribute the weight evenly when fully loaded.

Layering textiles

Layering in textiles can be used for a number of purposes, including structural support, insulation, comfort or to add body.

Interfacing

Interfacing is a non-woven, bonded fabric that can be sewn or ironed on to the outer fabric or lining. It is available in different colours and weights to provide light support and to stiffen or reinforce fabrics in order to improve the shape and add structure. It is most commonly used around necklines, armholes, waistbands, button stands, collars and cuffs. It is also used in decorative techniques such as **appliqué** to **stabilise** the fabric.

Interlining

Interlining is a layer of fabric added between the fabric and the lining of a garment, most commonly to add a layer of insulation. This is often used in suit jackets and winter coats to provide additional warmth. This layer of fabric also supports the structure of a garment.

Lining

Garments are often lined to improve comfort, and to hide seams and other construction methods. The **lining** is usually a lightweight fabric, such as polyester satin or nylon. The lining can also be a design feature – bright or patterned linings are often used inside plain suit jackets. As a lining adds another layer, it will also add to the warmth of the garment. On sheer fabrics, an underlining is used to provide opacity or to add some body to the garment. Chiffon dresses or skirts would have an underlining to prevent the garment being see-through.

Boning

Boning is a technique that dates back to sixteenth century corsetry and is named after the whalebones that were originally sewn into garments. Today corsets are a popular fashion item, back on trend by reinvention by the designer Vivienne Westwood – not necessarily as an undergarment. Medical corsets are used to treat back pain or protect people with spinal or internal injuries by restricting their movement.

Modern-day corsetry uses plastic or metal boning strips, which are sewn into reinforced seams to support the fabric, preventing creasing and buckling.

Piping

Piping can be inserted into seams to add structure to the shape and form of the product. This can also help the durability of the product. It can also be used purely as a decorative feature. Piping can be bought ready-made or it can be made by wrapping a piece of **bias binding** around a cord. The cord is available in different thicknesses, so it is easy to construct the piping to an exact specification. Piping can be customised and covered with **bias** cut fabric strips in patterns and colours to co-ordinate with the rest of the fabrics.

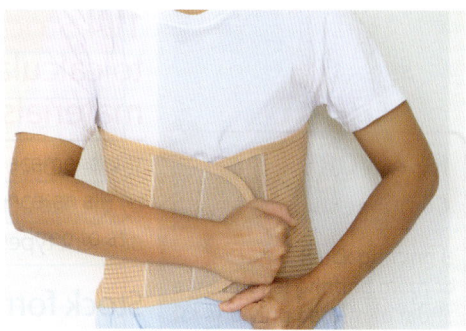

Figure 11.25 A modern torso support, inspired by original medical corsets

Figure 11.26 The contrast colour piping insert on the upholstery adds structure and support to the product, and helps prevent wear and tear. It is also decorative.

Activity

For the following products, consider what forces or stress they would be subjected to in use. Discuss what method a designer could use reinforce or strengthen each product.
- a loaded rucksack
- a tent
- a baby carrier
- active sportswear
- a shopping bag full of groceries.

KEY POINTS
- There are a number of methods to reinforce textile fabrics to improve structure and enhance shape.
- Fabric can be directly strengthened by applying interfacing to it.
- Components like boning and piping add structure and shape to products.
- Linings are used on clothing to conceal construction processes, improve wearability and add a layer of warmth.

KEY WORDS

Boning: metal or plastic strips used to add structure to products.

Bias binding: a strip of fabric cut on a 45° angle diagonally across the straight grain of the fabric, which has some stretch as a result of being cut this way; bias binding naturally bends around corners more easily, maintaining a smooth line.

Bias: this is the diagonal line which runs at a 45° angle to the selvedge edge and straight of grainline of the fabric.

Figure 11.31 Bespoke wedding dresses are made for individual clients.

Scales of production

One-off, bespoke or job production

One-off, or bespoke, products are often made by an individual or a small team. All are highly skilled, versatile workers with the ability to adapt to a range of processes and machinery. Products made this way are often commissioned as a unique piece by an individual client. The client usually has opportunities to attend fittings and make design decisions during the manufacturing process. Products made in this way take a long time to produce, as most of the work is detailed and done by hand. This type of product often uses high-quality fabrics and components and therefore is expensive to purchase. Many **haute couture**, designer gowns are made in this way. Saville Row in London is renowned for its expertise in producing high-quality men's tailoring. Bespoke suits and shirts are hand-made to order.

Batch production

Batch production is used to produce a specific number of identical products in a set timescale. The products are made by large teams of workers, working at various stages around the factory. This type of production utilises a mix of semi-automated machinery and hand assembly. Workers are specialised in one element of the construction process, such as collars or pockets. Each employee works through a batch of partial products, which are then passed around the production line until they are complete. While this is an efficient process it can make the job boring and repetitive. Batch production is quite flexible and can be changed to meet market demand. Repeat orders can be facilitated quite easily. Batch-produced products are usually of mid- to low quality. Seasonal clothing – summer or winter wear and items for seasonal events such as Halloween – is produced using batch-production methods.

Mass production

This method is used for products that are in constant high demand over a very long timescale – often several months to years! Products, such as socks and plain t-shirts, where the style does not change, are typical of products made by **mass production**. Variations are kept to a minimum. Many factories run 24 hours per day, in order to maximise output and profit, to meet demand. Workers are skilled or specialised in one element of the construction process. Equipment, workers and the supply of materials and components have to be well organised to ensure the production line runs smoothly. Increasingly **CAM** is used in mass production. Quality is controlled via computer, so instances of faulty products are low and products are consistent.

Manufacturing systems

Within mass and batch production, the production lines can be organised in different formats in order to maximise efficiency and output. Much depends on the type of product being manufactured. **Straight-line production** is where the work flows through a series of workstations in a straight line – the work is passed from one worker to the next either along a conveyor belt or on an overhead automated system. This system is often used in large-scale garment production. Each operation is timed to maximise output. The work is repetitive and can be quite boring for the workers.

KEY WORDS

One-off production: a single product.

Batch production: a limited number in a set timescale.

Mass production: Very large numbers made continuously over long periods of time.

CAM: computer-aided manufacture.

Straight-line production: work flows through a series of workstations in a straight line.

The **progressive bundle** system can operate within any large-scale manufacturing system. Bundles of garments or product parts are moved in sequence from one worker to the next. Each worker completes a single operation on each garment within a bundle. The garment parts are re-tied into bundles and passed to next worker. **Cell production** is a sub-system of manufacture and can operate within other systems. Groups of workers operate together to make whole or part products. These cells could be set up to manufacture the whole product, for example one cell works on one size while a different cell works on a different size. Alternatively, cells could be set up to manufacture a specific part of a product before it goes back on the main production run. This could apply to a cell completing, for example, the collars for a range of shirts, or completing a machine embroidered motif on a range of garments before they re-join the main production run.

Figure 11.32 An example of straight line assembly with bundles of work contained in the boxes which are passed along the central conveyor belt.

Activity

In groups, simulate a small production line in your class for a simple product that you have designed (for example, a simple glasses case). Consider all the jobs from design to finished product, and allocate everyone in your group a particular job. Each person only does one job several times over. That could mean sewing just one tiny part. Make up to ten products.

Consider:

- How repetitive was each job?
- Did anyone get quicker doing the same job?
- How was the quality of the products affected?
- Did anyone hold up production?
- How would you feel doing the same job day after day, month after month?
- How would it make you feel working repetitively in a less pleasant environment?

Evaluate your activity.

KEY WORDS

Progressive bundle production: bundles of garments or product parts are moved in sequence, from one worker to the next.

Cell production: small sub-assembly lines working on parts of a product or one size of a complete product.

KEY POINTS

- The scale of production depends on the number of products needed, the type of product, the timescale for manufacture, and the complexity of the product.
- Computerised machinery is increasingly being used in manufacturing to control production and improve quality. While this speeds up manufacture, it might lead to fewer workers.
- Assembly lines can be organised under different systems, including sub-systems such as cell production, to maximise efficiency.

Making models and finished **prototypes** is an important part of the **iterative design process**. Modelling will allow you to test, manipulate and modify your design ideas before making the final idea. You will need to use a wide range of equipment and tools and have a good understanding of the construction methods required to realise your ideas in 3D form.

Tools and equipment

There are a number of hand tools available to support you when you manufacture a textile product. The most common ones are listed in Table 11.5.

Sewing machines

Most modern domestic sewing machines offer wide range of facilities and stitches to complete many of the processes that are needed to make a textile product. Computerised sewing machines also have a facility to embroider original designs. All domestic machines have optional feet or specialist attachments for specific processes, such as attaching different types of zips, or a specialist attachment for sewing on buttons or making the button hole. To get a high-quality finish, the right attachment should be used. Different thicknesses and specialist needles are available for different fabrics used in textiles. A very fine needle is needed if sewing, for example, chiffon, but a thicker and stronger needle is needed for sewing denim. The wrong size needle can damage the fabric, whereas some needles will break if the fabric is too thick. You should always check the needle type is suitable for the fabric you intend to use.

An overlock machine cuts a straight edge on the material and over sews the edge to neaten the seam in one process. Up to four reels of thread are used in the process. Although there are other methods of neatening seams, this gives the most professional finish. In industry, overlockers are the most cost-effective method of constructing a seam. The blade on the machine is very sharp and must be used with care.

Metre rule	Useful for marking out and cutting out fabric; for measuring straight lines and hemlines.
Tape measure	Essential for taking body measurements and for measuring curved shapes or surfaces.
Craft knife	For hand cutting stencils or smaller templates.
Cutting mat	For use with the craft knife or with a rotary cutter. Cutting mats are pre-marked into squares which act as guides for cutting accurately.
Seam ripper or quick unpick	Often used to unpick faulty stitching; but the curved edge can also be used to cut open button holes and seams.
Pins	A temporary method of holding fabrics together or in place. Available in different thickness to suit different fabric types.

Table 11.5 Hand tools used in textile manufacturing

Figure 11.33 A range of specialist 'feet' for specific processes used in the construction of textile products

Industrial sewing machines and overlockers

Industrial sewing machines and overlockers are heavy-duty machines, specifically designed to withstand constant use. These machines have large motors that run much faster than domestic machines. They can also take large spools of strong thread to minimise snapping and time lost re-threading machines. These machines are able to sew with ease through heavy or tough materials, such as leather and denim.

Laser cutting

Laser cutting is controlled by a computer program in which the design is drawn as a 2D image (**CAD**). The laser strength and speed are set depending on the material to be cut. Once the fabric is placed into the cutter, the laser follows the digital design to quickly and accurately cut the design (CAM). Laser cutters can also be set up to etch the surface of a fabric, rather than cut all the way through. Intricate designs can be created on fabric that are not possible by any other means. The downside is that not all fabrics can be cut on the laser cutter, as some will melt and burn. With some fabrics, the laser leaves a burnt brown edge which can be unsightly. The laser can also be used to cut stencils and make blocks for block printing. Laser cutters are also used in industry to cut through multiple layers of fabric on an automated system following a digital lay plan that is stored in the computer's memory.

Pattern marking and cutting

Pattern cutting involves the use of paper or card templates, placed on the surface of the fabric and cut around to produce fabric pieces that are of accurate size and shape for the product being made.

- Commercial patterns contain templates that are printed on large sheets of pattern paper. These often include several sizes and variations.
- Basic blocks are usually made from thin card and are a basic template that can be adapted to produce a range of products.

Figure 11.34 A neat seam finish on an overlock machine

Figure 11.35 An intricate laser-cut pattern on a designer dress

KEY WORD

CAD: computer-aided design.

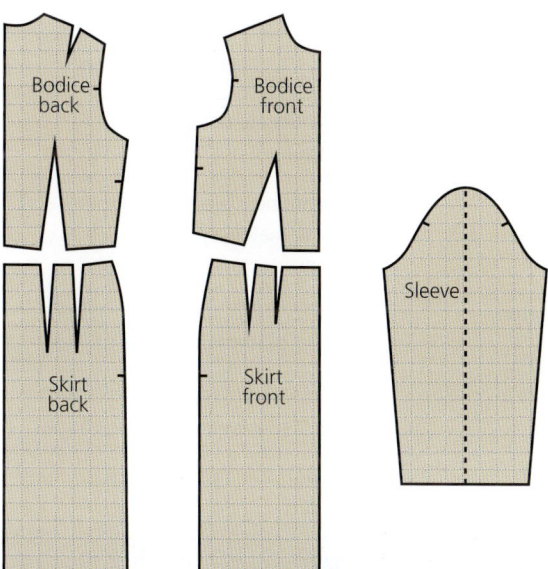

Figure 11.36 Basic blocks can be adapted easily to create pattern pieces to suit your design.

Commercial pattern pieces and basic blocks come printed with a range of important markings that must be followed accurately to ensure that the finished product is the correct size, shape and quality, as shown in Figure 11.37. Pattern pieces and basic blocks are marked with an arrow to show the direction of the grain line, and therefore how the pieces should be placed on the fabric for cutting. The straight grain runs vertically down the warp yarn in the fabric, and it is this grain line that is most commonly used in garment production, as it gives the best drape.

Fabrics can be laid lengthways and folded over so that selvedge edges come together, the templates are then laid out according to pattern instructions. Sometimes, fabrics can be laid out on a crosswise fold (folded along the width of the fabric) for a more efficient lay plan. A pattern can also be cut on the bias, which runs diagonally at a 45° angle to the straight grain. Fabrics cut on the bias are more flexible and can easily be sewn into curved shapes. Cutting on the bias often causes more wastage, so designers need to purchase more fabric when cutting patterns this way.

Pattern mark	Meaning of the mark	Why it is important
	Straight grain or grain lines	Template must be parallel to the selvedge edge, so the garment hangs as intended or lies flat
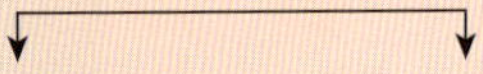	Place on folded edge	The edge of the template needs to be on a folded edge of the fabric, as the piece is symmetrical
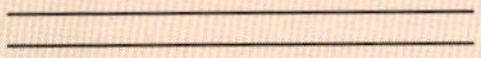	Adjustment lines to lengthen and shorten templates	The templates can be adjusted here to get a more personalised fit
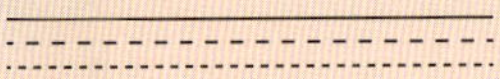	Cutting lines in various sizes	Cut along the desired size
	Stitching line	This is where stitches should be when joining pieces – if not adhered to, the product will not fit together
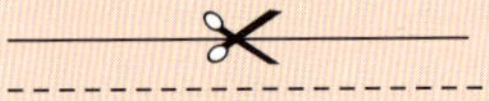	Seam allowance	The distance of the stitching line to the fabric edge, usually 1.5 cm
	Dots	Indicates the position of a component or shaping technique
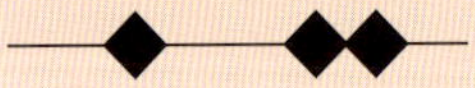	Notch	Indicate how pieces fit together and how to match a pattern, such as stripes
	Position of button	Transfer the mark onto the fabric for correct placement on the garment
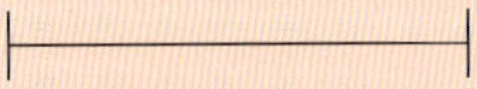	Position of button holes	Transfer the mark onto the fabric for correct placement on the garment
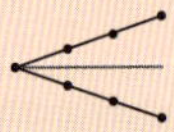	Position of dart	The dots need to match up to create the dart
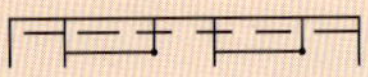	Placement of pleats and tucks	The lines need to match up to create the pleat or tuck

Figure 11.37 Pattern markings that must be followed accurately

WJEC EDUQAS GCSE (9–1) Design and Technology

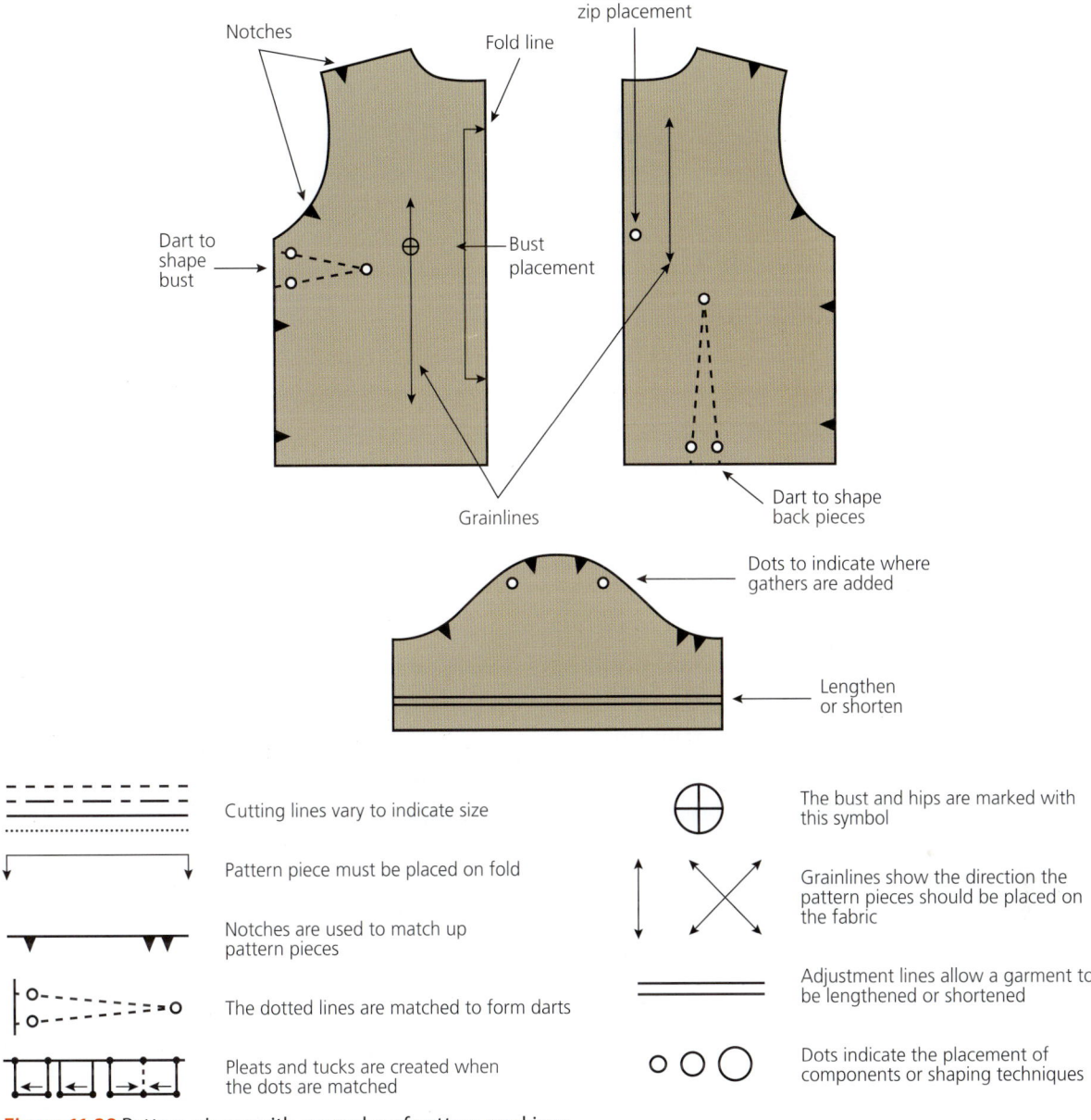

Figure 11.38 Pattern pieces with examples of pattern markings

There are several tools that can be used for transferring pattern markings to fabric accurately:

- Tailor's chalk – a small piece of hard chalk, used to temporarily mark fabric.
- Vanishing markers – pens containing vanishing ink that slowly fades on exposure to air, allowing marks to be temporarily made on fabric.
- Tracing wheel and carbon transfer – in this method of marking out pattern pieces, carbon paper is laid on top of the fabric, with pattern pieces on top. The carbon is transferred by the pressure applied when the tracing wheel is rolled along the surface of the pattern piece.
- Tailor's tacks – this method uses stitches to mark important details such as the position of a dart or button. Small loops of thread, which are later removed, are made through the fabric.
- In industry a hot notcher is used to mark small visible notches onto fabric to transfer important pattern marks. It is usually used to mark through several layers of fabric in large-scale production.

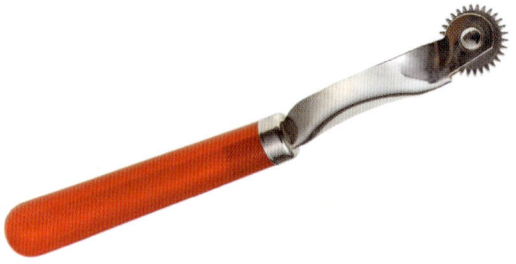

Figure 11.39 Tracing wheel

Figure 11.40 Tailor's tacks

Cutting tools

There are several tools/techniques that can be used for cutting fabric:

- Fabric shears – these are the most commonly used and easiest method for cutting fabric. Many other types of scissors are used in the construction of textile products. Small embroidery scissors, which have a sharp point blade, are essential for cutting intricate work. Pinking shears produce a zig-zag shaped cut along the raw edge of a seam, which prevents fraying.
- Rotary cutter – these incredibly sharp tools are rolled along the surface of the fabric, following the pattern lines. The surface underneath must be protected with a cutting mat to minimise damage.
- Laser cutting – this can be a quick and efficient way to cut out more complicated pattern pieces if you have access to a laser cutter in school. They can also be used to etch a pattern on the surface of the fabric.
- Band saw – when pattern cutting on a large scale, highly skilled workers use handheld band saws for cutting through up to 100 layers of fabric accurately and quickly. They follow a digital lay plan to reduce waste, and cutting is quick and efficient. The workers wear chainmail gloves to protect their hands from the sharp blades. Band knives and straight knives are used for the same purposes as a band saw.
- Automated die cutters – these are used for cutting constant shapes though several layers of fabric. They are usually used on small template pieces that may not be suitable for cutting on larger machines. The die cutter has a very sharp lower edge which, when laid onto the fabric and pressure is applied, will cut down through the layers.

Figure 11.41 Fabric shears are the most commonly used method for pattern cutting at home or at school

Figure 11.42 Rotary cutters are very accurate when cutting fabrics

Seam construction

This section focuses on the formation of seams that are suitable methods of joining for different fabrics and products. It is important that the correct type of seam is used to ensure the product is high quality and functions as expected.

Tolerances and seam allowances

It is equally important to use the correct **seam allowances** and **tolerances** throughout the manufacture of the product. The standard seam allowance used in textiles is 1.5 cm. If the correct seam allowance is not used consistently then the product parts will not fit together as intended, resulting in a poorer quality, often ill-fitting product.

The complexity of some textile products make it quite difficult to achieve total accuracy. For this reason, in industry, a permitted tolerance of a seam is about +/−1 cm (maximum). This, however, could still affect the size. Seam allowances which include the permitted tolerance are added to pattern pieces to allow enough fabric around the edge of the sewing line for errors. In order to achieve a high-quality product, the correct type of thread is needed for the fabric, as well as a suitable stitch type and good colour match where appropriate. It is important to test your stitch quality on the correct fabric before you start.

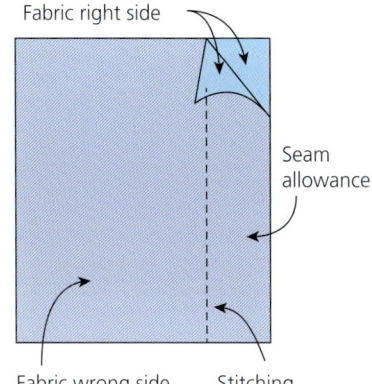

Figure 11.43 Plain seam

Plain seams

Plain seams are the most commonly used seam and can be finished neatly using a range of methods (for example, with an overlocker, pinking shears or bias binding). The seam allowance can be stitched together or pressed flat open with each edge neatened separately.

Plain seams are suitable for most fabric types.

French seams are enclosed, hiding any **raw edges**. This type of seam is suitable for sheer materials like chiffon, where the seams need to be almost invisible. It is often used on more expensive clothing.

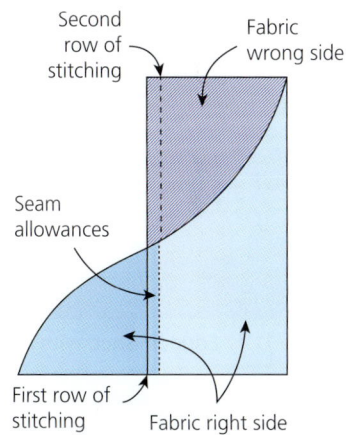

Figure 11.44 French seam

KEY WORDS

Seam allowance: the distance between the raw edge of the fabric and stitching line.

Tolerance: an allowance included in the seam allowance, for consistency when assembling a product.

Raw edge: the unfinished edge of a piece of material.

Flat-felled seams

Flat-felled seams are very strong, enclosed seams. Two rows of stitching strengthen the seams. The stitching on the top is often in a different colour thread to create a more distinctive look. Lapped seams and double stitched seams look very similar to a flat-felled seam. This type of seam is commonly used on denim and sportswear.

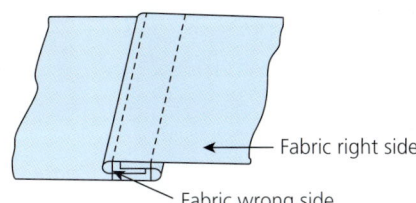

Figure 11.45 Flat-felled seam

Clipping seams

When a seam is sewn along a curve, particularly with woven fabrics, it will need to be clipped to allow the fabric to lie flat. Clipping involves the use of shears or specialist tools to cut into the seam allowance. This technique is commonly used around necklines and armholes to achieve a neat finish.

Figure 11.46 Seam finished with a zig-zag

Figure 11.47 Edge finished with a bias binding

Finishing seams

The aim of finishing seams is to neaten them and to prevent fraying. Common methods for finishing seams include:

- Overlocking – the overlocker trims off excess fabric along the seam and stitches around the raw edge, giving a neat and professional finish.
- Zig-zag – if you do not have access to an overlocker, machine sewing a zig-zag stitch along the raw edge of a seam can be just as effective. Pinking shears also cut a zig-zag finish.
- Seams can also be bound using a bias binding. This finish can also be used to neaten the edge of a fabric. This is often found on the seams of a tailored coat or jacket. It is also used on tents and waterproof clothing.

Adding shape or body

Fabrics, by nature, will lie fairly flat, and even knitted and non-woven fabrics will be difficult to shape. The methods in this section are used to add shape or body to fabrics in order to add interest and to improve fit and function.

Pleats

Pleats are formed by folding the fabric back on itself and sewing it into place. Pleating narrows the original width of the material quite significantly, while adding shape or body. There are different types of pleating which suit different purposes. Tucks are very similar to pleats and also give shape and form to the product. Pleats can be used as a decorative frill on products.

Gathers

Gathers are formed by sewing along the edge of the fabric with two parallel rows of long stitches. The thread ends, or tails, are then pulled to create the gathers. This technique narrows the original width of the material and gives fullness to the garment. Gathers are used throughout textiles on a wide range of textile products. While they are mainly used for adding shape, they are often used as a decorative feature.

Figure 11.50 Gathers are an easy way of adding shape and body to a product.

Figure 11.48 The pleats are stitched close to the waistband and lie flat but give shape to the skirt

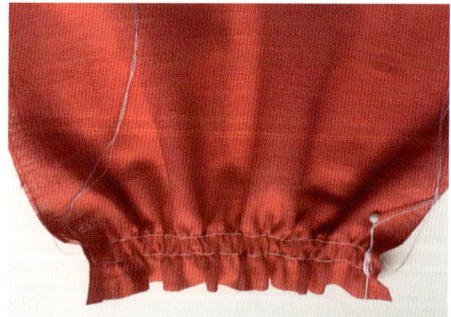
Figure 11.49 Gathers are formed by sewing two rows of stitching, and pulling up the thread ends to create gathers.

Darts

Darts are used to shape fabrics, improving the fit. They are made by creating folds in the fabric that taper to a point. These folds are often sewn into the bust, the back of bodices and waistlines, but can be used anywhere to give shape.

Edge finishes

There are a number of processes that can be used to finish the edge of the fabric in a textile product. The type of finish will vary and depend on the type of product being made – for example, the finish on a shaped neckline will be quite different from that used on a hem.

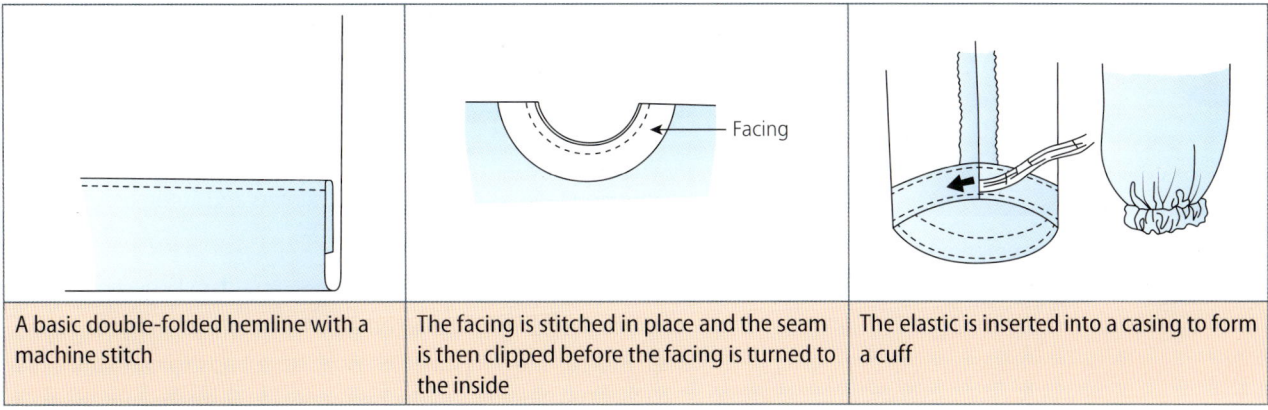

A basic double-folded hemline with a machine stitch	The facing is stitched in place and the seam is then clipped before the facing is turned to the inside	The elastic is inserted into a casing to form a cuff

Figure 11.51 Ways to finish edges

Computer-aided design and manufacture

Computer-aided design (CAD)

Computer-aided design has become a very important part of designing and making textile products. Designers can develop their ideas more effectively through CAD systems – designs can be revisited, manipulated and changed according to demand. Patterns and colourways are more easily developed through the basic design tools on most software systems. CAD is also considered a more sustainable and cost-effective way of developing designs as it often reduces the need for too many prototype products having to be made before manufacture.

A number of applications are available for image creation and manipulation when designing textile products. Examples include Adobe Illustrator, CorelDraw and Digital Fashion Pro. Hand-drawn sketches can also be transferred to the screen for dimensions and further refinement. Software packages are now available to view original 2D designs in a 3D format. CAD software allows designers to develop surface design for printing that can be transferred to relevant digital printing systems.

Digital lay planning and minimising waste

CAD software is also available to assist pattern cutters with the creation of digital lay plans, as shown in Figure 11.53. These plans show the manufacturer where to place each pattern piece on the fabric so that they follow the grain line and minimise wastage. Waste fabric is created during pattern cutting when small amounts of fabric are left around each pattern piece. These pieces are often unsuitable to use in other applications. Plotting layouts digitally enables manufacturers to **tessellate** the pattern pieces to maximise fabric usage. Fabric quantities are calculated based on the digital lay plans.

> **KEY WORD**
>
> **Tessellate**: how pattern pieces are fitted together to use the least amount of fabric.

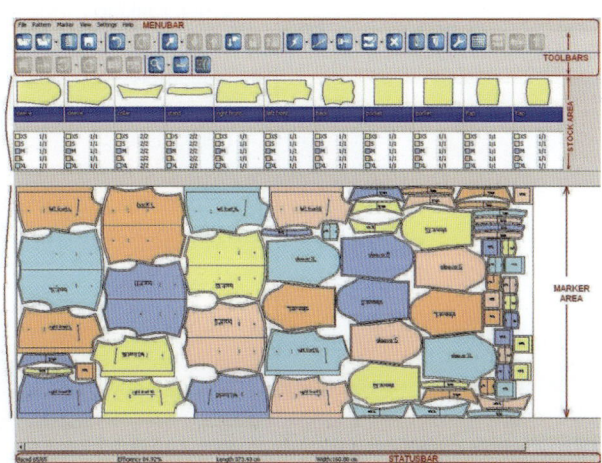

Figure 11.52 A digital lay plan enables designers to plan fabric layouts more efficiently to maximise fabric usage.

Figure 11.53 Multi-head computerised embroidery machines complete several designs at once.

Computer-aided manufacturing (CAM)

Computers are increasingly used to control sections of the manufacturing side of the textile industry. Some machinery is semi-automated in that it still requires some human input, but other machines are fully automated – this is known as CAM. These systems are expensive, but they speed up manufacturing, improve productivity and consistency, and reduce the risk of human error.

CAM applications include multi-head embroidery machines, digital printing on fabrics, laser cutters, 3D printers and automated fabric spreaders.

The automated fabric spreader is programmed to lay a set number of fabric layers. When the automated fabric spreader has reached that number, the template pieces will be cut according to the digital lay plan. The fabric can either be cut on a fully automated system or cut manually with a band knife or straight knife.

Activity

Make samples of the following construction techniques:

1   plain seam, but experiment with different finishes on the raw edges
2   French seam
3   flat-felled seam
4   gathers
5   tucks.

Mount each sample on paper or thin card and explain where each could be used on a textile product. Think of an actual product you might see or have seen each on – do the techniques change the shape of the fabric pieces? How?

KEY POINTS
- Modelling and testing of ideas are important aspects of the iterative design process. When making models and prototypes, the same construction processes should be used as they will appear on the final product.
- Machinery and equipment should be set up correctly and to suit the task ahead. Sewing machines need the correct needle, thread type and stitch for the task and fabric being used.
- You need to know why there are specialist attachments on a sewing machine and have an understanding of their importance.
- It is important to maintain consistent seam allowances when making textile products. The inside of a textile product should be the same high quality as the outside. This is part of quality control.
- You need to know what the pattern markings mean and how to use them when laying templates on fabric.
- You need to know and be able to describe methods of shaping textile products.

11.7 Appropriate surface treatments and finishes that can be applied for functional and aesthetic purposes

Surface finishes and treatments are applied to textile fabrics and products for a range of different reasons. In most cases, they are for aesthetic reasons – colour, texture, placement of motif, for example, but some finishes change the purpose of the fabric – for instance, an all-over print can change what the fabric is suitable for. Surface treatments are also referred to as embellishments or decorative techniques. Finishes apply to printing techniques.

Figure 11.54 Block printing is a traditional printing method for applying pattern to fabric. Paint or dye is applied to the relief pattern block on one side. The block is pressed onto the fabric to create pattern. The block is moved to form a repeat pattern.

Printing

There are many ways of printing onto textile fabrics. It is a process of applying dyes or pigment onto fabric to create pattern. Many of the industrial methods, such as screen printing and roller printing, can easily be adapted for school projects.

Flatbed printing

Flatbed screen printing is carried out on a conveyor production line, as illustrated in Figure 11.55. Each screen applies a different colour and design to the fabric as the fabric is moved along the conveyor belt. The conveyor belt stops at intervals, the screens come down and apply the design. At the end of the printing run, the fabric has a complete design on its surface. The fabric will go on to be fixed, washed and pressed.

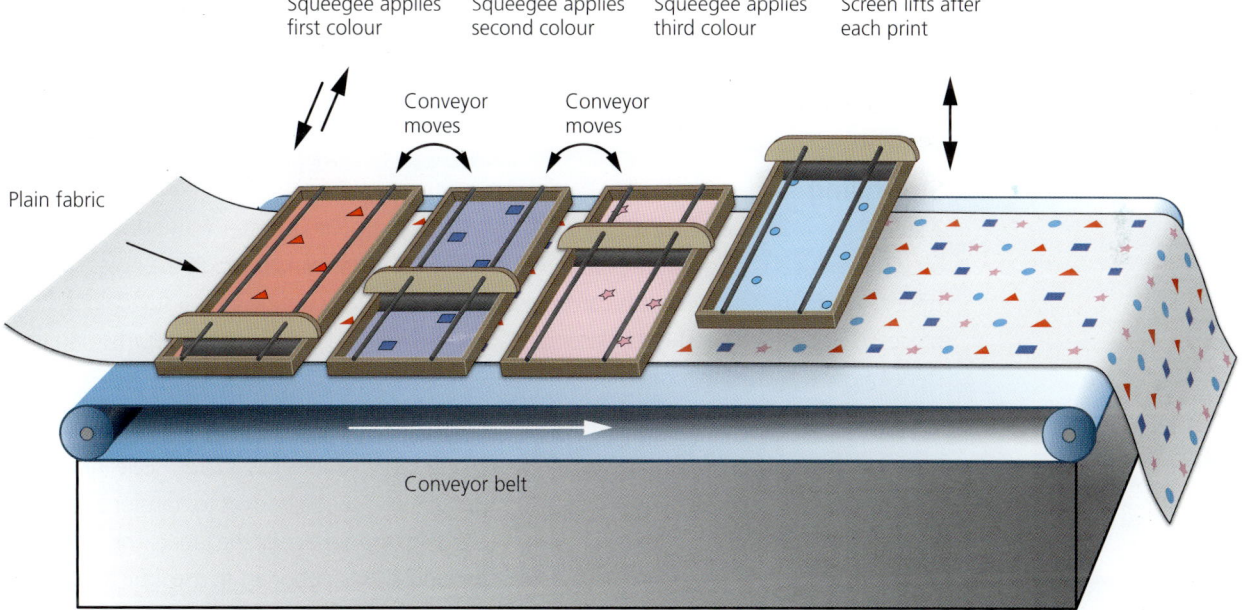

Figure 11.55 The flatbed printing process

Rotary screen printing

In rotary screen printing, cylinders are used instead of screens. The fabric design is created on metal sheets, which are then formed into a cylinder. The cylinders spin as the fabric passes underneath, printing a continuous pattern on to the surface. Each cylinder applies a single colour and design. Another name for this is roller printing.

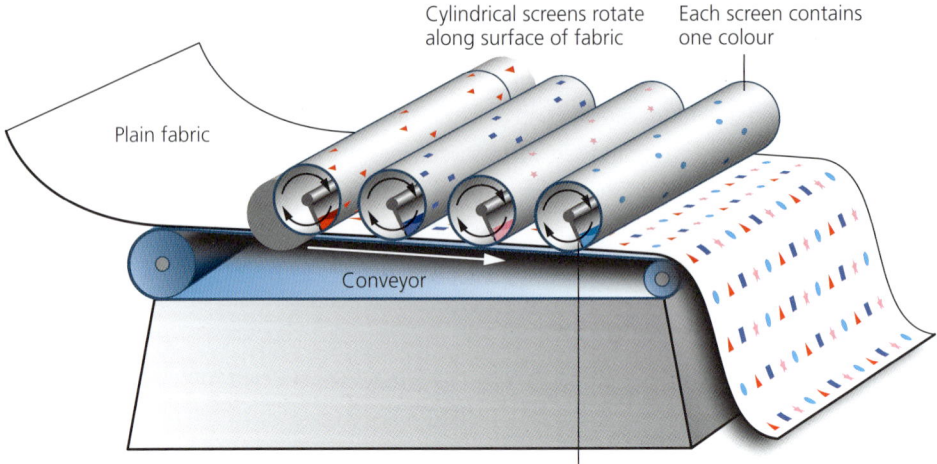

Cylindrical screens rotate along surface of fabric

Each screen contains one colour

Plain fabric

Conveyor

Squeegee ensures even flow of printing ink

Figure 11.56 The rotary screen printing process

Silk screen printing

In silk screen printing a fine mesh fabric, originally silk, is stretched over a wooden frame. Part of the screen is masked out with an opaque paste, the screen is laid face down on the fabric, printing ink is placed on the underside of the frame and a squeegee is used to drag the ink across the screen. The squeegee forces the ink through the fabric to leave the design on the material. The process can be repeated to build up complex designs. This process can be used with a stencil. The principles of screen printing are the same whether for a school project or on an industrial scale, however in industry several screens would be used.

Stencilling

A **stencil** is usually made from a thin sheet of card or plastic with a pattern cut out of it. It is used to produce a design on the fabric. Paint or dye is then applied through the holes in the stencil onto to the fabric. Stencils can be used with silk screen printing or as a standalone process. They can be hand-cut or laser-cut. Complex designs can be achieved by moving the stencil around and using more than one stencil in a design.

Digital fabric printing

Digital fabric printing uses large-scale inkjet printers and specialist dyes to transfer a digital image to the surface of the fabric. This type of printing allows designers to use intricate and detailed images. It also allows the designers to print many different sample pieces at the same time to evaluate designs before production.

Sublimation printing

Sublimation printing uses heat and pressure to transfer dye from specialist printer paper on to the fabric. This is a particularly effective method on fabric, as the process turns the dye into a gas that binds directly to the fibres, leaving a crisp design that is fully washable. In a similar way, an

Figure 11.57 Several designs can be tested quickly through digital printing directly onto fabric.

inkjet printer can be used to print a design onto specialist transfer paper. The design is then transferred to fabric to be fixed in place either with a heat press or an iron. Unlike sublimation printing, the image in this method lies on top of the fabric and is not considered as long lasting.

Discharge printing

A bleaching agent is applied to fabric, in the required design. The bleaching agent destroys the colour leaving a white or pale design. This works best on darker fabrics. To produce a coloured design, the bleach is mixed with a dye that will not react with it. The design produced will be in the colour of the dye.

Burnout printing

This process is most effectively used on knitted jersey type fabrics made from a polyester-cotton blend. A chemical, usually acid, is applied to the fabric in the required design. In industry this would usually be applied in a flatbed printing process. The acid destroys the cotton fibre, but the polyester resists, leaving a lighter thinner section on the fabric. It is an effective design and is widely used on fashion products.

Dyeing

The most common method of adding colour to fibres and fabrics is dyeing. Manufacturers can use natural or synthetic dyes, depending on the type of fibre to be dyed. Natural dyes work well on natural fibres and can be made from plants, minerals or insects. Synthetic dyes work on synthetic fibres, but can also give deeper or brighter colours when used with natural fibres. Synthetic fibres require the use of chemicals to enable them to take up the dye.

Fibres and fabrics can be dyed at various stages in the production process:
- **Fibre stage** – this is when the raw fibre is dyed before fabric construction to achieve consistent colour.
- **Yarn stage** – yarn dyeing will not give consistent colour in a woven or knitted fabric, but can be useful for creating stripes in woven fabrics like tartan.
- **Piece dyeing** – this is when an entire length of fabric is dyed. This method can produce inconsistencies in colour.
- **Garment dyeing** – this is when a completed garment is dyed. This can be beneficial in t-shirt production, where identical products can be dyed in a range of colours once they have been made.

There are other, more decorative methods of dyeing textile fabrics.
- Dip dyeing – where part of the fabric is dipped in the dye and is then gradually removed from the dye bath producing a graduated colour effect. Different parts of the fabric can be dipped in different colours to create some effective designs.
- Tie and dye – a traditional method of dyeing fabric. The fabric is tied or knotted in a variety of ways to produce unique and varied designs. This can be done to finished products, such as t-shirts, or fabric pieces. This is called a **resist method** of colouring fabric as the dye cannot penetrate where it has been tied, which creates the pattern.
- Batik is also a resist method of colouring fabric. Hot melted wax is applied to fabric in the desired pattern, once cooled the fabric is submerged in a dye bath, or the dye can be

KEY WORD

Resist method: a means of preventing dye or paint from penetrating an area on the fabric. This creates the patterns.

Figure 11.58 The batik flower has been hand painted, the white area indicates where the wax resisted the dye.

Figure 11.59 A hand-painted silk scarf – the white outline which separates the flowers is created by using gutta outline to create a barrier between the different sections.

Figure 11.60 A modern interpretation of an appliqué design

directly painted on. The process can be repeated several times to build up a more detailed design. The wax needs to be removed once the design is complete.

- Random – dyeing or colouring small sections of a piece of fabric or yarns. This could mean different sections having different colours. There is no regularity to the design.

Painting

Fabric paints can be applied directly onto textile fabrics to create the desired design. Fabric felt pens and pastel crayons can be used in much the same way. Specialist silk paints give a very delicate watery effect and can be used with gutta outliner, which acts as a barrier to separate sections of the design. Dimensional paints leave a raised, slightly 3D, surface on fabrics. They can be applied directly on to fabric from a squeezable bottle or tube and are a creative way to enhance other designs or create smaller details. Marbling is achieved by floating specialist fabric paints on specialist paste. The paints can be swirled into a suitable design and the pre-treated fabric is laid carefully on the paint and paste. The design is transferred to the fabric. Air brushing requires a specialist air-operated tool that sprays dye or paint onto fabrics. This is controlled by a trigger and creates a smooth, blended effect on the fabric.

Embroidery

Embroidery can be done by hand, which requires a lot of patience and skill as each stitch, of which there are many, is carefully applied to the fabric. Most embroidery we see on textile products is a form of machine embroidery. Embroidery is often further enhanced with beads and sequins. Types of machine embroidery include:

- Free machine embroidery – the fabric is secured in a frame and the machinist moves the fabric around freely to create a design. This is a skill that requires patience, but can be very effective.
- Machine embroidery – most sewing machines have the facility to stitch rows of decorative stitches which can be used to enhance any designs. Computerised machines offer the potential for further creativity, either by using pre-installed designs or with a suitable CAD package to create and then stitch an original design (CAM).
- Appliqué – a traditional way of applying a design to fabric by stitching separate pieces of fabrics onto a base fabric. Each piece has to be stitched securely to hold it in place. Traditionally, a satin stitch was used around the edges of each piece. These days, stitch techniques vary. There are endless possibilities for creative design work through mixing colour, textures, stitch type and number of pieces.
- Beadwork – beads are stitched individually by hand on to fabrics or are used to enhance other techniques such as appliqué. Beads can be placed and stitched randomly on a product or can be used to outline an area or in a cluster. Beads are available in many different shapes, sizes and material. Similar effects can be achieved using sequins or diamantes.

Activity

Follow this simple method for appliqué.

You will need: samples of fabrics, **Bondaweb**, embroidery scissors or sharp scissors, iron.

1   Cut a piece of fabric for the top design and iron a piece of Bondaweb to the back of it. Keep the paper backing on the Bondaweb.

2   Draw the shape on the back of the Bondaweb – paper side – making sure the design is reversed.

3   Carefully cut around the shape.

4   Peel off the backing paper and apply the design to the second piece of fabric, glue side down. Iron it in place making sure you protect the iron with a paper of a cloth.

5   Stitch the design in place using any suitable stitch.

The design can be added to by repeating the process for more parts.

Enhance the design further by hand stitching beads or sequins.

KEY WORDS

Bondaweb: a non-woven fabric with adhesive on both sides that allows two fabrics to be joined together. Heat is needed to activate the process.

Mordant: a chemical that is dissolved in a dye solution that sets the colour on the fabric. Salt does the same thing.

KEY POINTS

- Decorative techniques can appear on any type of textile product. The main purpose is to enhance the design and improve aesthetic appeal.
- Developing decorative ideas through trialling and testing are all part of the iterative design process.
- Paint effects, including pastel crayons and fabric pens, need to be fixed with heat to set the design.
- When dyeing fabrics, make sure a **mordant** is used to permanently fix the colour. Salt can be used for this process.
- A variety of decorative processes can be used together to create some imaginative and highly creative work.

11.8 Designing and making principles for natural, synthetic, blended and mixed fibres; woven, non-woven and knitted textiles

Selection of materials and components

When designing and making a textile product it is important to choose the correct materials and components. The fibre source and inherent properties, the construction method used to manufacture the fabric and industrial finishes applied will affect choice. Textile products also depend on smaller component parts to function. Some components are included for aesthetic reasons, and while they may not affect the function of the product, it might appear less appealing.

If, for example, you are going to make a young child's summer outfit as part of your non-examined assessment, you should consider the requirements of the user alongside the materials. As it is a summer outfit it would need to be cool to wear and comfortable for the child. A young child might get dirty while crawling and playing or spill drinks. The fabric needs to be absorbent to soak up spills and wash easily. As cotton is absorbent, it makes it cool to wear. Jersey is a knitted construction, so it will be comfortable to wear as it will stretch with movement. This means that cotton jersey may be the ideal fabric.

A young child may struggle with fastenings. Small components could present a choking hazard if they came off. Velcro® is a fastening a child could cope with and is not a choking hazard. However, it is not always a suitable choice, depending on the product. Popper fastenings or snap fasteners with no sharp edges and securely fastened in place might be more suitable. All of these need to be considered in order to make informed decisions.

Choosing manufacturing process and the development of templates

The most effective way of selecting the construction process is to model and test your ideas, preferably in the materials you are considering or something similar. The construction process will depend on the materials being considered and the purpose of the product. These were outlined earlier in the chapter. In garment construction, a **toile** could be made using pattern blocks or by following a simple commercial pattern. Although toiles usually refer to garments or clothing, the same principles apply to any textile product that is being developed.

Once the toile has been assembled and fitted onto a dressmaker's dummy, you can draw directly onto the toile to show intended changes in size, shape or structure. Use additional fabrics and techniques to develop the design of the product. These techniques could include cutting sections away, reshaping or adding sleeves, or creating shape by adding pleats or gathers. Seam types can be considered and tested as well as suitable edge finishes, such as hemlines and necklines.

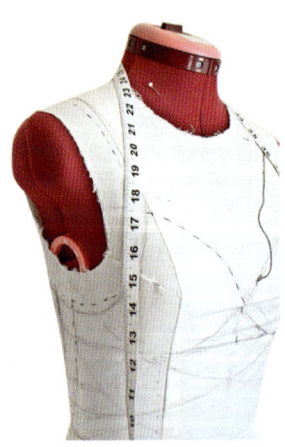

Figure 11.62 A designer has drawn the intended changes on the toile. The toile will be deconstructed to make new pattern templates.

Figure 11.61 A designer reshapes the toile on the dressmaker's dummy to develop and improve the design – all part of the iterative design process.

Following this iteration of design, the toile can be **deconstructed** and the pieces used to draft new pattern pieces for the final product. Modelling of ideas in a 3D form is an essential part of the iterative process – testing ideas to refine and develop them.

> **KEY WORDS**
>
> **Toile**: an early version or prototype of a garment, made in cheap substitute material to test the design, fit and form in order to develop the idea.
>
> **Deconstructed**: take something apart.

Use of specialist tools and equipment

For the main construction of any textile product in a school or college environment you will use a domestic sewing machine; some of these will be computerised and include more specialist features, such as embroidery. On all sewing machines, specialist foot attachments are available to complete some processes. In order to get a high-quality finish it is important to set the machine up correctly to suit a specific process. In order to insert an invisible zip, for example, you should use the specialist attachment – it is extremely difficult to get a good finish without one. If your machine does not have such an attachment, then consider an alternative zip fastener or fastening method.

Other specialist equipment includes overlockers for neat seam finishes, and laser cutters for cut work and engraving on fabrics. Laser cutters and 3D printers can be used to develop small unique component parts.

Applying appropriate finishes and techniques

Most commercially available fabric will already have a finish applied to it, depending on the intended purpose of the fabric. These finishes were discussed earlier in the chapter.

Some stitched decorative techniques, such as appliqué, need reinforcing in order to achieve a high-quality outcome. A non-woven material, such as Bondaweb or an iron-on interfacing, will suit this purpose. Once the fabric is stabilised it will lie flat while being stitched, giving a good finish.

Finishes for other decorative techniques, such as tie and dye, need to be considered during the process. Dyed fabric should be fixed with a mordant, such as salt, to ensure the dyes are permanent and will not wash out. Other techniques, such as painting, need specialist fabric paints that require fixing with a hot iron to permanently set the colour. You need to check the appropriate finishing process for the techniques being considered.

Throughout the construction of a textile product you should consider the quality of each process as you progress through manufacture. Seams, for example, on any product should be stitched with the correct thread type, stitch tension and needle for the chosen fabric. Regular pressing of seams and construction processes will also support a good finish. Take care that the iron is set to the correct heat setting, as some fabrics will melt if the temperature is too hot – it is a good idea to test a sample of the fabric first. A final visual check is important – trim all loose threads from stitching and a final press with the iron will improve the appearance of the finished product.

Activity

Find a textile product, such as a pair of shorts or a t-shirt, and carefully deconstruct it. Identify the number of different pattern pieces used and the construction processes. Consider how many different components were used and try to work out their specific purpose.

Lay the pattern pieces out, trace around them to create new templates. Remake the product in new materials. Repeat the process with more complex products.

Know it

1 The source of the fibre is an important aspect of choosing textile fabrics.
   a Name the two main sources of natural fibres.
   b Name one fibre that comes from each source.
   c Describe in detail the advantages of blending fibres for a range of textile fabrics. Include named examples in your answers to help illustrate your answer.

2 Textiles products are made using different scales of production.
   a Explain how a cell operates within a large-scale manufacturing facility.
   b Describe the benefits of bespoke clothing to a customer.

3 Textile fabrics are constructed in different ways.
   a Describe what is meant by the term 'pile weave'.
   b Explain why the templates for a teddy bear should all face the same way when laying the templates on acrylic fur.
   c Give two reasons why a designer would use a satin weave fabric for an evening dress.

4 When making a textile product, specific rules are followed to ensure the final product can function as intended.
   a Explain why it is important to follow pattern language when laying templates on fabric.
   b On the diagram below, draw the 'place to fold' instruction where it would normally be found and explain the importance of this.
   c Name the pattern mark shown as 'X' in the diagram and explain its importance in garment construction.
   d Describe the benefits of cutting templates on the bias when making textile products.

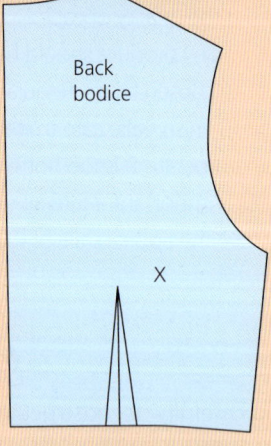

Figure 11.63 Pattern design

5 The finished dimensions of the cube floor cushion shown below are 30 cm × 30 cm × 30 cm.

Figure 11.64 Cube floor cushion

   a State how many pieces of fabric need to be cut to make the cube floor cushion if each side is going to be a different colour.
   b The standard seam allowance in textiles is 1.5 cm. This needs to be included in the templates for the cube floor cushion. Calculate the size of one template.
   c Calculate how many templates can fit across a piece of fabric that is:
      i 115 cm wide
      ii 150 wide
      iii State the width that would give best use of the fabric.
   d The floor cushion is made from cotton-coated PVC. Describe what this means and explain why it is a suitable fabric for the floor cushion.

6 The fashion industry has a big impact on the environment.
   a Explain why a 'throwaway culture' is having a negative impact of the environment.
   b Describe the benefits to the environment of upcycling your old clothes.

7 Finishes are applied to fabrics to improve their properties.
   a Name the chemical that is used in a flame-resistant finish.
   b Explain how this finish improves the functional properties of the fabric.

8 Analyse the impact that the intensive farming of cotton crops has on the ecosystem.

Exam practice questions

1 An electronic combination door lock is being developed. Three buttons – A, B and C – produce a logic 1 when pressed. A solenoid-operated lock should open for 5 seconds only when buttons A and C are pressed simultaneously.

   a Draw a circuit diagram of logic gates which will give a LOW output only when buttons A and C are pressed. [3 marks]

   b A monostable timer produces a 5-second output to operate the solenoid. Draw a circuit diagram of a monostable based around a 555 timer IC. [4 marks]

   c Calculate the monostable resistor value needed if a 47 µF capacitor is used (T = 1.1RC). [3 marks]

   d Explain the functional difference between a solenoid and a motor. [3 marks]

2 A student wishes to build a structure using lengths of flat metal bar of the type shown below.

The student finds that the bar is not very rigid.

   a Use sketches and notes to show four factors that affect the extent to which the metal bar will bend when it is subjected to loads. [4 marks]

   b Explain how triangulation is used to make a structure rigid. [3 marks]

   c Compare the use of a bevel gear system and a worm drive system when transferring the direction of a drive shaft through 90°. [4 marks]

3 A package made from thin card is shown below.

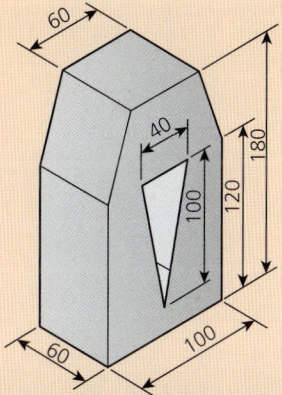

   a Draw the development net for the package. [8 marks]

   b The development net is to be made from one sheet of standard-sized card. State the size of card needed to make the net in one piece. [2 marks]

4 A prototype of the package is made before the package is mass produced.
Complete the table to show a suitable method of completing each process in the construction of the prototype and mass-produced package. [4 marks]

Process	Prototype (one off) method	Mass-production method
Printing the graphics on the development net		
Cutting out the net		

5 Give the name of a hardwood that you would use to make a garden bench. [1 mark]

   Explain why you have chosen this hardwood. [2 marks]

6 Use notes and sketches to explain how plywood gets its strength. [3 marks]

7 Use notes and sketches to explain the life cycle of an aluminium drinks can. [6 marks]

8 Name two permanent and two non-permanent methods of joining mild steel. [4 marks]

9 Give the name of a thermosetting polymer used to make a domestic electric plug. [1 mark]

   Explain why you have chosen this thermosetting polymer. [2 marks]

10 Use notes and sketches to describe the process of vacuum forming. [6 marks]

11 Study the picture of the fitted jacket below.

   a The jacket is lined. Explain the purpose of the lining. [3 marks]

   b An interlining has also been used. Describe where the interlining would be used and why it is needed. [3 marks]

12 Evaluate the use of the laser cutter when designing and making textile products. [6 marks]

Section 3

Core designing and making principles

Chapter 12 Develop and apply core knowledge,
    understanding and skills 270
Practice questions.. 306

Chapter 12
Develop and apply core knowledge, understanding and skills

Learning objectives

By the end of this chapter you should have developed a knowledge and understanding of:

- how contexts inform outcomes when designing products
- the collection of primary and secondary data
- how to write a design brief
- factors that influence the processes of designing and making

- how to test, analyse and evaluate your work
- how the work of past professionals can influence your ideas
- how to communicate design ideas
- developing a prototype
- making informed decisions, responding to feedback and further developing your ideas.

12.1 All design and technological practice takes place within contexts which inform outcomes

The context of a design is the settings or surroundings in which the final product will be used. In order for a design solution to be successful it must not just work, but work within the context it was designed for. The context of a design will incorporate many things such as:

- the surroundings or environment where it will be used
- the needs, wants and values of the **users** and other **stakeholders**
- the purpose of the end product.

Social, cultural, moral and environmental considerations may also influence and affect the **context**. A product that is designed properly within context will fulfil its purpose exactly, giving the users and stakeholders what they require with a minimum of interaction or inconvenience.

If design takes place without consideration of the context then it will invariably lead to a final product that does not fully meet the needs of the user or stakeholders and may even result in a product that is completely unsuitable. For example, if a chair designer was told to design a comfortable chair for use in a communal room they may design a chair similar to the one shown in Figure 12.1.

The design initially seems to be suitable and meets the need. However, if the context of the brief is an old people's home this design is completely unsuitable because the chair is much too low and laid back for an elderly person to sit comfortably in or get up from. It is, therefore, vitally important that we consider the context of a design problem when designing.

A useful method of considering the context of a design is to create a context map or task analysis showing all the possible factors that could or should influence the design, such as 'who', 'why', 'where', 'when', 'what', 'how'.

- **Who** are the primary users, secondary users and other stakeholders? For example, their age, gender, physical mobility.
- **Why** is there a need for this product? What is the problem? What are the restrictions on the design? For example, is this a problem specific to one particular person or user group, or is it needed for a specific reason or event?

Figure 12.1 The comfortable chair

- **Where** will the product be used? What type of environment will it be used in? For example, is it for use indoors or outdoors? Is it likely to be subjected to harsh weather or moisture? Will it have to operate in especially hot or cold conditions?
- **What** must the product do? What is its primary function? Are there any other secondary functions? For example, does it have just one main purpose or must it fulfil a number of different requirements?
- **When** is the product used? Is the product used at certain times of day/night? Is it used at certain times of the year? For example, is it used in the daytime when it is light or at night when it is dark? Will it just be used at certain times of year and then stored for long periods of time between uses?
- **How** is the product meant to function? How will it be stored, transported, maintained? How will the other items above affect the design? For example, will it have to function without making any noise? Will it need to be transported long distances, so have to be portable, etc.

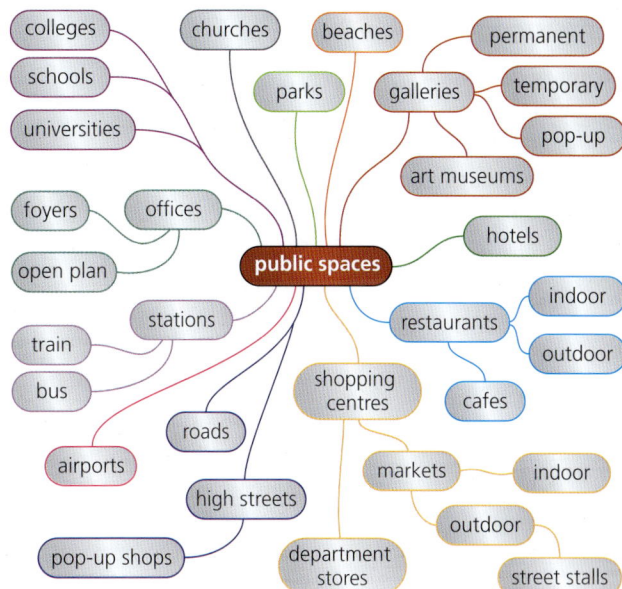

Figure 12.2 An example of a mind map

Many of the considerations will overlap and influence each other.

There are many different ways of creating or drawing a concept map, and you should use a method that helps you consider the entire context of the design problem.

Activity

You are the main user of the chair you are sitting on – it was designed for school students aged between 11 and 16 years of age.

Think about who the other stakeholders are.

What other people have an interest or will come into contact with the chair?

12.2 Identifying and understanding user needs: collecting primary and secondary data

Primary and secondary data

Considering the context of a design, research into the different factors that will or could influence the design and assessing the user and stakeholder needs will require many different kinds of data to be collected. You may be able to gather information from carrying out physical tests on something, questionnaires, surveys, interviews or studies you conduct yourself into the situation. Data gathered by yourself such as this is called **primary data**.

Primary data is any data collected by the designer themselves for the specific purpose of solving the problem. Primary data is also called 'first-hand' or 'raw' data. Collecting primary data is usually quite labour intensive, and as a result can be time consuming and expensive.

If you were designing a bespoke product for one particular client, then you would interview them, ask questions and test things out to see what they thought. However, if there were numerous stakeholders, then this process would need to be repeated with each of them. If the product you are designing is to be marketed and aimed at a wide user group, then you may need to carry out hundreds of questionnaires, interviews and tests across the spectrum of different users in order to collect enough accurate primary data.

Failure to carry out sufficient research can lead to inaccurate primary data, and in turn a product that does not fulfil all of the users' or stakeholders' needs.

Secondary data is 'second-hand' data which has already been collected by someone else for the same or a similar purpose. Secondary data is usually much easier to find than primary data, but because it has already been done, it may already be out of date. Secondary data can be gathered from a range of sources, such as the internet, websites, books, test reports, journals, etc.

Using secondary data can save a lot of time as it is much quicker than carrying out testing, interviews and questionnaires, etc., and is therefore much less expensive. However, the data collected is not as accurate as primary data because it is not specific to the designer's or user's exact needs. It will most likely have been collected for other purposes slightly different to those required. It may have been conducted on a slightly different user group or done some time ago when people's attitudes or opinions may have been different due to shifts in trends, beliefs, economic climate, etc. The methods used to collect the data and the reasons for doing so may also be significantly different to those required.

Needs, wants and values of the end user

One of the main considerations for any design must be the user group and their needs. While most products are designed for people, there are occasions when humans are not the main user. Custom-made or bespoke products are designed and made specifically for one particular person, and as a result can be expensive. However, the vast majority of products are designed for use by a particular group of people. The main person, or group of people, who will be using the product are known as the primary users. For example, the chairs in a secondary school classroom are designed with children aged between 11 and 16 years of age as the primary users.

Figure 12.3 Plastic school chair

Products also have other, secondary, users who will have an interest or come into contact with the product in one way or another. These are known as stakeholders. For example, the school chair may also be sat on by teachers when sitting next to a student, or by parents or younger children at parents' evenings or school events. Caretakers or cleaning staff will come into contact with the chair and while they may not sit on them, they will have to clean, stack or transport them around the school. The school management and governors will also hold an interest in the chair, as they will want it to be as inexpensive and long lasting as possible.

User	Need
Student (primary user)	Be comfortable to sit on and work (for extended periods of time)
Teacher	Be comfortable to sit on (for short periods of time)
Parent	Be comfortable to sit on (for short periods of time)
Cleaning staff	Be easy to wipe clean/easy to move around/lift up
Caretaker	Be easy to stack/easy to transport and store
Management	Be inexpensive/be long lasting
Maintenance staff	Be easy to repair/dispose of

Table 12.1 Stakeholders in a school chair and their needs

While it is not always possible to meet the needs of the user and all the stakeholders, a well-designed product will as far as possible meet the needs of the primary user and as many of the stakeholder needs as possible.

Collecting primary and secondary data

Surveys and questionnaires are an effective way of gathering information from people, providing the questions are well thought out and well worded. You can create a written questionnaire by hand on paper, or on computer. Questions can be open or multiple choice, depending on the type of information you require. Many people do not like to fill in lots of written answers, so the survey should be as easy to fill in as possible. By limiting the answers to a choice of three or four options this also means that you do not get irrelevant answers.

Finding people within your intended user groups to fill out surveys is of prime importance, but can sometimes be difficult. You must ensure that the people who fill out your survey or questionnaire fall in to the same user group as your intended users or the information collected will be inaccurate and result in a flawed final product. For example, if you were designing a product to assist an elderly person to complete a particular task, then it is pointless creating a survey and giving it to your classmates, as they will have completely different needs.

Many free online survey programs are now available, meaning you can email people you know who fit into your intended user group and conduct primary research and collate answers from people you may not necessarily have met.

Many students use the internet to collect images and information on existing products that are similar to what they may be designing. This is secondary research, as it is based on the reviews of others and/or the manufacturers' own claims. While this has some value, it is far better if you can find a 'real life' existing product which you can handle, use and test yourself.

Activity

Imagine you are designing a new phone. From the different information below, identify what is primary and what is secondary data.

- review of an existing phone from an internet forum
- technical details of an existing phone from a manufacturer's website
- measuring the phone with a ruler to find out its dimensions
- asking people questions about their phone
- results of a customer survey in *What Phone?* magazine
- finding out the best-selling phone from last year by asking a shop owner.

12.3 Writing a design brief and specifications

Design briefs

A design brief is a concise description of the task that the designer will undertake in order to solve the design problem or achieve what the client wants.

The design brief is not a long drawn-out description with lots of detail, but should be short and give a clear outline of what the required results of the design are. The design brief can sometimes be set by the **client** or decided by discussion between the client and designer.

Writing a clear and accurate design brief will help to ensure that the resulting design work and end product are what the client actually wants and not what the designer thinks they want. For this reason it is critical that the design brief makes it clear exactly what is required and that the designer continually refers back to the brief during the design process to check that what they are doing is working towards achieving this and they are not wandering off track.

Writing a design brief or specification

Before writing a design brief it is important that the full extent of the challenge or problem, and the context in which it is set, has been fully explored. By doing this, a clear and complete picture of the entire problem can be uncovered, and from this a definitive summary of the need. It may be that the problem facing the client is caused by something else and therefore the need of the client is different to what they actually think.

What a client wants and what they might actually need are not always the same thing. For example, a client may want a drinking bottle that can attach to a bicycle so that they can keep hydrated while out riding. The brief for the designer would be:

Design a drinking bottle that could attach to the client's bicycle.

However, by exploring the context of the problem and fully evaluating the actual needs of the client, the actual problem is that the client requires a way of remaining hydrated during long bicycle rides without stopping. Therefore, the brief should be:

Design a product that will keep the client hydrated while riding his bicycle without stopping.

A drinking bottle that attaches to the bicycle is one solution, but not necessarily the best solution, and may create other problems for the client themselves or other stakeholders. The bottle could fall off or be dropped, and holding and drinking from the bottle while riding may be dangerous.

The best solution may be a bottle that is worn by the client somewhere on their person and has a straw or tube that delivers the liquid directly into their mouth without the need for them to remove their hands from the handlebars.

When the brief focuses more on the **product** than the **problem** this can lead to **design fixation** and prevent alternative approaches to the problem from being considered or explored.

Once the brief has been decided and written, the specification must then be drawn up. The specification is a set of requirements that the product must meet or constraints that it must fit into. The specification can include specific **criteria** needed for the user or any of the stakeholders. Research carried out into the problem should also influence what goes into the specification.

KEY WORDS

Client: the person the designer is working for (this may or may not be the user).

Design fixation: when a designer limits their creativity by only exploring one avenue of design or relying too heavily on features of existing designs.

Criteria: specific goals that a product must achieve in order to be successful.

The specification for a product will usually cover areas such as:

- the primary and secondary functions that the product must achieve (what it must do)
- any specific requirements of the user/stakeholders
- materials, components that must be used or avoided
- maximum or minimum dimensions, weights and size constraints
- financial constraints (how much it should cost to produce)
- aesthetic factors (how the product must look or feel)
- anthropometric and ergonomic requirements
- environmental standards or constraints it must meet
- safety features and restrictions
- relevant manufacturing standards
- legal requirements
- how long it should be expected to last for.

Open specifications state criteria that the product must meet, but do not specify how it must be achieved. This gives the designer more freedom to explore different ways of achieving the outcomes and come up with different approaches.

Closed specifications are more detailed and state not only what must be achieved, but also how certain criteria must be met. This could be by specifying the tools, materials or processes that must be used to manufacture the product.

There are various websites and software packages available to assist GCSE students when writing a specification by providing prompts or questions about the product they are intending to design, such as ACCESS FM and SCAMPER.

Activity

You have been asked to design a portable overnight shelter for a group of six hikers.

Write a specification for the shelter with at least ten different criteria that the product must achieve in order to be successful.

12.4 Investigating environmental, social and economic challenges

Designers in today's society face many challenges when designing products. They must not only ensure that the product fulfils its purpose, but also consider the effect of the product on the environment and society. The designer has a responsibility to ensure that the choice of materials, processes or methods of disposal when designing are as environmentally friendly as possible, and do not offend certain cultures or have a negative impact on society. In order to achieve this, the designer must thoroughly investigate and weigh up the negative effects of manufacturing and producing a product against the positive impact of a new product on society.

Environmental considerations

Up until quite recently, manufacturers were mostly concerned with producing products as cheaply and quickly as possible, with little concern about the environmental impact of the product. Television advertising, social pressures to have the newest and most up-to-date products and the influences of fashion and trends have encouraged people to buy more

Designers have a responsibility to design products that can be made as cheaply as possible, but also to ensure that people are not being exploited in this way in order for the product to be manufactured. Designers should make sure clients they design for are following the guidelines for fair treatment of workers. They can do this by ensuring that the company follow guidelines set out by organisations such as Fairtrade (see Chapter 1), the European Institute for Crime Prevention and Control, the Gangmasters and Labour Abuse Authority, or AWARE (The Alliance for Workers Against Repression Everywhere).

Anthropometrical and ergonomic issues

Anthropometrics is the study of the sizes of people in relation to products. It uses statistics and measurements of different parts of the human body taken from people of different ages, genders and races. Anthropometric data is used by designers to determine the sizes, shape and forms of products or components so that they are fit for purpose and meet the needs of the intended user.

Anthropometrical data usually provides designers with the average sizes of the smallest 5 per cent (the 5th percentile), the mean (50th percentile) and the largest 5 per cent (95th percentile) of people measured.

In some cases, products are designed to fit the average person. In others, they may be designed to fit the largest or smallest. For example, a chair used in a primary school needs to be suitable for the average size of pupils aged between 4 and 7 years of age. The designer would use anthropometric data to decide on the most suitable height, width and depth of the chair.

The designer would use dimension 19 to decide on the height of the chair, dimension 8 to decide the width, and dimension 15 to decide the depth. Dimension 9 would be used to decide the height of the backrest (see Figure 12.4).

Ergonomics is the relationship between people and the products which they use. Ergonomic data can be used to make products more comfortable and easy to use by considering the shape of the human body and the force a person can apply to something. For example, when holding and turning a handle, the more comfortable the shape of the handle the easier it is to use. The larger the handle, the less effort or force is needed to turn it.

Ergonomics and anthropometrics are used together when designing products to ensure the outcome not only 'fits' the intended user but is as comfortable and easy to use as possible.

Activity

Design a pair of sunglasses for an adult man or woman.
- What three pieces of anthropometrical data will you need to collect in order to make the sunglasses the correct size?
- Use an available adult (such as a teacher or parent) and measure the relevant parts of their head and face.
- Use these measurements to make a cardboard prototype of your design and test how well they fit.

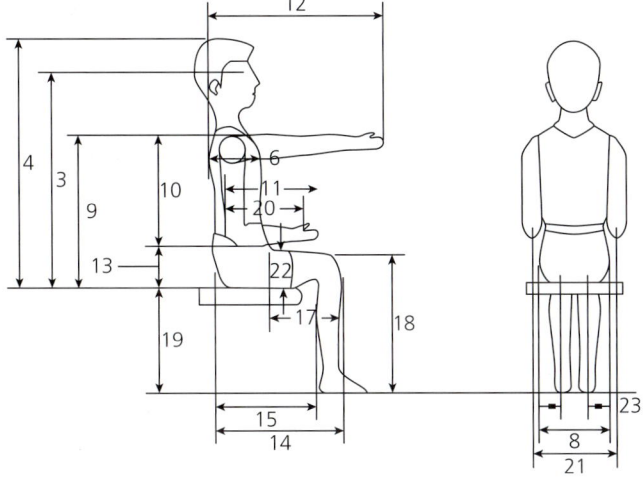

Dimension	5%	50%	95%
3	374	472	512
4	415	510	583
6	161	178	195
8	269	290	318
9	299	394	422
10	274	292	412
12	460	485	501
14	347	372	406
15	272	290	330
18	302	332	355
19	258	288	296
21	312	334	356

Figure 12.4 Anthropometric data for a seated child

KEY POINTS

- Designing without considering the context leads to a final product that does not fully meet the needs of the user.
- Insufficient research can lead to inaccurate primary data and a product that does not fulfil all of the users' or stakeholders' needs.
- Designers in today's society must consider the effect of the product on the environment and society.
- The use of anthropometric data ensures products 'fit' the intended users as much as possible.

12.5 Exploring and developing ideas and testing, critically analysing and evaluating work

Testing and evaluating ideas

Innovative design is about exploring new ways of doing things or trying to approach problems from different angles or perspectives. This is often one of the most difficult aspects of the design process because we are so used to seeing, using and living with existing products that we automatically re-create these when trying to design new products.

Another common practice is to think of a new way of solving a problem or to come up with a new idea or design for something, but then stick to this first idea you have instead of trying to develop and refine it. This is called **design fixation**.

To avoid design fixation and to get different perspectives on a problem in order to explore new ideas, designers can use different sources of information to help them:

- **Focus groups** – a focus group is made up of different people who each give their views and experiences of a problem or discuss their perceptions and attitudes towards an existing product or idea.
- **Existing solutions** – by looking at existing solutions to a problem or products designed to solve similar problems and considering which aspects work well or need improvement.
- **Biomimicry** – by looking at different aspects of the natural world, such as naturally occurring structures and features. Then considering how these methods, shapes or forms could be incorporated into the design. For more on how biomimicry works in design, see Chapter 2.

Once designers have explored different ideas, they can begin to come up with possible solutions to the problem that draw inspiration from the different avenues of exploration. As one idea begins to come to life through sketches, models or thinking, new ideas can develop and emerge as improved iterations of the original idea.

This creative process of selecting ideas, elements, materials and manufacturing techniques from initial ideas and using them in new ways to explore and produce newer and better designs or ideas that work in different ways is called **development**. Development is an important part of the creative design process where designers try out new things and make creative decisions based on what works and what does not.

Modelling is an integral part of the development process. Modelling allows designers to try out and test ideas or parts of designs by making scale models. Modelling and testing allows designers to see if a design will work or not and then make further decisions or developments in light of this. It may also show that a particular design will not work and lead the designer to abandon this idea in favour of another. Models and ideas that do not work are just as valid and important in the design process as successes and should not be viewed as a failure. More can often be learnt from a failed or unsuccessful model, and it is only by taking these risks and trying new things that designers can come up with innovative ideas. It may take numerous trials and failed attempts at something before a solution is reached, but each step along the way is a vital part of the development process.

Critical analysis and evaluation

Critical analysis and evaluation are another method of assessing the suitability of a design idea. They go hand in hand with development of ideas, but can also be done at any point in the design process. With each new idea or development of an existing idea, a critical analysis will assess the suitability of the design against given criteria. During the design process this will be the specification which the designer will refer back to constantly to check it meets the necessary requirements set out.

The critical analysis can be carried out by an individual, but is best done by a group of people such as the stakeholders or potential users of the product, in order to gain a range of views and perspectives. Usually, once the design ideas have been narrowed down and developed into two or three possible solutions, these will be drawn up neatly and/or modelled to give a clear picture of what the final product will look like and how it will function. These will then be presented to the user group to examine and try out.

The list of criteria will depend on the product, but will cover things such as:

- Product function
  - Does the product do what it is supposed to?
  - How well does it do this?
  - Is it easy to use?
  - Is it comfortable to use?
- Aesthetics of the product
  - Does it look appealing?
  - Does it feel nice?
- Anthropometrics and ergonomics
  - Is it the correct height, length, diameter, etc?
  - Does it suit all users?
  - Can it be adjusted to suit different users?
  - Will it fit where it is supposed to?
- Cost
  - Will the materials be expensive to purchase?
  - Will the manufacturing costs be acceptable?
  - Will the final price of the product be acceptable?
- Materials
  - Are the materials used of high quality?
  - Are the materials suitable for the product?
  - Are the materials easy to source/readily available?
- Construction methods
  - Is it well made?
  - Are the skills/processes required to make it readily available?
  - Is it quick to manufacture?
- Health and safety
  - Is it safe to use?
  - Does it meet relevant health and safety standards?
- Environmental considerations
  - Are the materials from a sustainable source?
  - Can the product be easily disassembled?
  - Can the materials be recycled?
  - Are the processes used harmful to the environment?

Refinement and modification

Following the critical analysis, the designer can re-evaluate the suitability of the prototype and make further changes or modifications to the design in order to address any areas where the design may not be meeting the criteria or is not performing well. Once the refinements have been made, the modified and revised design can then be re-analysed. If further improvements are still needed the design will be modified again and the same process repeated. Each new 'iteration' of the design should be a slightly improved version of the last, until the final iteration, which should meet all the criteria as much as possible and is the best possible solution. This cycle of refinement, analysis and re-designing is known as **'iterative design'**.

KEY WORD

Iterative design: a repeated cycle of quickly implementing designs or prototypes, gathering feedback and refining the design.

In groups of four or five:

- On your own, draw a design for a simple product, such as a toothbrush (5 minutes).
- In groups, pass your idea onto the next person in the group. Modify and refine the other person's design in one way (5 minutes).
- Repeat the process until you get your own design back, then draw a final idea incorporating the modifications done by others.
  Would you have thought of those things yourself?

12.6 Investigating and analysing the work of past and present professionals and companies

All successful designers will look at previous products or influences from significant design movements throughout the research and development of a new concept or iteration of a product. Inspiration can be gained about how technology has been used, how materials have been manipulated and, most importantly, what lessons can be learnt from previous successes and failures. There are a huge amount of influential designers and successful companies, many of which you may come across when researching your non-examined assessment (NEA) context, but some of the most well-known are introduced below.

Airbus

Airbus is a European company best known for their aircraft, but who also develop helicopters and have divisions that focus on military equipment and space travel. Airbus's range of civil passenger aircraft are used by most airline companies. Their flagship model is the A380, the world's largest passenger aircraft with the capacity to carry up to 800 passengers.

The development of this aircraft caused aeronautical engineers a huge amount of issues related to the sheer size and weight of the aircraft. Many composite materials were used to reduce the weight, and engineers even looked at biomimetics for inspiration. They studied how the structure and shape of an eagle's wing overcame similar issues, and this resulted in wing tips being installed on the A380's wings. Without these the wing span of the plane would be too large for any airport to accommodate the plane.

Generative design is used to optimise components or parts to reduce weight while maintaining strength. Airbus use CAD technology to create components that can be 3D printed in a variety of materials, particularly titanium due its excellent strength-to-weight properties. For example, the 3D printed version of the engine door cover hinge on the A380 is 65 per cent lighter than the previous cast version. For more on generative design, see the CAD section of Chapter 1.

Airbus components are manufactured all over the globe. The wing units are manufactured in Britain, the rear fuselage in France and the front fuselage in Germany. Transportation of goods is a vital part of the Airbus company's model. In 1984 Airbus manufactured their own super transporter, known as

Figure 12.5 Airbus A380

'Beluga' due to its distinctive whale shaped nose. This helped reduce the environmental impact, due to its huge capacity.

Airbus are constantly developing technology to improve the fuel efficiency of their planes, and reduce their carbon emissions and negative environmental impact. Airbus have already created an electric prototype aircraft and are working with other major manufacturers such as Rolls Royce and Siemens in the development of the first hybrid aircraft.

Figure 12.6 Airbus Beluga

Apple

Apple Computers is one of the most successful companies in the world. One thing that makes Apple stand out from its competitors is the importance that they place on innovation and design, and their constant drive to create the best products.

Apple were pioneers in the use of graphical user interfaces (GUIs). This concept of a desktop that has icons or small images representing files, folders and discs first appeared on the Apple Lisa computer in 1983, along with a cursor that was controlled by a mouse. Although we are now more familiar with touch-screen technology, the cursor and mouse have stood the test of time.

Apple products have an instantly recognisable style, using consistent shapes, colours and materials. However, early Apple products had similar uninspiring aesthetics as those found on most home computers and electronic devices. In the mid-1990s Apple appointed a British industrial designer, Jonathan Ives, who was responsible for the styling of the first iPod and iMac. Suddenly, **aesthetics** and the user experience were at the forefront of the company.

Many have drawn comparisons between Ives' style and that of the German designer Dieter Rams. Dieter Rams was head of design of the company Braun and is well known for creating the 'ten principles of good design', many of which can be seen influencing Apple products.

Apple are renowned for their product launches, which command worldwide interest and create a media frenzy. However, this has led to the problem of **obsolescence** (see Chapter 1). Apple has received criticism regarding software updates that do not work on older devices, and for developing their own port for connecting to peripheral devices. Most other electronic companies make use of a standard USB charging port, whereas Apple have had a host of unique systems, preventing the use of standard chargers, and more recently even headphones.

James Dyson

James Dyson is an English industrial designer renowned for creating innovative products by using new technologies and applying engineering principles. Initially trained as a furniture and industrial designer, Dyson's early work included the 'ball barrow', a variation on the standard wheelbarrow that used a large inflatable ball instead of a wheel to spread the load of the barrow, making it easier to push on soft ground and increase its manoeuvrability.

> **KEY WORDS**
>
> **Aesthetics**: factors that determine the looks of a product, including colour, size and texture.
>
> **Obsolescence**: when a product becomes unusable or out of date.

> **Activity**
>
> Use the internet to research the work of Ives and Rams and draw your own conclusions on the apparent similarities.

Figure 12.7 The original Dyson DC01

Dyson is well known for his approach to designing products that improve on the performance of existing solutions. Before the DC01 vacuum cleaner was released, dust from vacuuming was collected in a replaceable and disposable bag that was mounted on the vacuum cleaner. Dyson identified that this system performed poorly because as the bag became more full, the suction became less effective. Dyson had witnessed a local timber yard that had a large cyclonic extractor fitted for collecting wood dust and saw the similarities in the role they performed. He began to model and develop a miniaturised cyclone system capable of collecting dust without the need for a bag.

He went through a huge number of design iterations including 5127 prototype models. He struggled to gain market interest in the UK, and Dyson licensed his design to a Japanese company, using the funds raised from its sales to finally, 14 years after beginning its development, launch the DC01 in the UK.

Dyson has launched many other domestic products, including washing machines, fans and heaters, hairdryers and lighting. Dyson has a unique facility in Malmesbury where designers and engineers develop and test new products. In order to have confidence in the durability of their products they all undergo extensive testing before being released.

Dyson has always been an active supporter of design education. There is a Dyson School of Design Engineering at Imperial University and he has established an international competition to inspire the future design engineers. Winners of this award have included the 'eco bike helmet' and 'MOM', the inflatable incubator for use in refugee camps.

Figure 12.8 Dyson ball barrow

Phillippe Starck

Phillippe Starck is one of the most well-known and influential designers of recent times. His early career involved him manufacturing inflatable products, before establishing 'Starck products' in 1979. He released many designs himself, but is perhaps better known for his commissioned work for Italian homeware manufacturer Alessi and the lighting company FLOS.

His most commercially successful product is the aluminium lemon squeezer known as 'Juicy Salif'. It is said to be based on the shape of a squid, and its initial designs were sketched upon a napkin. It is an elaborate design for a lemon squeezer, but Starck has been quoted in saying 'My juicer is not meant to squeeze lemons; it is meant to start conversations'.

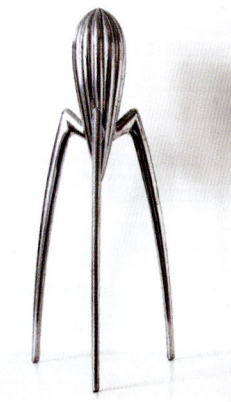

Figure 12.9 Juicy Salif

Other designs for Alessi that share similar aesthetic elements include the 'Hot Bertta' kettle, the 'Poe' radio and the 'Flo's lamp 'Ara'.

Starck's work is well known for pioneering manufacturing techniques and using materials that you would not immediately associate with a product. For example, the injection moulded polycarbonate chair, the 'Louis Ghost', is a one-piece moulded chair that uses no other fixings or fittings. Starck used transparent plastic, a material usually associated with cheap disposable products, in the manufacture of a high-end desirable piece of furniture.

Starck has also designed buildings, interiors, clothing, luggage and watches. One of his more controversial designs is the building known as the Asahi beer hall, in Tokyo. Part of the Asahi brewery headquarters, it features a large golden flame on its roof and is now considered one of Tokyo's most recognisable buildings.

Matthew Williamson

Matthew Williamson was born in Manchester in 1971, and it has been said that the grey nature of the city at that time inspired the use of colour in his collections. This is a major element in his signature style and was clear in his **debut collection** – Electric Angels in 1997.

Figure 12.10 Asahi beer hall

While studying at Central St. Martins, London, Matthew did a placement with the designer Zandra Rhodes, who was known for her use of chiffon and silk, dramatic use of colour and **embellishment** in her work. This strengthened his resolve in continuing to experiment with colour and texture. After graduating he was offered the position of accessories designer for the high-street store Monsoon. His bold use of colour, print, texture and heavy embellishment has had a lasting impact in the high street.

Williamson travelled to exotic locations to seek inspiration for his work. In particular, countries like Africa, India and Morocco have played a significant role in developing his signature style. He has a clear sense of who his customer is; she is a free spirit, a **bohemian**. His vision is to make women beautiful, to stop and take note, feel feminine and to enjoy wearing his designs. To him, fashion is about the woman not just the clothes.

Figure 12.11 Matthew Williamson's first collection, 'Electric Angels' in 1997, consisted of 14 pieces made in shades of shocking pink, orange and turquoise.

Williamson has stayed true to his original style and does not necessarily follow current trends. While colour has always been at the forefront of his designs, print and embellishments are important elements too. His prints often feature nature – dragonflies and butterflies, peacock feathers, as well as exotic plants. He has been widely credited with bringing colour and print back to the high street. His work has been highly influential and inspirational across all aspects of **contemporary fashion**, and more recently, interior design.

Activity

Conduct some further research in to the work of Matthew Williamson. Design a print inspired by the work of Matthew Williamson. This could be a placement (single) print or a fabric with an all-over design. Suggest what type of products the print could be used on. This could be an item of clothing, any accessories or a soft furnishing product. Extend your design task by sketching the product to show off your print design.

Activity

Using one of the companies or designers above, create a visual timeline of the key products manufactured.

12.7 Using different design strategies

You will be used to creating a range of design ideas both in your NEA work in Key Stage 4, but also much earlier in your technology lessons. The ability to create interesting and innovative designs relies heavily on the designer's ability to come up with unusual, outlandish and sometimes utterly crazy ideas. Sometimes this is difficult because we are afraid or embarrassed of designing ridiculous or silly products, or things that would not work. It is easier, therefore, to play it safe and come up with something the same as, or very similar to what already exists. Thinking like this stifles good design and leads to unexciting and mundane designs that follow 'the norm'.

As designers we should not be afraid of creating weird, stupid and crazy designs, but to use these ideas as a valid and valuable part of the designing thought process.

Many famous or successful inventions and designs have originated from mad ideas that someone has had. Even when the initial idea may have been not a particularly good one, there are often elements of the design which are worth exploring further and developing. This may lead on to a revised and improved version of the design or a completely new and different idea altogether.

Coming up with lots of design ideas is not always easy. The inspiration may be there, but often this is not enough. There are some simple strategies we can use to help us come up with a wide range of ideas.

Brainstorming

Brainstorming involves thinking of as many different ideas as possible and getting them written down or sketched as quickly as possible. The sketches are basic and should mean the designer can jump to the next idea, then to the next quickly while it is fresh in their mind. By being spontaneous and putting down what immediately comes into your head, many ideas can be summoned.

Brainstorming is often done in groups. Mind maps/spray diagrams are often used as a way of brainstorming ideas.

> **KEY WORD**
>
> **Brainstorming**: thinking of as many different ideas as possible and getting them written down or sketched as quickly as possible.

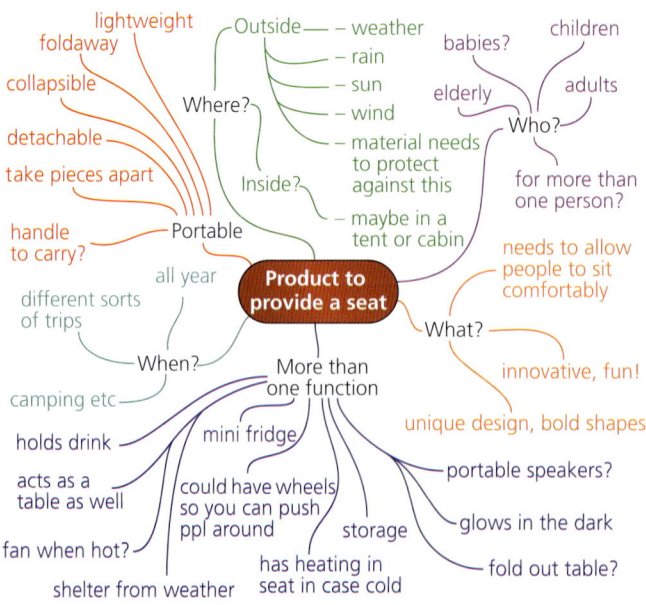

Figure 12.12 Mind map/spray diagram

When brainstorming ideas, the neatness of the sketches or writing is unimportant – it is about getting information and ideas down on paper as quickly as possible. The reasoning behind this is that during the brainstorming process, one idea often leads onto another which may be an off-shoot or development of the previous one. At this stage the more ideas that you can produce, the better.

Think of the solution to a design problem as a target and the ideas as shots at the target. The bullseye is the ideal (perfect design solution). The more shots you take at the target the more likely you are to get nearer the centre or hit the bullseye. In the same way, the more ideas you have – the more likely you are to have a really good idea that gets close to the centre of the target.

This is not the end of the design process but just the beginning! Once you have come up with an idea that is innovative and exciting you can follow this idea by refining, developing and experimenting with it to improve the idea and move it even closer to the centre of the target.

Collaboration

Many designers work in **collaboration** (in pairs or in groups). Usually, a design business will employ a number of designers who work together on specific design projects. For example, Seymour Powell (Richard Seymour and Dick Powell) invented the world's first cordless kettle for Tefal, and the pocket mobile phone. Similar collaborative firms include Bostock and Pollitt and Brahm and Swamp.

Figure 12.13 The first cordless kettles, as designed by Seymour and Powell

By discussing, sharing and working with each other designers can get a different perspective on a problem and one person's ideas will often feed the other. This process can mean designers bounce ideas back and forth between each other and refine elements or go down completely new avenues of investigation to explore different concepts and come up with designs they would not have thought of on their own.

Once a designer has created some initial ideas or concepts, they will often create a focus group comprising of the client, user and main stakeholders and present these ideas to them in order to gain feedback on the designs. This gives them a clear picture of which ideas are worth pursuing further or should be dropped. Ideally, the focus group should be involved throughout the design process to ensure this clear vision continues. This process of involving the user throughout the process to ensure the product meets their needs is known as user-centred design.

User-centred design

User-centred design is where the needs, wants, and requirements of the user are looked at and checked at every stage of the design and development process. This puts the user at the 'centre' of the design process with a view to getting the design closer to the user's requirements first time, so that less refinement and modifications are needed further along in the design process.

> **KEY WORDS**
>
> **User-centred design (USD)**: looking at and checking the needs, wants, and requirements of the user at every stage of the design process.
> **Design collaboration**: a number of designers working together on specific design projects.

The user-centred design process has four main stages:

- Specify the context of use – identify the users of the product, what they will use it for, and under what conditions it will be used.
- Specify requirements – identify any user goals that must be met for the product to be successful.
- Create design solutions – this part of the process may be done in stages, building from a rough concept to a complete design.
- Evaluate designs – evaluation through usability testing with actual users.

Systems thinking

Systems thinking is when you do not just think of the product you are designing, but consider it as part of a larger system or experience. Often when we buy a product, using it is only part of the experience. The opening of the packaging, maintenance of the product, use of the product and disposal or exchange of the product are all part of the experience of owning a product. By applying systems thinking, the designer considers the whole problem and how to provide the best service to the user.

For example, instead of just designing a mobile phone that is easy to use, looks good and works well, the designer will consider how the phone will be ordered, delivered and packaged to the user. They will consider how easy it is to download apps, sync to other devices, connect to the internet, etc. and how easy it is for the user to get technical help, get repairs carried out, upgrade, exchange and recycle the mobile phone. By ensuring the whole experience of owning the product from beginning to end is good – the user is more likely to purchase their next product from them.

12.8 Developing, communicating, recording and justifying design ideas

The successful communication of your thoughts and ideas is a crucial part of the design process. The process of creating an idea and developing it through to manufacture involves many different teams of people, and so the ability to communicate your thoughts clearly is important. In industry, designers will often need to pitch their early concepts to investors and stakeholders, explore customer and market feedback and test early iterations of their design. All of these stages of the design process require different styles of communication and all will have their place as you work through your NEA.

Formal and informal 2D and 3D drawing

Most designers will start creating concepts for an idea by freehand sketching. In the early stages, these sketches will be informal, and in some cases incomplete. As the designer quickly sketches shapes and basic detail, they may use brief annotation or suggest movement with the use of arrows. These freehand sketches are completed without the use of templates or drawing aids and there may be many lines on the page helping the designer refine the shape or profile of the drawing. These early sketches are sometimes referred to as thumbnails, as they tend to be small sketches that lack detail, but are effective ways to communicate a designer's initial thoughts.

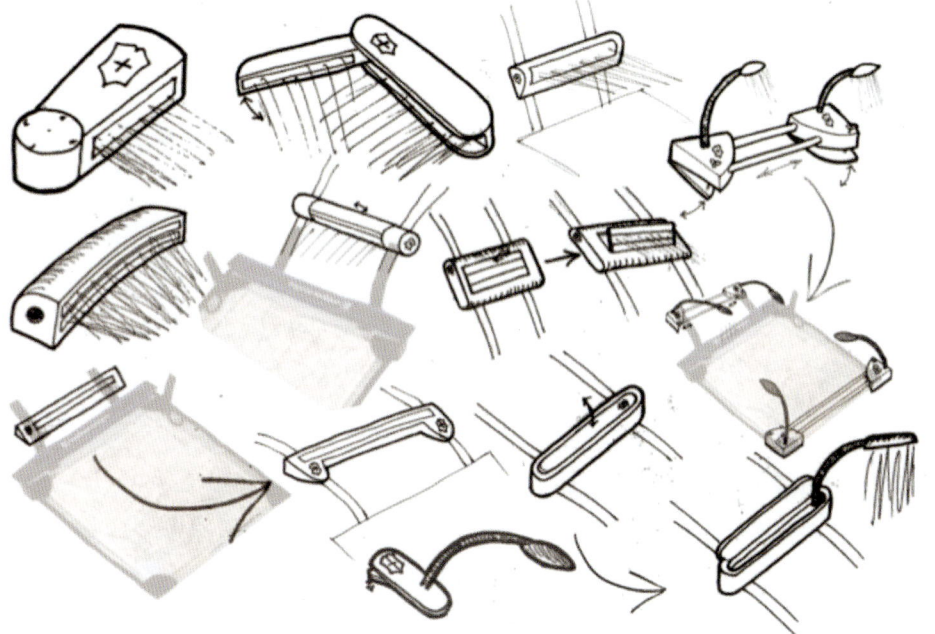

Figure 12.14 Thumbnail sketches used to present early design iterations

There are no rules when referring to informal drawings, and they can be 2D or 3D in style. 2D drawings are 'flat' and they generally show one view and no detail about depth. They are used when a designer may be developing the profile of a shape or providing detail of the front of a product such as arrangement of buttons, logos, etc.

3D drawings provide more detail and can be presented as either oblique, isometric or perspective drawings.

Oblique drawings

Oblique drawings are a very basic form of 3D drawing. They simply involve turning an existing 2D drawing in to 3D by adding or projecting a thickness to two sides of the original drawing. Using a 45° degree set square, lines of equal length are drawn from the extremities of the top and side of the original drawing and then joined up. It is an effective way of showing a little more detail, but will not look as accurate as other 3D drawing techniques.

Isometric drawing

Isometric drawing is more useful than oblique, as you can start to present detail that is slightly more in proportion. It also allows detail to be projected from all faces, allowing the drawing to provide greater information. Isometric drawing uses an angle of 30° for the projected lines – again a template or drawing aid can be used, and often isometric paper can be useful to help layout designs. Dimensions can be easily added to an isometric drawing.

Figure 12.15 An early 2D sketch of a vehicle

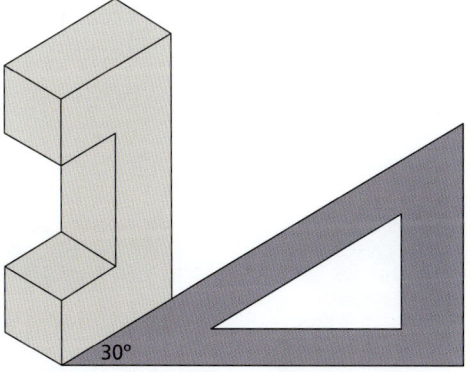

Figure 12.16 A 30° set square showing the angle used in an isometric drawing

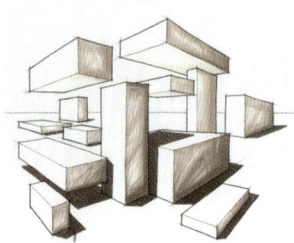

Figure 12.17 Two-point perspective

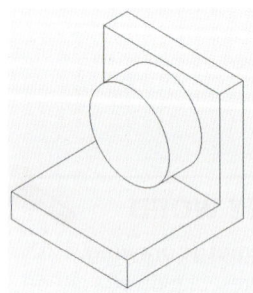

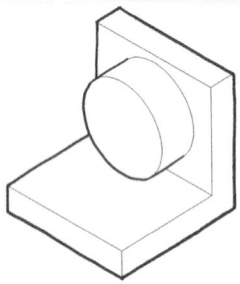

Figure 12.18 Thick and thin line technique

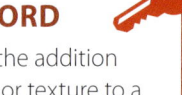

KEY WORD

Render: the addition of colour or texture to a design.

Perspective drawing

Perspective drawing is the most realistic representation of a product, as it mimics the way in which we see objects in reality, with objects appearing small as they become further away. When creating a perspective drawing, a vanishing point is created on an imaginary horizon line. The projected lines move away from the front edge of a drawing towards the vanishing point. Two-point perspective is similar and uses a vanishing point on either end of the horizon line. Dimensions are hard to add to a perspective drawing because the length of lines are not true representations of size.

Throughout the generation and presentation of ideas you will find that designers use a combination of media to communicate. Pencils are usually used to create the initial thumbnail sketches, before moving into black line as an idea becomes more refined. Shading can be added to suggest 3D features or marker pens can be used to suggest colour.

Thick and thin line technique

One of the most effective techniques that can be easily applied to initial sketches is the use of the thick and thin line technique. A thin black line can be used to ink in the details of the drawing and then a thicker line is used on all edges, where the detail on the adjacent edge is not visible. This is always the outside edge of a design, but may also incorporate the edges of shelves, etc.

Colour and shadow

Colour and shadow are some of the trickier elements to add to a sketch, but they are hugely important when representing fabric or presenting a textile idea. Coloured pencils and marker pens are both effective ways to add colour to a design. Applying flat colour to a surface is fairly straightforward, but adding shadow, depth or shading is more difficult. Marker pens can be used, and specific **rendering** markers are capable of providing a range of tone. More commonly 3D CAD systems are now being used to add colour to designs.

There are no hard and fast rules about the best sketch or communication method to use for a particular purpose. It is more important for designers to be able to communicate clearly and effectively. It can take many years to become proficient and natural, but just like any skill, it comes down to lots of practice and experimentation. There are lots of product designers that have uploaded tutorials for sketching and rendering; one of the most accessible is www.sketch-a-day.com.

Figure 12.19 Design sketches can be enhanced with the use of colour.

Figure 12.20 Combining marker pens and coloured pencils can be effective.

System and schematic diagrams

Not all design thinking is presented as visual sketches. When designing or planning systems or electronic circuits a different style of communication is more appropriate.

Systems diagrams are used to plan and lay out an overall solution to a problem. They are similar to a flow diagram in the way in which they present the solution in a series of sequential stages, but they are usually more general and give an overview of the system, rather than specific detail. A simple system diagram breaks a task or process down into an input, process and output. You can see examples of system diagrams in Chapter 3.

Schematics are a more detailed communication method and can be used to present a visual representation of a circuit or system. They use standardised circuit diagram symbols that can be universally recognised. For more on circuit diagrams, see Chapter 3.

Annotated sketches

It takes a great deal of skill and talent to create sketches which are able to fully communicate the thoughts of the designer. It is possible to suggest movement with arrows and apply shading to represent a material or surfaces texture, but the addition of annotation is needed to ensure that others can fully interpret a designer's ideas. Annotations should be clear and relevant to the design and used to provide clarification of the details of a design. This could refer to choice of material, finish or construction, as well as providing information about a function or feature that cannot be represented in a sketch. If a design has parallel features with an existing product, annotations could highlight this, for example 'USB charging socket' or 'removable battery compartment'. Weight and texture are also important elements to comment on, as they cannot be gained from a sketch.

Figure 12.21 CAD renders can be hard to distinguish from real products.

KEY WORD

Schematic: a visual representation of a circuit or system.

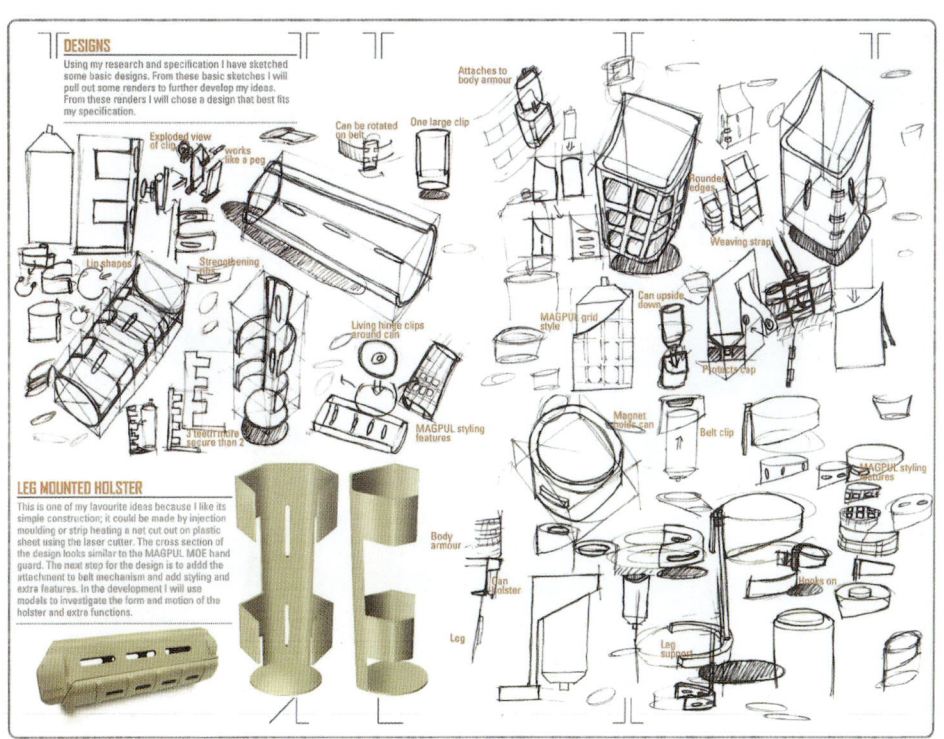

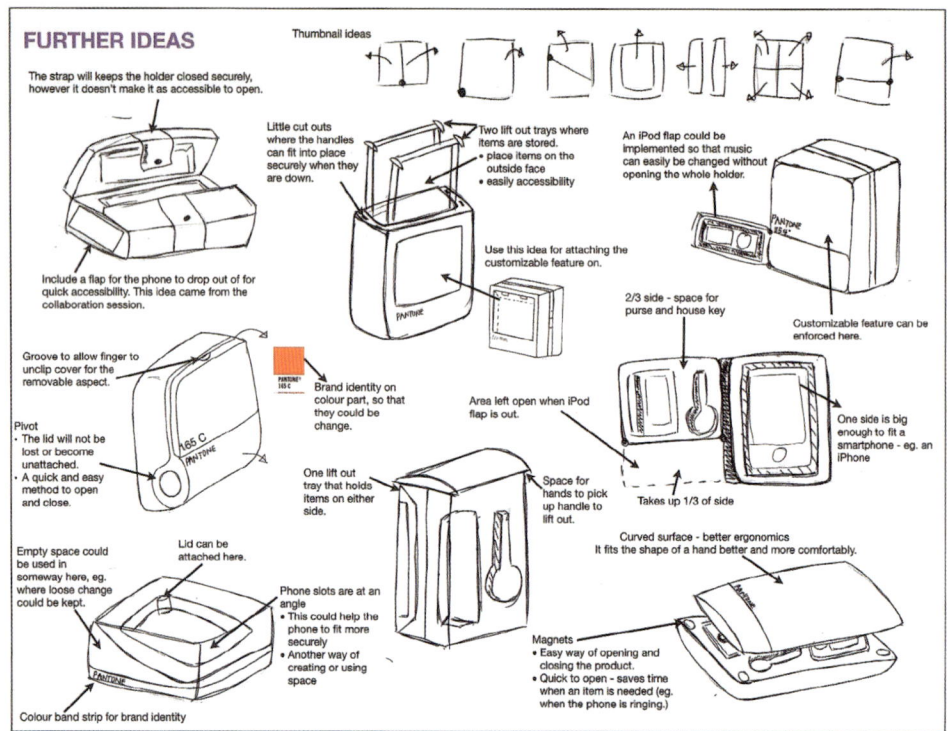

Figure 12.22 Annotated sketches for a design concept

In addition to annotations, designers working with fabrics and textiles may find it useful to attach swatches or small pieces of a specific fabric to their initial design ideas.

Figure 12.23 Fabric swatches are used to help present textile ideas.

Exploded diagrams

An exploded diagram is used to help communicate how the component parts of a product come together during assembly. If you have ever built a Lego® toy or assembled a piece of flat-pack furniture you will already be familiar with their principle. They are often found in instruction leaflets, where they are used to explain the order of assembly, but they are also useful to identify parts and part numbers in large complex products, such as engines and washing machines.

Exploded diagrams are challenging to complete by hand as you need to have a clear idea about how the drawing is going to look before starting. Many people find it easier to use a lightbox or tracing paper to help. Starting with a complete isometric or 3D drawing of your idea, trace each part and move the paper a small amount before sketching the next component.

Figure 12.24 Lego instructions

It is more straightforward to create exploded drawings with the help of a CAD program, as it is possible to copy, paste, group and move components into place easily. If you have drawn each of your components accurately and to scale, some CAD programs will explode the model for you and may even animate the process.

Models

Models are an excellent way to further develop an idea from an initial sketch. They can be used to model a complete product in full size or to a given scale, and they are also useful to test a small element of a design, such as a hinge or individual component.

Cardboard modelling

Cardboard is an excellent material to use when making initial models as it is cheap, readily available and can be easily cut, scored and joined with basic workshop tools. Cardboard has the added benefit of coming in thicknesses that can easily be used to represent acrylic and can also be laser cut, allowing designers to produce accurate 3D models.

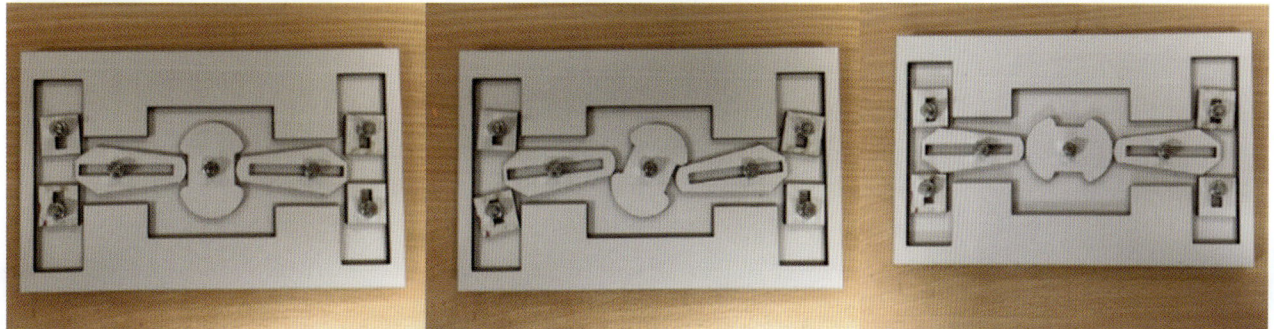

Figure 12.25 Card modelling of a mechanism

Foam modelling

Foam core is a paper and board material that is more rigid than cardboard and has the advantage of being faced with white or black paper. It can also be scored and joined easily and is frequently used in architectural models.

If a designer is looking to develop a model that is more organic in nature, they will most likely move into working with polyurethane foam. This is lightweight and can be easily cut, shaped and joined. This allows designers to make 3D representations that can be held and interacted with. It enables an element of ergonomics to be explored.

Figure 12.26 Blue foam modelling of a radio concept

Polyurethane foam is available in many different densities. The denser varieties can be machined by a CNC router and subsequently finished and sprayed to represent a finished prototype. These prototypes, or block models, can be hugely useful as they can give third parties and stakeholders a realistic impression of what the final prototype may look like.

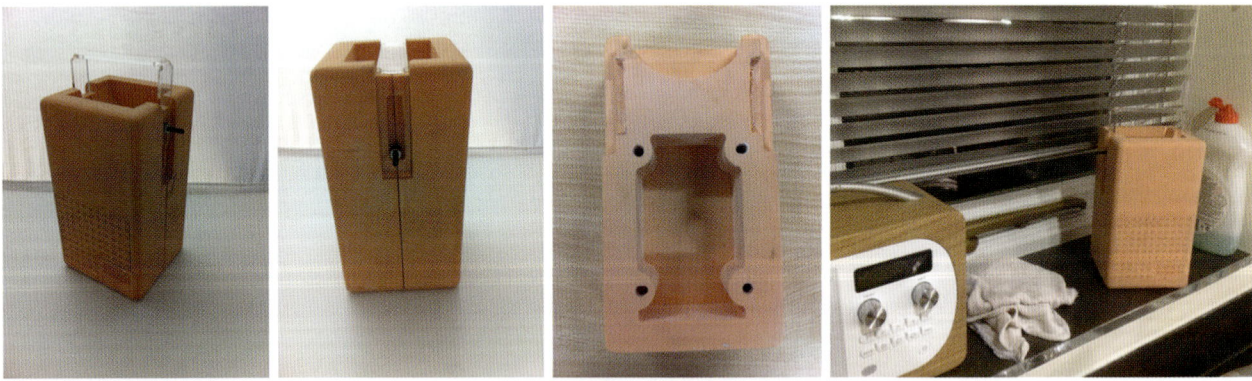

Figure 12.27 The radio concept being modelled and tested in dense polyurethane foam

Toiles

When working with textiles a designer may produce a toile – a full-scale version of the final piece, but manufactured from a cheaper material. A toile gives the designer an opportunity to fit the garment or design on to a model in order to make any further adjustments. They can also be used to determine the positioning of zips and fastenings. For more on producing a toile, see Chapter 11.

Figure 12.28 A textile toile

Electronic circuits

If **modelling** a system or electronic circuit a breadboard would be an appropriate method of developing and testing whether the design will work. It is useful, as it is quick to place and remove components, and multiple breadboards can be joined together if necessary. When the circuit is working correctly a formal schematic can be drawn up.

Presentations

Throughout the design process there will be occasions when design ideas need to be presented to a third party or stakeholder. Digital presentations, when a series of slides can be linked together and presented, are commonplace. Digital presentations have the advantage of being able to be emailed or shared electronically, and can also feature animations or videos to enhance the presentation.

Figure 12.29 Testing a circuit using a breadboard

Figure 12.30 A design student using presentation boards at a competition

Designers may also use physical presentation boards to convey and communicate their ideas to clients. These boards are usually a large format, such as A2 or A1, and may include initial sketches, exploded diagrams and 3D rendered images of their product.

Written notes

Written notes are useful when a designer is formalising their thoughts or providing a detailed summary of design decisions made. They are particularly important when a third party is viewing the work, as they would not have the benefit of understanding all aspects of the creative process to that date. In your NEA, you may find it useful to provide detailed notes throughout your folio to back up your informal design annotations.

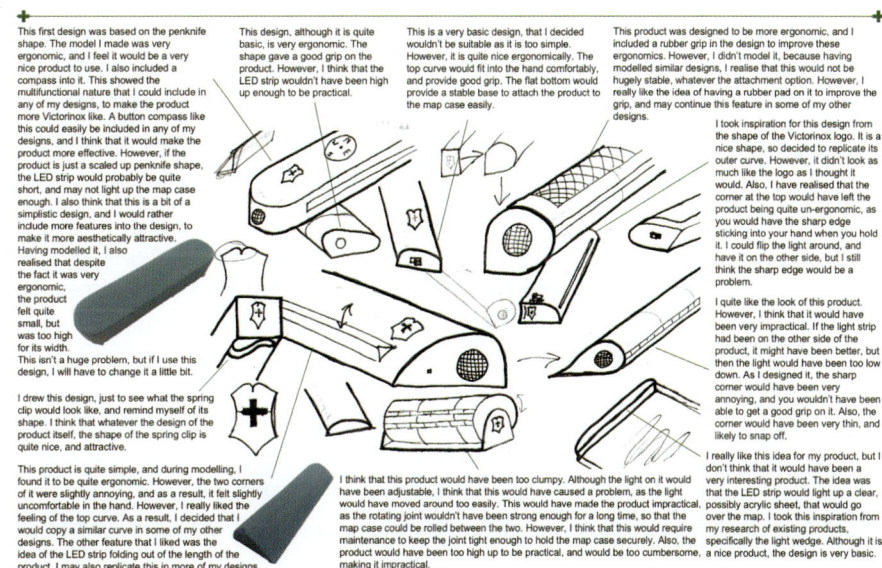

Figure 12.31 Folio page with written notes supporting the thumbnail sketches

Flowcharts

A **flowchart** is a graphical representation of a process or series of stages within a system. Flowcharts are generally written instructions or statements linked together by an arrow to indicate the order of the sequence. They are made easier to understand by the use of common shapes indicating different actions, as seen in Chapter 3, Figure 3.13. Decisions within a flowchart are often used as quality control checks, such as checking whether a dimension is correct or seeing if an input signal from a switch has been pressed.

They can be used when planning simple electronic programs or used to show the sequence of activities when manufacturing a component or product.

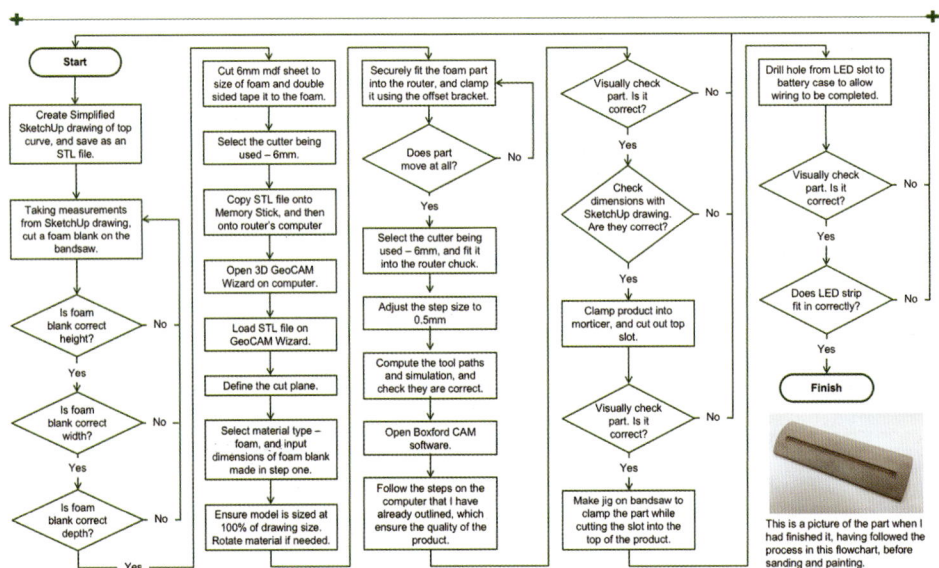

Figure 12.32 Flowchart

Working drawings

Working drawings are technical documents that provide details about a particular design or product. They can include information such as relevant dimensions, scale, materials and details about parts and components. They are sometimes referred to as engineering drawings, and they can be presented in many ways, but generally include a collection of 2D views of a product where relevant dimensions are included in mm. These are commonly referred to as orthographic drawings. They have a front view, side view and aerial view or plan. These three views will provide enough information for a third party to attempt successful manufacture. They can include sectional areas where details about internal features can be illustrated, and some also include a parts list.

The format and layout of the drawing should be based on the document published by the British Standards Institute. The use of a standardised approach means that the drawings should be able to be reliably interpreted.

Detailed working drawings can be easily generated from 3D CAD models at the click of a button.

When working with textiles, a working drawing is referred to as a 'flat'. This is a fully dimensioned drawing that includes technical details.

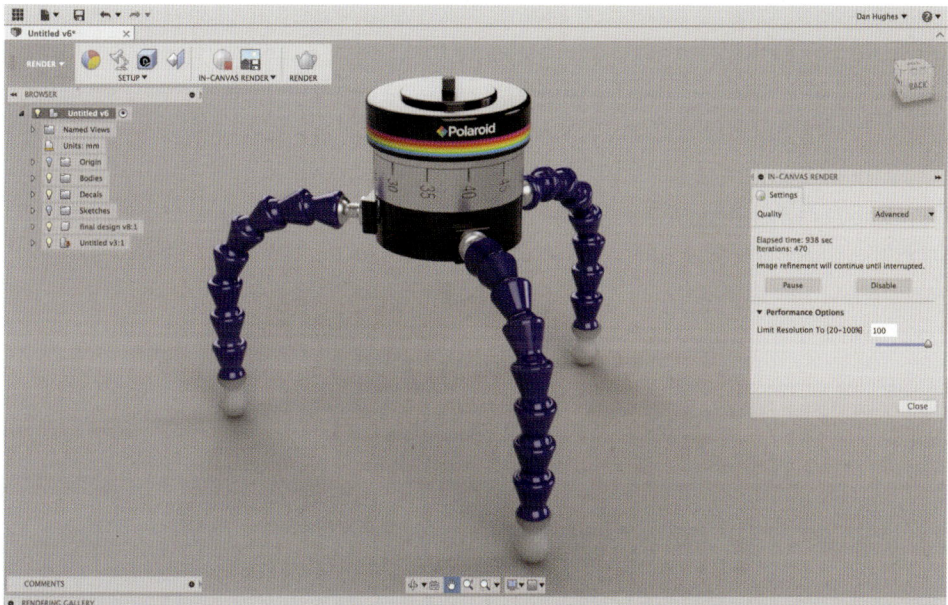

Figure 12.33 A rendered 3D CAD model of a tripod

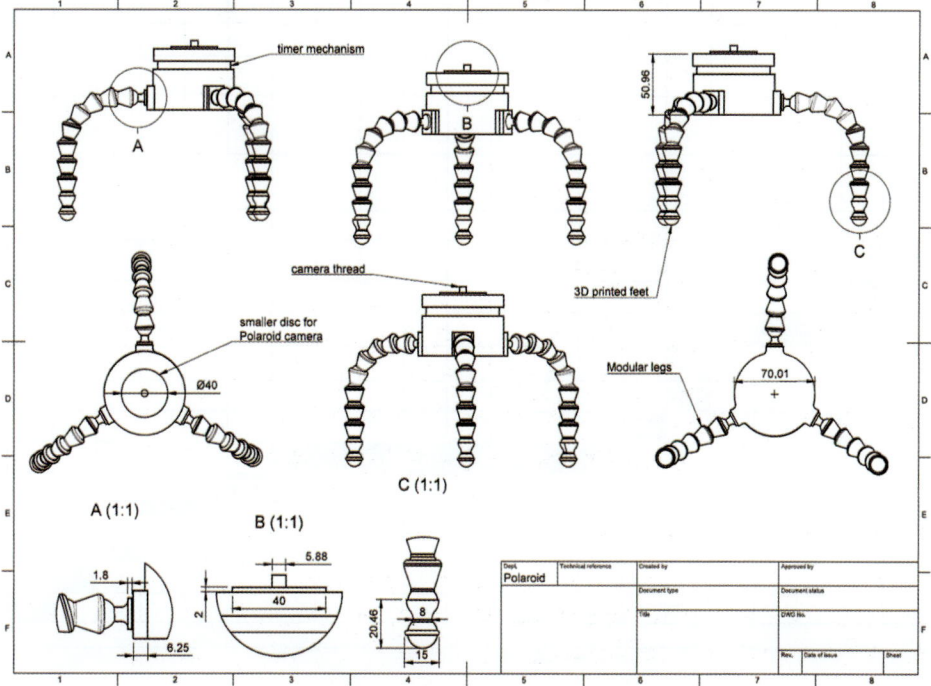

Figure 12.34 The working drawing generated from the tripod 3D CAD model

Schedules

Schedules play an important part in the design process, especially when in industry and when working to specific deadlines. It is sensible to plan out the time available to complete a project before commencing. This is often done through the use of a Gantt chart or timeline. In a Gantt chart the available time is laid out on one axis of a table, with the stages or tasks needed to be completed on another. This gives a rough plan of an extended period of time and helps the designer stay on target for completion. A task may take longer than anticipated and a designer may find that they will need to edit and amend the chart as the project progresses.

Other schedules can be used to plan when a particular resource, such as a machine, may be needed or when a material or component would need to be delivered. Manufacturing schedules become critical when working on a larger project or sharing a resource, such as a workshop or studio.

Design brief & Gantt chart – On this slide I will summarise the design brief and analyse the direction the project will go in and also create a Gantt chart to clarify the order and time frame of the project.

What – I'm going to make and design a beautifully hand crafted surfboard stand that reflects the authentic, elegant and natural style of surfing.
Why – The problem with surfboards today is that they are extremely brittle, since the 1960s boards have been made from fibreglass and foam, but this means they can easily crack and dent which lets the water in and the problem gets worse and worse. Therefore the purpose of making a surfboard stand is to help the user protect their board from everyday knocks.
Who – I'm going to design and make this surfboard stand for a good family friend of ours, Andy Strowbridge, he is a keen surfer that lives on the north coast of Cornwall.
Where – the client is planning to keep his surfboard in his living room, however this could change and he may move it into his garage depending on space. His living room is decorated with deep reds and dark wood, it has quite a traditional African feel to it.
When – As the Gantt chart suggests (if I stick to the timings) I will have completed the whole project in 25 weeks, however this is unrealistic because there are bound to be problems along the way, and communication with the client may be slow because we can't meet face to face.

Stage	1	2	3	4	5	6	7	8	9	10	11	12	13	14	15	16	17	18	19	20	21	22	23	24	25
Problem and contexts	█																								
Task analysis	█																								
Product analysis		█																							
Investigation into environment			█																						
Research into possible techniques/materials			█																						
Ergonomic and anthropometric research			█																						
Specification				█																					
Ideas and development					█																				
Evaluation of ideas						█																			
Modelling							█	█	█																
Engineered drawings										█															
Materials list										█															
Plan of manufacture											█														
Project manufacture												█	█	█	█	█	█	█	█	█					
Diary of manufacture																					█				
Client testing																						█			
Other user feedback																							█		
Evaluation																								█	
Improvements																									█

Figure 12.35 Gantt chart

Audio and visual recordings

Although not widely found in student NEA folios, audio and visual recordings can be a really useful resource for research, and also as a real-time source of product evaluation.

Recordings can be used at several stages of the design process. They provide a valuable resource when undertaking a focus-group exercise, where a group of people from a target market may be gathered together to discuss a problem or to observe issues with their interaction with a product. Observing this kind of exercise is useful, but being able to revisit it focusing on a particular aspect of investigation makes it a lot easier. Videos can also be used to document potential users interacting with a model of a product, and so help the designer identify common problems or the habits of a particular user. More frequently, in a school setting they can be used to record evaluation feedback on a model or a design. Most mobile phones are capable of taking high-quality videos and they can be easily embedded in to a digital presentation.

Figure 12.36 A still image from a video of a child testing a concept product

Mathematical modelling

Mathematical modelling has become more accessible to designers as the cost and availability of 3D CAD programs has fallen. Rather than physically testing a model, which could involve a great deal of expense, and in most cases would result in the model being tested to destruction, virtual modelling and mathematical modelling can be used.

It is possible to simulate and test a variety of factors, such as how an object would respond to a given force acting upon it (for example, how a bridge reacts to a given load), or to explore how a material or component may conduct heat. The results of the mathematical principles applied to the model are usually displayed visually as a range of colours. It is also possible to test the aerodynamic performance of a product using mathematical modelling.

Mathematical modelling allows designers to predict and fine-tune the performance of a product before having to manufacture the final prototype, therefore saving time, money and resources.

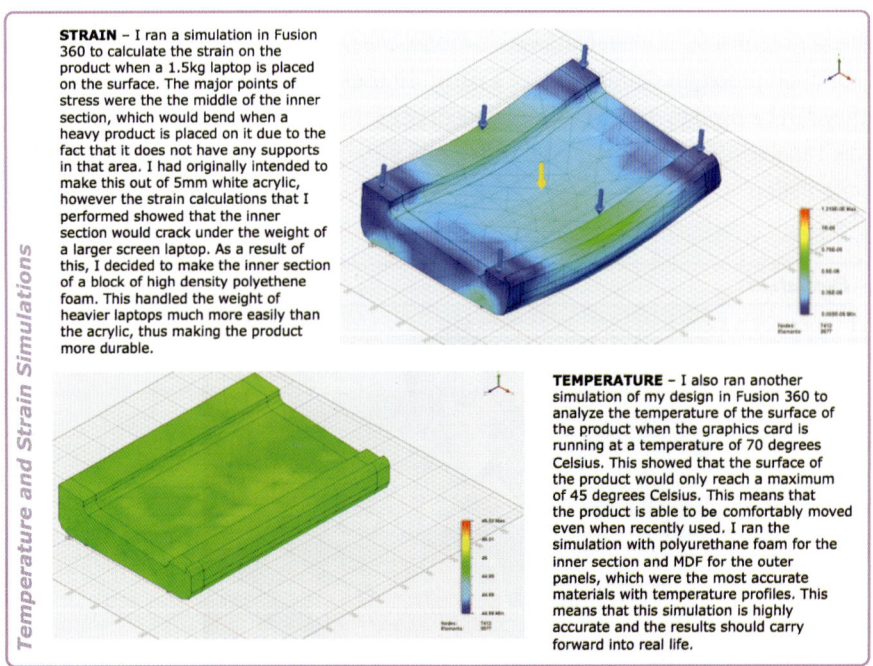

STRAIN – I ran a simulation in Fusion 360 to calculate the strain on the product when a 1.5kg laptop is placed on the surface. The major points of stress were the the middle of the inner section, which would bend when a heavy product is placed on it due to the fact that it does not have any supports in that area. I had originally intended to make this out of 5mm white acrylic, however the strain calculations that I performed showed that the inner section would crack under the weight of a larger screen laptop. As a result of this, I decided to make the inner section of a block of high density polyethene foam. This handled the weight of heavier laptops much more easily than the acrylic, thus making the product more durable.

TEMPERATURE – I also ran another simulation of my design in Fusion 360 to analyze the temperature of the surface of the product when the graphics card is running at a temperature of 70 degrees Celsius. This showed that the surface of the product would only reach a maximum of 45 degrees Celsius. This means that the product is able to be comfortably moved even when recently used. I ran the simulation with polyurethane foam for the inner section and MDF for the outer panels, which were the most accurate materials with temperature profiles. This means that this simulation is highly accurate and the results should carry forward into real life.

Temperature and Strain Simulations

Figure 12.37 Mathematical analysis tools being used to test a concept for a laptop stand

Computer-based tools

It is normal for design ideas to start as small hand-drawn thumbnail sketches before being developed into a more refined solution. CAD has a limited value at this early stage, although developments in computing hardware now allow designers to create digital drawings using styluses and graphics tablets, meaning that initial ideas can quickly appear on the computer. CAD systems become more important as ideas become developed and refined. Adjustments and edits can be quickly made to digital drawings and it is easy to undo changes if necessary.

As design ideas become more formal, it may be appropriate to create a 3D CAD model of an idea. In 3D software, colour or texture can be added and the model can be rotated to see different viewpoints. It can require a great deal of skill to make full use of all the facilities and functions that a CAD package includes. There are many basic programs available that allow for reasonable 3D modelling. One method of creating a 3D model is to import a 2D CAD drawing into a 3D CAD piece of software and then add depth and material options. This is a particularly useful function if you have used a 2D CAD drawing to laser-cut models at an earlier stage in the design process.

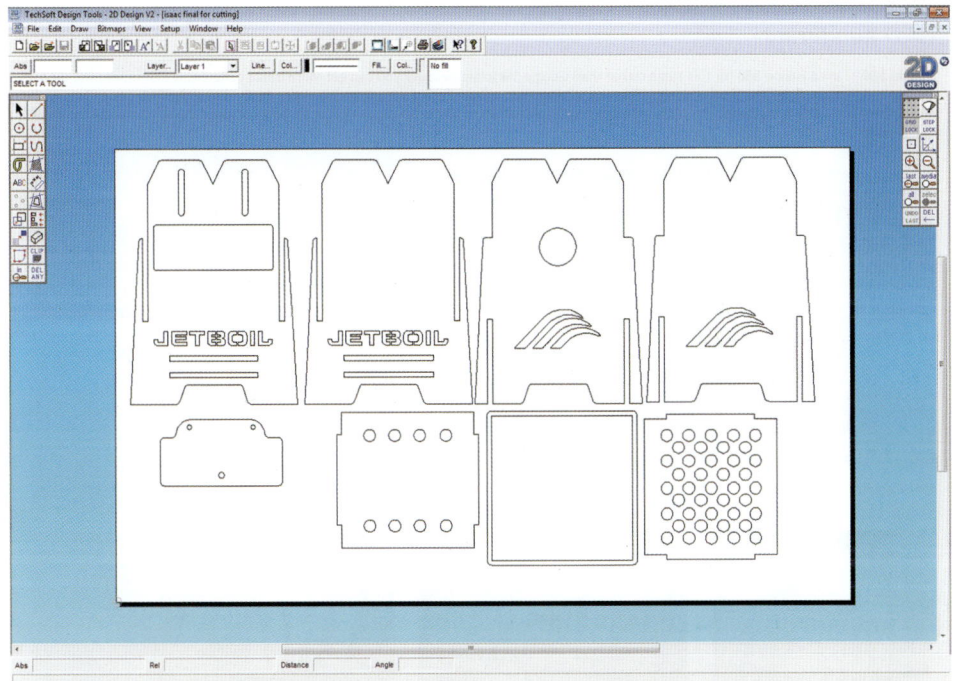

Figure 12.38 A 2D design drawing ready for laser cutting

Figure 12.39 A 3D CAD model generated from the 2D design drawing

The process of rendering (or adding a colour) is one of CAD's most powerful functions and some of the more powerful CAD programs can make the render of a design look almost photorealistic.

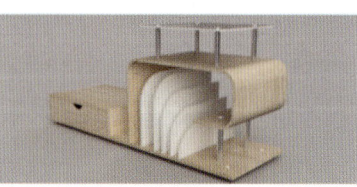
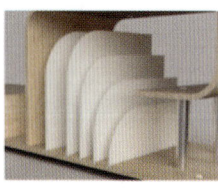

Figure 12.40 CAD rendering

Components such as nuts, bolts and hinges can be complicated to draw in a CAD program and can often be downloaded from an online component warehouse. These can then be imported into a drawing and scaled and moved into place.

Activity

Try using a 3D CAD program and create a 3D model of one of your recent projects. If you do not have a CAD system in school there are plenty of free versions available, such as 'TinkerCAD', 'Sketchup' or 'Autodesk fusion 360'.

KEY WORDS

Prototype: an early model of a product or part of a product to see how something will look or function.

12.9 Designing and developing prototypes

In order to develop an idea, the designer will often produce a **prototype**. Prototyping involves making a one-off version of the whole product or a specific part of the design. It may be made using slightly different materials or production methods, or be a scaled-down version of the product. By making a prototype, designers can test the design or parts of the design, find out the users' and stakeholders' views, and find if there are any problems with the design. From this, they see how successful the design is and make changes or further developments.

Prototypes can show up potentially fatal flaws in a design which can be addressed before the product goes into full-scale production. If used in the earlier stages of the design, this prevents the designer wasting time exploring an avenue or design path that will not work. It also prevents lots of time and money being put into the manufacture and production of a product that then turns out to be ineffective.

Prototyping is often done following the design ideas stage, once a final design (or a selection of the best potential designs) has been decided. However, it can also be used at any stage of the design process. The type of prototype used will depend on what stage during the process it is used and its purpose.

Low-fidelity prototypes

Low-fidelity prototypes are usually produced quite early on in the design process. They can be basic models of the product to give a simple visualisation of how it will look or they can be scale models of a particular part of the product (such as a mechanism or feature) to illustrate and test how it works. The prototype model may be made from simpler and different materials to that of the real product, such as paper or card instead of sheet metal, and plasticine or modelling clay instead of polymer or plastic.

Low-fidelity models are cheap and quick to make, and so allow the designer to try out numerous ideas and make lots prototypes, if required, that can then be thrown away if not successful. They allow designers to test crucial elements of their design early on and can give quick results allowing them to make changes early on in the design process.

Due to the simplicity and often low-quality nature of low-fidelity prototypes they are often not suitable for intended users as they will not exhibit the appearance, feel or function of the finished product.

High-fidelity prototypes

High-fidelity prototypes are usually made later, once a design has been developed considerably or a final design decided. They will look, feel and function as much like the finished product as possible and be made using the same materials and processes as far as is possible.

High-fidelity prototypes take much longer to produce and are more expensive than low-fidelity prototypes, but give a much more realistic idea of what the finished product will be like. This allows the users and stakeholders to give more accurate feedback on the product and see how well it meets their needs.

If significant changes are required to high-fidelity prototypes this can take a long time and delay the process, so it is important that they are only produced when the designer is confident that the final design is close to the finished product and any changes of refinements will be minor.

When making prototypes to develop your ideas remember the following:
- Making something instead of just drawing it will help you to see your idea in a different way and find how you can improve it further.
- Do not spend a long time building a prototype, as this will slow down the thought process and you will be less likely to change something if you have spent hours making it.
- Do not forget what the prototype is supposed to be testing, and try to let the user test the product if possible.
- Do not be afraid to fail! If the prototype does not do what you want, learn from this and use this knowledge to change or develop your design.

Figure 12.41 A low-fidelity prototype

Figure 12.42 A high-fidelity prototype

Activity

Practise making low-fidelity prototypes using paper, card, foamboard, Styrofoam, etc. Give yourself a strict time limit of about 10–15 minutes to make a low-fidelity prototype of a games console control pad.

12.10 Making informed and reasoned decisions and responding to feedback

Designers will need to make decisions at various stages throughout the design process. The number of decisions will depend on the complexity of the problem they are trying to solve or the type of product they are designing, as well as the requirements of the users, and many other factors.

Prototyping and asking for user feedback are two ways to test aspects of a design and gain valuable information that can help the designer make important decisions about key aspects of the design. The design brief and specification should be the reference points for all the decisions the designer will need to make and they should constantly refer back to these documents when making any sort of decision.

Once a high-fidelity prototype has been produced, a simple way that the designer can 'test' its features, characteristics, appearance and functions is to check them against the criteria set out in the brief and specification. In its simplest form this can just be answering a simple yes or no to each point in the specification. Any points that are not met are quickly identified and the designer can look at ways of rectifying them.

No matter how well a product or prototype is designed, it is likely that it will not meet all the criteria in a detailed specification, or it will only partly satisfy some of the criteria. In this case, the designer will consider how well it meets this point and look at ways it could be further improved.

Self-evaluation and referral to the specification will help provide some valid information on how well a product has performed against the brief and give the designer a basis for further decisions and improvements. However, the most effective and useful feedback about a prototype is from the intended user. There are several ways of getting feedback on your design.

User testing

User testing is about watching a user interact and use your product for its intended purpose to see how well it works, how easy it is to use and whether they actually like it. A user might be given the product to interact with for a set period of time and then be asked how well it fulfilled their need.

Focus groups

Focus groups can be used throughout the design process to check a product design is on track. Once a final prototype has been made, it can be presented to the group. Ideally, the group should represent the different stakeholders who will each have different needs. Their different initial reactions, concerns, and comments can be recorded. A focus group allows people to ask questions and state how they would like the product to be improved. This can

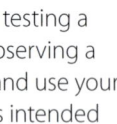

KEY WORDS

User testing: testing a product by observing a user interact and use your product for its intended purpose.

Focus group: group of people used to check a product design is on track.

have great advantages over single user testing because a wide range of responses are obtained, however the opinions may often be different and contradictory because of the different needs, and the designer then has the difficult decision of which user's needs are more important.

A/B testing

A/B testing is a form of user testing often used to choose between two different design ideas. The two different prototypes are given to an equal number of users and they are asked to do certain tasks using the product. The designer then looks at the results of the tests for the two products to see which design achieved the task the quickest or most efficiently, and uses this to make further decisions about the direction of the design. This type of testing is often used in industry to compare a new updated version of product to the existing one to see if it actually works better.

Surveys and questionnaires

Surveys and questionnaires are an easy way to gather a large amount of information from users. The right questions can reveal some extremely useful information about how well the product meets the users' needs, allowing the designer to make informed decisions about future modifications. However, the designer must ensure that the survey asks questions that will provide accurate information about the product, without being too constraining.

For example, compare the two questions below. Which is the most useful question to the designer?

- Question A – Were the controls easy to use? YES/NO
- Question B – Which features of the following controls did you find hardest to use?
    a the push on/off button
    b the sliding volume control
    c the adjustment knob.

There are a number of websites that allow designers to create online surveys, which can be used to gather and collate information from users around the world.

The different types of user feedback provide **qualitative data** (users' opinions) and **quantitative data** (what actually happened).

Quantitative data refers to data which gives specific counts and values in numerical terms, such as measurements like height, weight, volume, length, size, humidity, speed, age, etc. The data can be gathered from things such as surveys, experiments, or observations, etc. and presented in the form of charts, graphs, tables, etc.

Qualitative data is data that is observable by appearance, taste, feel, texture, etc. that cannot be specifically measured. Qualitative data can be collected from observations, focus groups, interviews and archive material. The data is not numerical but presented as spoken or written words rather than numbers.

Once any data is gathered it should be used by the designer to:
- evaluate the performance and suitability of the product
- make decisions about what needs to be improved
- implement the necessary modifications and changes to the design
- re-test and evaluate to check the effectiveness of the changes.

KEY WORDS

A/B testing: user testing to choose between two different design ideas.

Qualitative data: observations and opinions about a product.

Quantitative data: specific measurable data given in numerical form.

Activity

Visit an online survey website, such as SurveyMonkey.

Write a survey asking people about their opinions on an aspect of school life, such as canteen meals, sports facilities or uniform. Use a mixture of different question types and ask as many people as possible to complete the survey online.

KEY POINTS
- Critical analysis assesses the suitability of the design against given criteria.
- Prototypes can show up potentially fatal flaws in a design which can be addressed before the product goes into full-scale production.

Exam practice questions

1 The internet has had a massive impact on society. Discuss the impact and effects of the internet on society. [8 marks]

2 Using a specific item of clothing as an example, describe how the principle of systems thinking could be applied to clothing design. [4 marks]

3 Describe three different pieces of anthropometrical data that a designer would need to consider when designing a child's climbing frame and explain how these would be applied to the design. [6 marks]

4 What would be the most appropriate style of drawing to use in order to provide key dimensions to a manufacturer? [1 mark]

5 Identify five advantages that a physical model provides over a CAD render. [5 marks]

6 Explain the role that mathematical modelling plays when designing a shelf bracket. [4 marks]

7 Explain why exploded diagrams are useful to a consumer. [4 marks]

8 Following his appointment at Monsoon, describe the influence Matthew Williamson's style has had on high-street fashion. [6 marks]

Section 4

Preparing for assessment

Chapter 13 Component 1: Design and Technology in the 21st century 308

Chapter 14 Component 2: Design and make task 312

Chapter 13
Component 1: Design and Technology in the 21st Century

Learning objectives

By the end of this chapter you should have developed a knowledge and understanding of:
- when you will complete the written exam
- the different types of questions asked in examination papers
- tips for preparing for the exam and answering exam questions.

Component 1: Design and Technology in the 21st Century written exam accounts for 50 per cent of the total marks in your Eduqas Design and Technology GCSE.

When will the written paper be taken?

The written exam will take place in the summer exam period in the final year of your GCSE course. For most students this will be in May or June of Year 11, but your school will be able to tell you when your exam will take place.

How long will I have?

You will have **two hours** in which to complete the exam.

What format will the written paper take?

The exam paper will include a mixture of short-answer, structured and extended writing questions. The paper will be divided into two sections:
- **Section A** will include questions that assess core knowledge and understanding. You will need to answer **all** questions in this section.
- **Section B** will include questions that assess in-depth knowledge and understanding. You will need to answer **one** question in this section.

How will I be assessed?

The exam will assess your knowledge and understanding of technical principles and designing and making principles, as well as your ability to analyse and evaluate design decisions and wider issues in design and technology.

There are four assessment objectives (AOs) in the GCSE, but in the written exam you will only be assessed against AO3 and AO4.

Assessment objective	Component 1 weighting
AO3 Analyse and evaluate: - design decision and outcomes, including for prototypes made by themselves and others - wider issues in design and technology.	10%
AO4 Demonstrate and apply knowledge and understanding of: - technical principles - designing and making principles.	40%
TOTAL	**50%**

General advice on answering exam questions

- Read through the instructions on the front of the exam paper carefully. Make sure that you understand what to do.
- Read each question carefully (twice) before answering.
- Make sure you understand what the **command words** in the question mean. The table below shows some common command words you may encounter on the exam paper.

Command word	Explanation
State/name/give	Provide brief facts or examples.
Complete	Fill in missing information.
Describe	Provide characteristics or a brief account.
Explain	Provide details and reasons for how and why something is the way it is.
Calculate	Work out the value.
Discuss	Examine an issue in detail by addressing a range of key ideas and reasons for and against the issue.
Analyse	Organise information or subject matter into components/characteristics and address each in detail by close examination of the issue in question.
Justify	Present a reasoned case using supporting evidence to explain why something should happen in a particular way.
Evaluate	Make a judgement based on weighing up points for and against.
Assess	Make an informed judgement based on weighing up arguments for and against.

- Look at how many marks are available for a question. This may help guide you on how many points you need to include in your answer.
- For extended writing questions you may find it useful to plan your answer before you begin writing.
- Make sure you allow time to look through your answers at the end of the exam.

Types of exam questions

Short-answer questions

Short-answer questions require a short phrase, a short sentence or statement, or a simple one-word answer.

Example question

1 Pattern markings are used in textiles as a guide to laying out templates on fabrics.
   a State the name or meaning of the pattern markings show below.   [3 × 1 mark]

(i)	(ii)	(iii)

Candidate response

i	Balance mark (or notch)	[1 mark]
ii	Place along the straight grain	[1 mark]
iii	Place along a folded edge of the fabric	[1 mark]

In question 1a, the markings are instructions.

Example question

1 b Explain the importance of following pattern markings accurately when laying out templates on fabric when making textile products. [3 marks]

Candidate response
- Pattern markings indicate specific instructions for cutting out correctly and matching up specific things on a product. [1 mark]
- Failure to do this will mean pattern pieces will not fit together or hang correctly as intended. [1 mark]
- This will lead to an inferior product where the balance is not quite right and certain things are placed incorrectly. [1 mark]

Example question

2 Describe the benefits of having a bespoke item of clothing made for a client. [4 marks]

Answers to question 2 could mention:
- Bespoke is a single product made specifically for a single client. [1 mark]
- The products will be fitted perfectly to suit the individual client. [1 mark]
- It could be the only product of its type. [1 mark]
- The client has input to the design. [1 mark]
- The product is usually hand-made with attention to detail. [1 mark]
- The product is often of a higher quality than mass-produced products. [1 mark]
- The product is often made with more expensive/better quality fabrics and components. [1 mark]

Calculation questions

In calculation questions, it is important to show all calculations. Credit can be awarded for a suitable method even if the answer is incorrect. Other methods of calculation are acceptable where appropriate.

Example question

3 A student wants to use the laser cutter to cut a number of circular shapes from a piece of cotton fabric which measures 90 cm wide by 45 cm length.

The circular shapes are all 12 cm in diameter.

There is no gap between each circular shape when cut from the fabric.

Show all your workings.

a Calculate how many whole circular shapes can be cut from the piece of cotton fabric. [3 marks]

Candidate response
- 90 divided by 12 = 7 circles across the fabric [1 mark]
- Repeat the process to calculate how many full circles will fit down the length of fabric.
- 45 divided by 12 = 3 circles down the length [1 mark]
- Answer: 21 in total (7 × 3) [1 mark]

Example question

3 b Calculate the percentage of fabric that will be wasted after cutting the circular shapes. [5 marks]

Candidate response

- Surface area of rectangular piece of fabric:
  90 cm × 45 cm (width × length) = 4050cm^2 [1 mark]
- Surface area of total circular shapes:
  πr^2 × 21 (3.142 × 6 × 6) = 2375.35cm^2 [1 mark]
  (The diameter of the circle is 12 cm, so the radius is half this, so 6 cm.)
- To calculate the waste fabric:
  4050cm^2 − 2375.35cm^2 = 1674.65cm^2 [1 mark]
  (The rectangular surface area minus the surface area of the circular pieces.)
- To calculate the waste fabric as a percentage of the whole piece of fabric:

$$\frac{\text{Waste amount}}{(90 \times 45)} \times \frac{100}{1}$$ [1 mark for the right calculation]

$$\frac{1674.65}{4050} \times 100 = 41.37\%$$ [Correct answer: 1 mark]

> For question 3b, you will need to calculate the surface area of the rectangular piece of fabric and the surface area for 21 circular pieces.

Questions that require extended answers

This type of question requires an extended piece of continuous writing, so bullet points will not be acceptable. Quality of communication may also be assessed in this type of question.

Example question

4 Analyse the impact our ecological footprint is having on the environment. [6 marks]

You will need to consider the question carefully and try to identify the main issues. In this case, what is the ecological footprint and how do humans contribute to it? It is a good idea to include specific examples to help illustrate your answer. Briefly describe the impact that our ecological footprint is currently having on the environment (what is already happening), and if this practice continues to grow, what the potential consequences are for the future.

In a question where 'analyse' is the key word at the start you will be expected to make connections between different parts of your answer and show evidence of reasoning for any points you put forward.

The following points are examples of what you could refer to:

- The ecological footprint is a measure of the impact human activity has on the environment.
- Land is continually being cleared to allow for roads, buildings, infrastructure, etc.
- We need land to grow crops to feed ourselves, and grazing land for livestock.
- Land is needed for growing fibres for textiles.
- Forestry land is needed for timber supplies for wood products.
- Land is needed to dispose of the rubbish we create.
- The natural ecosystem is often destroyed to make way for a new purpose for the land to meet our needs; once cleared it may never recover.
- By clearing land masses some animals and other smaller creatures suffer if their natural habitats are destroyed; some could become extinct if they cannot adapt.
- Nature cannot keep up with the demand we make on the land, we are in danger of creating an ecological deficit – using far more than can be naturally replaced.

Chapter 14
Component 2: Design and make task

Learning objectives

By the end of this chapter you should have developed a knowledge and understanding of:
- the iterative process of design
- the structure of the non-examined assessment (NEA) and the contextual challenge
- the format, style and approaches to the NEA
- the assessment criteria for the NEA
- the evidence and information needed within your portfolio of work.

Introduction

The non-examined assessment (NEA) is a design and make task worth 50 per cent of your marks for your GCSE qualification in Design and Technology. It is an opportunity for you to demonstrate the skills, knowledge and understanding that you have gained while studying for this qualification. As part of your assessment you will be expected to produce a portfolio of evidence that shows your design journey from **contextual challenge** to finished prototype product.

The iterative design process

The **iterative process** of design is based on a cycle of modelling and prototyping. Ideas need to be tested, **analysed** and refined in an ongoing process to make a **prototype** product that fulfils a real-life need.

Think – test – reflect

Trialling of ideas leads to reward – a more refined, improved idea, and the potential for a new approach to a problem or even a better product! Each iteration (most recent version) of the product moves it closer to fulfilling the needs and wants of the client market or **stakeholders**. This cyclic process of design is a reflection of what happens in industry; this is what all products and clothing have gone through.

> **KEY WORDS**
>
> **Iterative process**: an ongoing cyclic process of developing ideas through modelling and testing.
>
> **Analysing**: deconstructing information to find connections and logical chains of reasoning.
>
> **Prototype**: the first or early models of an idea. This term could also apply to a finished concept model.
>
> **Stakeholder(s)**: a person or people who have an interest in or would use your product.

Contextual challenges

The exam board will set three different contextual challenges each year. They will be available on 1st June in the year before your final year of study. The contextual challenges are very broad and are intended to be a starting point for you to consider your project. You can consider and interpret the many different design possibilities that could arise from the exploration of any challenge. Try to avoid any preconceived ideas and keep an open mind to other possibilities as your ideas evolve. There are no restrictions on what materials to use, but it is suggested you focus on an area of particular interest and strength. You will need to apply specialist knowledge, understanding and skills to realise your ideas.

Here is an example of a contextual challenge:

The interpretation of colour

Colour can be used as a means of communication and education, for cultural and aesthetic reasons, but can also represent emotion – fear, excitement, anger, joy. Explore the ways colour can influence choice and use this information to design and manufacture a product with colour being central to its function or purpose.

There are many ways to interpret this challenge, for example:
- Colour can be used to enhance the home – lighting, soft furnishing, furniture, control devices …
- Colour is educational/informative – primary/bright colours on children's toys, warning mechanisms and devices, display products, branding …

The important point is to explore and consider as many ideas as possible. Consider a few options in a little more detail and from that follow a more defined route.

General guidance

You will have approximately 35 guided hours in which to complete your design and make task. As you follow the iterative process of design you will be expected to manage your time effectively as you develop, test and refine your ideas. It is very much a personal journey! You can prepare notes, sketch ideas and conduct tests outside normal lessons and this can be referred to as and when needed. However, the work presented in your portfolio and the manufacture of the product must take place in the school or college environment, under teacher supervision. Your teacher needs to be sure it is your work that is presented for assessment.

Format of the NEA

There is no set format to presenting your portfolio of work. It is the content and focus of the work that is most important. Some schools will favour an informal approach, such as a sketchbook (A3 or A4) in which all the research is recorded alongside the development of ideas, similar to a working document that tracks how your design is evolving. It is anticipated that the research/investigation – assessment strand (a) – and the generating and development of ideas – assessment strand (c) – will take place concurrently, with one aspect influencing the other. The second part of the portfolio should be a more formal section that outlines all the technical details needed for a third party to manufacture your product. The portfolio of work could be in digital or electronic format, or a mixture of both. Obviously, the finished product needs to be included alongside any test pieces to complete the portfolio of evidence you put forward for assessment. The content will be discussed in more detail further into the chapter.

Assessment

Your portfolio of work will be marked out of 100, and assessed according to the five assessment strands outlined below. These strands are all linked to the iterative design process. It should be noted that strand (e) will be addressed throughout the portfolio of work through evaluative commentary and decision making that should be evident while designing, developing and testing your ideas and during the manufacture of your final prototype product.

	Assessment criteria		Marks
(a)	Identifying and investigating design possibilities		10
(b)	Developing a **design brief** and **specification**		10
(c)	Generating and developing design ideas		30
(d)	Manufacturing a prototype		30
(e)	Analysing and **evaluating** design decisions and prototypes		20
		Total	100

(a) Identifying and investigating design possibilities

You will be given the opportunity to consider the three contextual challenges set by the examination board. You can choose just one or consider all three at least initially, but the main point is to explore the contexts and identify a number of possible **design opportunities**. You can present your thoughts as a mind map or thought shower, but you must ensure that a **client** or **potential user** is at the core of your thinking.

> ### KEY WORDS
> **Design brief**: a statement of intent outlining what is to be designed and made.
> **Design specification**: a list of features the product must have in order to be successful.
> **Evaluating**: appraising and making judgements on information and issues.
> **Design opportunities**: areas to explore where a real-life need has been identified.
> **Client** or **potential user**: the person or persons who will likely need, want or use your product.

There are a number of things to consider, all centred around your chosen contextual challenge.

For example:
- Consider whether a particular event or occasion, place, location or process presents an opportunity based on the chosen contextual challenge. Explore the issues and try to identify a real need.
- The profile of your potential client – lifestyle choices, age, gender, ethnicity, their needs and wants. Can you identify a product or need specific to someone or a group of people? If so what type of products? What are the issues? What do you need further information on – materials, processes, function, aesthetics, technical requirements, and so on.
- Your starting point could be an existing product that you would like to develop further and improve upon. It could be a sketched idea you already have that fits into one contextual challenge. In a similar way, explore the issues that surround your initial thoughts.

There are multiple starting points from which to analyse and consider the contextual challenges. The more effort you make at this stage the more successful you will be in identifying multiple starting points. Whichever way you choose to start, the important part is to record all your thoughts.

Figure 14.1 An exploration of the issues that could arise from a contextual challenge; in this example a number of design opportunities have been identified.

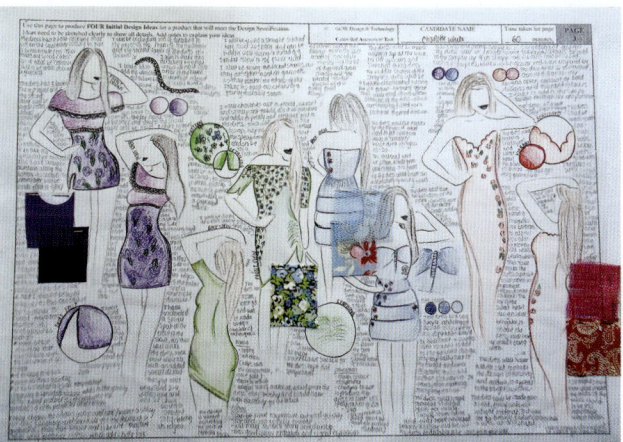
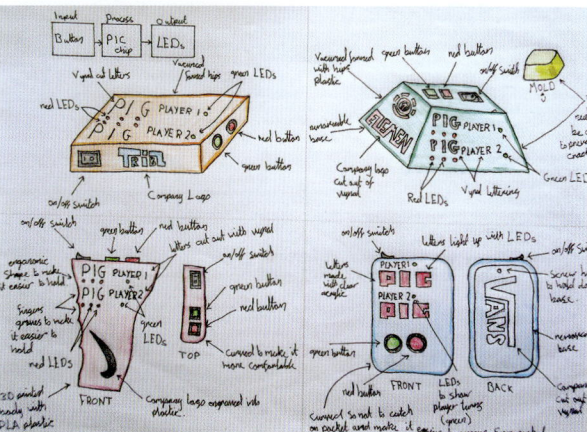

Figure 14.2 Sketching of ideas can start at any point and should continue while further research is being conducted.

Once you have identified possible design opportunities, you will need to conduct some research and investigation. This needs to be focused, relevant, and linked to the context. You can use a range of strategies, but choose those that will be of most use. **Primary research** will give you more specific information related to your task and client needs while **secondary research** is useful for more general information, for example about current trends or materials and processes.

There are many research and investigative strategies you could use to gather the information you may need. The following are offered as general guidance:

1   Product analysis – the analysis of a competitor product. Consider, for example, the form, style and function, materials and construction processes, quality issues, performance characteristics, environmental/sustainability factors, overall strengths and weaknesses. Be sure to identify, analyse and record what is of value to your design. Consider how the information could be used effectively.

2   Interview, conduct a survey or questionnaire with your potential clients or users – this should directly influence the decisions you make and drive your design thinking forward. Keep all questions focused – avoid anything that is unnecessary, and include an analysis of your results.

3   Studying the work of professionals, past or present is a useful tool. Analyse what makes them and their products successful. You could also simply take inspiration from their work for your designs. Again, make sure there is a purpose to this activity.

4   Analyse current trends – this could be done in local stores or online. Identify key factors and record how this helps move your design thinking forward. You could also disassemble an existing product to find out how it fits together. This could lead to a better understanding of materials, components and processes that you could use. Be sure to analyse your findings.

5   Produce a mood board or concept board – collect images, materials, colours and text that can help focus your ideas and gain a visual understanding of the task ahead. Again, focus on client needs and views, avoiding unnecessary information.

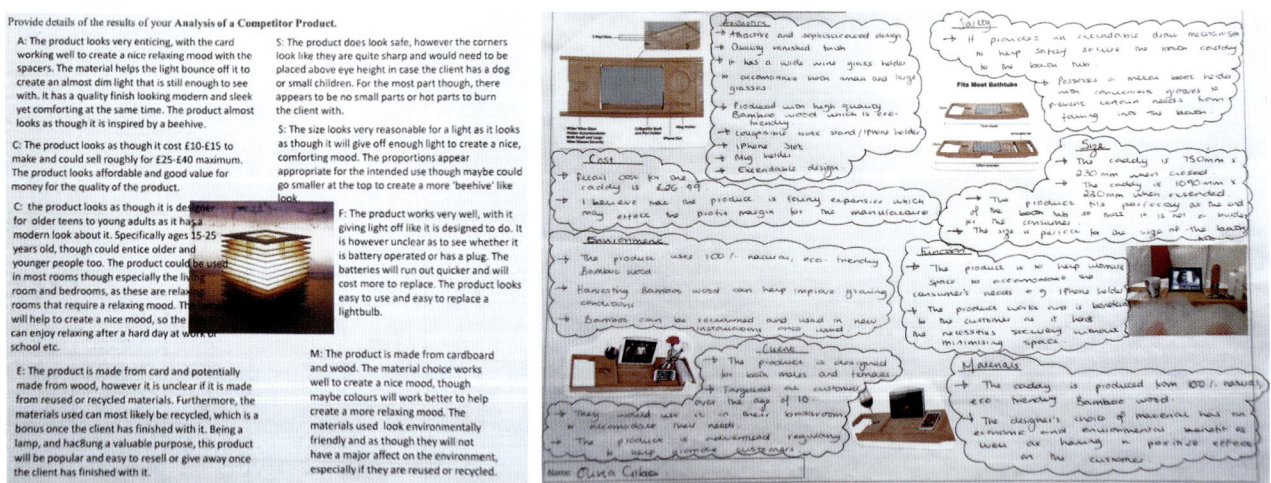

Figure 14.3 Product analysis is a useful way of identifying strengths and weaknesses in competitor products. You could analyse one product in depth or a range of similar products as a comparative exercise.

My potential user is a female in the 18–28 age group. My client is a 23-year-old female. She lives with her friends in a shared house in a trendy part of the city. She has recently finished university and has started her first job. She earns her own money and uses it to pay her way in the house and to fund her shopping habit. She likes going running with her friends to keep fit and healthy. She couldn't live without her iPhone and iPad. She drives a Mini car, but often walks to keep her carbon footprint low and show some consideration for the environment. She is increasingly aware of issues of sustainability and environmental issues, and is moving towards buying organic food. She relaxes at weekends with her friends – she may go to a few nightclubs or parties – this helps take away the stresses of her working life. She is fashion-conscious and has the latest trends in her wardrobe. Her clothes are stylish yet practical. Her favourite places to shop are H&M, River Island and Topshop. She also buys online. She enjoys most genres of music, but mainly listens to indie bands and chart music.

The products that would appeal to her must reflect her lifestyle – fashion-forward, but practical to reflect her work life and partying. She would very much like sustainable eco-friendly products that fit in with her increasing 'green consciousness'.

Figure 14.4 Clients or potential users should be at the forefront of your design thinking throughout the project. A written lifestyle profile that clearly describes their needs, wants and values is a useful way of setting out their requirements.

Throughout the research and investigation you should be narrowing down your ideas to a more defined range of possible design challenges and be moving closer to setting your final design brief.

Towards the end of this assessment strand, you will need to have a clear idea of what you intend to make and the rationale behind that decision. Before a final decision is made, you might find it helpful to consult potential users for feedback on your first thoughts and ideas.

Designing and modelling ideas should be taking place alongside your initial research. Modelling and testing ideas may prompt you into further research later in the process as you uncover potential design problems. This is all part of the iterative process of design and should be in evidence in your portfolio of work.

The activities carried out in this section form part of the more informal section of your portfolio.

(b) Developing a design brief and specification

When you feel you have conducted sufficient detailed research you will need to summarise your thoughts and explain any decisions before writing a final design brief and design specification. You need to demonstrate you have a clear understanding of the task ahead and that the needs, wants and interests of potential users have been considered.

The design brief

The final design brief is a statement that clearly sets out what you intend to make and includes the rationale for your decision. It should be based on the exploration of ideas that have arisen from the contextual challenge, and show that you have considered a range of problems or opportunities before this point. Avoid narrowing down your options too much at this point by being too specific about any design features such as colour and specific materials or being too descriptive about the final prototype product. Remember, the design brief is a statement of intent – you have not designed it yet!

The design specification

After broad and detailed research, you should have some understanding of the details and features that need to be included in the design of your prototype product if your design is to be realised and successful. The design specification is a list of features which you believe to be most important. The specification should include both **objective** and **measurable criteria**, with the needs and wants of potential users clearly identified. Try to include key technical terms (for example, function, aesthetics, dimensions, and so on).

KEY WORDS

Objective criteria: realistic and achievable points setting out the purpose of the product.

Measurable criteria: specific points that are measurable, such as weight or size.

You will be expected to refer to your design specification throughout the iterative process of design. Use it to direct and inform the development of the prototype product. Each iteration should be compared to the criteria within the specification; this will enable you to stay on track throughout the design stage. You should include reference to the specification by including evaluative comments in your sketchbook/informal portfolio as your designs evolve.

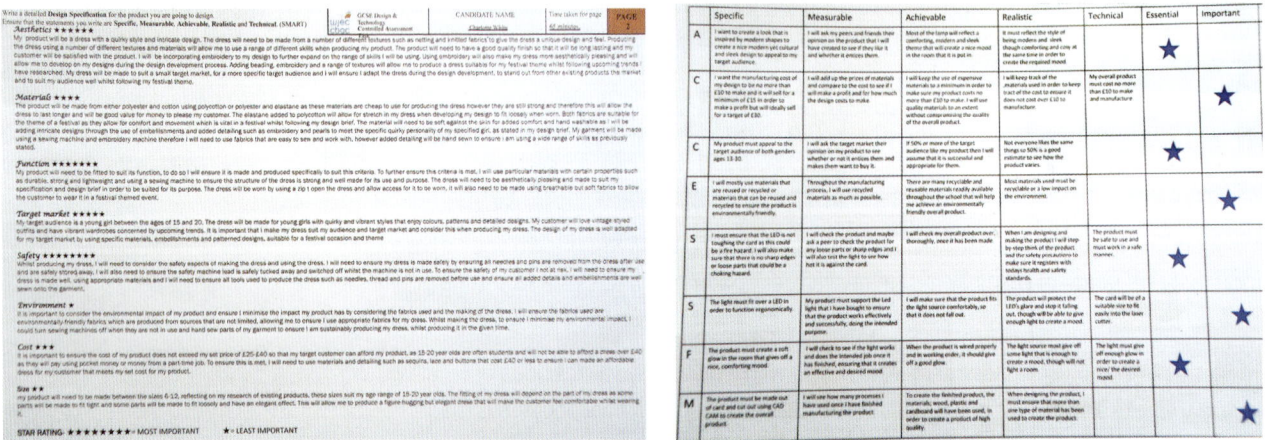

Figure 14.5 The specification should contain a broad outline of the essential and desirable qualities your product must have. It should also include measurable criteria that the product can be tested against.

The activities carried out in this section form part of the formal section of your portfolio.

(c) Generating and developing design ideas

The iterative design process is not viewed as a linear process. Initial ideas can be considered from the very beginning of the design task, including when the contextual challenges are first issued. Your initial thoughts could be in the form of a cardboard model or sketch. Research, designing and some modelling should take place simultaneously – each process informing and directing the others. It will not matter if your sketchbook/folio has evidence of both side by side in the early stages; the important point is that it is all included and you are applying the iterative process.

You will need to show you have considered a range of design strategies, techniques and processes in the development of your ideas in order to access the highest assessment band. Provided the research you conduct directly informs design decisions, this addresses a small part of assessment band (c). You will, however, need to consider a wider range of design strategies. The table below outlines some of those possibilities and is intended for guidance purposes only.

Design strategies, techniques and approaches	
Freehand sketches	These can be presented in any medium as a quick method of recording initial ideas and identifying possibilities. As ideas progress as a result of testing, sketches can be more refined and show more detail – close ups, exploded diagrams, construction processes, etc.
CAD modelling	Can be used in many ways – to develop the product in its entirety, to develop parts or sections (for example, circuits, component parts) or to develop print, pattern or embellishment as well as for final presentation drawings. This includes designing for use on the laser cutter or CNC machines.
Mock-ups	Practical testing of ideas – test out component parts by physically modelling the ideas. This could mean construction processes (joints, seam types), toiles, vacuum forming, foam block modelling, dimensions, printing techniques, testing applied finishes or how materials perform/react in use.
Card and paper modelling	An economical way to test concept ideas is to use paper or card. If a foam block model has been developed for a prototype product, for example, to test the user interface, use paper! Scaled card modelling can be used to test the shape, form and proportion of a product before manufacture. Paper can be used to develop a toile and templates for textile products.
Empathy modelling	To gain an understanding of a very specific user you need put yourself in their situation, either in real life or through a simulated setting to gain a better understanding of the issues they might face.
User/wearer trials and experience modelling	Involve potential users in the design process. When a product is close to being realised, get it tested in a real-life situation – use/wear the product. One of the best ways to test your product is through the experience of actually using it.
Rapid prototyping	Where technology exists, use it to develop and test components or whole products through 3D printing.
Virtual modelling	3D CAD modelling of ideas, views from various angles. Test ideas before manufacture.

You need to be selective over the strategies you use and work within what is available in your school or college. The important point is that modelling takes place and that ideas evolve as a result of testing. During the development of your ideas it is anticipated that materials and components, construction processes and techniques, dimensions, functional requirements and manufacturing constraints will be considered as part of an integrated approach. Social, moral and economic factors should also be considered as part of the research and inform design decisions where appropriate. Photographic evidence of all test pieces can be pasted into the sketchbook and analysed, but all test pieces, where possible, should be presented for assessment.

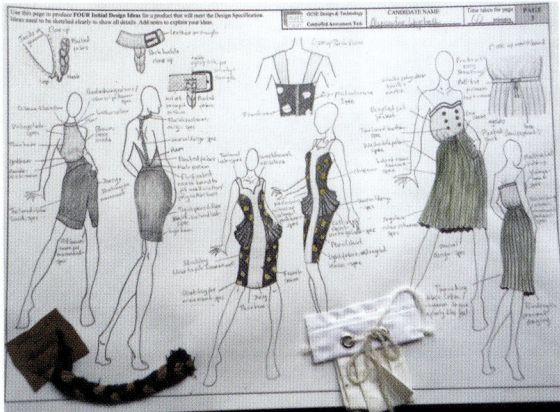
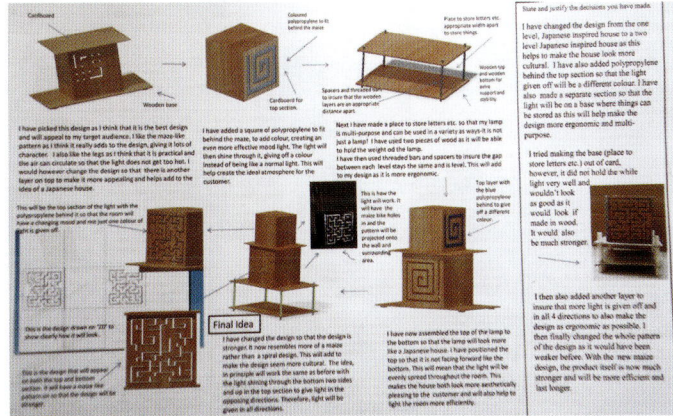

Figure 14.6 Initial ideas can be presented in any format or media. The examples shown also indicate that some practical testing is taking place alongside.

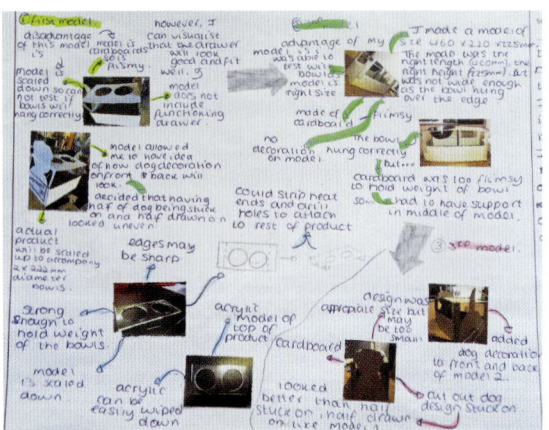

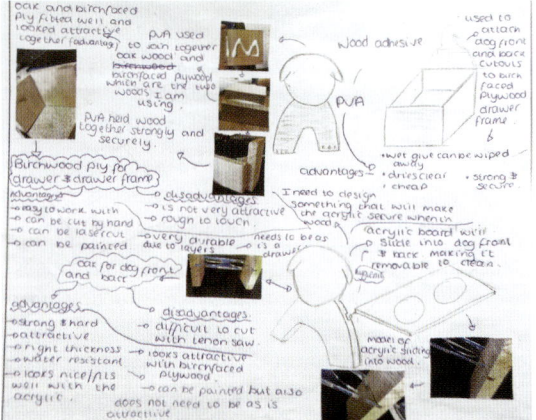

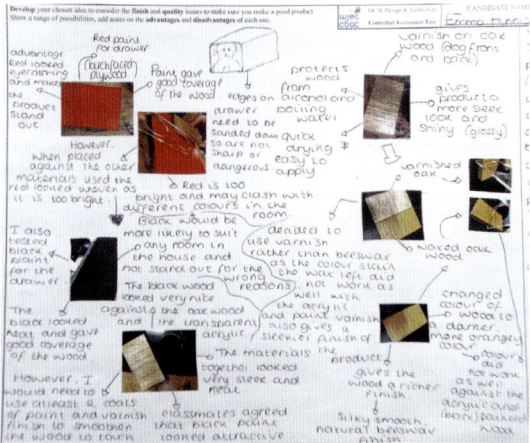

Figure 14.7 The informally presented work shows photographic evidence that the iterative design process is being followed through modelling and testing ideas along with evaluative commentary.

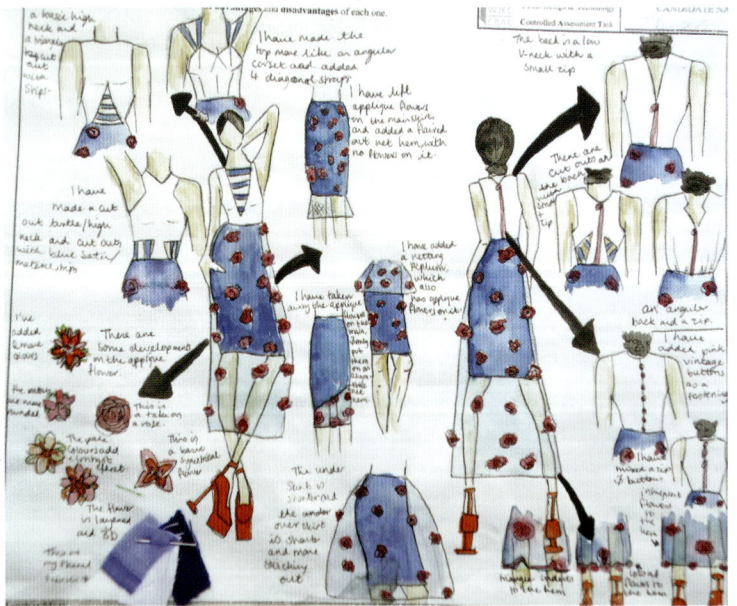

Figure 14.8 The development of style, form and materials has been considered, but a toile in calico supports the development even further.

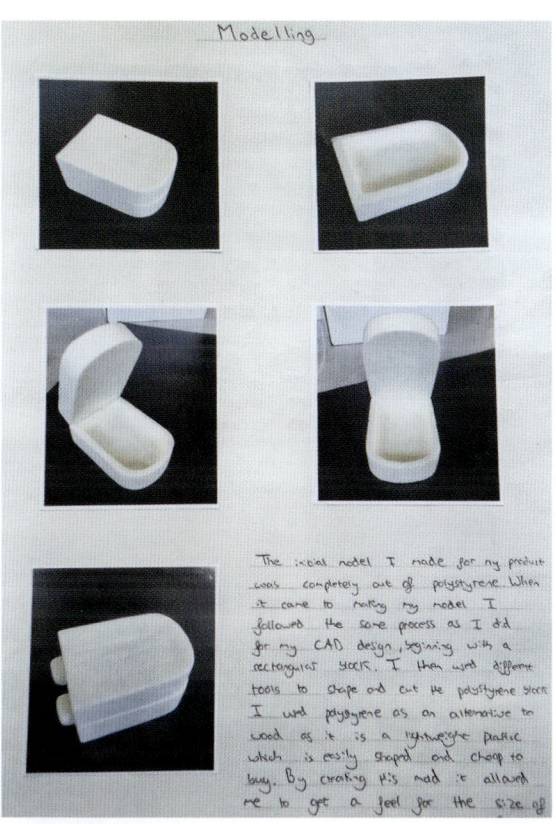

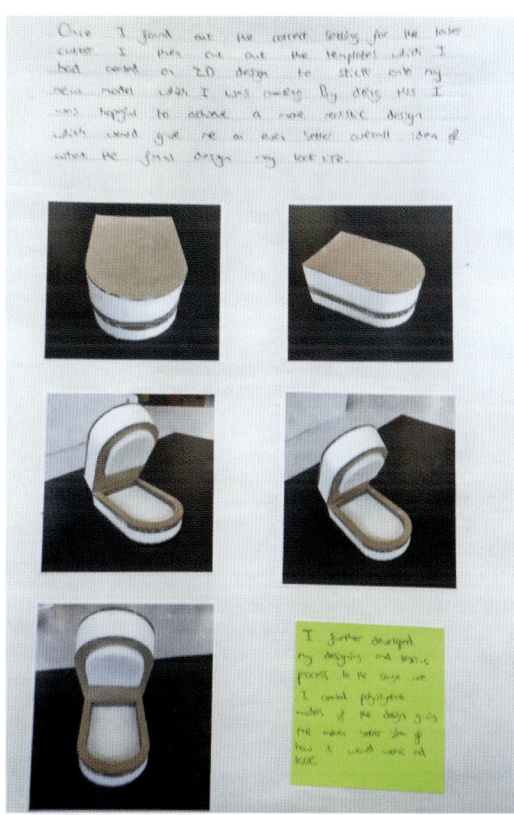

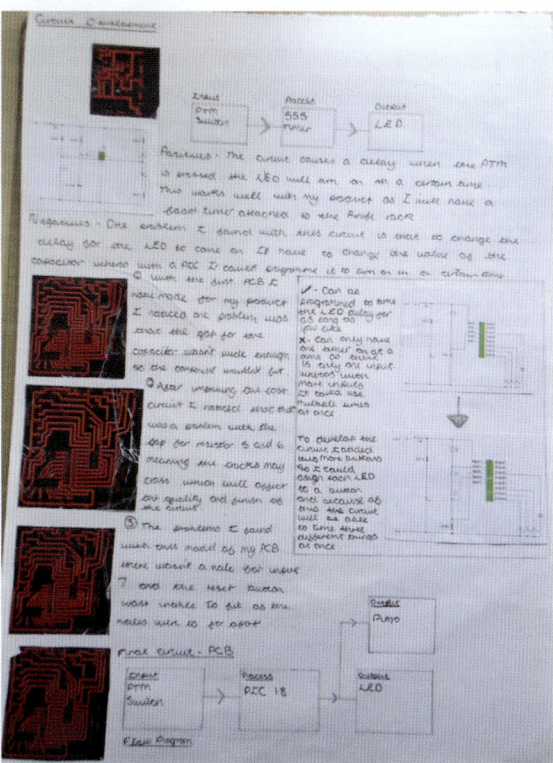

Figure 14.9 Iterations, methods of testing and modelling ideas is dependent on the materials and products being developed. In this example, the first iteration is for the casing, through foam block modelling and card. The second iteration is for the circuit, which will then lead to further testing.

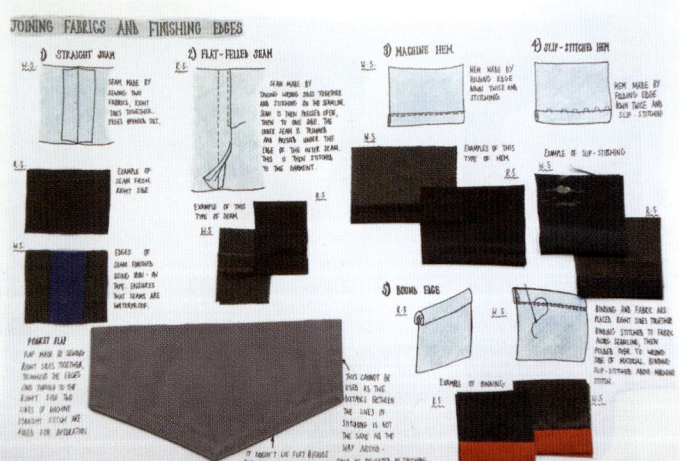

Figure 14.10 Iterations for woven, non-woven and knitted textiles in this example include quilting fabrics, machine embroidery designs, sublimation printing and seam construction methods. Practical testing of processes is taking place alongside sketched ideas.

The activities carried out in this section form part of the more informal section of your portfolio.

For the final part of this assessment strand a final presentation drawing will be required along with the technical details needed for a third party to realise your idea. All critical measurements and dimensions, tools and equipment and settings for specific machinery should be included in this section. The format for presenting this information will be dependent on the product type.

The latter part of this section forms part of the more formal section of your portfolio.

Figure 14.11 Presentation drawings can be in any format and style. You should also consider showing different views, different angles and, where appropriate, exploded diagrams to show specific details.

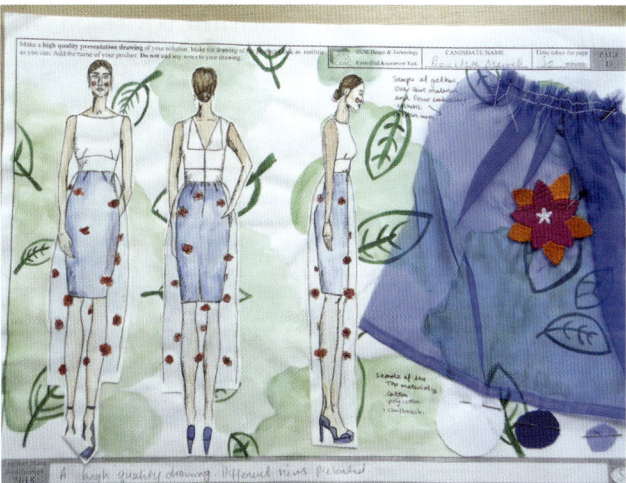

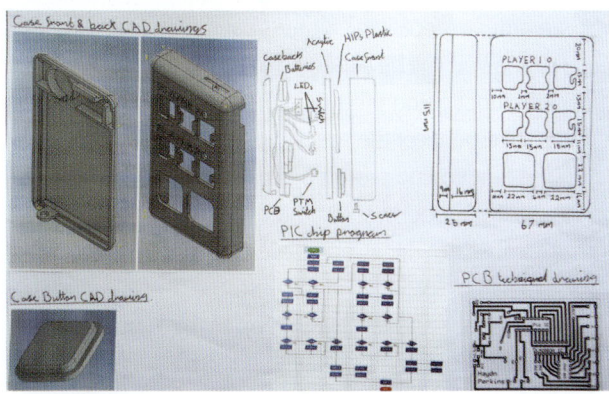

Figure 14.12 The technical details need to be sufficiently detailed for a third party to manufacture your product – all important dimensions are required as well as reference to processes, equipment and settings for machinery. The style of presentation for this will vary depending on the product. The details shown here are for an electronic device, a lighting product and a dress.

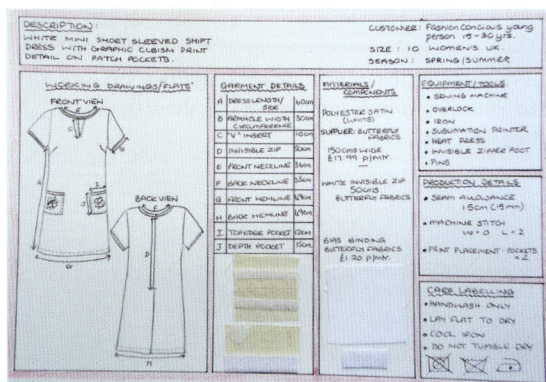

(d) Manufacturing a prototype

Through modelling and testing your ideas you will have a fair understanding of the stages needed to manufacture your product. You will be expected to present these stages in a logical sequence of steps – in other words a plan for making. It should be sufficiently detailed that a third party could follow it to manufacture the same product. The plan should show details of specific processes and stages, including reference to tooling and equipment, a suitable and achievable timeline, acknowledgement of potential constraints and a means of evaluating and testing the product throughout the manufacturing process.

The sequence for making forms part of the formal section of your portfolio.

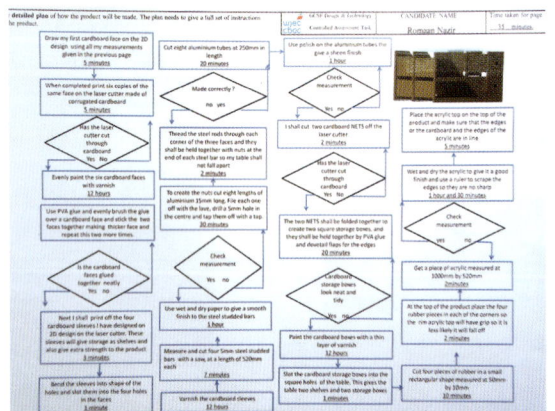 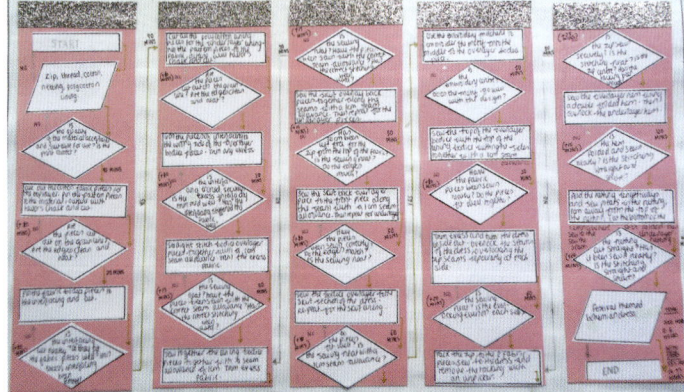

Figure 14.13 The sequence for making can be presented as a flowchart showing details and stages of processes, quality considerations, equipment needed, a suitable timeline and potential constraints.

Figure 14.14 An alternative way of presenting the sequence for making is in a tabular format, but it must still show the same considerations as a flowchart.

In order to access the highest band for this assessment strand you will be expected to produce a high-quality, fully functioning prototype product that meets all the requirements of the specification and is fit for purpose. The functioning prototype could be a fully developed concept model that resembles a finished artefact, but does not necessarily have all the internal features of a real-life product. In this case, the concept model should look and feel like the real thing. Your prototype product could be a fully finished artefact that could be used immediately – a functioning device with a control system, a suite of graphic products, a storage or lighting item, or a fully wearable item of clothing or accessory. Whatever the product, appropriate materials and components should be used. Processes and techniques should be executed to a high standard, showing good use of machinery and tools, and attention must be paid to the accuracy and quality of the finish.

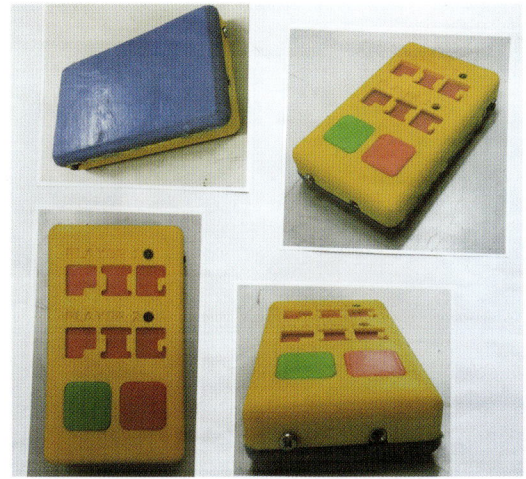

Figure 14.15 The finished device is a score tracker for a specific game. The casing is high quality and neatly finished, but it also contains a fully functioning circuit.

Figure 14.16 The environmentally friendly lighting product is manufactured from 60 per cent recycled cardboard. It is a high-quality, fully functioning product made with precision and attention to detail.

(e) Analysing and evaluating design decisions and prototypes

Throughout the iterative process of designing and the manufacture of the finished prototype product you must show evidence of evaluating and analysing your design decisions and outcomes as an ongoing process.

Part of this final assessment strand is assessed in the earlier sections of the portfolio, but the main focus at this stage is a critical, objective appraisal of the final prototype. You are expected to reference the design brief and specification criteria, the needs, wants and views of potential users, and outline the strengths and weaknesses of your prototype product. It is highly recommended that you test your product, in situ if possible, or conduct a full user or wearer trial. You can include photographic evidence to support any commentary along with sketched ideas and notes for further improvements and modifications.

This final appraisal should be included in the formal section of your portfolio.

Figure 14.17 The summer dress is a high-quality, fully functioning wearable product. It should be noted that the internal finishing of seams is equally important in textile products, as it can affect the external appearance.

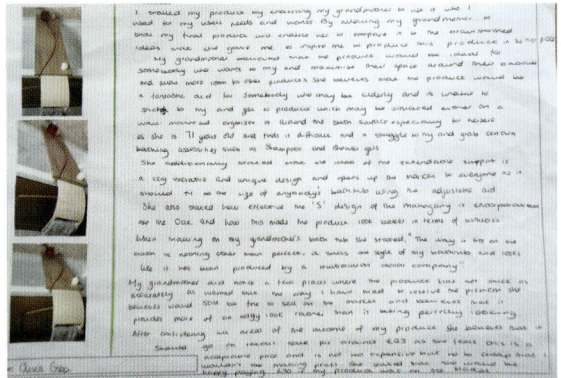

Figure 14.18 Testing your prototype product in situ will give you a better understanding of the success of your product. This should also include the views of the potential client or users.

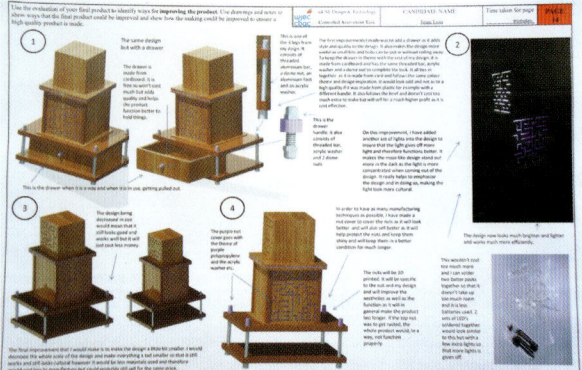

Figure 14.19 Based on testing and obtaining the views of potential users, you should put forward ideas for modifications and improvements. The improvements could be for functional or aesthetic reasons, or improvements to manufacture.

Summary of evidence needed for assessment

- Informal sketchbook/folio which fully demonstrates the iterative process.
- Formal portfolio which includes all technical details for manufacture.
- A finished prototype product.
- Supporting models, prototypes, tests and iterations.

KEY POINTS

- June 1st – contextual challenges are published.
- Guided hours means time set by and agreed with your teacher to complete the NEA in the classroom.
- Research needs to be focused, relevant and linked to the context.
- You must show evidence of evaluating and analysing your design decisions and outcomes as an ongoing process.
- Client and potential users are important and should be considered throughout the iterative process.
- Modelling is an essential requirement and must be in evidence throughout the folio of work.
- The manufacturing specification needs to include all the technical details to manufacture the product.
- The sequence for making must be sufficiently detailed to allow a third party to follow in order to make the same product.
- Your product should be finished to a high standard and be fit for purpose.
- The final evaluation should be a well-written and articulate appraisal of the prototype product.
- It is a good idea to test your prototype in situ to get a better understanding of how it performs in reality.

Glossary

A/B testing: user testing to choose between two different design ideas.

Absorbent: the ability of a fibre to suck up moisture.

Additive manufacture: the process of building up a physical shape layer by layer.

Aesthetics: factors that determine the looks of a product, including colour, size and texture.

Alloy: a mixture of two or more different metals.

Amplifier: a subsystem to increase the magnitude of an analogue voltage.

Amplify: to make something larger.

Analogue sensor: a sensor to measure 'how big' a physical quantity is.

Analysing: deconstructing information to find connections and logical chains of reasoning.

Anneal: heating a metal to increase its elasticity.

Applied finishes: processes applied to fabrics to add to their properties or even improve them.

Appliqué: a decorative feature made by stitching one fabric shape onto a different fabric to create pattern.

Aramid synthetic fibre: a non-flammable heat resistant fibre at least 60 times stronger than nylon.

Assembly line: a line of workers and equipment in a factory. A product is gradually assembled as it moves through each stage of the line until it is completely assembled.

Astable: a subsystem to produce a continuously pulsing output at a specific frequency.

Automated production: the use of automatically (computer) controlled equipment or machinery to manufacture products.

Autorouting: a PCB design software function to optimise the pattern of tracks.

Availability: what shape, form a material is and how easy it is to access.

Batch production: making a small number of the same or similar product.

Bauxite: ore that contains aluminium.

Bending strength: the ability to resist being bent.

Bespoke: a one-off design to a unique specification.

Bias binding: a strip of fabric cut on a 45° angle diagonally across the straight grain of the fabric, which has some stretch as a result of being cut this way; bias binding naturally bends around corners more easily, maintaining a smooth line.

Bias: this is the diagonal line which runs at a 45° angle to the selvedge edge and straight of grainline of the fabric.

Billet: a rectangular bar of metal that can be processed into a smaller form by rolling.

Biodegradable: the ability of a material, substance or object to break down naturally in the environment through the action of microorganisms, thereby avoiding pollution.

Biodiversity: the balance of many different living creatures living side by side in a particular habitat.

Biomimicry: taking ideas and mimicking features from nature.

Blow moulding: a method of shaping thermoforming polymer by heating it and blowing it into shape.

Bondaweb: a non-woven fabric with adhesive on both sides that allows two fabrics to be joined together. Heat is needed to activate the process.

Boning: metal or plastic strips used to add structure to products.

Brainstorming: thinking of as many different ideas as possible and getting them written down or sketched as quickly as possible.

CAD: computer-aided design.

CAM: computer-aided manufacture.

Carbon fibre reinforced polymer (CFRP): a thermoforming polymer reinforced with carbon fibre.

Cell production: small sub-assembly lines working on parts of a product or one size of a complete product.

Cellulosic fibres: natural fibres from plant-based sources.

Chassis: the support structure for a mechanical system.

Circular economy: extracting maximum value from resources, which are then kept in use for as long as possible, recovered and regenerated into new products instead of thrown away.

Clearance hole: a hole large enough for a screw to slide through.

Client or **potential user**: the person or persons who will likely need, want or use your product.

CNC: Computer Numerically Controlled.

Coarseness: a measure of the rough texture found on abrasive papers.

Coating: an additional outer layer added to paper.

Colour separation: separate colours (cyan, magenta, yellow and black) printed in different combinations to create other colours.

Compensation: payment, usually money given to someone as a result of loss.

Components: smaller items that help products function as intended, or add-on non-functional features such as lace edges, buttons, ribbons, toggles.

Composite: a material manufactured from a combination of two materials with desirable properties.

Compressive strength: the ability to resist being squashed.

Context: the settings or surroundings in which the final product will be used.

Continuous flow production: products are made 24/7, making use of computer-aided machines (CAM).

Conversion: converting tree trunks into planks.

COSHH: regulations regarding the Control Of Substances Harmful to Health.

Cost: what the financial cost of a material is relative to other materials.

Counterfeit: an imitation of something valuable, sold with the intention to defraud or deceive someone.

Cracking: the processing of naptha to produce a monomer.

Cradle-to-cradle design: an approach to the design of products that models human industry on nature's processes, viewing materials as nutrients circulating in healthy, safe metabolisms.

Criteria: specific goals that a product must achieve in order to be successful.

Cross filing: a method of shaping metal.

Cross grain: horizontally across the fabric from selvedge edge to selvedge edge.

Cultural awareness: understanding the differences in attitudes and values between people from other countries or other backgrounds.

Cultural factors: how cultural background can influence the design of a metal product.

Culture: the ideas, customs, and social behaviour of a particular people or society.

Current: a measure of the actual electricity flowing.

Debug: find and remove errors in a microcontroller program.

Deconstructed: take something apart.

Deforestation: the large-scale felling of trees which are not replanted.

Deforming: the process of changing the shape of a material by applying force, heat or moisture.

Design brief: a statement of intent outlining what is to be designed and made.

Design collaboration: a number of designers working together on specific design projects.

Design fixation: when a designer limits their creativity by only exploring one avenue of design or relying too heavily on features of existing designs.

Design opportunities: areas to explore where a real-life need has been identified.

Design specification: a list of features the product must have in order to be successful.

Development: the creative process of selecting ideas, elements, materials and manufacturing techniques from initial ideas and using them in new ways to explore and produce newer and better designs or ideas.

Digital sensor: a sensor to detect a yes/no or on/off situation.

Dip coating: the process of coating a metal in a thermoforming polymer.

Dowel: a cylindrical timber moulding of consistent cross-section.

Drape: how a fabric hangs, flows when handled.

Draw filing: a method of smoothing the edge of metal.

Drilling: the process of making a hole in the Earth's surface to extract liquids or gas.

Driver: a subsystem to boost a signal.

Ductile: the ability of a material to be stretched out.

Ecological deficit: a measure to indicate that more natural resources are being used than nature can replace.

Ecological footprint: a measure of the impact that human activity has on the environment.

Ecosystem: the natural and delicate balance of plant life, soil and animals that live interdependent lives.

Effort: the input force on a lever.

Electroluminescent: a material that provides a visible light when exposed to a current.

Embedding: permanently installing a microcontroller into a product.

Environmental directive: a type of law to provide protection for the environment.

Environmental factors: how the material affects the environment during sourcing, processing, manufacture, use and final disposal.

Ethical factors: how the moral standards of society can influence the design of a product.

Evaluating: appraising and making judgements on information and issues.

Exploitation: treating someone unfairly in order to benefit from their work.

Exploited: unfairly taken advantage of.

Extrusion: a length of material with a consistent cross-section.

Fabric construction: the way a fabric has been made – for example, knitted or woven.

Fabric specification: a list of guidelines used by designers to ensure the correct fabric is used for a product.

Face edge: the surface of a piece of wood that is known to be straight and true.

Face side: the surface of a piece of wood that is known to be straight and true.

Fast fashion: a recent trend involving the quick transfer of new collections from the catwalk into stores. Fast fashion is often on trend, low quality and low in price.

Fastenings: a means of joining fabrics together, for example zips or poppers.

Feedback: achieving precise control by feeding information from an output back into the input of a control system.

Ferrous metals: metals that contain iron.

Fibre: a fine hair-like structure.

Filament: a very and fine slender thread; the extruded material that is used in a 3D printer.

Finish: an applied coating to a material in order to protect or improve aesthetics.

Finite resources: non-renewable sources that cannot be replaced in a sufficient timeframe to allow further human consumption.

Flowchart: a graphical representation of a process.

Fluidised bath: an aerated powder which flows like a fluid.

Focus group: group of people used to check a product design is on track.

Force: a push, pull or twist.

Forest Stewardship Council (FSC): organisation that promotes environmentally appropriate, socially beneficial, and economically viable management of the world's forests.

Fossil fuels: finite resources that cannot be replaced.

Fractional distillation: the processing of crude oil to produce naptha.

FSC: See Forest Stewardship Council.

Fulcrum: the pivot point on a lever.

Function: what a product will do and how it will work.

Functionality: how well a product fits its purpose.

Fuse: the melting and joining of powder particles into an even layer.

Gain: the amplification factor of an amplifier.

Galvanising: the process of coating a metal in zinc.

Geotextiles: textiles associated with soil and various aspects of construction, drainage and support.

Glass-reinforced plastic (GRP): a thermoforming polymer reinforced with glass fibres.

Global warming: a rise in temperature of the Earth's atmosphere caused by pollution and gases.

Gloss: a shiny surface finish with high lustre.

Grams per square metre (gsm): the weight of paper and card.

Greenhouse gas: atmospheric pollution which traps heat at the Earth's surface.

Handle: the level of comfort against the skin.

Hardening: a heat treatment process that hardens steel.

Hardwood: timber that comes from deciduous trees.

High-fidelity prototype: a detailed and very accurate prototype similar to the final product.

High-volume production: many products are made, making extensive use of machinery and manufacturing aids.

Hydrophilic membrane: ability to repel and release moisture.

Insecticides: chemicals used to kill or suppress insects that destroy vegetation and crops.

Insulation: a means of adding warmth and keeping warm.

Integrated circuit (IC): a microchip.

Interactive textiles: fabrics that contain a device or circuit that responds and reacts with the user.

Interfacing: a bonded fabric, which when fused to a different fabric adds strength; connecting sensors and output devices to electronic control circuits.

Isometric drawing: a 3D representation of a design using 30° angles for all projections of depth.

Iterative design process: the development of an idea through to realisation by repeatedly testing, modelling and refining the idea.

Jigs: a mechanical device to aid production.

Laminated: layers of wood glued together.

Laminating: a method of bending wood by slicing into thin veneers and gluing back together.

Lamination: process of joining materials together with heat or adhesives.

Lay plan: how pattern templates are laid out on a piece of material in order to cut out accurately.

Lever arm length: the distance between the force and the fulcrum.

Lever: a rigid bar that pivots on a fulcrum.

Life cycle: the stages a product goes through from beginning (extraction of raw materials) to end (disposal).

Linear economy: raw materials are used to make a product, and waste is thrown away.

Lining: a layer of fabric in the same shape as the outer layer which adds supports and conceals the construction processes.

Linkage: a component to direct forces and movement to where they are needed.

Load: the output force from a lever.

Logic gate: a digital integrated circuit component whose output logic state depends on the combination of states on its inputs.

Low-fidelity prototype: a quick prototype that gives a basic idea of a product's looks or functions.

Lustre: a gentle shine or soft glow.

Managed forest: a forest where new trees are planted whenever one is cut down.

Manufactured boards: man-made boards that are available in large flat sheets.

Market pull: a new product is produced in response to demand from the market.

Marking out: the process of applying a drawing on to a material.

Mass production: many products are made, making extensive use of machinery, manufacturing aids and the use of CAM.

Measurable criteria: specific points that are measurable, such as weight or size.

Mechanical advantage: the factor by which a mechanical system increases the force.

Mechanical system: takes an input force (or motion) and processes it to produce an output force (or motion).

Mechanism: a series of parts that work together to control forces and motion.

Member: a part in a structure.

Micro-encapsulation: the process of applying microscopic capsules to fibres or fabrics.

Microfibre: an extremely fine, specially engineered fibre.

Micron: one thousandth of a mm (0.001 mm) – used to specify the thickness of card.

Milling: a method of cutting metal to produce slots, grooves and flat surfaces.

Modelling: the process of testing or developing a product in 3D that can be held or interacted with.

Monocoque: structural system where loads are supported through an object's external skin.

Monomer: a molecule that can be bonded to others to form a polymer.

Monostable: a subsystem to produce an output pulse of a specific period.

Mordant: a chemical that is dissolved in a dye solution that sets the colour on the fabric. Salt does the same thing.

MOSFET: a type of transistor, used as a transducer driver.

Motion: when an object moves its position over time.

Natural polymers (biopolymers): polymers made from natural sources, such as corn starch.

Natural timber: timber that has come directly from a tree.

Non-ferrous metals: metals that do not contain iron.

Non-renewable: energy sources which are not replenished.

Objective criteria: realistic and achievable points setting out the purpose of the product.

Obsolescence: when a product becomes unusable or out of date.

One-off production: one product is made.

Opacity: the quality of lacking transparency or translucence.

Open cast mining: mining ore by scraping and removing the top surface of the ground.

Oxidise: a chemical reaction with the air which changes the surface of the material.

PAR: planed all round.

PBS: planed both sides.

Pesticides: chemicals used to kill or suppress pests that destroy vegetation and crops.

Phase-changing materials: encapsulated droplets on fibres and materials that change between liquid to solid form within a temperature range.

Pilot hole: a hole into which a screw cuts its own thread.

Pinion: a small input gear.

Planing: smoothing the surface of rough sawn-timber on one or more sides using a plane.

Plasticisers: give flexibility to polymers.

Polymer: a scientific term for a substance or fibre that has a molecular structure made up of much smaller units which are bonded together; can be natural or manufactured.

Polymerisation: the blending of different monomers to produce a certain plastic/polymer.

Potential divider: two resistors, used to produce a known output voltage signal.

PPE: the range of protective equipment or clothing worn when working with a material.

Preparation: the process of preparing a timber ready for a surface finish to be applied.

Preservative: an additive for timber that increases its durability.

Press forming: a method of shaping thermoforming polymer by heating it and pressing it between two halves of a mould.

Primary data: data gathered by yourself 'first-hand'.

Primary research: research you conduct yourself, such as an interview to gather first-hand information.

Primer: the first coat of paint, designed to bond to the surface.

Printed circuit board (PCB): the support and connections for the electronic components in a product.

Program flowchart: a set of instructions that tells a microcontroller what to do.

Progressive bundle production: bundles of garments or product parts are moved in sequence, from one worker to the next.

Protein fibres: natural fibres from animal-based sources.

Prototype: the first or early models of an idea. This term could also apply to a finished concept model.

PSE: planed square edge.

Pulp: raw material from trees used to make paper.

Qualitative data: observations and opinions about a product.

Quantitative data: specific measurable data given in numerical form.

Quantum tunnelling composites: materials that change from insulators to conductors when under pressure.

Quilting: process of layering three materials together and stitching through to improve its characteristics.

Rating: the maximum value of a specified quantity that a component can handle.

Raw edge: the unfinished edge of a piece of material.

Ream: pack of 500 sheets.

Recyclable: a material suitable for processing using tertiary recycling methods.

Recycled paper: paper made from wood pulp using some re-pulped paper.

Reinforcement: extra material added to increase strength.

Relay: a component to allow control of a high voltage/current device from a low voltage/current circuit.

Render: the addition of colour or texture to a design.

Renewable: energy sources which will not run out.

Resist method: a means of preventing dye or paint from penetrating an area on the fabric. This creates the patterns.

Rigid: can withstand forces without bending or flexing.

Rotational velocity: the same as rotational speed, usually measured in rpm.

Schematic: a visual representation of a circuit or system.

Screen printing: a printing process for adding detail or text to polymer products.

Seam allowance: the distance between the raw edge of the fabric and stitching line.

Seasoning: reducing the moisture content of timber.

Secondary data: data collected by others 'second-hand'

Secondary research: information that relies on other people's findings.

Self-finishing: a surface which requires no further treatment to protect it or improve its appearance.

Selvedge: the sealed edge of the fabric.

Sensor: the 'eyes and ears' of an electronic system.

Shaft: a rod which carries rotation to different parts of a mechanism.

Signal: a voltage representing a physical quantity.

Smart material: a material whose properties change in response to an external change in environment.

Social factors: how the social background of a group of people can influence the design of a metal product.

Softwoods: timber that comes from coniferous trees.

Spur gear: a gear wheel with teeth around its edge.

Stabilise: make more rigid and stronger, prevents movement.

Stabilisers: added to polymers to reduce UV degradation and brittleness.

Stakeholder(s): a person or people who have an interest in or would use your product.

Steam bending: a method of bending wood by steaming, bending and cooling.

Stock form: the standard shapes and sizes of materials that are commonly available.

Straight grain: indicates the strength of the fabric in line with warp yarns.

Straight-line production: work flows through a series of workstations in a straight line.

Strip heater: a machine that produces bends in thermoforming polymer by heating it up.

Stroke: the linear distance moved in a reciprocating system.

Structure: object constructed from several parts.

Subroutine: a small program within a larger program.

Subsystem: the interconnected parts of a system.

Surface decoration: techniques to add detail, such as pattern to fabrics.

Surface mount technology (SMT): the industrial method of using robotic assembly to manufacture miniaturised electronic circuit boards.

Sustainability: producing goods and services without impacting on the needs of future populations.

Sustainable design: product design which minimises the environmental impact of manufacturing and using the product.

SWG: Standard Wire Gauge – a measurement of the wall thickness of a metal tube.

Synthetic: derived from petrochemicals or man-made.

Synthetic polymers: polymers that come from crude oil.

Systems thinking: considering a design problem as a whole experience for the user.

Technology push: a development in materials, components or manufacturing methods leads to the development of a new product.

Tempering: a heat treatment process that removes the brittleness from hardened steel.

Template: a 2D shape that aids cutting out a shape.

Tensional strength: the ability to resist being pulled apart.

Tessellate: to arrange shapes to interlock, thus avoiding waste when cutting out of a sheet.

Tessellation: an arrangement of shapes closely fitted together, especially of polygons in a repeated pattern without gaps or overlapping.

Texture: a raised surface that adds to the feel and handle of a fabric.

Thermoforming polymers/fibres: polymers that can be softened by heating, shaped and set over and over again.

Thermosetting polymers: polymers that can only be heated and shaped once.

Throwaway culture: the rise of fast fashion has made clothing far more affordable for consumers. The incredibly low prices in some high-street stores have resulted in a throwaway culture, meaning that consumers do not feel the need to keep clothing that is no longer in fashion, and happily dispose of it.

Throwaway society: a society that excessively consumes and wastes resources.

Thyristor: a latching transducer driver.

Toile: an early version or prototype of a garment, made in cheap substitute material to test the design, fit and form in order to develop the idea.

Tolerance: an allowance included in the seam allowance, for consistency when assembling a product.

Torque: a turning force.

Torsional strength: the ability to resist being twisted.

Transducer: a device to convert an electrical signal into a physical output.

Triangulation: adding cross-members to a structure to increase rigidity.

Turning: a method of producing cylindrical items in metal.

Twill weave: recognisable by the characteristic diagonal line pattern created by the weft yarn going over two warp yarns and under one, with a 'step', or offset, between rows to create the diagonal pattern.

User testing: testing a product by observing a user interact and use your product for its intended purpose.

User: the person or group of people a product is designed for.

User-centred design (USD): looking at and checking the needs, wants, and requirements of the user at every stage of the design process.

UV (ultraviolet) light: outside the human visible spectrum at its violet end.

Vacuum forming: a method of shaping thermoforming polymer by heating it and sucking it around a mould.

Velocity ratio: the factor by which a mechanical system reduces the rotational velocity.

Veneer: a very thin section of natural timber.

Vinyl: a self-adhesive polymer, available in a range of colours, suitable for CNC knife cutting.

Virgin fibre paper: paper made entirely from 'new' wood pulp.

Voltage comparator: a subsystem to compare two analogue input voltages, and produce a digital output.

Voltage: the electrical 'pressure' trying to make an electric current flow.

Warp: yarns that run along the length of fabric.

Wasting: the process of shaping material by cutting away unwanted parts.

Weft: yarns that run across the fabric.

Index

3D models 297
3D printing 11, 106–7
3D router 11, 166–7, 220
3D shapes 10

A

A/B testing 305
acrylic 60, 231
additive manufacture 11
    see also 3D printing
adhesives 107, 133–4, 162–3, 218–9
aesthetics 283
air seasoning 141
Airbus 282–3
alloys 56, 175
aluminium 55–6, 109, 174, 179
annealing 174
anodising 197
anthropometrical issues, and design 278–9
anti-static textiles 240
Apple 283
aramid synthetic fibre 28, 60
assembly line 2
astable 73–4
audio recordings 299
automated production 2, 5
autorouting 100

B

balsa 143
batch production 99, 127, 154–5, 184
battery energy 22
beech 142
belt drives 46–7
bending strength 150, 181
bespoke design 98–9
    see also one-off production
bevel gears 85–6
bias binding 243
binding methods 130–1
biodegradeable material 202, 237
biodiversity 149, 236
biomass energy 19, 20
biomimicry 25, 280
biopolymers 202
blackening 197
bleaching agents 116, 240
bleed-proof paper 113
blow moulding 221
board
    card 113
    curving for strength 123

ecological footprint 116
    foam 114
    laminated 114–5
    life cycle 117
    properties 114
    sheets 114
    stiffening 123
    stock forms 125
    structural integrity 123–4
    surface finishes 136–8
    thickness 48
    types 50–1
bonded textiles 227
boning 243
box joints 161
boxboard 51
brass 56, 109, 175, 179
brazing 108, 192
breathable fabrics 27
bridges 181
bronze 56, 175, 179
brushing 239
burnout printing 261
butt joint 151
buzzers 79

C

calendaring 239
callipers 186–7
cam lock 164
cams 88
    cam and follower 45
capacitors 72–3
car industry
    and pollution 20
    robot technology 2
    see also motor vehicles
carbon dioxide 20
    see also greenhouse gases
carbon fibre reinforced polymer (CFRP) 25, 209
carbon footprint 16
carbon neutral 16, 20
card 113
    making principles from 138
cardboard 50–1, 114
    see also board
cardboard modelling 293
cartridge paper 49, 113
case binding 131
casings for electronic components 94–5
cast iron 55, 173, 179
casting 106
catches 218

cedar 143
cell production 249
child labour 277–8
chipboard 54, 145
circuit diagram 32
circular economy 13, 89, 276
clockwork wind-up power 21
clothing see textiles
cloud-based technology 9
CNC lathe 194–5
coal 19
coated textiles 233–4
collaboration 287
colour separation 130
communication, technology 4–5
competition, and pricing 5
composite materials 25–6
compound gear train 82–3
compressive strength 150, 181
computer numerically controlled (CNC) machines 9–11
computer-aided design (CAD) 8–11, 100, 166, 301–2
computer-aided manufacturing (CAM) 9–11, 100, 128–30, 155, 166–7, 194–5, 214, 219
conductive fibres 26
consumer choice, and new technologies 3
consumer rights 6–8
Consumer Rights Act 2015 6–8
counterfeit goods 6
continuous flow production 155, 185
copier paper 49, 113
coping saw 103
copper 56, 174, 179
corner blocks 164
Corriflute 114–5
corrugated cardboard 51, 113–4
corsetry 243
costs
    calculating 125–6
    metals 183
    polymers 207, 212
    product design 153–4
    of prototyping 121
    textiles 246
    timber 148
cotton 59, 231, 232
cracking 201
cradle-to-cradle design 276
cradle-to-cradle production 13

crank and slider 87
crease resistance 240
critical analysis 280–1
cropland 17
crude oil 200–1
cruise control 34
culture
    and design 277
    impact of technology 4–5
current 66
cutting 132
    materials 102
    tools 102

D

data collection 271–2, 273, 304–6
debossing 136
decals 223
deforestation 120, 145, 149
design
    3D models 297
    anthropometrical issues 278–9
    brainstorming 286–7
    brief 274–5
    collaboration 9, 287
    collecting data 271–2, 273
    context 270–1
    critical analysis 280–1
    cultural awareness 277
    drawings 288–93
    economic challenges 277–8
    end user 270, 272–3
    ergonomics 278
    fixation 279
    flowcharts 296
    models 293–4
    presentations 295
    process 270–3
    research 282
    responding to feedback 304
    schedules 298
    schematic diagrams 291
    social challenges 276–7
    strategies 286
    systems thinking 288
    testing ideas 279–80
    tools and equipment 300–1
    user-centred 287–8
    working drawings 296–7
    written notes 295
    see also computer-aided design (CAD)

die cutting 138
dip-coating 110, 196
discharge printing 261
drawings 288–93
dressmaker's dummy 264
drilling 104
    metals 186, 188–90
    polymers 216
    timber 160–1
duralumin 176
dyeing fabrics 261–2
Dyson, James 283–4

E
ecological deficit 17
ecological footprint 17–8, 88
    current 66
    metal extraction 177
    polymers 204
economy
    circular 13, 89
    linear 13
elastane 231
electric cars 8, 21–2
electric oven 33–4
electricity
    generation 18–22
    mains power 22
    see also energy
electroluminescent material 23
electromagnet 79, 80
electronic components
    astable 73–4
    benefits and limitations
        of 91
    calculating cost of 98
    capacitors 72–3
    casing and protecting 94–5
    logic gates 76–7
    monostable 72
    output components 78–80
    process components 71–2
    stock sizes 95–6
    thyristor 72
    transistors 71–2
    voltage amplifier 75–6
    voltage comparator 74–5
electronic systems
    input devices 70
    input sensors 30–2
    integrated circuits (ICs) 30
    microcontrollers 30–2, 34–7
    modelling 295
    Ohm's law 66–7
    output devices 33
    programmable 34
    resistance 66–7
    signals 30
    subroutine 35–7
    subsystems 30, 68–78

switch sensor 32
switches 70
system diagram 30, 68
thermistor 32, 71
voltage 66
embossing 136, 239
embroidery 262
    computer numerically
        controlled (CNC) 10
emerging technologies
    see new and emerging
        technologies
enamelling 197
energy
    efficiency 13
    fossil fuels 8, 19
    non-renewable 18–9
    renewable 8, 18–22
    sources of 18–22
enterprise, impact of new and
    emerging technologies 2–4
environment
    carbon footprint 16
    deforestation 120
    environmental directives 12
    ethical responsibilities 92
    friendly product design 276
    global warming 16
    landfill 204
    and linear economy 13
    and metal products 179
    and paper production 116
    and polymers 204, 206–7
    sustainability 7–8, 12
    and timber products 147
environmental impact 14–5
    and design 275–6
epoxy resin 163, 193
ergonomics, and design 278
ethics
    and the environment 92
    and trade 7
    and use of materials 148–9,
        180, 208
European Ecolabel 12–3
exploded diagrams 293
exploitation 16

F
fabric
    construction 226–9
    specification 230–1
    stock forms 244–6
    types 244–5
    see also textiles
Fairtrade 15–6
fast fashion 237
fastenings 245
feedback, responding to 304
felted textiles 227–8

ferrous metals 54–5, 173–4
fibres 231–3
filing tools 103, 187–8
finishing techniques *see* surface
    finishes
fire-resistant textiles 28
fixings 107, 163–4, 190–1, 217–8
flame resistance 240
flexography printing 129
flowchart programs 35
flowcharts 296
foam board 114, 138
foam modelling 294
Foamex 115
focus groups 280, 304–5
folding 122
food packaging 117–8
force 41, 87
    and timber products 150
    withstanding 92–3, 122
Forest Stewardship Council
    (FSC) 116, 146
forestry 17
fossil fuels 8, 16, 17, 19, 20
fractional distillation 200–1
frame construction 162

G
galvanising 196
Gantt chart 298
garment construction *see*
    textiles
gas 19
gears 45–6
    bevel 85–6
    compound gear train 82–3
    simple gear train 81
    worm drive 84–5
geotextiles 28
geothermal energy 19, 21
glass reinforced plastic (GRP)
    25, 209
glazing textiles 239
global production 4–5, 7
    ethical factors 7, 121
    and job losses 5
global warming 16
grazing land 17
greenhouse gases 16, 20, 236

H
hacksaw 103
hand cutting tools 102
hardboard 54, 145
hardening 174, 181–2
hardwoods 52–3, 142–3, 148
    see also timber
haute couture 248
hazardous substances 92

health and safety, hazardous
    substances 92
hemp 59, 231
high-fidelity prototypes 303
high-volume production 213–4
hinges 218
hybrid cars 21–2
    see also electric cars
hybrid technology 8
hydroelectric energy 19, 21
hydrophilic membrane 233

I
Industrial Revolution 2
industry
    impact of new and
        emerging technologies
        2–4
    see also industries by name
infrastructure 17
input devices 70–1
input force 41
input sensors 30–2
interactive textiles 26
interfacing 242
interlining 242
internet, and global production
    4–5
inverters 76–7
isometric drawing 289

J
jelutong 142
jigs 101, 155, 184, 213
joining methods 107
    metals 190–3
    polymers 217–8
    timber 151, 161–2
just-in-time manufacturing
    99–100
jute 59

K
Kevlar® 25–6
kiln seasoning 141
knitted textiles 61, 228–9
knock-down fittings 164

L
laminating 51, 136–7, 165
landfill 204
laser cutting 10–1, 106, 166, 195,
    212, 220, 251
lathe 193–4, 219, 220
layout paper 49, 113
legislation, consumer rights 6–8
levers 41, 42–3
life cycle, of product 3–4, 14
    environmental impact 14–5
lifestyle, impact of technology
    4–5

light-dependent resistor (LDR) 31–2, 71
light-emitting diode (LED) 33, 78
light output 78
linear economy 13, 276
linear motion 40
linen 59, 232
lining 242
linkages 43
logic gates 76–7
loop stitching 130
loudspeakers 79
low-fidelity prototypes 303

M

machine screws 191
mahogany 143
'make-use-recycle' strategy 13
manufactured boards 53–4, 143–4, 148, 153
manufacturing
    just-in-time 99–100
    systems 248–9
    see also computer-aided manufacturing (CAM); production
market pull 3
marking-out 102, 132
    metals 186–7
    polymers 214–5
    timber 156
    tools 156–7
mass production 2, 99, 129, 155, 184
materials
    availability 119
    biodegradable 202
    biomimicry 25
    calculating cost of 98
    composites 25–6
    electroluminescent 23
    fibres 59–62
    influences on choice of 118
    interactive textiles 26–7
    joining methods 107
    for medical applications 24
    new and emerging technologies 3
    phase changing 27
    properties 119
    selecting 90–1
    self-finishing 109
    shape memory alloys (SMAs) 24
    smart 23–8
    stock forms 96
    strengthening 122
    see also board; metals; paper; textiles; timber

mathematical modelling 299–300
measuring tools 157–8
mechanical advantage (MA) 87
mechanical components 41–2
    belt drives 46–7
    cam and follower 45
    gears 45–6, 81
    levers 42–3
    linkages 43
    pulleys 43
    strengthening 92–4
mechanical devices 87–8
mechanical systems 41
medium-density fibreboard (MDF) 54, 144
mercerising 239
metals 54–5
    alloys 56, 175
    annealing 174
    availability 179
    billets 183
    costs 179–80, 183
    cutting 187
    drilling 188–90
    ecological footprint 177
    environmental impact 179
    ethical factors 180
    extrusions 183
    ferrous 54–5, 173–4
    forming 188
    hardening 174, 181–2
    joining methods 190–3
    life cycle of products 178
    machining 193–5
    making principles for 198
    marking-out 186–7
    non-ferrous 55–6, 174–5
    recycling 178
    selecting 178–9
    smelting 176–7
    social footprint 177, 180
    sources of 176
    specialist techniques 185–6
    standard wire gauge (SWG) 183
    stock forms 97, 182–3
    strength of 181
    surface finishes 196–7
    tempering 174, 182
    tools and equipment 187–8
    working with 105–8
    see also production
microcontrollers 30–2, 34–7
micro-encapsulation 24
microfibres 26, 60
micrometer 187
milling machines 193–4, 219, 220

miniaturisation 91
mining 177, 180
mobile technology 5
modelling 293–4, 299–300
monostable 72
moth proofing 240
motion
    linear 40
    oscillating 40
    reciprocating 40
    rotary 39–40, 79
motor vehicles
    cruise control 34
    electric cars 8
    energy sources 21–2
mounting board 114

N

naphtha 201
natural polymers 59
new and emerging technologies
    electric cars 8
    energy efficiency 13
    ethical factors 7
    hybrid technology 8
    impact of 2–5
    market pull 3
    materials 3
    product life cycle 3–4
    robot technology 2
    sustainability 7–8, 12–3
    technology push 3
nickel 23
nitinol 24
non-ferrous metals 55–6, 174–5
nuclear energy 19
nuts 191
nuts and bolts 107, 190
nylon 60

O

oak 143
obsolescence 89, 283
offset lithography printing 129
Ohm's law 66–7
oil 19
    environmental impact 204
    see also crude oil
oil finishing 197
oils 169–70
one-off production 126, 154, 184, 213
one-off prototyping 98–9
operational amplifier 74
oscillating motion 40
output components 78–80
output devices 33
output force 41
oxidising 109

P

paint finishes 170, 197
painting fabrics 262
panel trim fixings 218
paper
    bleaching agents 116
    chemical pulping process 112
    coating 135
    ecological footprint 116
    environmental impact 120
    folding for shape 132–3
    folding for strength 122
    laminating 136–7
    life cycle 117
    making by hand 111
    making principles for 138
    mechanical pulping process 112
    pulp 50, 111
    recycled 50, 112–3
    sizes 48–9
    sources of 111
    surface finishes 135
    types 49–50, 113
    weight 48
perfect binding 131
personal protective equipment (PPE) 160
perspective drawing 290
pewter 176, 179
phase-changing materials (PCMs) 27
photochromic pigment 24
piezo sounder 79
pine 143
piping 243
planing wood 159
plasma cutter 195
plastic
    recycling 8
    waste 236
plastic rivets 134
plywood 54, 144, 150–1
polishes 170
polishing 222
polyester 60, 233
polymerisation 201
polymers 57–8
    additives 204
    aesthetics 206
    bending 104
    biopolymers 202
    blow moulding 221
    computer-aided manufacturing (CAM) 214, 219
    costs 207, 212
    cutting 215

deforming 217
drilling 216
ecological footprint 204
environmental impact 206–7
ethical factors 208
forming 216, 221–2
functionality 206
joining methods 217–8
life cycle of products 205
line bending 216
machining 219
marking-out 214–5
natural 59
plasticisers 210
prototyping 223–4
recycling 204–5
reforming 217
selecting 206
shaping 215
social footprint 204, 207
sources of 200–1
stabilisers 210
stock forms 97, 210–2
strength of 208–9
strengthening 209
surface finishes 222–3, 224
synthetic 60, 200
thermoforming 57–8, 202–3
thermosetting 58, 203, 208–9
vinyl cutting 220
see also production
polymorph 24
polypropylene 60
pop rivets 107
potential divider 71
powder-coating 109–10, 196
pre-press 129–30
preservatives 169
press forming 222
primary data 271–2, 273
primer 109, 197
principles, designing and making 138–9
printed circuit board (PCB) 36, 91
printing
  burnout 261
  colour separation 130
  digital 260
  discharge 261
  flexography 129
  offset lithography 129
  pre-press 129–30
  screen 127–8, 223, 259–60
  stencilling 260
  sublimation 260–1
  super calendering 135

as surface finish 223, 259–60
product, life cycle analysis (LCA) 3–4
product design, calculating cost of 153–4
product life cycle analysis (LCA), environmental impact 14–5
production
  alternative processes 98–9
  batch 99, 127, 154, 184, 213
  bespoke 98–9
  computer-aided design (CAD) 8–11
  computer-aided manufacturing (CAM) 9–11
  continuous flow 155, 185
  cradle-to-cradle 13
  global 4–5, 7
  high-volume 213–4
  jigs 101, 155, 184, 213
  line 2, 8–9
  mass 99, 129, 155, 184
  metals 184–5
  one-off 126, 154, 184, 213
  polymers 213–4
  straight-line 248
  techniques 8–11
  textiles 247–8
  timber 154–5
  see also manufacturing
program flowcharts 35
progressive bundle production 249
prototyping 98–9, 100–1, 198–9, 223–4, 302–3
  assembly 107–8
  high-fidelity 303
  low-fidelity 303
  marking-out 132
  techniques 102–8, 132–4
  true cost of 121
  see also computer-aided design (CAD); computer-aided manufacturing (CAM)
pulleys 43
  pulley and belt drive 83–4
pulse frequencies 73–4

Q
qualitative data 305
quantitative data 305
quantum tunnelling composite (QTC) 23
questionnaires 305
quit 234–5

R
rack and pinion 47, 87
railway sleepers 146
ratchet and pawl 87
reciprocating motion 40
recycling 13, 88–9, 116–7
  metals 178
  paper 50, 112–3
  polymers 204–5
  textiles 236, 237–8
  throwaway culture 237
  timber 146
recycling technologies 8
reinforcing timber 150
renewable energy 8, 18–22
resistance 66–7
resources
  ecological footprint 17
  finite 236
  see also materials
Restriction of Hazardous Substances (RoHS) 92
reverse motion 43–4
rigidity 93–4
rivets 107, 134, 190, 218
robot technology 2
roof trusses 150
rotary motion 39–40, 79
routing 10
  computer numerically controlled (CNC) 10
rusting 109

S
saddle stitching 130
sanding 159, 215
sawing
  metals 187
  polymers 215
  wood 158–9
scan fitting 164–5
scissors, as mechanical system 41
Scots pine 143, 150
screen printing 127–8, 223, 259–60
screws 107, 163–4, 191, 217–8
seams 255–6
seasoning timber 140–1
secondary data 272, 273
self-finishing materials 109
self-tapping screws 217
sewing machines 250–1
sewn binding 130
shape memory alloys (SMAs) 24
shaping
  polymers 215
  techniques 103
  wood 159–60
shrink resistance 240

silk 59, 231, 233
silver 175, 179
smart materials 23–8
smelting 176–7
social footprint 145–6, 148, 177, 180, 204
  see also ecological footprint
social isolation, and new technologies 5
social media 5
softwoods 53, 143, 148
  see also timber
solar photovoltaic (PV) energy 19, 21
soldering 108, 191–2
solenoid 79
sound output 79
spiral binding 131
sportswear 25, 60
stabproof materials 25–6
stain resistance 240
stainless steel 175
stains 169
stakeholders 270
standard wire gauge (SWG) 183
staples 134
Starck, Phillippe 284–5
steam bending 147, 165–6
steel 55, 173, 175, 179
  finishing 109
stencils 128
stock forms
  board 125
  electronic components 95–6
  materials 96
  metals 97, 182–3
  polymers 97, 210–2
  textiles 244–6
  timber 96–7, 152–3
stonewashing 241
stool joints 162
straight-line production 248
street lights 33
strength
  of metal products 181
  of polymer products 208–9
  strengthening materials 92–4
  of structural systems 93–4
  of timber products 150
structural systems, strengthening 93–4
Styrofoam 114, 139
sublimation printing 260–1
subroutine 35–7
sugar paper 113
sun-protective clothing 27
super calendering 135

surface finishes 109–10, 135–8, 147
  applied finishes 238–9
  chemical 239–40
  decoration 239
  metals 196–7
  polymers 222–3, 224
  textiles 238–43, 259–62, 265
  textured 223
  timber 168–70, 171–2
surface mount technology (SMT) 91
surveys 305
suspension bridges 181
sustainability 7–8, 12–3, 17
  carbon footprint 16
  in design 89
  ecological footprint 17–8
  six Rs of 13–4
  see also environment
switch sensor 32
switches 70
synthetic polymers 60, 200
systems thinking 288

T
tape binding 131
technical textiles 26–8
technology
  cloud-based 9
  communication 4–5
  mobile 5
  push 3
  robot 2
  see also new and emerging technologies
tempering 174, 182
templates 128
tenon saw 103
tensile strenght 181
Tensol cement 218
tessellation 156
textiles 59–62
  anti-static 240
  bespoke design 248
  biodegradeable 237
  biodiversity 236
  bonded 227
  breathable fabrics 27
  coated 233–4
  costs 246
  crease resistance 240
  darts 256–7
  decoration 239
  dyeing 261–2
  ecological footprint 235
  embroidery 262
  environmental impact 235–6
  fabric specification 230–1

fancy yarns 232
fastenings 245
felted 227–8
fibre blends 231
fibres 231, 232–3
flame resistance 240
gathers 256
geotextiles 28
insulation 239
interactive 26
knitted 61, 228–9
lamination 233
layering 242
moth proofing 240
non-woven 227–8
painting fabrics 262
pattern marking and cutting 251–4, 257–8
pattern pieces 246–7
pleats 256
quilting 234–5
recycling 236, 237–8
seam making 255–6
selecting 263–4
selvedge 226
shrink resistance 240
social footprint 236–7
spinning 231–2
stain resistance 240
stock forms 244–6
stonewashing 241
straight grain 226
structural integrity 241
surface finishes 238–43, 259–62, 265
technical 26–8
templates 264–5
thermo-regulating 27
threads 245
toile 264–5, 294
tools and equipment 250–1
warp 226–7
water-repellent 240
weft 226
and working conditions 236–7
woven 61, 226–7
see also materials
textured finishes 223
thermistor 32, 71
thermochromic pigment 24
thermoforming polymers 24, 57–8, 202–3
thermo-regulating smart textile fabrics 27
thermosetting polymers 58, 203
threads 245
throwaway culture 237, 276

thyristor 72
timber 52
  aesthetics 147
  availability 147
  biodiversity 149
  chipboard 145
  costs 148, 153
  defects in 141–2
  deforestation 145, 149
  drilling 160–1
  environmental impact 145–6, 147
  ethical factors 148
  finishes 53
  finishing 109
  functionality 147
  hardboard 145
  hardwoods 52–3, 142–3, 148
  impact of forces and stress 150
  joining and fixing 151
  joining methods 161–2
  laminating 165
  life cycle of products 146
  manufactured boards 53–4, 143–4, 148, 153
  manufacturing methods 171
  marking-out 156
  medium-density fibreboard (MDF) 144
  planing 159
  plywood 144, 150–1
  recycling 146
  reinforcing 150
  sanding 159
  sawing 158–9
  seasoning 140–1
  selecting 147
  shaping 159–60
  and social footprint 145–6, 148
  softwoods 53, 143, 148
  sources of 140
  steam bending 147, 165
  stock forms 96–7, 152–3
  strength of 150
  surface finishes 147, 168–70, 171–2
  types 142–3
  veneering 166
  veneers 152–3
  see also production
titanium 24
toiles 264–5, 294
torsional strength 181
tracing paper 49
transducer 68
transistors 71–2

transportation, and sustainability 14
triangulation 94
turning 106

U
user-centred design 287–8
user testing 304
UV (ultraviolet)
  light 136
  protective fabrics 27

V
vacuum forming 104–5, 221–2
varnish 136, 169
velocity ratio 81
veneered board 54
veneers 152–3, 166
video recordings 299
vinyl cutting 128, 220
vinyl decals 223
virgin fibre paper 49
viscose 231
voltage 66
  and relays 80
voltage amplifier 75–6
voltage comparator 74–5

W
washers 191
waste disposal
  ecological footprint 17, 88
  legislation 88
  plastic 236
  see also environment
Waste Electrical and Electronic Equipment (WEEE) directive 88
wasting 102, 132, 156, 186
water
  ecological footprint 17
  as energy source 19
  ingress 94–5
  and paper production 120
water-repellent textiles 240
wave power 19
welding 108, 192, 219
Williamson, Matthew 285
wind turbine energy 19, 21
wood, as fuel 19
wool 59, 231, 233
  see also knitted textiles
working conditions, textile industry 236–7
working drawings 296–7
World Energy Council 12
worm drive 84–5
woven textiles 61, 226–7

Y
yarn 232–3
  see also textiles